SERVING DIVERSE CONSTITUENCIES

MODERN APPLICATIONS OF SOCIAL WORK

An Aldine de Gruyter Series of Texts and Monographs

SERIES EDITOR

James K. Whittaker

SERVING DIVERSE CONSTITUENCIES

Applying the Ecological Perspective

ROBERTA R. GREENE and MARIE WATKINS
Editors

ALDINE DE GRUYTER
New York

About the Editors

Roberta R. Greene is Professor and Dean of Indiana University, School of Social Work. Dr. Greene is the author of *Social Work with the Aged and Their Families;* and co-author with Betsy S. Vourlekis of *Social Work Case Management,* and co-author with Paul H. Ephross of *Human Behavior Theory and Social Work Practice* (all: Aldine de Gruyter). Dr. Greene is also the author of numerous journal articles dealing with the application of conceptual frameworks to social work practice.

Marie Watkins is Research Associate for Community Outreach of the Indiana University School of Social Work. In addition to this role, Dr. Watkins teaches graduate and undergraduate courses related to social work practice with individuals and family groups.

ALDINE DE GRUYTER
A division of Walter de Gruyter, Inc.
200 Saw Mill River Road
Hawthorne, New York 10532

This publication is printed on acid free paper ∞

Library of Congress Cataloging-in-Publication Data

Serving diverse constituencies : applying the ecological perspective / Roberta R. Greene and Marie Watkins, editors.
p.   cm. — (Modern applications of social work)
Includes bibliographical references (p.   ) and index.
ISBN 0-202-36109-8 (cloth : alk. paper). — ISBN 0-202-36110-1 (paper : alk paper)
1. Social work with minorities.   2. Multiculturalism.   3. Social work with children.   4. Social work with the aged.   5. Social work with the handicapped.   6. Social work with gays.   I. Greene, Roberta R. (Roberta Rubin), 1940— .   II. Watkins, Marie. III. Series.
HV3176.S3   1998
361.3'2—dc21   98-2007
                                                                        CIP

Manufactured in the United States of America
10 9 8 7 6 5 4 3 2 1

To my grandchildren
Carlin, Sondra, Orla, Evan, Colin, and Zoe

Thank you to all contributors, Dee Barnes,
Kimberly Ham and Mary Roberts,
and as always David Greene

RG

Contents

Preface

With the adoption of the Council of Social Work Education Curriculum Policy Statement in 1992, social work educators are further challenged to deliver a curriculum that integrates human behavior theory, social work practice methods, and diversity content. This book provides principles for ecologically framed and diversity-sound social work practice across several fields of practice. It also explores how to conduct ecologically and culturally sensitive research and social policy initiatives. Therefore, it is intended to address knowledge, attitudes, and skills across curriculum content areas. Themes of health and well-being, resilience, bicultural competence, and empowerment are explored.

Introduction

Social workers in the twenty-first century will increasingly serve diverse constituencies. The contributors to this text have applied the ecological or person-environment perspective to several areas of social work content to help meet the increased demand for diversity-sound social work practice.

Chapters 1–4 provide the integration of ecological and diversity principles as they may be used in social work assessment and intervention. Chapter 5 examines child welfare practice as it relates to the issues of attachment, bonding, grief and loss, permanent placement, and family reunification. Chapter 6 describes a practice approach to school social work that is child centered, family focused, and based on community partnerships. It contrasts the deficit model with concepts of resiliency and bi-cultural competence. Chapter 7 continues the theme that children and youth are best understood from a strengths perspective. Youth are viewed as community assets who through their positive development can contribute to improving the environments in which they live. Chapter 8 examines the cultural ecology of aging. Through the exploration of the life course, it provides a better understanding of indigenous theories of successful aging as it relates to group processes.

Chapter 9 further illuminates how mental health services can be derived from a strengths and empowerment perspective. It focuses on the culture and worldview of mental health consumers and their families. Chapter 10 discusses how marriage enrichment programs for African-American couples contribute to increased quality of life and marital satisfaction. It provides a curriculum guide for enrichment group leaders. Chapter 11 explores the world of developmentally disabled persons and the issues that arise from social barriers that prohibit their full participation in society. Chapter 12 examines ecologically-based research as method that can empower study participants. It suggests that collaborative research questions should seek knowledge that enhances participants' competence. Chapter 13 asks whether it is possible to create culturally sensitive public policy. It explores public policy as a philosophical statement, a political process, a product, a practice, and a pathway to action. Chapter 14 presents the ecological dimensions of family members living with HIV disease—their strains and supports. An empirically-grounded and culturally sensitive approach to service, program, and policy development is provided.

Roberta R. Greene
Marie Watkins

1

Ecological Perspective
Meeting the Challenge of Practice
with Diverse Populations

ROBERTA R. GREENE and LISA McGUIRE

As we enter into the 1990s [and beyond], the demand for culturally competent [social work] practice—a legacy of the 80s fueled by demographic forces and critical interest in ethnicity—will continue to shape practice.
　　　　　　　　　　　　　—K. L. Chau, *Ethnicity and Biculturalism:*
　　　　　　　　　　　　　Emerging Perspectives of Social Group Work

A look ahead to the twenty-first century, and social work's second century, [suggests] that the profession's dual, yet one-dimensional, focus appears to be in the process of transformation to a multi-dimensional focus on diverse person(s) in diverse environments.
　　—C. B. Germain, "Human Behavior and the Social Environment"

Despite the persistent myth of a single melting pot or homogeneous society, the United States actually comprises "multicultural environments" (Caple, Salcido, & di Cecco, 1996, p. 369). The racial and ethnic content of the U.S. population is more diverse now than at any time in the 20th century (U.S. Bureau of the Census, 1994). Using census designations, nearly one in four U.S. citizens identified themselves as black, Hispanic, Asian and Pacific Islander, or American Indian (Gould, 1996). Other multicultural environments include, but are not limited to race, ethnicity, socioeconomic class, national or regional origin, sexual orientation, age, physical and mental ability, and gender (Ewalt, Freeman, Kirk, & Poole, 1996).

In light of the changes in the demographic composition of the U.S.

1

population, along with other political, economic, environmental, and ideological shifts, such as attacks on affirmative action programs, it is imperative that the social work profession meet the challenge of culturally competent practice. In essence, social workers prepared for the complexities of 21st-century practice will need to work effectively with diverse people in diverse environments. Clearly, use of an integrated theoretical approach will become essential to enhance practitioners' abilities to operate within a variety of cultural contexts, be responsive to the socialization patterns of various cultures, be tested with the client and thus learn to self-correct, be descriptive rather than judgmental and prescriptive, and gain the potential to apply skills to multicultural populations (de Anda, 1997). Currently, however, there is no single theory on which social workers can rely to selectively serve diverse clients (Greene, 1994; Ho, 1987).

This book makes the case that the ecological perspective can serve as a framework for social work practice with diverse populations. A major reason for adopting the ecological perspective is its multitheoretical base. Because of the broad constituencies of social work, theory bases other than those encompassed in the person-environment approach are not holistic enough to individualize clients, whether the client is an individual, family, group, or community. Historically, clients "with problems that were unresponsive to particular methods were simply left out of social work's purview and services" (Meyer, 1988, p. 277). However, the ecological perspective permits multiple views—ranging from the personal to societal—to be systematically considered.

Another advantage of the ecological perspective is it provides a framework to address content about a client's culture and historical era, gender, ethnicity, and other factors related to relative political power, power differentials, and worldview (Germain, 1979). Because the perspective allows for the inclusion of such "contextual variables," it has the means for serving clients across cultural boundaries and for providing more culturally sensitive interventions and services (Meyer, 1988, p. 279).

Ecological assumptions share so much in common with diversity concerns that the perspective can be used as a framework to expand the diversity dimension of social work practice. Ecological and diversity principles are not only complementary but are so interwoven in social work history and philosophy [e.g., as is apparent in the National Association of Social Workers (NASW) 1997 Code of Ethics, here appended as Table 1.1] that their tenets can serve as the template for, or nucleus of, 21st-century practice. The following chapters explore the legacy of the person-environment approach and how it has converged with diversity issues to enhance social work practice with diverse populations. The goal is to

Table 1.1. Ecological and Diversity Principles: Tenets for Practice as Evident in the *NASW Code of Ethics*

Preamble

The primary mission of the social work profession is to enhance human well-being and help meet the basic human needs of all people, with particular attention to the needs and empowerment of people who are vulnerable, oppressed, and living in poverty. A historic and defining feature of social work is the profession's focus on individual well-being in a social context and the well-being of society. Fundamental to social work is attention to the environmental forces that create, contribute to, and address problems in living.

Social workers promote social justice and social change with and on behalf of clients. "Clients" is used inclusively to refer to individuals, families, groups, organizations, and communities. Social workers are sensitive to cultural and ethnic diversity and strive to end discrimination, oppression, poverty, and other forms of social injustice. These activities may be in the form of direct practice, community organizing, supervision, consultation, administration, advocacy, social and political action, policy development and implementation, education, and research and evaluation. Social workers seek to enhance the capacity of people to address their own needs. Social workers also seek to promote the responsiveness of organizations, communities, and other social institutions to individuals' needs and social problems.

The mission of the social work profession is rooted in a set of core values. These core values, embraced by social workers throughout the profession's history, are the foundation of social work's unique purpose and perspective:
- service
- social justice
- dignity and worth of the person
- importance of human relationships
- integrity
- competence

Ethical Principles

The following broad ethical principles are based on social work's core values of service, social justice, dignity and worth of the person, importance of human relationships, integrity, and competence. These principles set forth ideals to which all social workers should aspire.

Value: Social Justice
Ethical Principle: Social Workers Challenge Social Injustice

Social workers pursue social change, particularly with and on behalf of vulnerable and oppressed individuals and groups of people. Social workers' social change efforts are focused primarily on issues of poverty,

(continued)

Table 1.1. Continued

unemployment, discrimination, and other forms of social injustice. These activities seek to promote sensitivity to and knowledge about oppression and cultural and ethnic diversity. Social workers strive to ensure access to needed information, services, and resources; equality of opportunity; and meaningful participation in decision making for all people.

Ethical Standards

The following ethical standards are relevant to the professional activities of all social workers. These standards concern . . . social workers' ethical responsibilities in practice settings, . . . social workers; ethical responsibilities as professionals, . . . social workers' ethical responsibilities to the social work profession, and . . . social workers' ethical responsibilities to the broader society.

Some of the standards that follow are enforceable guidelines for professional conduct, and some are aspirational. The extent to which each standard is enforceable is a matter of professional judgment to be exercised by those responsible for reviewing alleged violations of ethical standards.

1.05   Cultural Competence and Social Diversity

            (a) Social workers should understand culture and its function in human behavior and society, recognizing the strengths that exist in all cultures.

            (b) Social workers should have a knowledge base of their clients' cultures and be able to demonstrate competence in the provision of services that are sensitive to clients' cultures and to differences among people and cultural groups.

            (c) Social workers should obtain education about and seek to understand the nature of social diversity and oppression with respect to race, ethnicity, national origin, color, sex, sexual orientation, age, marital status, political belief, religion, and mental or physical disability.

4.   Social Workers' Ethical Responsibilities as Professionals

4.02   Discrimination

            Social workers should not practice, condone, facilitate, or collaborate with any form of discrimination on the basis of race, ethnicity, national origin, color, sex, sexual orientation, age, marital status, political belief, religion, or mental or physical disability.

Source: National Association of Social Workers (1997).

further "a viable person-environment model to understand human behavior within a diversity framework" (Greene, 1994, p. 20).

This chapter describes the historical evolution of the ecological perspective and explores how the perspective has been used to unify the professional mission of social work, provide social work with conceptual unity, and define its professional purpose. The chapter also outlines the major assumptions underlying the ecological approach to social work practice. Chapter 2 discusses diversity principles derived from the social work literature, drawing together assumptions sufficiently broad enough that they may serve as generic guidelines for cross-cultural practice. Chapters 3 and 4 present an integrated approach to person-environment and diversity issues intended to guide social work assessment and intervention. Chapters 5–11 illustrate the use of the ecological perspective and diversity principles in various fields of social work practice. Chapters 12–14 explore how ecological and diversity principles can enhance the social work profession's research and policy commitment to serve diverse populations.

PERSON-ENVIRONMENT APPROACH
AND THE SOCIAL WORK MISSION

The eco-systems perspective [was] partially in response to . . . a half-century-long pursuit of a single holistic framework to support social work practice theory. Given the proliferation of disparate treatment models, this unifying idea seems vital for the future coherence of practice in social work.

—C. Meyer, "The Eco-Systems Perspective"

Over the past several decades, the terms *ecological perspective* and *person-environment approach* have often been used interchangeably. Generally speaking, the person-environment approach requires that the social worker use a mind-set that allows for a focus on both the person and the environment in the social work process. Figure 1.1 illustrates the person-environ

> The person-environment perspective has solidified social work's mission, established a conceptual reference point, and delineated the practitioner's role.

ment concept as a multitheoretical orientation adopted for social work practice that enables simultaneous attention to person-environment in assessment and intervention (Greene, 1991a, 1991b, 1991c).

Conceptual Point of Reference

The ecological perspective, a continuing and major theme in the historical development of social work, is a conceptual point of reference

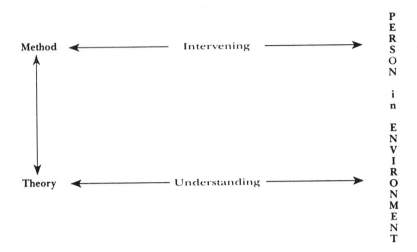

Figure 1.1. Person-in-environment, theory, and method.

(Greene & Ephross, 1991). Although there have been recent critiques about the abstract nature and adequacy of the empirical base of the perspective (Wakefield, 1996a, 1996b), there is little doubt that the person-environment theoretical construct has emerged as a major organizing framework in social work practice (Germain & Gitterman, 1995).

One of the most pervasive questions facing the profession today and that is at the heart of a continuing struggle in the profession's conceptual development is, What is the balance between unity and diversity in the conceptual definition of social work practice (Austin, 1986; Mandel School of Applied Social Sciences, 1996; Meyer, 1987)? Bartlett (1970) has expressed the challenge of conceptual unity best: A key feature of social work is the range of people served and the programs and services that have "suddenly opened out like a fan" (p. 15). Bartlett argued that, to be an effective profession, social work must use adequate words and holistic concepts. Without such a central concept, she believed social work would neither achieve a coherent knowledge base nor be able to serve its various clienteles.

Siporin (1980) was equally concerned with "conceptual constraints imposed by [the multiplicity] of social work methods" (p. 46). He, too, argued that the social work profession needed a conceptual point of reference and suggested that the ecological perspective could be such a reference point. He contended that the ecological perspective allows social workers to account for complex variables, assess the dynamic interplay of variables, draw conceptual boundaries around the case, and determine what interventions are needed.

Purpose of Social Work

Defining the professional purpose of social work, or its common practice base, has been difficult partly because practitioners must intervene in so many situations to achieve their dual purpose: to improve social conditions and to enhance individual, family, and group social function. An examination of the historical path of social work to professionalization provides another reason for the difficulty experienced in articulating a common purpose. Social work began as a voluntary activity among family, friends, social support structures—including settlement houses, and individual citizens with concern for others—such as religious leaders. It was not until the early 1900s that philanthropists engaged in specialized training at agencies, training schools, and, later, universities. With the publication of Richmond's (1917) *Social Diagnosis* and her focus on study, diagnosis, and treatment, social workers implemented a more defined practice approach.

From the 1920s until the late 1950s, social work was fragmented by field of practice specializations, such as child welfare or medical social work, and split by method specialties, including casework, group work, and community organization (Dinerman & Geismar, 1984; Ramsay, 1994). Theorists who called for unity in the conceptual base of social work also argued for a common purpose within social work practice to represent "the important facets and components of the profession's practice as a whole" (Bartlett, 1970, p. 46). Meyer (1987) expressed the need for an organizing social work framework based on the person-environment concept: Direct practice in social work is a "mosaic of methods and skills based upon many kinds of knowledge and guided by multiple theories" (p. 409). Meyer added that "what weaves all of these threads together" is the central purpose of social work to effect the best possible adaptation between person and environment (ibid.).

In 1959, the chairpeople of the Council on Social Work Education (CSWE) Curriculum Study (Boehm, 1959) and the NASW Committee on the Working Definition of Social Work (Bartlett, 1970) met to address the core practice domain of social work. The outcome was a central definition of the nature and purpose of social work on which the key aspects of social work education were articulated. *Social work* was defined as

> a profession concerned with the restoration, maintenance and enhancement of social functioning. It contributes, with other professions and disciplines, to the prevention, treatment and control of problems in social functioning of individuals, groups and communities. (Boehm, 1959, p. 1)

In the definition, *social functioning* encompasses the interacting effects of personal attributes and environmental characteristics on individual, group, and community behavior (Boehm, 1959). The adoption of social function as the domain of social work practice provided the profession with a clarification of the social worker's role as well as with a unifying theoretical anchor for human growth and behavior (Butler, 1959; Middleman & Goldberg, 1987; Pincus & Minahan, 1973).

Social Worker's Role

As the foundation of social work practice, the ecological perspective served as a catalyst for the "reconceptualization of [the] professional task [of social work] from a narrowly defined clinical role based on a deficit model of human functioning, to a much broader professional repertoire" (Whittaker, 1986, p. 40). From the vantage point of ecological theory, *clinical social work* was defined as "the mode of social work action that aims to help people, in individualized ways, to attain an adaptive goodness of fit between themselves and their society" (Siporin, 1983, p. 193). Thus, the social worker's role became centered around assisting people to cope with difficult life tasks (Bartlett, 1970; Gordon, 1969). Using the ecological perspective, social workers became better prepared to offer therapeutic insight and provide community resources, and practitioners engaged in administrative or community-level work also gained a more holistic perspective.

A Unifying Human Behavior Base

Today, the ecological perspective is often considered the social work's profession's unifying human behavior base. This was not always the case. In the past, social work theorists long argued for a more comprehensive theoretical approach to explain the complexities of human function in the social environment (Bartlett, 1970; De Hoyos, 1989; Souflee, 1993; Strean, 1971).

Although the profession has its roots in social and personal change, the following brief historical review suggests considerable tension has existed between the two points of intervention and reveals the use of different theoretical approaches on which practitioners grounded their practice (Ephross-Saltman & Greene, 1993). In the early days of the profession, social workers adopted theories from the social sciences to solve the social problems confronting their clients. During the 1930s, social work practitioners adopted many Freudian psychoanalytic principles of human behavior. This shift involved a strong emphasis on Freud's three-part personality system including the *id*, which houses drives, instincts, or tension-producing features; the *ego,* which consists of reality-based decision-making properties; and the *superego,* which involves values and ideals (Goldstein, 1986). The social worker's use of this framework led to a focus on the individual and his or her *intrapsychic,* or internal, mental phenomenon (Greene & Ephross, 1991; Janchill, 1969). The trend to emphasize the person continued with contemporary psychoanalytic thinking such as ego psychology, which centers on clients' *ego function,* or their conscious, adaptive mastery of the environment. There was also a focus on object relations theory, which emphasizes a client's ability to form relationships. These psychoanalytic approaches were most prevalent in social work practice for several decades; and some practitioners today still use these approaches to enable them to understand personality dynamics.

In the 1960s, a movement to broaden and conceptualize the profession's dual commitment to person-environment modified the emphasis on personality dynamics (De Hoyos, 1989). This increased interest in the person-environment can be traced to several factors. *General systems theory,* a content-free abstract model that explains stability and change among social phenomena, became the most widely used theoretical model among social work educators (De Hoyos, 1989). General systems theory was instrumental in moving social work to a conceptual scheme for understanding the interactions among a number of variables (see Greene, 1991). Systems theory was considered a valuable model because it drew attention to the need for social workers to explore the multiple systems in which people function (Greene, 1991).

A central premise of the ecological approach, derived from systems thinking, is that behavior is a complex outcome of person-environment transactions at multiple systems levels. As such, the development of the ecological approach was a natural outgrowth of systems theory. The ecological approach allows for several theories to be brought together to better explain the person-environment connection.

With general systems theory as a central element, the ecological approach further expanded the person-environment scope of social work practice. For example, theorists such as Germain (1978) urged that the two most prevalent theories in social work practice—ego psychology and general systems theory—be merged. Practitioners, who were increasingly concerned with the environmental systems, soon viewed the ecological perspective as a means of holding "ego and environment together in their formulations and actions" (Gitterman & Germain, 1976, p. 3).

The distinguishing feature of the ecological perspective became its "potential for integrating the treatment and reform traditions of the profession" (ibid., p. 4). Whittaker, Schinke, and Gilchrist (1986) argued that the ecological perspective was so deeply rooted in social work tradition that it cut across various fields of practice. The ecological approach was increasingly applied in all methods and practice models (Aponte, 1979; Hartman, 1979; Whittaker & Garbarino, 1983).

During the 1970s, the reemphasis on the person-environment focus converged with the growing civil rights movement. The increased use of the ecological perspective was fueled by its historical timing and by the need to better address sociocultural aspects of human behavior (Miller, 1980). Social work educators challenged the profession to "break loose from the tendency to see social work practice in terms of one culture, class, or nation" (Sanders, 1974, p. 86). Furthermore, social workers increasingly perceived personality theories as "culture-bound" (Germain, 1979, p. 11). The attraction of the ecological perspective was its call for an examination of the exchanges in the past and present ecological environments within a particular culture. Thus, the popularity of the ecological perspective can be attributed to its greater focus on people and their physical-social-cultural environment and on how people interact with and obtain community resources (Siporin, 1980).

ECOLOGICAL PERSPECTIVE: A PARADIGM SHIFT

[A paradigm shift is] a profound change in the thoughts, perceptions, and values that form a particular vision of reality.
—F. Capra, *The Turning Point: Science, Society and the Rising Culture*

[A paradigm shift] is rather as if the professional community had been suddenly transported to another planet where familiar objects are seen in a different light and are joined by unfamiliar ones as well.
—T. S. Kuhn, *The Structure of Scientific Revolutions*

Nondeterministic View of Human Behavior

The ecological view of human behavior in the social environment was heralded as a paradigm shift (Whittaker et al., 1986). *Paradigms* are the entire configuration of beliefs, values, and techniques that are shared by members of a professional community (Schriver, 1995). The paradigm shift in the case of the ecological perspective involved the view that behavior needed to be understood from a nondeterministic vantage point, that is *a* does not cause *b*. Rather, behavior is viewed as an outcome of a complex mediation between the many factors involved in person-environment.

> The ecological perspective represents a human behavior paradigm shift.

An additional shift in emphasis included the idea that the person-environment is a unitary system in which people and their environments reciprocally shape each other. Just as the environment affects the person, the person can influence his or her environment.

Transactional Approach

In the ecological perspective, the term transactional refers to the reciprocal people-environment exchanges that bridge the person-environment relationship. The idea that people and environments are parts of a unitary system is a key feature of the ecological perspective.

> Because ecology considers the organism to be inseparable from the environment—together constituting a transacting system—an ecological metaphor can avoid dichotomizing person and situation and direct our attention to the transactions between them. (Germain, 1973, p. 326)

This idea helps operationalize the social worker's role. Whether working with a person and the family, a patient and the ward, or a resident and the nursing home, the practitioner should view the development and well-being of each person as dependent on the nature of the person's transactions (Libassi & Maluccio, 1982). For example, because it focuses "on the adaptive aspects of human beings in continuous transactions with the physical and social environments" (p. 223), Gary (1996) used the ecological perspective to guide research on how Africa-American men perceive racial discrimination in U.S. society. The relationship among discrimination, demographic, sociocultural, and stressor variables was better understood through their transactional effects.

Goodness-of-Fit and Habitat. The terms *goodness-of-fit* and *habitat*, borrowed from the science of ecology, avoid dichotomizing person-environment. Goodness-of-fit refers to "the extent to which there is a match between the individual's adaptive needs and the qualities of the environment" (Dies, 1955, p. 46). Environmental forces are understood to support or undermine personal development. Similarly, a person may have positive and or negative effects on his or her environment. This mutual relationship of person-environment is not constant but evolves over time in relation to the individual's habitat. Habitat(s) are more than physical environments; they include a client's family and friend; neighborhood, church, and school; social geography and climate; laws, institutions, and values, for example.

Coulton (1981) illustrated the use of the concept person-environment fit as it relates to the health care environment. She pointed out that, when there is congruence between a person's needs, capabilities, and aspirations and the resources, demands, and opportunities in the health care environment, goodness-of-fit is nurtured. However, when there is lack of fit between an individual's needs and the health care system, an individual's health and mental health can be negatively affected. Coulton encouraged social workers in health care to use person-environment fit as a practice framework. Using this framework, social workers would examine the fit of all aspects of care: the physical dimensions, that is, spatial and climatological characteristics; the psychosocial dimensions, which encompass interpersonal and relationship aspects of performance; the behavioral dimensions, which involve behaviors demanded by the environment; and the economic dimensions, such as costs and available economic resources. Examining fit also would involve exploring a client's adaptation to the environment and working to ensure it could be more compatible by enhancing social supports, linking patients to activities, and providing material resources.

Contextual View of Development and Positive View of Growth

Social work theorists have increasingly questioned the bias of the alternative life stage approach to development. They have debated whether any fixed, determined sequence of life tasks sufficiently addresses an understanding of human development within an individual's personal history and his or her sociocultural setting (Germain, 1994; Kropf & Greene, 1993). Borrowing from developmental psychology and other disciplines, the ecological perspective has offered an alternative explanation: a "context-specific" approach to development (Boxer & Cohler, 1989; Sophie, 1986). From an ecological perspective, "there is no such thing as context-free development" (Garbarino, 1986, p. 20). Rather, the social worker realizes that development occurs in the context of the mutual influences of people and their environment(s).

The ecological perspective also combines concepts from disciplines such as humanistic psychology that deal with positive growth-producing experiences, reinforcing the emphasis on the nature of healthy human development (Maslow, 1970; Rogers, 1961). Ecological theorists have proposed that people are innately predisposed to act on their environments. Individuals are born with developmentally instigating characteristics, such as a baby's smile, that enable them to invite or discourage reactions from the environment. In this manner, the individual is influenced by the environment, can encourage a response from the environment, and thereby can influence the subsequent course of his or her growth (Bronfenbrenner, 1989).

Adaptiveness across the Life Course

Ecological theorists also believe that people have an innate capacity to act on and to master their environments. The contextual approach to development recognizes that people are goal directed and can achieve positive growth and societal change (Bronfenbrenner, 1989). In this positive view of adaptiveness, the attainment of well-being is a lifelong process of active person-environment exchanges, involving physical, emotional, familial, organizational, political, and economic factors related to human growth and development (Germain & Gitterman, 1987).

Because of its positive approach to adaptiveness, a contextual view enhances the understanding of human behavior across the life course:

> The ecology of human development is the scientific study of the progressive, mutual accommodation, *throughout the life course,* between active, growing human beings, and the changing properties of the immediate settings in which the developing person lives, as this process is affected by the relations between these settings, and by the larger contexts in which the settings are embedded. (ibid., p. 188)

Because the ecological perspective considers an individual's growth processes over the life course within his or her sociocultural context, it is particularly useful in working with diverse populations. For example, how older adults function is better understood as a process of transactions between the developing person and his or her specific environments over time in numerous encounters. Therefore, the practitioner often obtains a client's life story through a life review or the reviewing of memories. Such a process may allow for a better understanding of the client's present function.

Multilevel Attachments: Assessment and Intervention

Another reason the ecological perspective is viewed as a departure from earlier social work approaches is that it uses a multilevel assessment and intervention process based on systems theory. At the more personal or intrapsychic level of assessment, the ecological perspective emphasizes a number of complementary concepts including stress, self-efficacy, and mastery. These terms are often used to understand a similar life experience encompassing a personal sense of power or strength (Gutierrez, 1990). The idea that the processes of stress, self-efficacy, and mastery are expressions of person-environment relationships, rather than an expression of only the person or the environment, made an important contribution to understanding client well-being.

Another major contribution to the social work profession involves the ecological approaches to family-centered social work (Hartman & Laird, 1987; McGoldrick, 1989). From an ecological view of the family, the family system is understood within its internal and external context as well as its diverse form. Perhaps the most dramatic effect of the ecological approach is its influence on the view of what constitutes a family. More than 30 years ago, family theory was designed based on the traditional, white, middle-class family: an employed father and a stay-at-home mother. Today, the family is no longer a single unit with clearly defined rules, roles, and relationships (Poverny & Finch, 1988). Increasingly, social workers are engaging in practice with single parents, stepfamilies or blended families, gay partners, and other diverse family forms. Therefore, many social workers have come to prefer a self-definition of who comprises the family:

> The family is a social system consisting of individuals who are related to each other by reasons of strong reciprocal affection and loyalties, comprising a permanent household or cluster of households that persist over time. (Terklesen, 1980, p. 2)

Just as the ecological view has broadened what constitutes a family, so, too, it has expanded the definition of *parent*. According to Pennekamp and Freeman (1988), social workers can be more effective in their interventions when using the current definition of a parent:

> The definition of "parents" must include single parents, either mothers or fathers; joint custodial, divorced parents; stepparents; current partners of parents involved in some aspects of caregiving; extended family members such as grandparents; substitute families such as foster parents and group home and institutional counselors acting as primary caregivers; and persons who have created families of choice. (p. 246)

To examine the connection of an individual and his or her family to the wider environment, ecological theorists frequently use Bronfenbrenner's (1979) conceptualization of the nature of the ecological environment (Figure 1.2). Bronfenbrenner visualized the environment as a set of nested structures, similar to a set of Russian dolls. An individual's environment comprises systems at four levels that are "ever-widening concentric circles of environment that surround the (developing) individual, moving from the most near to the most remote" (p. 22). One level is the *microsystem*, an immediate setting involving activities and interpersonal face-to-face relationships. *Microsystems* are the small-scale systems such as families, peer groups, day care centers, and schools. Another level, *mesosystems*, refers to linkages between two or more systems. *Exosystems* en-

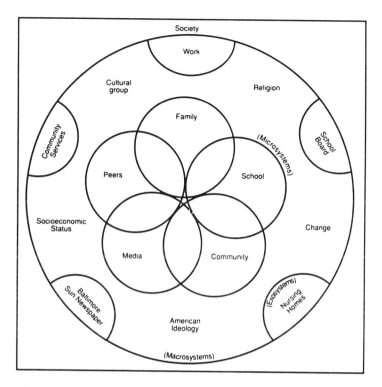

Figure 1.2. An ecological model of human development. Adapted with permission from Bronfenbrenner, U., *The Ecology of Human Development,* Cambridge, MA: Harvard University Press, 1979, p. Q48.

compass linkages between systems in which the person may not be involved. *Macrosystems* include the broad elements of society, such as legal or ideological contexts. A macrosystem consists of the overarching social, political, legal, economic, and value patterns of a given culture.

The connection and influences among various systems are central to the ecological paradigm. For example, the adaptation of a child diagnosed at birth with a physical or mental challenge involves a developmental process that includes the child, the family, and social and cultural contexts (Bauer & Shea, 1987). Bauer and Shea suggested that it is particularly important to understand the legal context of the Education of the Handicapped Act (P.L. 94-457), which mandates better education for physically challenged children. The act provides funding to states to plan, develop, and implement a comprehensive, multidisciplinary, interagency, statewide system of early intervention services. This legal action—truly an ecological approach—has brought about a change from unidimensional child-centered services to comprehensive services that encompass the needs and concerns of families, financial needs, and child care.

The broadest context in which behavior is examined is the macrosystem. The effects of macrosystem processes are far-reaching. Furr (1997) best defined the macrosystem as "the organized social and cultural patterns that envelope human behavior" (p. 17), particularly economic and governmental systems. Longres ([1900] 1990) also has captured the societal context of such macrosystem effects:

> Economic conflict pits owners, management, and the professional classes against the skilled and unskilled labor they hire. Conflict shows up as disputes in the workplace and over the distribution of wealth and income in a society. Ethnic struggles, on the other hand, are struggles over national and cultural identity: the language we speak, the holidays we celebrate, the legal and religious systems we espouse. . . . They are also struggles over national physical identity: the phenotype of our gods and mythical heroes; the physiognomy of our idealized selfhood, the physical image we project. . . . Not unusually, they are also quarrels about the nature of home and the proper household, over the suitability of marital and sexual partners. (pp. 39–40)

Macrosystem issues relate to a national ethos that somehow envelopes all. For example, despite the focus of social work on the person-environment, not enough attention has been given to seasonal issues (Elwell, 1994). Elwell has suggested that, because major religious holidays prevail as societal cultural events, they may be a time of heightened stress and return to childhood memories. Therefore, she has urged social workers to consider the effects of these holidays on clients and on themselves. Furthermore, social workers must think environmentally as well as globally (Hoff & Polack, 1993). The diminution of the Amazon rain forest is just one example of why social workers should not view the environment as an unlimited resource. In addition, given the internationalization of the economic system, which has resulted in the reorganization of economic and political opportunities worldwide (Austin, 1996), social workers who are concerned with social and economic justice will inevitably become involved.

FURTHER ECOLOGICAL ASSUMPTIONS

Professional [social work] practice . . . focuses on the transactions between
people and their environments that affect their ability to accomplish life tasks,
alleviate distress, and realize individual and collective aspirations.

—C. B. Germain, "Human Development
in Contemporary Environments"

Just as the ecological perspective focuses attention to the ongoing, contextualized process of human development, the ecological perspective itself has evolved in the changing context of social work practice as discussed earlier in this chapter. Therefore, there is no clear agreement about what constitutes the basic principles of the ecological perspective. However, a list of principles or themes (Table 1.2) was derived based on a review of the literature (Garbarino, 1986; Germain, 1979; Germain & Gitterman, 1986, 1987; Greene, 1991; Meyer, 1988), and a Delphi Survey among social work educators. An expert panel of faculty members who teach human behavior and the social environment from across the country participated in two Delphi Survey rounds. The initial round of the survey included 154 statements, but also left space for respondents to add statements. Respondents were asked to rate each statement in terms of their relative importance as principles upon which the ecological perspective was based. The final list numbered eighty-two statements.

To provide a framework for analysis, each statement was coded as to whether it described (1) theoretical knowledge, (2) attitudes and values, or (3) practice concepts. In addition, statements were coded as to the level of the environment: microsystem, mesosystem, and macrosystem (Bronfenbrenner, 1979) but also including multiple levels and transactions among those levels.

Attitudes and Values of the Ecological Perspective

With renewed emphasis on critical thinking in social work education, it is important to examine the underlying attitudes and values associated with the ecological perspective. From the initial list of 16 statements representing the attitudes and values of the ecological perspective identified in the readings, six (38%) remained through both rounds of the study (presented in Table 1.2, under "Attitudes and Values").

Theoretical Knowledge

Statements relating to theoretical knowledge of the ecological perspective made up the largest initial category with 119 statements. After two

Table 1.2.   Ecological Principles

Theoretical Knowledge

The ecological perspective builds on the science of ecology that emphasizes the interdependence of systems.

The ecological perspective recognizes that the person's environment is multifaceted and multileveled.

The ecological perspective provides a holistic view of people.

The ecological perspective recognizes the interrelatedness of each person to his or her environment.

The ecological perspective recognizes that human relatedness is necessary throughout the life course.

The ecological perspective sees human behavior as influenced by the connections of social networks.

The ecological perspective characterizes people-environment exchanges as continuous and reciprocal.

The ecological perspective focuses on person-environment as a unitary system that accommodates and adapts to each other over time.

The ecological perspective requires an understanding of
- emotional,
- physiological,
- psychological,
- environmental,
- cultural,
- socioeconomic,
- political,
- historical,
- physical and mental ability, and
- gender factors.

The ecological perspective examines multiples levels of social environments including
- friends,
- family,
- neighborhoods,
- communities,
- networks,
- workplaces,
- recreational sites,
- religious institutions,
- political and economic institutions,

(continued)

Table 1.2. Continued

- social space and time,
- educational institutions, and
- "hidden communities" (such as the gay community).

The ecological perspective attempts to understand people within all levels of organization from the individual to collectivities.

The ecological perspective recognizes that severe, persistent stress disrupts social function.

The ecological perspective views stress as varying with
- social class and
- ethnic membership.

The ecological perspective views coping and mastery as the two major instruments of adaptation.

The ecological perspective views mastery as a joint product of personal and social resources.

The ecological perspective examines persons and their environments and how they achieve goodness-of-fit or adaptive balance.

The ecological perspective views problems as arising when humans do not receive sufficient nutrients or environmental support (energy, resources).

The ecological perspective identifies that stress may occur in life transitions from
- environmental pressures and
- interpersonal processes.

The ecological perspective explores societal and institutional stressors such as poverty, unemployment, and oppression.

The ecological perspective assesses transactions between the person and environment at all levels of systems affecting the client's adaptiveness.

The ecological perspective considers problems to be located in the interface between person and environment; that is, maladaptive transactions within the life space.

The ecological perspective strives to understand problems of living within the totality of life space.

The ecological perspective allows for ideas from many theories including
- ego psychology,
- empowerment theory,
- humanistic psychology,
- social goals model of group work,

(continued)

Table 1.2. Continued

- role theory,
- stress theory,
- human ecology,
- general systems theory,
- ecological development,
- the Life Model, and
- chaos theory.

The ecological perspective views identity and self-esteem as arising from a widening sphere of human interaction.

The ecological perspective views the environment as having a context through
- time,
- space,
- physical environments, and
- social network and institutions

The ecological perspective views self-esteem as transactional in nature.

The ecological perspective views the relative weight of biological or genetic and environmental factors in accounting for differences between and among humans.

Attitudes and Values

The ecological perspective is broad enough to encompass any treatment model.

The ecological perspective provides a broad context for social work practice.

The ecological perspective intends to capture the complexity of cases in their real-life context.

The ecological perspective rejects linear causality.

The ecological perspective implies a heuristic view of practice that fits with naturalistic models of knowledge building.

The ecological perspective considers human relatedness as a biological and social imperative.

Practice Concepts

The ecological perspective strives to bring out the adaptive potential of people and the nutritive properties of environments.

The ecological perspective provides a practice framework for multimethod practice: casework, group work, and community organization.

(continued)

Table 1.2. Continued

The ecological perspective targets problems in living including environmental pressures.

The ecological perspective is a theory for change that uses many types of interventions.

The ecological perspective explores interventions that influence the interacting forces in the client's life space.

The ecological perspective seeks interventions that affect the goodness-of-fit among a client and his or her environment at all systems levels.

The ecological perspective is action oriented, working for a better person-environment fit.

The ecological perspective strives to use natural helpers and informal helping systems.

The ecological perspective supports the client's personal ability to help himself or herself.

The ecological perspective asserts that professional action may be directed to the person, the environment, or the interaction between the two.

The ecological perspective allows clinicians to view cases holistically.

The ecological perspective includes the idea of environmental modification or intervention.

The ecological perspective does not prescribe what specific direction a social worker should take.

rounds of the survey, 56 statements regarding theoretical knowledge remained, representing 53% of the initial set of statements (presented in Table 1.2, under "Theoretical Knowledge"). The largest number of the theoretical knowledge statements related to micro-, or individual, issues (66%). The next largest number were related to macro- (45%) and multi-level (42%) principles.

Practice Concepts

In addition to theoretical knowledge building and attitudes and values, social work as a profession has been concerned with the pragmatic implications of theory for practice. Twenty-seven (27) of the initial statements related to practice concepts and 15 (55%) of them remained through both rounds of the study (presented in Table 1.2, under "Practice Concepts").

LIMITATIONS OF THE ECOLOGICAL PERSPECTIVE

Critics recently have challenged the usefulness of the ecological perspective (Brower, 1988; Furr, 1997; Wakefield, 1996a, 1996b). For example, Goldmeier and Fandetti (1991) questioned whether the ecological model fully accounts for how an individual internalizes aspects of the external environment. Although he recognized the contribution of the perspective to understanding behavior and its value as a tool for working with people, Brower (1988) contended that the approach is too abstract to be operationalized as a practice model. For example, he asked "What does it mean for a person to 'shape' an environment? . . . To make it 'one's own?' . . . Are there limits to how much power one has over his or her environment?" (p. 413).

Furthermore, social constructionists and feminist theorists have questioned the general systems theory component of the ecological approach. Systems theory is based on a structuralist view of human function that makes the assumption that universal principles describe societal structures and communication patterns. However, theorists and practitioners have increasingly disputed the assumption that there are neutral, value-free, or universal laws to explain people's behavior in social systems. Rather, they have contended that the helping process is not devoid of social, political, and cultural concerns as once believed (Greene, 1991). The theorists and practitioners have particularly criticized family treatment approaches, which they say endorse the normative nuclear family and its traditional gender roles, as well as accepting social and political assumptions about the nature of U.S. society. As a result of these criticisms, further modifications have been made to family treatment models (see Hare-Mustin, 1989, 1990; Hoffman, 1990, 1992).

Wakefield (1996a, 1996b) proposed still another question: "Does social work need a generic practice perspective in order to be a coherent, unified, and clinically effective profession?" (p. 1). He acknowledged that the influence of the ecological perspective on social work practice has been so profound that, to some degree, the validity of the perspective has been linked to the profession's intellectual credibility. He concluded, though, that the ecological perspective does not offer a way to combine competing theories into a coherent framework, does not provide a means for determining which causes at which level are important, and does not guide the practitioner to decide what action to take in a case. The chapters that follow attempt to address these concerns.

REFERENCES

Aponte, H. J. (1979). The negation of values in therapy. *Family Process, 24,* 323–338.

Austin, D. M. (1986). *A history of social work education.* Social Work Education Monograph Series. Austin: Unviersity of Texas at Austin School of Social Work.

Austin, D. M. (1996). The profession of social work in the second century. *Social work in the 21st century,* 396–407.

Bartlett, H. M. (1970). *The common base of social work.* Washington, DC: NASW Press.

Bauer, A. M., & Shea, T. M. (1987). An integrative perspective on adaptation to the birth or diagnosis of an exceptional child. *Social Work in Education, 9*(4), 240–251.

Boehm, W. (1959). *Curriculum study* (Vols. 1–12). New York: Council on Social Work Education.

Boxer, A. M., & Cohler, B. J. (1989). The life course of gay and lesbian youth: An immodest proposal for the study of lives. *Journal of Homosexuality, 17*(3–4), 315–355.

Bronfenbrenner, U. (1979). *The ecology of human development.* Cambridge, MA: Harvard University Press.

Bronfenbrenner, U. (1989). Ecological systems theory. *Annals of Child Development, 6,* 187–249.

Brower, A. M. (1988). Can the ecological model guide social work practice? *Social Service Review, 62*(3), 411–429.

Butler, R. (1959). *An orientation to knowledge of human growth and behavior in social work education* (Vol. 6). New York: Council on Social Work Education.

Caple, F. S., Salcido, R. M., & di Cecco, J. (1996). Engaging effectively with culturally diverse families and children. In P. L. Ewalt, E. M. Freeman, S. A. Kirk, & D. L. Poole (Eds.), *Multicultural issues in social work* (pp. 366–381). Washington, DC: NASW Press.

Capra, F. (1983). *The turning point: Science, society and the rising culture.* Toronto: Bantam.

Chau, K. L. (1991). *Ethnicity and biculturalism: Emerging perspectives of social group work.* New York: Haworth.

Coulton, C. J. (1981). Person-environment fit as the focus in health care. *Social Work, 26*(1), 26–35.

Council on Social Work Education (1969). Curriculum policy for the master's degree program in graduate schools of social work. New York: Author.

de Anda, D. (Ed.) (1997). *Controversial issues in multiculturalism.* Needham Heights, MA: Allyn & Bacon.

De Hoyos, G. (1989). Person-in-environment: A tri-level practice model. *Social Casework, 70*(3), 131–138.

Dies, L. P. (1955). *Nature and nature's man: The ecology of human communication.* Ann Arbor: University of Michigan Press.

Dinerman, M., & Geismar, L. L. (1984). *A quarter-century of social work education.* National Association of Social Workers, ABC-CLIO, & Council on Social Work Education.

24   Roberta R. Greene and Lisa McGuire

Elwell, M. E. (1994). Christmas and social work practice. *Social Work, 39*(6), 750–752.

Ephross-Saltman, J. E., & Greene, R. R. (1993). Social workers perceived knowledge and use of human behavior theory. *Journal of Social Work Education, 29*(1), 88–98.

Ewalt, P. L., Freeman, E. M., Kirk, S. A., & Poole, D. L. (1996). *Multicultural issues in social work.* Washington, DC: NASW Press.

Furr, L. A. (1997). *Exploring human behavior and the social environment.* Needham Heights, MA: Allyn & Bacon.

Garbarino, J. (1986). Where does social support fit into optimizing human development and preventing dysfunction? *British Journal of Social Work, 16(Supplement),* 23–37.

Gary, L. E. (1996). African-American men's perception of racial discrimination: A sociocultural analysis. In P. L. Ewalt, E. M. Freeman, S. A. Kirk, and D. L. Poole (Eds.), *Multicultural issues in social work* (pp. 218–240). Washington, DC: NASW Press.

Germain, C. B. (1973). An ecological perspective in casework practice. *Social Casework, 54*(6), 323–331.

Germain, C. B. (1978). Space: An ecological variable in social work practice. *Social Casework, 59*(9), 519–522.

Germain, C. B. (Ed.) (1979). *Social work practice: People and environments.* New York: Columbia University Press.

Germain, C. B. (1987). Human development in contemporary environments. *Social Service Review,* 565–580.

Germain, C. B. (1994). Human behavior and the social environment. In F. G. Reamer (Eds.), *The foundations of social work knowledge* (pp. 88–121). New York: Columbia University Press.

Germain, C. B. & Gitterman, A. (1986). The life model approach to social work practice revisited. In F. J. Turner (Ed.), *Social work treatment.* pp. 618–643. New York: Free Press.

Germain, C. B., & Gitterman, A. (1987). Ecological perspectives. In A. Minahan et al. (Eds.), *Encyclopedia of social work* (18th ed.) (pp. 488–499). Silver Spring, MD: NASW Press.

Germain, C. B., & Gitterman, A. (1995). Ecological perspective. In R. L. Edwards and J. G. Hopps (Eds.), *Encyclopedia of social work* (19th ed.) (pp. 816–824). Washington, DC: NASW Press.

Gitterman, A., & Germain, C. B. (1976). Social work practice: A life model. *Social Service Review, 50*(4), 3–13.

Goldmeier, J., & Fandetti, D. V. (1991). Self psychology in child welfare practice. *Child Welfare, 70*(5), 559–570.

Goldstein, E. G. (1986). Ego psychology. In F. J. Turner (Ed.), *Social work treatment* (pp. 375–406). New York: Free Press.

Gordon, W. E. (1969). Basic constructs for an integrative and generative conception of social work. In G. Hearn (Ed.), *The general systems approach: contributions toward a holistic conception of social work* (pp. 5–11). New York: Council on Social Work Education.

Gould, K. H. (1996). The misconstruing of multiculturalism: The Stanford debate and social work. In P. L. Ewalt, E. M. Freeman, S. A. Kirk, and D. L. Poole (Eds.), *Multicultural issues in social work* (pp. 29–42). Washington, DC: NASW Press.

Greene, R. R. (1991a). Carl Rogers and the person-centered approach. In R. R. Greene and P. H. Ephross (Eds.), *Human behavior theory and social work practice* (pp. 105–122). Hawthorne, NY: Aldine de Gruyter.

Greene, R. R. (1991b). Eriksonian theory: A developmental approach to ego mastery. In R. R. Greene and P. H. Ephross (Eds.), *Human behavior theory and social work practice* (pp. 39–78). Hawthorne, NY: Aldine de Gruyter.

Greene, R. R. (1991c). The ecological perspective: An eclectic theoretical framework. In R. R. Greene and P. H. Ephross (Eds.), *Human behavior theory and social work practice* (pp. 261–296). Hawthorne, NY: Aldine de Gruyter.

Greene, R. R. (1994). *Human behavior theory: a diversity framework*. Hawthorne, NY: Aldine de Gruyter.

Greene, R. R., & Ephross, P. H. (1991). *Human behavior theory and social work practice*. Hawthorne, NY: Aldine de Gruyter.

Gutierrez, L. M. (1990). Working with women of color: An empowerment perspective. *Social Work, 35*(2), 149–153.

Hare-Mustin, R. T. (1989). The problem of gender in family therapy theory. In M. Mc Goldrick, C. M. Anderson, & F. Walsh (Eds.), *Women in families: A framework for family therapy* (pp. 61–77). New York: Norton.

Hare-Mustin, R. T. (1990). Sex, lies and headaches: The problem is power. In T. J. Goodrich (Ed.), *Perspectives for family therapy* (pp. 61–83). New York: Norton.

Hartman, A. (1979). The extended family. In C. G. Germain (Ed.), *Social work practice: People and environment* (pp. 282–302). New York: Columbia University Press.

Hartman, A., & Laird, J. (1987). Family practice. In A. Minahan et al. (Eds.), *Encyclopedia of social work* (18th ed.) (pp. 575–589). Silver Spring, MD: NASW Press.

Ho, K. H. (1987). *Family therapy with ethnic minorities.* Newbury Park, CA: Sage.

Hoff, M. D., & Polack, R. J. (1993). Social dimensions of the environmental crisis: Challenges for social work. *Social Work, 38*(2), 204–211.

Hoffman, L. (1990). Constructing realities: An art of lenses. *Family Process, 29(1),* 1–12.

Hoffman, L. (1992). A reflective stance for family therapy. In S. McNamee and K. J. Gergen (Eds.), *Therapy as social construction* (pp. 7–24). Newbury Park, CA: Sage.

Janchill, M. P (1969). Systems concepts in casework theory and practice. *Social Casework, 15*(50), 74–82.

Kropf, N. P., & Greene, R. R. (1993). Life review with families who care for developmentally disabled members: A model. *Journal of Gerontological Social Work, 21*(1 / 2), 25–40.

Kuhn, T. S. (1970). *The structure of scientific revolutions* (2nd ed.). Chicago: University of Chicago Press.

Libassi, M. F., & Maluccio, A. N. (1982). Teaching the use of ecological perspectives in community mental health. *Journal of Education for Social Work, 18*(3), 94–100.

Longres, J. F. ([1900] 1990). *Human behavior in the social environment*. Itasca, IL: F. E. Peacock.

Mandel School of Applied Social Sciences (1996). *White paper on social work education—today and tomorrow*. Cleveland, OH: Case Western Reserve University

Maslow, A. (1970). *Motivation and Personality* (2nd ed.). New York: Harper & Row.

McGoldrick, M. J. (1989). Women through the family life cycle. In M. J. McGoldrick, C. M. Anderson, and F. Walsh (Eds.), *Women in families: A framework for family therapy* (pp. 200–226). New York: Norton.

Meyer, C. (1987). Direct practice in social work: Overview. In A. Minahan et al. (Eds.), *Encyclopedia of social work* (18th ed.) (pp. 409–422). Silver Spring, MD: NASW Press.

Meyer, C. (1988). The eco-systems perspective. In R. A. Dorfman (ed.), *Paradigms of clinical social work* (pp. 275–294). New York: Brunner/Mazel.

Middleman, R. R., & Goldberg, G. (1987). Social work practice with groups. In A. Minahan et al. (Eds.), *Encyclopedia of social work* (18th ed.) (pp. 714–729). Silver Spring, MD: NASW Press.

Miller, S. (1980). Reflections on the dual perspective. In E. Mizio and J. Delany (Eds.), *Training for service delivery to minority clients* (pp. 53–61). New York: Family Service of America.

National Association of Social Workers (1978). *Code of ethics of the National Association of Social Workers*. Washington, DC: Author.

Pennekamp, M., & Freeman, E. M. (1988). Toward a partnership perspective: Schools, families, and school social workers. *Social Work in Education*, 246–259.

Pincus, A., & Minahan, A. (1973). *Social Work Practice: Model and Method*. Itasca, IL: Peacock.

Poverny, L. M., & Finch, W. A. (1988). Gay and lesbian domestic partnerships: Expanding the definition of family. *Social Casework*, 116–121.

Ramsay, R. (1994). Conceptualizing PIE with a holistic system of social work. In J. M. Karls and K. E. Wandrei (Eds.), *PIE Manual Person-in-environment: The PIE classification system for social functioning problems* (pp. 171–196). Washington, DC: NASW Press.

Richmond, M. (1917). *Social diagnosis*. New York: Russell Sage Foundation.

Rogers, C. R. (1961). *On becoming a person*. Boston: Houghton Mifflin.

Sanders, D. S. (1974). Educating social workers for the role of effective change agents in a multicultural, pluralistic society. *Journal of Education for Social Work, 10*(2), 86–91.

Schriver, J. M. (1995). *Human behavior and the social environment: Shifting paradigms in essential knowledge for social work practice*. Needham Heights, MA: Allyn & Bacon.

Siporin, M. (1980). Ecological systems theory in social work. *Journal of Sociology and Social Welfare, 7*, 507–532.

Siporin, M. (1983). The therapeutic process in clinical social work. *Social Work, 28*(3), 193–198.

Sophie, J. (1986). A critical examination of stage theories of lesbian identity development. *Journal of Homosexuality, 12*(2), 39–51.

Souflee, F., Jr. (1993). A metatheoretical framework for social work practice. *Social Work, 38*(3), 317–331.

Strean, H. S. (1971). *Social casework theories in action.* Metuchen, NJ: Scarecrow.

Terklesen, G. (1980). Toward a theory of the family cycle. In E. A. Carter and M. McGoldrick (Eds.), *The family life cycle: A framework for family therapy* (pp. 21–52). Hawthorne, NY: Aldine de Gruyter.

U.S. Bureau of the Census (1994). *Statistical abstract of the United States: 1994* (114th ed.). Washington, DC: Government Printing Office.

Wakefield, J. C. (1996a). Does social work need the eco-systems perspective [Part I] *Social Service Review*, 1–32.

Wakefield, J. C. (1996b). Does social work need the eco-systems perspective [Part II] *Social Service Review*, 183–213.

Whittaker, J. K. (1986). Integrating formal and informal social care: A conceptual framework. *British Journal of Social Work, 16*, 39–61.

Whittaker, J., & Garbarino, J. (1983). *Social support networks: informal helping in the human services.* Hawthorne, NY: Aldine de Gruyter.

Whittaker, J. K., Schinke, S. P., & Gilchrist, L. D. (1986). The ecological paradigm in child, youth, and family services: Implications for policy and practice. *Social Service Review*, 483–503.

2
Diversity Defined

ROBERTA R. GREENE, MARIE WATKINS, JOHN McNUTT,
and LUISA LOPEZ

The concept of multiculturalism is in itself controversial, leading to varied and sometimes opposing definitions that span the continuum from abstract construct examined in relation to various theoretical models to a very concrete labeling of the populations to which it refers . . . others focusing on specific needs, services, and policies related to multicultural populations.

—D. de Anda, *Controversial Issues in Multiculturalism*

The social work profession has not always had a broad view of diversity. The approach to diversity and culturally competent social work practice has evolved over time, becoming increasingly broad and inclusive. For example, Cooper (1973) proposed that diversity encompasses "the capacity [of the social worker] to value difference as a positive phenomenon, and to guard against the need to measure everyone by a single standard of behavior" (p. 78). Hooyman (1996) contended that diversity not be considered synonymous with multiculturalism per se. Rather, for the practitioner "to fully incorporate diversity is to promote the full humanity of all voices which have been marginalized in our society" (p. 20).

This chapter reviews the evolution of the social work definition of diversity and the effects of this expansion on culturally competent social work practice. Major concepts and principles from the diversity literature are discussed. The chapter explores the need for an overarching theoretical model for effective cross-cultural social work.

CONTENT FOR CULTURALLY COMPETENT
SOCIAL WORK PRACTICE

[Cultural competence] refers to . . . communities of interest . . . communities not
explicitly racial or ethnic. For example, I will refer to a school for the deaf, the
experiences of elderly street women, a psychiatric clinic, and a drug house. . . . I
am interested in how the concept of culture can be used to better understand a
variety of communities and differing ways of life.

—J. W. Green, *Cultural Awareness in the Human Services:*
A Multi-Ethnic Approach

Perhaps one of the more challenging issues facing the social work profession is the identification of the necessary content for effective social work practice with diverse populations. Human diversity is not unidimensional, but multidimensional; it encompasses many sources for effective practice. To engage in culturally competent social work, practitioners must have sufficient knowledge that encompasses demographic, historical, and socioeconomic information about a diverse group; and skills that comprise interpersonal

> The parameters of diversity content have dramatically expanded over time.

interactions, the gathering of information, the development of relationships, and the construction of effective interventions. Further, practitioner attitudes must involve feelings, perceptions, and worldviews that will enhance their practice with diverse populations (Greene, 1994). *Knowledge competencies* are gained through a cognitive process of learning about cultural similarities and differences such as dress, foods, celebrations, family structure, or immigration experiences. *Affective competencies* are the respectful affective responses to cultural similarities and differences. *Skill-based competencies* are techniques and styles that apply to the problem-solving and change process, for instance, how the social worker interviews clients or intervenes to affect racist policies (Grant & Haynes, 1996).

In addition, the practitioner's ability to work with diverse populations requires knowledge that draws on and integrates content from social welfare policy, research, social work methods, and human behavior. Not all theories of human behavior in the social environment have equal utility in addressing diversity and cross-cultural and ethnic concerns. To effectively deliver cross-cultural social work services, practitioners must be armed with theories that are as universal as possible in their application (Greene, 1991a, 1991b, 1991c). Theories of human behavior that tend to be more universal in nature are generally more applicable to the diversities that characterize U.S. society and allow for human differences within cultures.

Culturally competent practice requires that practitioners shift their feelings, thoughts, and behaviors in response to others whose life experiences differ from their own (Grant & Haynes, 1996). Social work services that allow for diversity and are delivered in a culturally sensitive manner also must consider a client's gender and life-style, including sexual orientation.

Cultural Approach to Diversity

Several of the assumptions of the diversity literature mesh with those of the ecological perspective. A key assumption relevant to both bodies of literature is that humans are a culture-producing and cultural-produced species and are best understood within a broad cultural and historical context (Luria, 1978; Vygotsky, 1929). *Culture,* which encompasses the values, knowledge, and resources that people learn to view as appropriate and desirable, is assumed to have a powerful influence on behavior (Greene, 1994). It establishes the parameters that guide and often limit or structure thinking and behavior (Berger & Federico, 1982). Historically, social workers have attempted to integrate an understanding of a client's psychological dynamics and cultural life (Hamilton, [1940] 1951). Caseworkers borrowed from sociology and anthropology to help define and examine culture as a shared value and belief system (Kluckhohn & Stodbeck, 1961). Practitioners explored the general influences of a client's culture, including how culture contributes to the maintenance of behavioral styles and traditions (Leighton, 1959). Within this context, theories that have sought to explain how children are socialized and customs that have been passed from generation to generation permeate the literature (Austin, 1948; Hollis, 1950; Perlman, 1957).

Because cultural norms and values are uniquely configured for each reference group, practitioners who engage in cross-cultural communication must be particularly sensitive to social boundaries and be prepared to move beyond the present limits of their own personal experiences. At the same time, it is safe to assume that social workers can expect a continuum of attachment to cultural beliefs or that characteristics of a group may not be relevant to a particular group member (Pinderhughes, 1989). Thus, the culturally competent social worker will be a learner (Green, 1995).

As social workers have become aware of the role of culture in service delivery, they increasingly have realized that the notion of culture-free service delivery is an illusion. Culture is likely embedded in the programming and structuring of the helping process (Pinderhughes, 1989). A recurrent theme in the more recent social work literature has emphasized the importance of understanding how help-seeking behavior is shaped by culture and how this socialization affects the practitioner's ability to assess and intervene with clients across cultures.

Categorical Approaches to Diversity

Cultural competence was first equated with ethnic competence and services to minority clients. *Ethnicity* is an orientation toward a group of people that shares a sense of common ancestry, and is maintained by and structured by similarities in culture and language (Longres, [1900] 1990). Hence, ethnicity plays a critical role in an individual's self-identity. An ethnic group may be considered a community or social system, and, as such, is another concept that typifies ecological thinking.

The literature contains many useful sources on social work with ethnic minority clients as communities based on a common identity. For example, Lum (1986) proposed that minority social work should focus on individuals, families, and communities who have historically faced oppression because of their ethnic and socioeconomic status. Working with ethnic minorities is a person-to-person approach that must consider discrimination and devalued status. According to Chau (1991), the group work practitioner of the 21st century will attempt to meet the challenge of strengthening and affirming ethnic identity and will most likely have to accomplish this goal in multiethnic rather than single-ethnic groups.

Over the past three decades, historical and social events in the United States have brought about an increase in the number of groups that have advocated for themselves and sought redress for inequalities. For example, women as well as gays and lesbians have become increasingly better informed consumers of social work services. As a result of such advocacy, their concerns have received more attention in social work practice. Feminist theorists have encouraged practitioners to rethink family therapy models and examine the devalued societal status of women (Suarez, Lewis, & Clark, 1995). In large measure, feminist theorists have urged social workers to address inaccuracies and biases in the established theory and research base concerning women (Kravetz, 1982). Communities based on a common interest have produced a rich body of literature that focuses on women and women's issues. The literature on gay males and lesbians describes advocacy for social work interventions that address the affectional ties and sexual orientation of family members (Berger, 1987, 1983; Crawford, 1988; Roth & Murphy, 1986; Shernoff, 1984). For example, Roth (1989) pointed out that, in psychotherapy with lesbian couples, the practitioner needs to consider individual issues, female socialization, and the social context. The female couple often is not socially sanctioned as a family unit; therefore, the full commitment of each person to the other requires that she deal with stigmatization. Social workers' sensitivity to issues such as social oppression has gained prominence in the literature on the helping process (Anderson & Henderson, 1985).

Specific Client Populations

The literature has tended to focus on specific knowledge, attitudes, and skills for working with a particular client population. Hence, equating diversity with specific populations, the definition of cultural competence has generally become population based. According to Greene (1994), the groups often discussed include

- minority groups, who are defined by limited political power,
- ethnic groups, which are characterized by a shared peoplehood,
- women, in terms of gender roles and power issues,
- the aged population, which is affected by devalued status,
- members of certain social classes, in terms of their economic and educational advantage or disadvantage,
- developmentally disabled people, who are perceived as challenged by mental or physical ability,
- people of varying sexual orientations, who are affected by misconceptions and discrimination about their affectional ties,
- religious groups, which are defined by their spiritual needs, religious beliefs, and practices,
- oppressed populations, who face discrimination and limited political power (p. 5).

Because of the profession's growing interest in diversity issues, definitions of the diverse populations appear in many social work documents. The primary source is the Council on Social Work Education (CSWE) *Curriculum Policy Statement* (CPS) (CSWE, 1992). Through the mandate of the CPS, content in schools of social work must emphasize the effects of discrimination, economic injustice,

> The social work profession has increasingly expanded its commitment to serve diverse client groups.

and oppression on client well-being. Professional social work educators are required to prepare students who understand and appreciate human diversity. On graduation, social workers are expected to understand clients' varied experiences, needs, and beliefs and be able to serve diverse populations through differential assessment and intervention (CSWE, 1996).

Table 2.1. CSWE Curriculum Policy Statement for Master's Degree Programs in Social Work Education

---

Diversity

M6.6   Professional social work education is committed to preparing students to understand and appreciate human diversity. Programs must provide curriculum content about differences and similarities in the experiences, needs, and beliefs of people. The curriculum must include content about differential assessment and intervention skills that will enable practitioners to serve diverse populations.

Each program is required to include content about population groups that are particularly relevant to the program's mission. These include, but are not limited to, groups distinguished by race, ethnicity, culture, class, gender, sexual orientation, religion, physical or mental ability, age, and national origin.

Promotion of Social and Economic Justice

M6.7   Programs of social work education must provide an understanding of the dynamics and consequences of social and economic injustice, including all forms of human oppression and discrimination. They must provide students with the skills to promote social change and to implement a wide range of interventions that further the achievement of individual and collective social and economic justice. Theoretical and practice content must be provided about strategies of intervention for achieving social and economic justice and for combating the causes and effects of institutionalized forms of oppression.

Populations-at-Risk

M6.8   Programs of social work education must present theoretical and practice content about patterns, dynamics, and consequences of discrimination, economic deprivation, and oppression. The curriculum must provide content about people of color, women, and gay and lesbian persons. Such content must emphasize the impact of discrimination, economic deprivation, and oppression upon these groups.

Each program must include content about populations-at-risk that are particularly relevant to its mission. In addition to those mandated above, such groups include, but are not limited to, those distinguished by age, ethnicity, culture, class, religion and physical or mental ability (p. 140).

Source: Commission on Accreditation, *Handbook of Accreditation Standards and Procedures,* Alexandria, VA: Council on Social Work Education, 1992.

The most recent CSWE curriculum standards address diversity and include but are not limited to "groups distinguished by race, ethnicity, culture, gender, sexual orientation, religion, physical or mental ability, age, and national origin" (CSWE, 1992; see Table 2.1). The intent of the standards is to encompass any individual or group that experiences the consequences of social and economic injustice. In this context, *diversity* applies to individuals or groups who have been marginalized and or denied access to power, goods, and opportunities.

Limitations of the Categorical Approach

Green (1995) has argued that categorical explanations of cultural differences often fail to sufficiently consider issues of diversity among groups and in intergroup relationships. He has cautioned against the uncritical adoption of a "categorical approach to diversity" (p. 23). According to Green, there are two differing views of ethnicity: (1) a categorical perspective, which attempts to explain differences between and among groups by the degree to which members follow distinctive cultural traits, for example, their manner of eating, dressing, or behaving, and (2) a transactional approach, which focuses on the way in which people of different groups interact and communicate to maintain their sense of cultural distinctiveness. He believes the *transactional* view, which is based on an ecological view of how people interact across systems, better explains how people from different backgrounds relate to one other.

Because of the growing demands within the profession for better ways to provide services within an increasingly culturally diverse social system, parameters related to cultural diversity are ever expanding (Tully, 1994). As the concept of culturally competent social work practice continues to evolve, the complexity of addressing diverse cultural environments is becoming more clear. It is reasonable to assume, then, that social workers will need to move beyond the limited view of working with specific diversity groups to a more contemporary vision of cross-cultural practice. Such a vision points to a multiple group perspective that allows for a broader focus on manifold worldviews (Longres, 1996) (see Chapters 3 and 4).

Social workers who can work effectively with people and communities other than their own are generally considered *culturally competent* (Crompton, 1974). Cultural competence focuses on ethnographic information in an effort to understand specific clients from diverse communities. Being "familiar with social service issues, individualizing the client, demonstrating empathy, identifying the ecological context of problem resolution, and communicating effectively" are central to the concept of cultural competence (Green, 1995, p. 1). Thus, the concept of cultural competence has "expanded to include experiences related to class identity, sexual identity, and other experiences where power [is] significant" (Pinderhughes, 1989, p. xiii).

Focus on Self-Awareness

To engage in culturally competent social work practice, practitioners need to make a conscious effort to achieve self-awareness. Several authors have developed questionnaires to assess sensitivity to diversity issues among social workers (Ho, 1991; O'Neil, 1984). Palmore (1977) created the Facts on Aging: A Quiz. In addition, O'Neil developed a Cultural Sensitivity Exercise that covers the practitioner's ethnic or cultural identity and memories; a Self-Assessment of Homophobia, which assesses fear of homosexuality or antagonism toward homosexuals; a Self-Assessment of Gender Sensitivity, which addresses personal attitudes and possible stereotypical ideas regarding gender roles; and a Self-Assessment of Value Orientation, which encompasses values that may conflict with human welfare services. In addition, Ho (1991) provided an Ethnic-Sensitive Inventory to enhance practitioner skills with minorities (Table 2.2).

MAJOR CONCEPTS FOR CULTURALLY COMPETENT SOCIAL WORK PRACTICE

To be oppressed is to be rendered obsolete almost from the moment of birth, so that one's experiences of oneself is always contingent on an awareness of just how poorly one approximates the images that currently dominate a society.
—I. I. Goldenberg, *Oppression and Social Intervention*

Self-Esteem and Positive Self-Identity

The concepts of self-esteem and positive self-identity are central to the diversity literature. Identity and self-esteem are largely shaped by early childhood relationships within the child's natural environments (Figure 2.1). However, enhancement of identity and self-esteem can continue throughout the life course through an ever-widening circle of positive relationships. The ecological approach to identity and self-esteem proposes that a positive sense of self-esteem is more likely when the environment supports a person's general success and the person is able to act with a greater degree of competence. Competence can only be understood by examining successful performance in specific social contexts (Germain & Gitterman, 1986).

Social workers may draw on a rich array of concepts to better understand their diverse constituencies.

Sotomayor (1971) contended that self-concept is the most vulnerable psychological component in the transactions between minorities of color

Table 2.2. Ethnic-Sensitive Inventory

In working with ethnic minority clients, I

A. Realize that my own ethnic and class background may influence my effectiveness.
B. Make an effort to assure privacy and/or anonymity.
C. Am aware of the systematic sources (racism, poverty, and prejudice) of their problems.
D. Am against speedy contracting unless initiated by them.
E. Assist them to understand whether the problem is of an individual or a collective nature.
F. Am able to engage them in identifying major progress that has taken place.
G. Consider it an obligation to familiarize myself with their culture, history, and other ethnically related responses to problems.
H. Am able to understand and "tune in" the meaning of their ethnic dispositions, behaviors, and experiences.
I. Can identify the links between systematic problems and individual concern.
J. Am against highly focused efforts to suggest behavioral change or sensitivity.
K. Am aware that some techniques are too threatening to them.
L. Am able at the termination phase to help them consider alternative sources of support.
M. Am sensitive to their fear of racist or prejudiced orientations.
N. Am able to move slowly in the effort to actively "reach for feelings."
O. Consider the implications of what is being suggested in relation to each client's ethnic reality (unique dispositions, behaviors, and experiences).
P. Clearly delineate agency functions and respectfully inform clients of my professional expectations of them.
Q. Am aware that lack of progress may be related to ethnicity.
R. Am able to understand that the worker-client relationship may last a long time.
S. Am able to explain clearly the nature of the interview.
T. Am respectful of their definition of the problem to be solved.
U. Am able to specify the problem in practical concrete terms.
V. Am sensitive to treatment goals consonant to their culture.
W. Am able to mobilize social and extend family networks.
X. Am sensitive to the client's premature termination of service.

Source: Adapted from Ho (1991, pp. 60–61).

and the majority population. Several theorists have discussed the idea that identity formation for African-American teenagers may be more difficult because of the negative massages they receive from the dominant society (Chestang, 1984; Gibbs & Moskowitz-Sweet, 1991; Logan, 1981). Chestang's (1980) *Character Development in a Hostile Environment* outlines the developmental difficulties people face when they experience racist dynamics of the larger society. He suggested that the black experience involves *social injustice*, the denial of legal rights; *societal inconsistency*, the

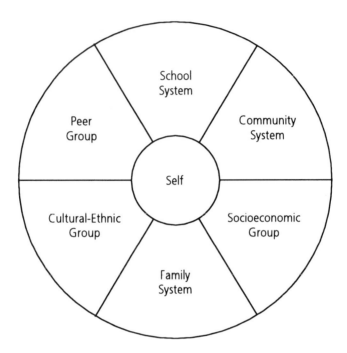

Figure 2.1. The child's ecosystem as a perspective for assessment. Source: Allen-
    Meares, Lane, and Oppenheimer (1981). Reprinted with permission.

institutionalized disparity between word and deed; and *personal impo-
tence,* the loss of autonomy, a diminished sense of self-worth, and low
self-esteem. Chestang challenged the idea that minority group members
fail because of individual deficits. Rather, the three conditions he described are socially determined and institutionally supported and are the
very factors that undermine personal development.

It is increasingly understood that self-worth is a community phenomenon fostered by a sense of trust, common values, and cohesion in communities. In a study of rates of violence in urban neighborhoods, *collective
efficacy* was defined as "a shared vision, if you will, a fusion of a shared
willingness of residents to intervene [in the lives of children], [to build]
social trust, a sense of engagement, and ownership of public space" (Butterfield, 1997, p. 11). The director of the study, a psychiatrist in the Department of Public Health at Harvard, reported that the most important
predictor of collective efficacy, and the most effective means of reducing
teen violence, was a "willingness by [community] residents to intervene
in the lives of children" (ibid.).

Dual Perspective

Although schools of social work have historically offered courses to address minority concerns and taught strategies to confront racism, ethnocentricism, and sexism, in 1970 CSWE gave high priority to the development of such educational programs (Echols, Gabel, Landerman, & Reyes, 1988). It was argued that "in a pluralistic society composed of different racial, ethnic, and socio-economic groups, the goal of social work education must be to train social workers to meet the needs of its total client system" (Norton, 1978, p. 1). In addition, CSWE published the dual-perspective framework, which often is considered the cornerstone of social work practice with minority clients. The framework suggested a cognitive and attitudinal context that not only explored the problems that may accompany minority status, but the richness and benefits of minority contributions to society.

A *dual perspective* is an outgrowth of systems thinking that views every individual as part of two systems: the larger system of the dominant society and the smaller system of the individual's immediate environment (Figure 2.2). The culturally competent social worker who has a "conscious awareness of the cognitive and attitudinal levels of the similarities and differences in the two systems" (Norton, 1978, p. 3), is better able to provide more culturally sensitive services and assist the client to tap into natural support systems for strength (Delgado & Delgado, 1982).

The dual perspective helps social workers evaluate disparate systems and determine where the client's major sources of stress lie. Practitioners should understand that minority individuals develop two self-images: (1) a personal self-image derived from the nurturing systems of the family and immediate community and (2) the social self-image developed through the society's sustaining political, economic, and educational systems (Norton, 1978). The social self-image is particularly affected by prejudice and discrimination often found in social institutions.

Norton (1993) has contended that the dual perspective continues to be useful; however, she urged that it be revisited and combined with an anthropological-ecological approach. This combination would improve the framework by preventing stereotyping, illuminating the universal goals of societal organization, and exploring the early socialization of children.

In his article "Reflections on the Dual Perspective," Miller (1980) recounted a conversation with a minority student that captures the full meaning of the dual perspective:

> For a Chicano like myself it can be very hard. I have found that I am lonely for a people, a culture, a way of life—I have missed my people. Not just my

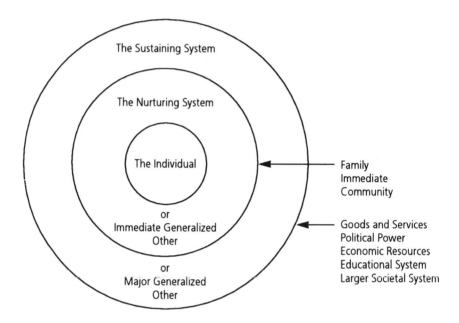

Figure 2.2.   The dual system of all individuals. Source: Norton (1978, p. 5).

family, but the Chicanos and the Chicano way of life. I miss speaking our language with a group of people. I miss our food and the many varieties of it, miss seeing others like me at restaurants and the movies, miss my people and culture. But aside from that, there is the matter of rethinking what I know and believe. Minority students who have achieved high success in the educational system are often hurt most, because they have to exchange their way of life and their values so as to fit into the mold of that system. I have had to do that for a little while, but I have not given up my way of life and values. I have only placed them aside for a while. Once I return to San Antonio and the barrio, I will again be myself with one difference: I will know how to think like the people that are in control of things; and I will have credentials which they recognize. I will not think like them all the time; only when I want to communicate with them. (p. 59)

Biculturalism

Working with bicultural clients is an important aspect of cross-cultural social work. Definitions of a bicultural perspective focus on an individual's ability to move effectively from his or her own ethnic community to the larger society (Chau, 1991). In large measure, minority individuals may learn more of their traditional culture at home, acquiring dominant cultural patterns from public schooling, content on mass media, and mass marketing techniques (de Anda, 1984; Valentine, 1971).

Socialization patterns and the maintenance of cultural differences in different contexts are related to an individual's development and sense of well-being. The extent and success of movement between a person's own nurturing environment and the larger society's sustaining environment differs among individuals and the various cultures involved. As Longres ([1900] 1990) so aptly put it, "Minority group members must know both what is expected of them if they are to be successful within their own community and what is expected of them if they are to be successful in the majority community" (p. 172). In interviews of 151 healthy Cuban-Americans to ascertain their views on biculturalism and to determine how a bicultural perspective affects mental health, Gomez (1990) found that subjective mental health was positively related to an ethnic group member's degree of biculturalism. The more bicultural, or the greater the comfort in both cultures, the Cuban-American was, the higher his or her sense of personal well-being.

Because the term *bicultural* is qualitative and dynamic, it may mean more than moving from one culture to another (Bilides, 1991). The term may be used to refer to movement between cultural contexts such as between social classes. In an application of biculturalism to workplace issues, Van Den Bergh (1991) proposed that, because the workplace is increasingly diverse, it is useful for employers to provide group experiences that socialize employees and enhance their sense of belonging to the organization. Homosexuality is another aspect of diversity in which the concept of biculturality may be applied. Lukes and Land (1990) suggested that "even if sexual minorities do not have a culture in the traditional sense, there are several reasons for examining sexual minorities from a cultural context" (p. 155). Among these is that it gives the social worker a better understanding of structural, political, and life-style differences, a further realization of how sexual minorities may be rejected by the larger society, and an increased acceptance of self-definition.

Ethnosystems

Connectedness with one's own and other cultural groups is viewed as a central dynamic in understanding human behavior between and among diverse groups. Building on a systems understanding, Solomon (1976) proposed that race or ethnicity is the primary organizing feature in U.S. society. She coined the term *ethnosystem* to refer to a collective of interdependent ethnic groups bound by unique history and culture and held

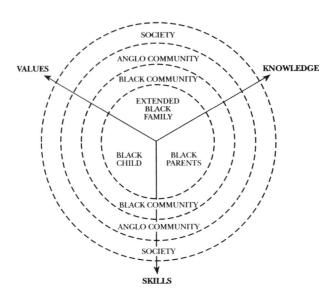

Figure 2.3. A framework for understanding the behaviors of an ethnosystem. Source: Bush, Norton, Sanders, and Solomon (1983, p. 112). Reprinted with permission.

together by a single political system (Figure 2.3.). Each ethnosystem has a relative amount of power and control of resources; that is, each group has an unequal proportion of the overall systems resources. This idea is a central dynamic in race or ethnic relations. The concept may be used to better understand how each family and individual interacts with the larger society in accessing a fair share of societal resources.

In addition, the ethnosystem concept is useful in understanding how people as members of groups have different social histories, life experiences, and social contexts that relate to personal well-being. For example, Pinderhughes (1989) adopted an ecological metaphor in her discussion of the relationship of cultural connectedness to mental health. She argued that the state of mental health is facilitated by a positive sense of connectedness with one's own cultural group. Such a connection allows a person to set goals to validate, preserve, and enhance his or her chosen identity; facilitates healthy relationships and group interaction; provides respect for the person's belief system; and enables a person to achieve mastery of his or her environment and to maintain self-esteem.

> Diversity concepts explain a range of behavior from internal to macro-level processes.

Power and Empowerment

Understanding the relationship among human growth and development, power, and powerlessness is also central to cross-cultural social
work practice (Pinderhughes, 1989; Solomon, 1976). Major social work
theorists who have examined how power affects human function have
proposed that power deficits are a major problem for devalued or marginalized individuals and communities (Solomon, 1976; Pinderhughes, 1989).
For example:

The diversity literature has examined and the ecological approach addresses how societal power may be withheld from a client on the basis of
personal or cultural characteristics such as skin color, ethnicity, and sexual orientation. Both the literature and the ecological approach have embraced action to redress power inequities.

Power, a complex controversial construct, is an individual, interpersonal, and societal phenomenon. Power is the capacity to influence for one's
own benefit the forces that affect one's life space" (Pinderhughes, 1989,
p. 154). The concept of power may be used to explore a person's sense of
mastery and competence; understand one person's undue influence over
another; examine stratification of goods and resources within a society;
and understand denial of access to societal institutions.

The term *hierarchy*, which is closely linked to the notion of power,
addresses the ranking and control of various members of a system. Hierarchy may be thought of as a "ladder of success" or the pecking order
within a system. Such unequal distribution of power, which may stem
from a disproportionate share of and access to education, health, housing,
and employment, leads to vertical stratification of individuals and families in society.

At the personal level, such societal inequities may lead to a sense of
powerlessness. *Powerlessness* is the inability to manage emotions, skill,
and knowledge in a way that leads to successful role performance and
personal gratification. That is, the feeling of being able to control one's
own destiny is important to psychological well-being. Moreover, an individual, group, or community may be unable to obtain an equitable share
of resources. In addition to the devaluation of the powerless individual or
group, power differentials need to be understood for their effect on fair
treatment in the legal system, labor and housing market, and educational
practices (Davis, Leijenaar, & Oldersma, 1991).

There can be a destructive cycle between discrimination, poverty, and powerlessness in which the failure of the larger social system to provide needed
resources operates in a circular manner. . . . The more powerless a community the more families within it are hindered from meeting the needs of their

members and from organizing the community so that it can provide them with more support. (Pinderhughes, 1983, p. 332)

Power should be considered a factor in the client-social worker relationship (Pinderhughes, 1989). In fact, because practitioners control needed resources and access to forms of expertise, some theorist consider power asymmetry between social worker and client to be unavoidable (Simon, 1994). Thus, equalizing power within the relationship and arriving at mutually established goals are central to effective cross-cultural social work practice. The concept of power anticipates that the practitioner will use *empowerment techniques,* a process whereby an individual gains power and interpersonal influence. Empowerment techniques, such as working with the client to obtain denied resources, are helpful to individuals, families, and groups. Such techniques also help communities "rediscover their own capacities and to modify their environments to conform to rights, needs, and goals" (Solomon, 1976, p. 21). In addition, empowerment helps build support systems and reduce societal discrimination (Greene, 1991a, 1991b, 1991c).

Institutional Racism

In U.S. society, the term *race* has come to "refer to differences between people based on color" (Pinderhughes, 1989, p. 89). Race also is a social concept that too often defines social discourse, such as "making moral evaluations" (Green, 1995, p. 12). *Racism,* often equated with prejudice, is a form of prejudging and expecting certain behaviors from specific individuals. Racism not only can occur on the interpersonal level, but occurs at the level of society when racial differences are seemingly legitimized by societal arrangements. A single institution is not necessarily the problem. Rather, it is the way a total network of systems works together to reinforce discrimination and lack of access (Pinderhughes, 1989).

Every society creates institutions to perform certain functions, for example, the family or kibbutz to offer socialization; the legal and correction system to assure social control; schools and universities to provide education; and churches, synagogues, mosques, and so forth to supply religion (Anderson & Carter, 1990). Institutional arrangements regulate day-to-day interactions. Society's institutional structures reflect the general norms and values of society including attitudes toward race, religion, age, or women.

All social institutions, including schools, hospitals, and "even" social service agencies, are usually governed by the prevailing ideologies and routines. As people interact with social institutions by seeking information, help, resources, and so forth, they encounter these societal norms of what constitutes "good behavior" (Goffman, 1961). Behaviors and values, such as racism, that dominate general U.S. society, are likely to be embedded in institutions:

> This "institutional racism" implies that the negative valuation of minority individuals and communities has resulted in their experience of systematic disadvantage from the policies, procedures, value sets, and normative behaviors in our major social institutions. (Solomon, 1976, p. 16)

Power arrangements, brought about by the negative valuations based on membership in a stigmatized group, can affect anyone who is consistently excluded or deemed expendable (Goldenberg, 1978). Power differentials are also institutionalized in social arrangements and may account for other forms of discrimination: such as ageism, "a process of systematic stereotyping of and discrimination against people because they are old" (Butler, 1969, p. 12); or sexism, a means of continuing "the inferiority [status] of women embedded into the norms and beliefs of the society by means of language, socialization processes, and cultural stereotyping" (Longres, [1900] 1990, p. 207).

Institutional racism is a product of these institutionalized social arrangements that embody oppression and bias. For instance, public schools may fail to provide African-American students with quality education and marketable skills, whereas hospitals may not provide equal access to services (Burman & Allen-Meares, 1996). Race, then, takes on a "cultural significance as a result of the social processes that sustain majority-minority status" (Pinderhughes, 1989, p. 9).

Social and Economic Justice

At one time, economics and social work were closely aligned disciples. Early social workers often came from the ranks of persons trained in economics, such as Francis Perkins (Austin, 1986). Social workers have long had and continue to build on their commitment to social and economic justice (Beverly & McSweeney, 1987). This commitment to the rights of the poor and the oppressed is demonstrated in the stands taken by social work organizations. For example, CSWE's recent accreditation standards mandated that all professional social work education programs incorporate content on social and economic justice into their curricula (CSWE, 1992), while the current National Association of Social Workers Code of Ethics renewed the profession's mission to enhance human well-being and the well-being of society (NASW, 1997).

Economic and social justice has both an awareness aspect and an interventive aspect. The *awareness aspects* means an appreciation of the nature
of economic and social justice and when and why economic and social
injustice occurs. The *interventive aspect* refers to the ability to intervene in
economic and social institutions and processes. To carry out the commitment to enhance general well-being, social workers need to have an understanding of models of social and economic justice and how they relate
to ecological theory and diversity theory. Ideas from these models may
then be incorporated into social work practice in the professions' efforts to
build healthy social systems. One of the enduring ethical questions that
confronts any profession is What is just? How we answer this question
defines many of our social relationships, particularly those that deal with
the allocation of resources. Few would argue for the value of injustice.
Justice, however, means different things to different people. The major
positions on social and economic justice are the conservative approach,
the liberal approach, and the communitarian approach (McNutt, 1994).

Conservative *approaches* to social and economic justice argue for the
greatest good for the greatest number (Ericson, 1990). A just society is
defined as a society that maximizes the amount of benefits that it can
provide to its members. From a conservative approach, inequality and
even poverty may be in the interest of a just society because they motivate
people to greater effort (Gilder, 1980). Government action that interferes
with the market is seen as unjust (except in a few limited circumstances)
because it reduces economic efficiency and thus limits the production of
social assets (Friedman, 1962).

While conservatives advocate a limited social safety net, they believe
there is no justification for state-sanctioned redistribution of income. From
this viewpoint, redistribution of income and other assets works against
the cause of economic efficiency, and thus social and economic justice,
because it destroys incentives to produce. The market, not the government, is seen as the source of ultimate justice. Rather, individual rights are
important to the conservative approach to social and economic justice.
Individual action, motivated by self-interest and managed by the market
system, is expected to lead to optimal output and thus maximal justice.
Diversity of the population is viewed as a characteristic that makes economic systems more competitive and adaptable. In addition, the market
should discourage racism, discrimination, and oppression as a waste of
economic resources and efficiency.

On the other hand, liberal thought on social and economic justice does
not share the assumptions about the efficacy of the market system. The
liberal approach to social and economic justice contends that government
action is the means to a just society. Rawls (1971), whose ideas about
social and economic justice are representative of the liberal position, ar-

gued that justice means fairness in human relationships that involve the allocation of social resources.

There are a number of principles that flow from the basic assumption that fairness is the central criterion of social and economic justice. The individual is seen as the basic unit of concern, without regard to individual traits and characteristics. To consider an individual solely by his or her traits would invite unfairness. This position is in conflict with feminist thinkers who argue that people cannot be separated from context (Cochran, 1989).

The liberal approach gives primary attention to basic needs, such as food, clothing, shelter, education, and health care. The right to fulfill basic needs is considered superior to the fulfillment of preference needs, such as the luxuries of some well-off persons. This viewpoint means that the state is responsible to see that economic redistribution occurs to the point that basic human needs are fulfilled. The idea of entitlements, safety nets, and the welfare state reflect this principle.

Individual rights, ensured by state action, are another important part of Rawls's liberal (1971) model. Rights are unconditional and are not related to individual characteristics. The liberal model seeks to protect diverse groups through the development of individual rights. Racism, discrimination, and oppression are seen as violations of fairness and individual rights—and as therefore wrong. This is true of both overt discrimination and institutional racism.

Communitarianism breaks with both the liberal and conservative approaches' focus on the centrality of the individual by placing a central emphasis on community and institutions. Communitarians fear the rise of individualism, which they blame for the breakdown of community and social institutions (Etzioni, 1993). Whereas liberals and conservatives are held responsible for the proliferation of individual rights, communitarians argue for a balancing of rights and responsibilities as a way to support community, replenish institutions, and rebuild social fabric. Etzioni (1993) argued that a communitarian approach to social justice should include individual responsibility for oneself, responsibility for those near to the person, community responsibility, and—in exceptional cases—societal responsibility.

Communitarians reject both liberal and conservative ideas about rights without context. Communitarians propose that diversity is encouraged by healthy, functioning, and responsive communities. These communities use informal means to protect and encourage diversity. State action is unnecessary and may even have negative impacts.

All three approaches—the conservative, the liberal, and the communitarian—agree that it is in society's interest to protect diversity and ensure some level of social and economic support for the poor and oppressed.

Conservative approaches see discrimination and oppression as a waste of economic resources, which lead to economic inefficiency and thus to lower levels of production, which is bad for society. Liberal approaches see discrimination and oppression as a violation of the fairness principle and of individual rights. Communitarians see discrimination and oppression as an aspect of the breakdown of community. While all of these approaches start at different places, all stress that diversity must be encouraged for the good of society and of individuals.

OVERARCHING DIVERSITY PRINCIPLES
FOR SOCIAL WORK PRACTICE

A final reason for examining cross-cultural encounters in social work has to do with how the profession has conceptualized its involvement with ethnic [and a variety of] communities generally. Despite years of work with minority clients, practitioners have only recently considered their relations with minority communities systematically.
—R. R. Greene, *Human Behavior Theory: A Diversity Framework*

The social work literature contains rich theoretical and practice principles as well as value stances that taken together document the commonality of issues among theorists concerned with culturally competent social work practice. This section summarizes principles gleaned from

> A major challenge for the social work profession is the development of a more systematic and sensitive approach to serving diverse constituencies.

the literature, and presents the results of a pilot survey to summarize major themes (Table 2.2.).

The diversity principles may be categorized by knowledge, encompassing cognitive or factual information; attitudes, comprised of affective or value-laden content; and skills, including methods of assessment and intervention. These three components of diversity content overlap and cut across all social work curriculum areas: social welfare policies and services, social work practice, social work research, human behavior in the social environment, and field practicum.

The knowledge component refers to the information needed to develop an accurate understanding of the client's life experiences and life patterns. This information may range from an understanding of internal mental processes to political and economic concerns. Knowledge diversity principles most frequently found in the literature include:

- Diversity–sound practice requires a model.
- Diversity practice requires the ability to think critically.
- Diversity content encompasses practice methods, social policy, human behavior in the social environment, research, and field education
- Diversity content encompasses the selective and differential use of knowledge, skills, and attitudes pertaining to all areas of social work practice.
- Theory-building for social work practice with diverse constituencies should reevaluate concepts such as normalcy and deviance.
- Diversity practice involves the use of knowledge or research conducted in a culturally congruent manner to people involved in the study.
- Diversity practice requires an understanding of multiple theories such as

systems thinking	an ecological perspective
ego-psychodynamic approach	psychotherapeutic principles
symbolic interaction	life span developmental stages and tasks
social construction	cognitive behavioral theory

- Diversity practice requires an understanding of such concepts as

self-identity	biopsychosocial function
stress	person-environment
the dual perspective	the person is political
mastery of the environment	

- A diversity framework views culture as a source of cohesion, identity, strength, strain, and discordance.
- A diversity framework needs to provide an understanding of a culture's adaptive strategies.
- Diversity practice requires an understanding of bicultural status.
- The scope of diversity practice encompasses all populations at risk.
- Diversity content provides an understanding of a range of individuals and groups affected by social, economic, and legal biases; distribution of rights and resources; or oppression.
- Diversity practice requires an understanding of the person's behavior as guided by membership such as families, groups, organizations, and communities including:

family	diverse family forms
partner	peers
cohort	work colleagues
schoolmates	social network
intergroup relations	kin network

geographic isolation   reference groups
religious affiliations   political affiliations

- Diversity practice requires that social workers understand the process of inclusion and exclusion.
- Diversity practice requires social workers to understand that individuals and groups may
  have limited access to resources,
  live in environments damaging to self-esteem,
  live in unsafe environments ,
  have a history of oppression,
  experience their environment as hostile,
  have various ties to their land and physical environment,
  have previous history with health and human services.
- Diversity practice takes an understanding of the effects of
  institutional racism   institutional sexism
  institutional ageism   institutional homophobia
  institutional class barriers
  institutional barriers to physically
      challenged people

To be an effective social worker with diverse populations requires that an understanding of client (system) function be joined with practitioner self-awareness. Feelings and attitudes toward a particular client population, especially when hidden and negative, have the potential to interfere with effective social work practice. Therefore, affective learning, usually considered experiential, involves an exploration of practitioner attitude. Attitude diversity principles frequently addressed in the literature include:

- Diversity practice recognizes that social work practice cannot be neutral, value free, or objective.
- Diversity practice requires an appreciation for attitudinal differences between clients and social workers regarding
  autonomy   use of space
  self-determination or choice   relationship to the earth
  intuition   individuation
  group or collective orientation unique familial obligation
  rationality   family caregiving responsibilities

  interrelatedness   separation
  hierarchy   timing of life events
  role performance   intimacy
  trust   interdependence

self-disclosure	authority
competitiveness	power
productivity	experience with violence
use of time	privacy

- Diversity practice requires education/training involving a shift in feelings, thoughts, and behaviors.
- Social workers who are culturally sensitive appreciate differences.
- Diversity practice requires that social workers be nonjudgmental.
- Diversity practice requires that social workers understand that their decisions may be culture bound or ethnocentric.
- Diversity practice requires social workers to be self-aware, open to cultural differences, and aware of their own (preconceived) assumptions of diverse groups values and biases.
- Diversity practice requires social workers to understand their own and the client's belief systems, customs, norms, ideologies, rituals, traditions, and so forth.
- Diversity practice requires social workers appreciate and confront their own privilege.
- Diversity practice requires social workers to use processes that value the client.
- Diversity practice requires social workers to uphold the profession's commitment to social justice.
- Theory-building for social work practice with diverse constituencies should critically reevaluate underlying values of practice models.
- Diversity practice requires an appreciation for what it means to be a member of a group devalued in U.S. society.
- Diversity practice requires an appreciation for how marginalization affects human function.
- Diversity practice requires reexamination of Anglo-centric views or further incorporation of nondominant culture views in the helping process.
- Diversity practice calls for social workers to understand how client issues are compounded by poverty.
- A diversity framework helps social workers to understand the client in the context of whether the client believes obtaining services is stigmatizing.

To work effectively across various client communities, practitioners must be prepared to use their practice skills differentially. Skills for diversity practice generally include interacting appropriately, gathering information in a culturally sensitive manner, and constructing helpful and meaningful interventions (Greene, 1994). Skill diversity principles that appear frequently in the literature include:

- Diversity practice involves the integration of skills and theory grounded in the reality of the client. Diversity practice recognizes differences in help-seeking patterns, definition of problems, selection of solutions, and interventions.
- The most effective social workers in diversity practice differentially use assessment and intervention strategies.
- In diversity practice, social workers direct change efforts at any level of intervention or at multiple levels from personal problems to environmental restraints.
- Diversity practice requires that social workers sincerely convey signals of respect congruent with the client's cultural beliefs.
- Diversity practice requires that social workers have a strong ability to develop client trust, mutual respect, acceptance, and positive regard.
- Diversity practice requires that social workers effectively work with feelings of anger, suspicion, and distrust.
- Diversity practice requires social worker be learners.
- Social workers who practice effectively with diverse clients use a strengths perspective.
- Diversity practice can be enhanced through ethnographic interviewing skills.
- Diversity practice requires social workers to appreciate and use appropriate

language	terms or words
visual clues	facial expressions
self-revelation	cadence
tone	

- The most effective social workers in diversity practice
  explore issues of authority or equality in the therapeutic relationship,
  use a relationship-oriented style,
  promote role equity, where culturally appropriate,
  reduce barriers to optimal client functioning,
  act as cultural brokers,
  understand multiple meanings or voices,
  aid the construction of new client stories or meanings,
  use client expertise,
  use client-centered outcome measures.
- Effective diversity practice may
  examine intrapsychic phenomenon,
  give attention to the effects of stigma on self-esteem,
  use and interpret knowledge from the dominant culture,

use and interpret knowledge from the client's culture.

- Diversity practice identifies and uses the client's definition of successful coping strategies.
- Effective social workers in diversity practice assess a client within the context of his or her

culture	religion
sociopolitical life	gender
historical	age
life course or cohort	sexual orientation
biological context	physical challenges and abilities
social class	mental challenges and abilities
community	

- A diversity framework should encompass an understanding of the client within the context of protection by federal, state, or local laws.
- A diversity framework helps social workers to understand the client in the context of

nationality	immigration status (newness)
citizenship status	economic integration
physical appearance	family characteristics
living environment	educational history
health status	

- Social workers in diversity practice assess a client within the context of his or her pathway to the United States, and whether his or her pathway was voluntary or involuntary; or, if an original American, within his or her place of origin.
- Diversity practice promotes a client's sense of self-efficacy and mastery of his or her environment.
- Diversity practice enhances or restores client's psychosocial function and seeks to redress structural inequities at the societal level.
- Diversity practice aims to increase personal, interpersonal, or political power of individuals, families, groups, and communities through empowerment techniques.
- Diversity practice aims to promote a sense of the collective, increase access to resources and to co-created client-social worker solutions.
- Diversity practice includes attention to mutual-aid systems.
- The most effective social workers in diversity practice use a blend of formal and informal resources, including

folk healers	interpreters
cultural guides	grassroots support
natural helpers	paraprofessionals
political activists	

- The most effective social workers in diversity practice explore and try to correct insensitive services that lead to agency underuse.
- Agencies involved in effective diversity practice
  are engaged with the community,
  reexamine and address issues of community power differentials,
  provide access to other resources,
  are consumer oriented,
  use participatory management techniques,
  work to bring down barriers among staff, social workers, and clients,
  provide in-service training relative to diversity,
  examine and enhance program development with community members,
- Diversity practice requires the incorporation of cultural information into agency procedures, structures, and services.

SELECT MODELS OF CROSS CULTURAL SOCIAL WORK

At a minimum, a model for culturally responsive social and health services would require . . . [defining] a model of cross-cultural social work and caring services. The model must be systematic, and it must take account of cultural complexity in a genuinely pluralistic society.

—J. W. Green, *Cultural Awareness in the Human Services:*
A Multi-Ethnic Approach

There is growing recognition that social work needs overarching principles and models to address the profession's diverse constituencies. Some social work theorists have begun the difficult task of systematically developing overarching models and principles for effective cross-cultural practice (Chau, 1990; Devore & Schlesinger, 1987; Green, 1989). The following are several theorists who have had a major effect on this effort.

Devore and Schlesinger

Devore and Schlesinger (1987) examined the intersect of ethnicity and social class and developed a model that would enable social workers to be more "attuned to ethnically distinctive values and community practices" (p. 516). They (Devore & Schlesinger 1987a) also suggested that practitioners need to think through the effects of their own ethnicity in the provision of ethnic-sensitive social work services. This thought process

involves discovering "ME—not always nice, sometimes judgmental, prejudiced and non-caring" (p. 83). Such ethnic-sensitive practice, according
to Devore and Schlesinger, is based on three major principles: (1) social
workers must give simultaneous attention to individual and systemic
concerns as they emerge out of client need and professional assessment,
(2) practitioners must adapt their practice skills to respond to the particular needs and dispositions of various ethnic and class groups, and (3)
practitioners must recognize that the "route of the social worker" affects
problem definition and intervention.

Green

Green's (1982, 1995) model for ethnic competence in social work practice requires that social workers conduct themselves in a way that is
congruent with the behavior and expectations that members of the group
being served see as appropriate among themselves. He has defined five
major features of ethnic-competent practice: (1) awareness of one's own
cultural limitations; (2) openness to cultural differences; (3) a client-
oriented, systematic learning style; (4) use of cultural awareness; and (5)
acknowledgment of cultural integrity. Through ethnographic approaches,
Green (1989) has applied principles of cross-cultural practice to minorities
and other cultural groups. For social workers to respect and celebrate a
client's diversity, he argued, they must extend their cultural knowledge
by assuming the role of social work-learner.

Ho

M. K. Ho (1987) proposed an ecological approach to culturally sensitive
family practice. According to that approach, a culturally competent family
therapist

- recognizes that some of the assumptions of a particular human
  behavior theory may be antithetical to a particular cultural orientation,
- uses theory-based practice differentially,
- considers the family's sociopolitical history and present situation,
- is congruent with the family's belief system and ethical and value
  orientation,
- is accepting of the way in which a particular family defines its
  problem and expresses help-seeking behaviors,
- identifies and works within a particular family's form,

- bases his or her practice on a culturally sound examination of family structure and communication patterns,
- may, at times, deliver services in other than the English language or using a social intermediary,
- recognizes the way culture shapes individual and family life experiences as well as developmental transitions,
- is sensitive to the influences of culture on a family's role differentiation and process of self-definition,
- selects skills and techniques differentially to achieve congruence with a family's culture,
- uses a multisystems approach,
- uses natural support systems and helpers, such as healers and religious leaders,
- selects goals culturally congruent and mutually satisfactory to the family's goals,
- is open to the family's ideas about what is effective for them (as summarized in Greene, 1994, p. 156).

Feminist Theorists

Several feminist thinkers have applauded the use of feminist theory to address diversity (Van Den Bergh, 1995). Theorists have applied feminist principles to women of color (Suarez et al., 1995), the aging of women (Brown, 1995), and the integration of lesbian or gay male experiences in practice and education (Donadello, 1986). Other theorists have discussed the combined use of the ecological perspective with feminist principles to broaden and reinforce both visions (Kissman, 1991). These combined frameworks would generally offer a perspective that examines "a multidimensional view of potential strengths in the external environment in which women and men interact" (p. 23). The feminist theorist Collins (1986), in calling for a social science paradigm that would adequately explain female experiences, indicated that the congruence embodied in the social work person-environment approach and the feminists' "the person is political" is compelling. According to Collins, both the ecological framework and feminist thought are integrated approaches that examine transactions between people and their environments.

These are among several models that provide a rich background to inform many aspects of cross cultural-social work practice. However, more needs to be done to further conceptualize an overarching model for culturally competent social work practice. The need for general diversity practice principles stems from the realization that it is impossible to acquire in-depth knowledge about all diverse clients. Furthermore, a single profile does not fit all members of any specific diversity group. For example, Solomon (1976) pointed out that general information about a particular group is helpful only in establishing hypotheses about a client's situation, and cannot substitute for an exploration about the client's reality.

To work effectively with diverse constituencies means the social worker must develop a multicultural worldview that responds to increasingly complex environments. This perspective-building requires a framework that "can help all groups in society orient their thinking at a transcultural level" (Gould, 1996, p. 36). Transcultural models suggest that this is not the equivalent of adding one more group as part of the social work curriculum or adding one more group to practice competency. Rather, transcultural models "deal with the diversity of the world within ourselves" (Hartman, 1990, p. 291).

The following chapters suggest how the social work profession may combine major diversity principles with the ecological perspective to create an integrated approach to social work practice with diverse populations across fields of practice. Perhaps this combined approach will provide another focus in the ongoing challenge to serve the diverse constituencies of social work.

REFERENCES

Allen-Meares, P., Lane, B. A., & Oppenheimer, M. (1981). A child's natural habitat. Paper presented at the Second National Conference of School Social Workers, Washington, D.C., May 7–9.

Anderson, R., & Carter, I. (1990). *Human behavior in the social environment: A social systems approach* (4th ed.). Hawthorne, NY: Aldine de Gruyter.

Anderson, S. C., & Henderson, D. C. (1985). Working with lesbian alcoholics. *Social Work, 30*(6), 518–525.

Austin, D. (1986). *The history of social work education.* Austin: University of Texas, School of Social Work, Monograph in Social Work Education #1.

Austin, L. N. (1948). Trends in differential treatment in social casework. *Journal of Social Casework, 29,* 203–211.

Berger, R. M. (1983). What is homosexual: A definition model. *Social Work, 28*(5), 132–135.

Berger, R. M. (1987). Homosexuality: Gay men. In A. Minahan et al. (Eds.), *Encyclopedia of social work* (18th ed.) (pp. 795–805). Silver Spring, MD: NASW Press.

Berger, R. M., & Federico, R. (1982). *Human behavior: A social work perspective.* New York: Longman.

Beverly, D., & McSweeney, E. (1987). *Social welfare and social justice.* Englewood Cliffs, NJ: Prentice Hall.

Bilides, D. G. (1990). Race, color, ethnicity, and class: Issues of biculturalism in school-based adolescent counseling groups. *Social Work with Groups, 13*(4), 43–58.

Brown, C. (1995). A feminist life span perspective on aging. In N. Van Den Bergh (Ed.), *Feminist Practice in the 21st Century* (pp. 330–354). Washington, DC: NASW Press.

Burman, S., & Allen-Meares, P. (1994). Neglected victims of murder: Children's witness to parental homicide. *Social Work, 39*(1), 28–34.

Bush, J. A., Norton, D. G., Sanders, C. L., & Solomon, B. B. (1983). An integrative approach for the inclusion of content on Blacks in social work education. In J. C. Chunn, P. J. Dunston, & F. Ross-Sheriff (Eds.), *Mental health and people of color*. Washington, DC: Howard University Press.

Butler, R. N. (1969). Directions in psychiatric treatment of the elderly: Role of perspectives of the life cycle. *Gerontologist, 9*(2), 143–138.

Butterfield, F. (1997). Study links violence rate to cohesion of community. *New York Times,* August, p. 11.

Chau, K. L. (1990). A model for teaching cross-cultural practice in social work. *Journal of Social Work Education, 26*(2), 124–133.

Chau, K. L. (1991). *Ethnicity and biculturalism: Emerging perspectives of social group work.* New York: Haworth.

Chestang, L. W. (1980). Character development in a hostile society. In M. Brown (Ed.), *Life Span Development* (pp. 40–50). New York: Macmillan.

Chestang, L. (1984). Racial and personal identity in the black experience. In B. W. White (Ed.), *Color in a White Society* (pp. 83–94). Silver Spring, MD: NASW Press.

Cochran, C. (1989). The thin theory of community: The communitarians and their critics. *Political Studies, 32,* 422–435.

Collins, B. G. (1986). Defining feminist social work. *Social Work, 31*(3), 214–219.

Cooper, S. (1973). A look at the effect of racism on clinical work. *Social Casework, 54*(2), 76–84.

Council on Social Work Education (1992). *Curriculum policy statement for master's degree programs in social work education.* Alexandria, VA: Author.

Council on Social Work Education (1996). *Handbook of accreditation standards and procedures.* Alexandria, VA: Author

Crawford, S. (1988). Cultural context as a factor in the expansion of therapeutic conversation with lesbian families. *Journal of Strategic and Systemic Therapies, 7*(3), 2–10.

Crompton, D. W. (1974). Minority content in social work education—Promise or pitfall? *Journal of Education for Social Work, 10*(1), 9–18.

Davis, K., Leijenaar, M., & Oldersma, J. (Eds.) (1991). *The gender of power.* Newbury Park, CA: Sage.

de Anda, D. (1984). Bicultural socialization: Factors affecting the minority experience. *Social Work, 29*(2), 101–107.

de Anda, D. (Ed.) (1997). *Controversial issues in multiculturalism.* Needham Heights, MA: Allyn & Bacon.

Delgado, M. & Delgado, D. (1982). Natural support systems: Source of strength in Hispanic communities. *Social Work, 27*(1), 83–89.

Devore, W., & Schlesinger, E. G. (1987a). *Ethnic-sensitive practice* (2nd ed.). Columbus, OH: Merrill.

Devore, W., & Schlesinger, E. G. (1987b). Ethnic-sensitive practice. In A. Minahan et al. (Eds.), *Encyclopedia of social work* (18th ed.) (pp. 512–516). Silver Spring, MD: NASW Press.

Donadello, G. (1986). Integrating the lesbian/gay male experience in feminist practice and education. In N. Van Den Bergh and L. B. Cooper (Eds.), *Feminist visions for social work* (pp. 283–298). Silver Spring, MD: NASW Press.

Echols, I. J., Gabel, C., Landerman, D., & Reyes, M. (1988). *An approach for addressing racism, ethnocentrism, and sexism in the curriculum.* In C. Jacobs and Bowles, D. (Eds.), Ethnicity and race: Critical concepts in social work, 217–230. Silver Spring, MD: NASW Press.

Ericson, D. (1990). Social justice, evaluation and the educational system. In K. Sirotnik (Ed.), *Evaluation and social justice: issues in public education* (pp. 5–22). San Francisco: Jossey Bass.

Etzioni, A. (1993). *The spirit of community.* New York: Crown.

Friedman, M. (1962). *Capitalism and freedom.* Chicago: University of Chicago Press.

Germain, C. B., & Gitterman, A. (1986). The life model approach to social work practice revisited. In F. J. Turner (Ed.), *Social Work Treatment* (pp. 618–643). New York: Free Press.

Gibbs, J. T., & Moskowitz-Sweet, G. (1991). Clinical and cultural issues in the treatment of bi-racial and bi-cultural adolescents. *Families in Society,* 579–592.

Gilder, G. (1980). *Wealth and poverty.* New York: Bantam.

Goffman, E. (1961). *Asylums: Essays on the social situation of mental patients and other inmates.* New York: Doubleday/Anchor.

Goldenberg, I. I. (1978). *Oppression and social intervention.* Chicago: Nelson Hall.

Gomez, M. R. (1990). Biculturalism and subjective mental health among Cuban Americans. *Social Service Review, 64*(3), 374–389.

Gould, K. H. (1984). Original works of Freud on women: Social work references. *Social Casework, 65*(2), 94–101.

Gould, K. H. (1996). The misconstruing of multiculturalism: The Stanford debate and social work. In P. L. Ewalt, E. M. Freeman, S. A. Kirk, and D. L. Poole (Eds.), *Multicultural Issues in Social Work* (pp. 29–42). Washington, DC: National Association of Social Workers.

Grant, D., & Haynes, D. (1996). A developmental framework for cultural competence training with children. In P. L. Ewalt, E. M. Freeman, S. A. Kirk, and D. L. Poole (Eds.), *Multicultural Issues in Social Work* (pp. 382–398). Washington, DC: NASW Press.

Green, M. (1989). *Theories of human development: A comparative approach.* Englewood Cliffs, NJ: Prentice Hall.

Green, J. W. (1982). *Cultural Awareness in the Human Services.* Englewood Cliffs, NJ: Prentice Hall.

Green, J. W. (1995). *Cultural awareness in the human services: a multi-ethnic approach* (2nd ed.). Needham Heights, MA: Allyn & Bacon.

Greene, R. R. (1991a). Carl Rogers and the person-centered approach. In R. R. Greene and P. H. Ephross (Eds.), *Human behavior theory and social work practice* (pp. 105–122). Hawthorne, NY: Aldine de Gruyter.

Greene, R. R. (1991b). Eriksonian theory: A developmental approach to ego mastery. In R. R. Greene and P. H. Ephross (Eds.), *Human behavior theory and social work practice* (pp. 39–78). Hawthorne, NY: Aldine de Gruyter.

Greene, R. R. (1991c). The ecological perspective: An eclectic theoretical framework. In R. R. Greene and P. H. Ephross (Eds.), *Human behavior theory and social work practice* (pp. 261–296). Hawthorne, NY: Aldine de Gruyter.

Greene, R. R. (1994). *Human behavior theory: a diversity framework.* Hawthorne, NY: Aldine de Gruyter.

Hamilton, G. ([1940] 1951). *Theory and practice of social casework.* New York: Columbia University Press.

Hartman, A. (1990). Our global village. (Editorial). *Social Work 35,* 291–292.

Ho, M. K. (1987). *Family therapy with ethnic minorities.* Newbury park, CA: Sage.

Ho, M. K. (1991). Use of Ethnic-Sensitive Inventory (ESI) to enhance practitioner skills with minorities. *Journal of Multicultural Social Work, 1*(1), 57–67.

Hollis, F. (1950). The psycho-social approach to the practice of casework. In R. Roberts and R. Nee (Eds.), *Theories of social casework.* Chicago: University of Chicago Press.

Hooyman, N. R. (1996). Curriculum and teaching: Today and tomorrow. In *White paper on social work education—today and tomorrow* (pp. 11–24). Cleveland: Case Western Reserve University Press.

Kissman, K. (1991). Feminist-based social work with single-parent families. *Families on Society, 72*(2), 23–28.

Kluckhohn, F., & Stodbeck, F. L. (1961). *Variation in value orientations.* Westport, CT: Greenwood.

Kravetz, D. (1982). An overview of content on women for the social work curriculum. *Journal of Education for Social Work, 18*(2), 42–49.

Leighton, A. L. (1959). *My name is legion.* New York: Basic Books.

Logan, S. L. (1981). Race, identity, and Black children: A developmental perspective. *Social Casework, 62*(1), 47–56.

Longres, J. F. ([1900] 1990). *Human behavior in the social environment.* Itasca, IL: F. E. Peacock.

Longres, J. F. (1996). *Human behavior in the social environment.* Itasca, IL: F. E. Peacock.

Lukes, C. A., & Land, H. (1990). Biculturality and homosexuality. *Social Work, 35*(2), 155–161.

Lum, D. (1986). *Social work practice and people of color: a process-stage approach.* Monterey, CA: Brooks/Cole.

Luria, A. R. (1978). *Cognitive development: Its cultural and social foundations.* Cambridge, MA: Harvard University Press.

McNutt, J. G. (1994, November). Liberal and communitarian views of social justice: implications and dilemmas for policy and program evaluators in the Clinton era. Paper presented at the 1994 Conference of the American Evaluation Association, Boston.

Miller, S. (1980). Reflections on the dual perspective. In E. Mizio and J. Delany (Eds.), *Training for service delivery for minority clients* (pp. 53–61). New York: Family Service of America.

National Association of Social Workers (1997). *Code of ethics of the National Association of Social Workers.* Washington, DC: Author.

Norton, D. G. (1978). *The dual perspective: inclusion of ethnic minority content in the social work curriculum.* New York: Council on Social Work Education.

Norton, D. G. (1993). Diversity, early socialization, and temporal development. *Social Work, 38*(1), 82–91.

Perlman, H. H. (1957). *Social casework: A problem solving process.* Chicago: University of Chicago Press.

Pinderhughes, E. (1983). Empowerment for our clients and for ourselves. *Social Casework, 64,* 331–338.

Pinderhughes, E. (1989). *Understanding race, ethnicity and power: The key to efficacy in clinical practice.* New York: Free Press.

Rawls, J. (1971). *A theory of justice.* Cambridge: Harvard University Press.

Roth, S. (1989). Psychotherapy with lesbian couples: In M. McGoldrick, C. Anderson, and F. Walsh (Eds.), *Women in families: A framework for family therapy* (pp. 286–307). New York: Norton.

Roth, S., & Murphy, B. C. (1986). Therapeutic work with Lesbian clients: A systemic therapy view. In J. C. Jansen and M. Ault-Riche (Eds.), *Women and family therapy* (pp. 78–88). Rockville, MD: Aspen.

Shernoff, M. J. (1984). Family therapy for lesbian and gay clients. *Social Work, 29*(4), 393–396.

Simon, B. (1994). *The empowerment tradition in American social work.* New York: Columbia University Press.

Solomon, B. B. (1976). *Black empowerment: social work in oppressed communities.* New York: Columbia University Press.

Sotomayor, (1971). Mexican-American interaction with social systems. *Social Casework, 51*(5), 316–322.

Suarez, Z. E., Lewis, E. A., & Clark, J. (1995). Women of color and culturally competent feminist social work practice. In N. Van Den Bergh (Ed.), *Feminist practice in the 21st century.* Washington, DC: NASW Press.

Tully, C. T. (1994). Epilogue: Power and the social work profession. In R. R. Greene (Ed.), *Human behavior theory: A diversity framework* (pp. 235–243). Hawthorne, NY: Aldine de Gruyter.

Valentine, C. A. (1971). Deficit, difference, and bicultural models of Afro-American behavior. *Harvard Educational Review, 41,* 135–141.

Van Den Bergh, N. (1991) Managing biculturalism at the workplace: A group approach. *Social Work with Groups, 13*(4), 71–84.

Van Den Bergh, N. (Ed.) (1995). *Feminist practice in the 21st century.* Washington, DC: National Association of Social Workers.

Vygotsky, L. S. (1929). The problem of the cultural development of the child. *Journal of Genetic Psychology, 36,* 415–434.

3

The Ecological Perspective, Diversity, and Culturally Competent Social Work Practice

ROBERTA R. GREENE and GLENNA BARNES

To remedy some of the cultural biases and stereotypes, it has been recommended that the [practitioner] be trained to take the context into account before arriving at a specific diagnosis. . . . [The diagnosis or assessment] should focus on the entire context, open to multiple, interacting influences, and thus provide more flexibility. The absence of a contextual orientation often negates the complexity and diversity of human experience.

—L. Comas-Diaz, "Cultural Considerations in Diagnosis"

Given the many determinants of human behavior, the merger of the ecological perspective—which involves the personal, psychosocial, cultural, political, and economic contexts—with diversity populations—which include groups based on gender, age, sexual orientation, and physical and mental ability as well as minority, ethnic, and religious groups—offers a rich context for social work assessment and intervention. This chapter and Chapter 4 integrate principles derived the ecological and diversity literature to provide a theoretical orientation for culturally competent social work practice.

As late as 1991, Aponte decried the fact that there were relatively few therapeutic models that simultaneously addressed emotional distress and social problems, and especially the demands on the poor and minority populations. He is among a number of theorists who urged a broad focus on the ecology of the community as a means of serving diverse populations (Allen-Meares & Lane, 1987; Castex, 1992; Matsuoka, 1990). These other theorists have combined the ecological perspective with a focus on diverse client groups. For example, Allen-Meares and Lane (1983, 1987) applied the ecological approach in assessing the adaptive behavior of children and youths. Kirschner (1979) grounded social work practice in ecosystems theory to better understand and intervene in an individual's reaction to aging, family tensions, and an unresponsive environment. Moreover, Bauer and Shea (1987) used the ecological perspective to further understand the exceptional child within personal, familial, social, and cultural contexts. Gwynn and Kilpatrick (1981) outlined an ecological approach for working with African-American male clients.

> The ecological perspective is a social work practice approach that draws on a multifaceted conceptual base that addresses the complex transactions between people and their environments. A broad framework that synthesizes ideas from a number of human behavior and practice theories, the ecological perspective offers a rich, eclectic social work knowledge and practice base.
>
> —R. R. Greene, "The Ecological Perspective: An Eclectic Theoretical Framework"

The central purpose of clinical social work is to conduct an assessment of the person-in-situation and to carry out interventions based on that assessment (Ewalt, 1980). Meyer (1987) expressed well the social work goal to intervene in any part of the person-group-environment gestalt:

> The core professional task in the direct practice of social work is to assess the relationships among the case variables. The practitioner must determine what is salient or prominent and in need of intervention, what is relevant and therefore appropriate to do, and what balance or imbalance must be maintained or introduced. Thereafter, the introduction of interventions can be drawn from the repertoire of approaches. (p. 415)

Ecological assessment addresses the totality of the client's life experience and contexts as a harmonious whole. Overall, assessment from an ecological perspective is a broad exploration of life problems. This holistic view is based on the work of Lewin (1935), who first used the term *field* to describe this totality of coexisting facts that are mutually interdependent. The concept of field, derived from Gestalt psychology, proposes that all factors in an individual's life form a harmonious whole or larger pattern of reality (Murphy & Jensen, 1932). When the practitioner uses the concept in assessment, he or she is better able to understand the client's problem within the totality of the client's life experiences and contexts. The practitioner also may use this mind-set to direct interventions anywhere in the client's life space.

A major contribution of the ecological perspective is that it provides a guide for the assessment of the client's entire ecosystem. The ecological perspective provides a context for a social work assessment process in which the practitioner systematically defines the various components of the client's life situation, his or her attachments to others, and the manner in which the client copes and masters life. This process requires a holistic, dynamic exploration of the client's function within his or her milieu, including the larger geographic, political, and economic environments.

Ecological assessments emphasize that client difficulties may stem from a combination of internal, interpersonal, and systemic factors. Using the ecological perspective, the social worker recognizes that a client's problems may rest with a combination or internal, interpersonal, and systemic factors, such as family, social networks, workplace, and economy. Through the assessment, the social worker should consider the person in all of his or her critical systems. The goal of this exploration of multiple systems is to determine the client's sources of stress, for example, interpersonal problems or discrimination in employment. The practitioner then links the assessment to intervention and client strengths to enhance a client's coping and problem-solving capacity as well as systems engagement (Strean, 1971).

From an ecological perspective it is critical then that the social worker pay attention to both personality or internal factors as well as an array of larger systems issues (e.g., unemployment and community violence). The environment to be examined includes all "situational forces that work to shape behavior and development of the individual in a particular setting" (Greene, 1991, p. 294). In addition, assessment from an ecological viewpoint encompasses the broad concerns of time, social change, and demographic information, and an exploration of such issues as pollution, the stress of unemployment, crowding, and the complexity of biomedical technology (Germain, 1984). Ecological assessment generally includes data collected on the social worker's direct observation of and information from the client and his or her significant others; and information on the client's sociocultural context, that is, culture, gender, ethnicity, and other factors related to relative political power and worldview.

Another key feature of an assessment from the ecological perspective is the examination of goodness-of-fit between person and environment. Goodness-of-fit refers to the extent to which there is a match between a client's *adaptiveness*--a positive process of self-development and engagement with people and institutions—and the quality of his or her environment (Germain & Gitterman, 1987). Problem definition and resolution from an ecological perspective is then intended to address the imbalances in person-environment fit, or the balance between internal and external resources (Allen-Meares, 1985). Through this process of accounting for the goodness-of-fit between the client system and other environmental systems, the practitioner and client define life problems and assets and seek resolutions.

> *Accurate assessment of the person-problem-situation configuration must be undergirded by awareness of the cultural ecology within which this configuration is embedded.*
> —M. M. Dore and A. O. Dumois, "Cultural Differences in the Meaning of Adolescent Pregnancy"

Eclectic Approach

Perhaps the most critical feature of the ecological perspective as an assessment method is that it combines major concepts from many disciplines to form a multitheoretical approach for understanding human behavior as the mutual and progressive accommodation between person and environment (Table 3.1). In addition to ego psychology and general system theory, other disciplines that have been incorporated into the perspective include ecology, which emphasizes the organism and environment as a unitary system; evolutionary biology, which encompasses a study of the adaptation of species over time and across the life span; ethology, which involves a study of animals in their natural environment; and anthropology, which focuses on on-site interaction with people to gain increased understanding of their culture.

There are no particular theories or treatment approaches integral to the ecological perspective. Therefore, at each level of analysis, the social worker selects a theory as an assessment tool. When assessing a client at the personal level, the social worker may choose from psychoanalytic, behavioral, cognitive, or other theories. To examine family functioning, the practitioner may select from an array of insight-oriented or structural approaches (Ackerman, [1972] 1984; Bowen, 1978; Minuchin, 1974). Therefore, it is critical that social workers purposefully select their assessment theories and strategies.

As an eclectic framework, the ecological perspective is not one theory, but a mind-set that requires the practitioner to explore an individual's situation within the broad context of all of the pertinent social systems. To accomplish this holistic goal, the social worker draws on a number of complementary theory bases as a resource in assessment and intervention. Each theory base in its own right may be limited to explaining phenomena at only one or two systems levels (Figure 3.1). For example, the practitioner using the ecological perspective might adopt constructs from ego psychology (Goldstein, 1986), object relations (Applegate, 1990), or attachment theory (Bowlby, 1973) to explain an individual's internal life; role theory (Blumer, [1937] 1969; Kluckholn & Strodbeck, 1961) or anthropology (Mead, 1930) to explore a person's interpersonal life; network theory (Swenson, 1979) to assess support systems; or Marxism (Burghardt, 1986) to examine the forces shaping the individual's political environment. The social worker's assessment requires integration of information related to these various systems (Allen-Meares & Lane, 1987).

As stated earlier, the ecological perspective may be thought of as a blueprint for organizing the social worker's approach to assessment and intervention. By examining various systems levels, the client and social worker learn about the opportunities and constraints of organizational, community, institutional, and societal systems (Miley, O'Melia, & Dubois, 1995). The levels of ecological systems are depicted in Figure 3.1..

In sum, an ecological approach to assessment requires an understanding of human behavior at multiple levels. The ecological perspective may be portrayed as a "complex configuration of nested and interlocking systems" (Miley et al., 1995, p. 54) (see Figures 1.2. and 3.1.). This configuration guides the social worker in a systematic analysis in which the practitioner moves from system to system to better understand the multiple forces contributing to the client's concerns. The social worker needs to understand each systems level in its own right and then to target a system or several systems for intervention. Fandetti and Goldmeier (1988) provide an example of a multilevel cultural assessment for planning of interventions in social work practice in health care settings (Table 3.2).

USE OF ECOLOGICAL CONCEPTS IN ASSESSMENT

The following concepts were selected to guide ecological—or multisystems-level—assessment at the personal, micro-, meso-, and macrolevels within a diversity context. At each phase, assessment aims to identify the stressors, the presenting need(s), client strengths, and the possible life solutions.

Focal System

From an ecological viewpoint, the client system may be a person, a family, a hospital ward, a housing complex, or a particular neighborhood (Meyer, 1987). At first, this description of what constitutes the professional social worker's task seems broad and complex. However, Longres

Table 3.1. Select Theoretical Foundations of the Ecological Perspective

Time Frame	Major theorist(s)	Theory	Major theme	Concepts adopted for practice
1859	Darwin	Evolutionary theory	Evolving match between adapting organism and environment	Goodness of fit
1917	Richmond	Social diagnosis	Improving socioeconomic conditions through personal adjustment	Social treatment
1930	Coyle	Social goals model of group work	Interacting processes of groups	Task roles, reciprocal relations
1932	Murphy Jensen	Gestalt	Perceiving figure-ground configuration	Analysis of total experience
1934	G. H. Mead	Role theory	Studying social functioning as a transactional process	Pattern of behavior and social positions
1957 1934 1937	Perlman G. H. Mead Blumer	Symbolic interaction	Establishing meaning	Self, generalized other
1940 (pub 1969)	Gordon Hamilton	Social diagnosisImproving economic and social conditions as well as intrapsychic functioning	The importance of socioeconomic conditions to personal well-being	
1949	M. Mead	Anthropology	Interacting within cultural environments	The importance of ethnographic data and information about personality development
1959	Maslow	Humanistic psychology	Providing growth-inducing life experience	Caring therapeutic relationships
1961	Rogers			

1931, 1951	Lewin	Field theory	Understanding the life space	Person-in-environment
1953	Lorenz	Ethology	Studying animals in their natural setting	Critical periods
1956	Selye	Stress theory	Coping with stress	Adaptive mechanisms
1960	Searles			
1963	Bandler	Ego psychology	Promoting the ego's effectiveness; personal competence	Integrity of ego and functions, coping, competence
1958	Hartman			
1959	White			
1959	DuBos	Environmental biology Human ecology	Promoting adaptive environments	Transactions
1973	Bowlby	Attachment theory	Forming relationships through active transactions	Attachment, relatedness
1968	Bertalanffy	General systems theory	Examining systems change	Synergy, open systems, reciprocal causality
1969	Gordon	Ecological development Developing process-person context	Micro-, meso-, exo-, and macrosystems	
1979	Bronfenbrenner			
1972	Chestang	Empowerment	Affecting one's life space beneficially	Reciprocal power
1976	Solomon			
1978	Pinderhughes			
1980	Germain	Life model	Intervening in the life space	Common practice base, life experiences, time, space, ecological maps
1983	Gitterman Meyer			

Source: From Greene and Ephross (199, pp. 266–267).

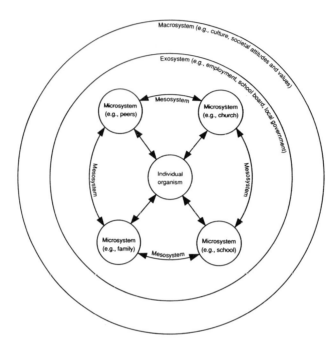

Figure 3.1. The levels of the ecological system. From Hefferman, J., Shuttles-
worth, J., and Anbroseno, R., *Social Work and Social Welfare*, West Publishing,
St. Paul, MN (1988). Reprinted with permission.

([1900] 1990) has outlined six steps that delineate or set boundaries for a
systems analysis:

1. Identify the system to be assessed.
2. Identify the condition in that system to be understood.
3. Identify the factors about the system itself that contribute to the
    condition.
4. Identify the factors in the social context of the system that contrib-
    ute (or assist) with the condition.
5. Identify the resources that exist within the system itself.
6. Identify the resources that exist within the environment of the
    system (pp. 47–48).

The use of a systems analysis requires that the social worker designate
a *focal system*, a system chosen by the practitioner to receive primary
attention in assessment and intervention (Anderson & Carter, 1990;
Longres, [1900] 1990). After the social worker has identified the focal

Table 3.2. Steps in a Multilevel Cultural Assessment

Micro: The Person

> Assess the person's cultural orientation, for example, languages spoken, religion professed, and primary client's generation of immigration.
>
> Evaluate the importance of intraethnic group variations affecting the person's orientation.
>
> Consider the person's class membership as a mediating factor.
>
> Select ethnically compatible solutions to personal problems.

Mezzo: The Family, Client Group, and Treatment Team

> Assess the ethnically based dynamics of the family, client group, or team.
>
> Assess the responsiveness of a group or team, whose members themselves may reflect different ethnic orientations.
>
> Evaluate the importance of intraethnic group variations in families, groups, and treatment teams.
>
> Consider class membership as a mediating factor.
>
> Select ethnically compatible solutions at the family, group, or treatment team level.

Macro: The Local and Nonlocal Community

> Understand family boundaries with the larger community in intervention and planning.
>
> Facilitate community responsiveness to ethnic cultural needs.
>
> Be aware of local, state, and national policies affecting the integration of the ethnic groups.

Source: Fandetti and Goldmeier (1988, p. 173).

system and its members, the client and social worker will explore the inside dimensions of the system, the outside dimensions of the system, the connections between the inside and outside dimensions, and the way in which the system moves through time (see Miley et al., 1995).

> Assessment requires identification of a focal system to receive primary attention.

Assessment of the Person

An assessment of a person involves understanding his or her biopsychosocial function. Biological factors include genetic endowment, life expectancy, and physical aspects of health and well-being. Social factors encompass the capacity to carry out social roles with respect to other members of society. Psychological processes generally involve coping strategies and capacities of the individual vis-à-vis environmental demands (Birren, 1969; Greene, 1986).

The need to understand a client's stress levels and coping capacities or strengths is central to an ecological approach to assessment (Searles, 1960; Selye, 1956). According to the ecological approach, coping is more than an individual or internal process. Stress occurs when there is "an imbalance between a person's perceived demands and his or her perceived capability to use resources to meet these demands" (Greene, 1991, p. 295). It is difficult to predict how a given individual will respond to prolonged stress. However, the reaction to stress is related to the individual's

> Practitioners need to comprehend client's stress levels and ability to cope with stress.

coping mechanisms and to the nature of the societal structures that are contributing to the stress (Brooks, 1974). Through this understanding, the social worker can better help clients seek needed resources and work to alleviate institutional barriers related to stress. For example, based on an examination of the relationship of ecological status—race, income, age, educational level, and marital status—to life stress and schizophrenia, Land (1986) proposed that life events requiring an adaptive response to the environment exacerbated the nature of the disease. She used the term *social stressor* to refer to "a personal life event, such as bereavement, marriage, or loss of a job, that alters the individual's social setting or ongoing life pattern" (p. 254).

In their investigation of the particular patterns of coping among Vietnamese refugees, Timberlake and Cook (1984) found that the traditional Vietnamese family's cohesive extended relationship network was key to restoring refugee clients' self-image and feelings of competence. Effective coping also involved individual coping mechanisms, family coping patterns, and community building in their new country. The authors emphasized that the social worker, when examining stress and coping issues, needs to examine the responsiveness of various institutions to a client's psychosocial needs and cultural characteristics.

To aid them in the assessment process, social workers may consult the Person-in Environment System (Karls & Wandrei, 1994), a classification system for social function problems that provides indexes for the assessment of a client's coping levels. The Coping Index enables the practitioner to identify the degree to which the client is able to balance social role functions with his or her own internal resources, as well as to record the social worker's judgment of the client's ability to solve problems, the client's capacity to act independently, and the client's ego strength, insight, and intellectual capacity.

The Coping Index comprises six levels:

- Outstanding coping skills: The client's ability to solve problems; to act independently; and to use ego strength, insight, and intellectual ability to cope with difficult situations is exceptional.
- Above-average coping skills: The client's ability to solve problems; act independently; and to use ego strength, insight, and intellectual ability to cope with difficult situations is more than would be expected in the average person.
- Adequate coping skills: The client is able to solve problems; can act independently; and has adequate ego strength, insight, and intellectual ability.
- Somewhat inadequate coping skills: The client has fair problem-solving ability but has major difficulties in solving the presenting problems; acting independently; and using ego strength, insight, or intellectual ability.
- Inadequate coping skills: The client has some ability to solve problems but it is insufficient to solve the presenting problems; the client shows poor ability to act independently; and the client has minimal ego strength, insight, and intellectual ability.
- No coping skills: The client show little or no ability to solve problems; lacks the capacity to act independently; and has insufficient ego strength, insight, and intellectual ability (p. 33).

Self-efficacy, the perceived ability or power to be effective in regard to one's environment (Bandura, 1977; White, 1959), is another internal and external developmental process included in an ecological approach to assessment. The concept is related to a sense of internal competence or clients' sense of purpose. From an eco-logical perspective, it is understood

> Social workers assess client efficacy or confidence to act on the environment.

that development of efficacy—the belief in personal ability "to produce and to regulate events in one's life" (Bandura, 1986, p. 122) and the confidence to act on one's environment—is linked to the availability and accessibility of environmental resources (Maluccio, 1981).

The practitioner must understand, within a broad societal context, the factors that influence a client's efficacy. For example, findings from a study of psychological traumas and depression among a sample of Vietnamese people in the United States revealed that refugees' efficacy or well-being was moderated by ecological variables, including English-speaking ability, economics, marital status, education, and premigration stresses (Tran, 1993).

The social worker needs to assess efficacy within a specific life domain or activity. For example, people's perception of themselves as capable or effective begins when they are young children and successfully transact with their environment by walking, crawling, and manipulating objects. In the adult, examples of a strong sense of efficacy include presenting a paper in class or standing up for one's rights at the workplace.

Efficacy is often best understood by assessing a client within his or her home environment. Assessment and interventions in the home environments for older adults who live alone are an important ecological approach to social work practice in the field of aging (Kropf & Greene, 1993). Frail older adults fear falling, for example, which contributes to low self-efficacy (Tinetti & Powell, 1993). Because older adults may not feel as efficacious in their home environment, they may curtail their social engagements because they fear going out. When older adults are less mobile, their movements may become more awkward and their bones more brittle, thereby resulting in a downward spiral in physical, emotional, and social function.

The assessment of home hazards provides a picture of the older adult's function within the household. The practitioner should consider the following factors in such an assessment: lighting—accessibility and brightness; carpets and rugs—slipperiness and state of repair; chairs and tables—stability to support a person's weight; heating—comfort and the danger of physical damage; cabinets—accessible heights; floors—slipperiness; and gas ranges—marked clearly, and safety of use for the older adult. Other factors are the safety and accessibility of bathroom fixtures, such as the toilet seat or medicine cabinet, and the safety, lighting, and configuration of stairways (Tideiksaar, 1986).

Overall, efficacy is a dynamic feature of a person's internal and external life and, as such, can be enhanced through positive interaction with the environment. Gutierrez (1990), whose interest lies in developing clients' ability to act on their environment, suggested the use of empowerment techniques for increasing self-efficacy among women of color. She proposed that an ecological analysis of a client from the strengths perspective would include an examination of personal control and the ability to affect others, as well as an examination of and equity in the distribution of community resources.

Assessment of Relationships

A fundamental assumption of ecological thinking is that people are connected to others as well as to social institutions. From the ecological perspective, *individuation,* becoming one's own person, and *interdependence,* a positive reliance on others, are inseparable processes. Therefore, the ecological perspective views the formation of relationships as an important aspect of assessment. Concepts that address relationship formation include *attachment,* how people form affectional ties, and *relatedness,* a form of attachment behaviors involving emotional and social exchanges among people and their natural environment.

> Assessment encompasses how clients engage with people and their natural environment.

Attachment is thought to be derived from early parenting and the ongoing quality of caregiving relationships throughout the life course (Ainsworth & Bell, 1974). Ecological theorists are concerned with people's attachments in families, in groups, to social support networks, and to their larger society. An understanding of the extent and quality of such attachments is essential to the process of social work assessment and intervention.

Family-Level (Microsystem) Assessment. The first level of attachment is a person to his or her family. The ecological concept of goodness-of-fit has allowed for a better understanding of diverse families within the context of their broader environment. The family is perceived as a unit, and it is the unit characteristics that the practitioner assesses. The social worker generally examines current patterns of communication and interaction among family members. For example, the child with developmental delays might be central to the social worker's evaluation, but the social worker must consider and understand siblings, other family members, and the interaction among these members (Bosch, 1996). The practitioner must also assess interactions between the family and its environments. A major source of resources may be informal support systems.

> Key to the assessment process is determining the goodness-of-fit between the family and their environment.

Determining the goodness-of-fit between the family and environmental system in the following four interrelated areas of living is central to the assessment: (1) life transitions, such as births and deaths; (2) status-role changes and crisis events, such as retirement or illness; (3) the unresponsiveness of the environment; for example, unemployment or homelessness; and (4) communication and relationship difficulties, such as role conflict (McPhatter, 1991).

Hartman (1979), a leader in family-centered practice, has described how a family adapts using its connections to educational, religious, health, safety, recreational, political, economic, neighborhood, and ethnic systems, among others. The assessment goal is to understand the nature of the family's problem at a particular time. The mutual construction of genograms and ecomaps often guides assessment. A *genogram,* a chart of

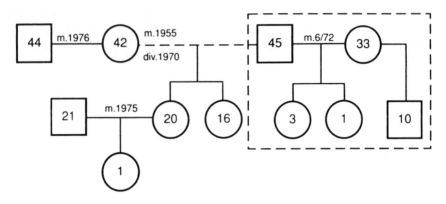

Figure 3.2. Model for a family genogram. From Hartman, A., "Diagrammatic Assessment of Family Relationships," *Social Casework, 59,* 473. Copyright © 1978. Reprinted with permission of Social Casework.

family members across at least three generations, is useful in gathering information on family structure and function (Hartman, 1978) (Figure 3.2). The *ecomap* portrays the fit or lack of fit among family, microsystem, and macrosystem environments, and extends the social worker's assessment to the various systems with which the family interacts (Figure 3.3).

As social workers' concern about the social, economic, and political contexts of family treatment grew, their assessments became equally broad in their areas of interest. For example, Congress (1994) proposed the combined use of the ecomap and genogram with culturally diverse families. She described the use of a *culturagram,* an empowerment tool to assist social workers in obtaining information on the client's reasons for immigration, length of time in the country, legal or undocumented status, language spoken, contact with cultural institutions, and other areas such as health, beliefs, and values (Figure 3.4).

Because of the broad ecological definitions of the nature of family and parenthood (see Chapter 1), the number of family-centered approaches has proliferated since the 1970s. There is a small but growing body of literature on how to use the approaches with ethnic minority families (K. H. Ho, 1987; McGoldrick, Pearce, & Giordano, 1982; Mokuau, 1990). These approaches examine how the family system participates within society and call for the infusion of the family's values, traditions, and culture into the design and development of practice (Red Horse, Lewis, Feit, & Decker, 1978; Sotomayor, 1971), for example M. K. Ho's (1987) conceptual framework for culturally sensitive family therapy with ethnic minorities.

Theorists also have modified ecological family practice models for work with inner-city families (Bryant, 1980). In addition, the ecological

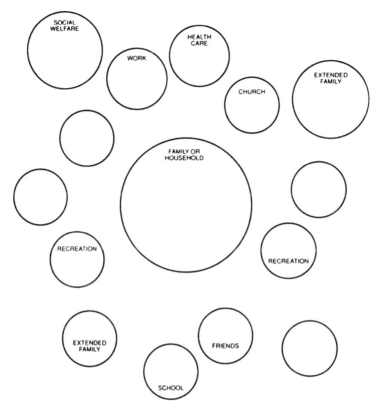

Figure 3.3. A sample ecomap. From Hartman, A., "Diagrammatic Assessment of Family Relationships," *Social Casework, 59,* 469. Copyright © 1978. Reprinted with permission of Social Casework.

approach has been applied in social work practice with single-parent families. To better understand the dynamics of single-parent families and to develop preventive and intervention strategies to resolve postdivorce problems, Howard and Johnson (1985) suggested the practitioner: examine divorce as a transition or life crisis; explore the influence of the social environment, including family, social supports, and community agencies; assess the global social environment, including cultural expectations; understand the structure of the single-parent family as a unique family form; explore the individual family's unique characteristics; and synthesize the interaction of all these components. The ecological approach has been applied in other practice areas. Johnson's (1986) seven-question guide organizes ecological assessment and informs intervention decisions with dementia patients and their families. The questions are as follows:

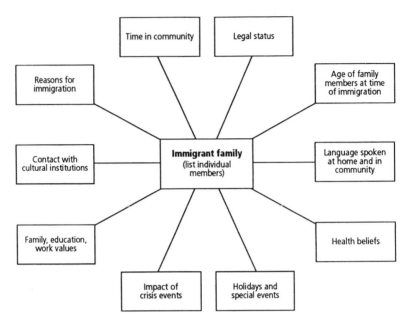

Figure 3.4. Culturagram. From Congress, E. P., "The Use of Culturagrams to Assess and Empower Culturally Diverse Families," *Families in Society,* 532. Copyright © 1994. Reprinted with permission of *Families in Society.*

(1) What physiological factors are present? (2) What environmental or situational factors are present? (3) What culturally based conflicts are present? (4) What are the living arrangements? (5) Can educational or skills training help? (6) Can group experience help? (7) Can individual or family counseling help? (p. 488).

Mesosystem Relationships

Understanding mesosystem relationships is another arena for social work assessment and intervention. *Mesosystems* refer to an individual's relationships between two or more settings, such as the family, school, workplace, and neighborhood. School social workers often use an ecological approach involving school and home to solve seemingly child-related problems (Allen-Meares, 1985). Ecological thinking also has provided a useful framework for understanding the dynamics of inner-city changes, especially urban renewal gentrification (London, Bradley, & Hudson, 1980). Another example of using ecological approaches to better understand the social organization of mesosystems is Joseph and Conrad's

(1980) parish neighborhood model. Use of that model enables social workers to focus on neighborhood, family, church, and voluntary associations to combat funding problems and the scarcity of resources.

This concept of connectedness reinforces the need for the social worker to look beyond the individual and his or her family and examine a person's social supports, systems connections, and sociocultural risks and opportunities (Garbarino, 1986). Assessment at the mesolevel involves an examination of the interaction between and among systems (Montalvo, 1974). For example, when a clinical social worker addresses a situation involving a child's difficulty at school, it is critical that he or she enter and engage the relevant family and school systems in the assessment and intervention (Bryant & Zayas, 1986). A child's seemingly unacceptable behavior in the classroom may stem from any number of factors in these systems (see Chapter 6). The following broad assessment outline developed by Allen-Meares (1985) assists social workers to gather information so that they may understand a child's ecosystem:

The Child.   What is the child's educational, psychological, cultural/ethnic, and social background? What is the child's medical, developmental, and behavioral history?

The Family.   What is the family's socioeconomic and educational status? What is the quality of its relationship with the child? What are its expectations for the child, its approaches to discipline, and its view of the school? Identify the family's parenting skills and internal resources, including its degree of mobility and the parent's marital and employment stability. What stressful events have had an impact on the quality of the family's life?

The School.   What are the characteristics of the school's atmosphere and academic expectations, the quality of teachers, and the flexibility of the educational program? Is the school responsive to children of different ethnic and socioeconomic backgrounds? How willing is it to reach out to parents? What degree of humaneness and flexibility is there in the school's policies and educational programming?

Peer-Group Affiliation.   What is the status of the child in his or her peer group? What are the child's friendship patterns and level of social skills? How do peers see the child? What expectations do they place on the child?

The Community.   What types of behavioral patterns are reflected by community members? What degree of congruence is there between expectations the community places on its members and those the school places on students and parents? What differences are there in the ethnicity and economic and educational status of educational staff and community members? (pp. 107–108)

Pennekamp and Freeman (1988) have suggested that the formation of family-school partnerships involving children, their families, their schools, and community services is the "new frontier" for school social workers

(p. 248). Hence, the authors have argued that social workers are helping to develop communication between mesosystems (see Chapter 6). Accordingly, they urged social workers to involve neighbors, the community at large, social agencies, and businesses, as well as evaluate the effects of macrosystems as they relate to national values, legislation, policies, and funding patterns.

Exosystems Assessment

Increasingly, theorists are recognizing that people act simultaneously within several systems. This level of interdependent action across systems is the exosystem. *Exosystems* involve linkages between two or more systems, any one of which may not necessarily play a direct role but nevertheless will have a meaningful effect on a person's life, for example, the workplace of a child's parents. In a study on women's adult development, Brennan and Rosenzweig (1990) concluded that women's development cannot be explained using an individualistic approach. Rather, practitioners may best understand women by examining key life domains that deal with the interplay among the women's relationships, roles, and work.

Social Supports Assessment

According to a person-environment view, even if social workers are assessing an individual client, they must understand the client within the context of their participation in social support networks. *Social support networks,* a set of relational linkages and communication pathways that influence the behavior of its members, such as friendship groups or neighborhood councils (Gitterman & Germain, 1981), are of interest to social workers in assessment (Litwak, 1985).

> Awareness of a client's social supports enables social workers to effectively match client needs and resources.

They focus attention on the helpfulness of family, friends, and neighbors, thus allowing for the best match between client needs and resources. Social workers familiar with ecological views of the nature of support systems increasingly have assessed social networks to learn of their availability to clients.

A large body of literature exists on measuring social networks. Social network assessments generally include a portrayal of a client in relationship to his or her family, significant others, friends, and neighbors (Swenson, 1979). An assessment of the content and structure of networks is equally valuable. The structure includes the number of social ties; the types of ties, such as kin or partner; and the interconnectedness of ties. This analysis sheds light on the people who potentially are available and may have an interest in the client. For example, Biegel, Shore, and Gordon (1984) developed a questionnaire for network assessment that examines closeness between and among relationships. The network assessment enables practitioners to determine who the client can confide in, from whom he or she derives satisfaction in the relationship, and what network members may be willing to do for the individual (Table 3.3).

Networks are the entire web of relationships in which individuals participate directly and indirectly (Pearlin & Schooler, 1978). Networks provide the support upon which a person can draw. This concept is important to the ecological perspective because it focuses the social worker's attention on the institutional and organizational resources available

Table 3.3. Network Assessment Evaluation Questionnaire

1. "Is there any one person you feel close to, whom you trust and confide in, without whom it is hard to imagine life? Is there anyone else you feel very close to?"
2. "Are there other people to whom you feel not quite that close but who are still important to you?"
3. For each individual named in (1) and (2) above, obtain the following:
   A. Name
   B. Gender
   C. Age
   D. Relationship
   E. Geographic proximity
   F. Length of time client knows individual
   G. How do they keep in touch (in person, telephone, letters, combination)
   H. Satisfaction with amount of contact—want more or less? "If not satisfied, what prevents you from keeping in touch more often?"
   I. "What does individual do for you?"
   J. "Are you satisfied with the kind of support you get?"
   K. "Are there other things that you think he or she can do for you?"
   L. "What prevents him or her from doing that for you?"
   M. "Are you also providing support to that individual? If so, what are you giving?"
4. "Now, thinking about your network, all the people that you feel close to, would you want more people in it?"
5. "Are there any members of your network whom you would not want the agency to contact? If so, who? Can you tell us why?"
6. "Are you a member of any groups or organizations? If so, which ones?"
7. "Are you receiving assistance from any agencies? If so, what agency and what service(s)?"

Source: Biegel, D. E., Shore, B. K., & Gordon, E., *Building support networks for the elderly,* Sage Publications, Beverly Hills, CA (1984, p. 148). Reprinted by permission of Sage Publications.

to the client. However, the scope and richness of networks vary. Some networks are clearly more extensive and resourceful than others. Moreover, some individuals may be more active in forming attachments and viable affiliations, which are critical factors to assess in the client person-environment fit.

Assessment also needs to encompass how and if social supports and efficacy may vary given age, gender, ethnic, racial, or cultural contexts. For example, De La Rosa (1988) argued that minority individuals who have strong natural support systems cope better with racism, crime, poverty, and poor housing. His study of Puerto Rican individuals who received more support from their natural support systems found that they were less likely to experience stress and emotional difficulties, substance abuse, and family problems. However, not everyone facing the same situation exhibited the same response. Linking the concept of social supports and coping and the concept of self-efficacy may provide a better understanding of the differences observed in people's responses to common problems (Pearlin & Schooler, 1987).

A model for linking networks in social work practice with institutionalized older adults was developed by Wells and Singer (1985). Realizing that the social networks of institutionalized older adults often are diminished, Wells and Singer created a demonstration project to strengthen the mutually supportive nature of existing networks, to establish new networks of peer support from the community, and to create linkages among a variety of community networks. This networking also involved establishing social work student units that facilitated activities among networks (see Chapter 7).

Agency Assessment

The political, economic, and social aspects of the social worker's professional authority represent important considerations in any assessment process (Dworkin, 1990). In forming a helping alliance, the practitioner must examine the political and economic environment, as well as ethnic and gender issues and their effect on the client–social worker relationship. The social worker's recognition of his or her power in the helping relationship and how he or she perceives societal concerns in that process strongly influence assessment and later interventions that may help clients gain control of their environment (Hasenfeld, 1987).

> Agency assessment addresses the climate for services to diverse client populations.

Social workers who use an ecological approach also view issues of agency accessibility and availability of human services as important aspects of practice. In her early work on the ecological approach, Germain

(1976) cautioned that an agency's policies and approach to time can affect client progress. She observed that "how the rhythm, tempo and timing of an organization's activities mesh with temporal patterns of those who use its services is rarely considered in program development or evaluation" (p. 425). She observed that some agencies dehumanized their procedures by following the book to shape their services.

Clients may perceive arbitrary or culturally insensitive organizational strategies as power abuses, contend Gitterman and Miller (1989). Therefore, Doelker and Lynett (1983) have proposed that the additional staff development needed in agencies should be guided by the ecological perspective. That is, agencies should devise programs and learning activities that meet the needs of a specific staff within the context of that agency and its clientele.

The Child Welfare League of America's (1993) *Cultural Competence Self-Assessment Instrument* is a resourceful tool that enables agencies to assess their climate in terms of their provision of services to diverse populations. Although the instrument was developed to provide a structured format to examine issues of culturally competent child welfare services, social workers may adapt it for use with other service delivery systems. Using the instrument, agencies may be better able to recognize the effect and relevance of cultural competence on all agency management and service functions; to identify the areas related to decision-making, policy implementation, and service delivery in which competence is essential; to assess what changes are needed and who should assume responsibility for each change; and to develop strategies to address cultural competence issues (Child Welfare League of America, 1993, p. ix).

Macrosystems Assessment

Social analysts (DuBois, 1969; Lemann, 1986; Wilson, 1985) have long urged social workers to give attention to social dislocations and urban crises. From the ecological perspective, social workers are equally concerned with these issues of inequality.

> Assessment at the macrosystem level explores the large-scale societal context.

The systematic oppression and disenfranchisement of individuals and groups are, of necessity, included in the assessment and intervention agenda. The macrosystem may be considered a blueprint for historical change and collective reward. It encompasses contextual variables such as sociocultural and institutional resources, including legal, health, educational, social, media, and technological services.

From the ecological perspective, human problems result when the goodness-of-fit between the needs of an individual and the broad resources of the macrosystem become strained. For example, in an examination of the relationship between racial discrimination and its effects on employment, education, and social isolation, McAdoo (1993) found that assessment of the overall community system is critical to the ecological perspective. In work with the Latino community, Hardy-Fanta (1986) revealed that a community needs assessment dealing with issues of environmental stress, such as poverty, powerlessness, inadequate housing, unemployment, health problems, and racism, must not receive secondary attention to treatment of interpersonal problems. She combined group and community approaches, contending that comprehensive planning for Latino groups should reaffirm the validity of natural groups.

Global Issues Assessment

Ecological models of assessment are also concerned with global issues. Attention to the environment of the earth, including global warming, the burning of fossil fuels, deforestation, and increasing drought, is essential (McLain Park, 1996). Expanded use of the ecological approach to social work practice enables the social worker to recognize the worldwide and local social dimensions of the environmental crisis, such as health problems, urban stress, and industry relocation.

INTERVENTION

An ecological definition of the problem offers the professional a greater variety of possibilities for intervention than exists when problems are seen only in the context of psychological causation.
—C. Kirschner, "The Aging Family in Crisis: A Problem in Living"

Step back from the client and holistically perceive him or her in interrelationship with the environment. [This] stimulates the clinician to use a broad repertoire of interventions that are suitable for the varying needs of a particular case.
—C. H. Meyer, "The Eco-Systems Perspective"

Improvement of Goodness-of-Fit

The major goal of social work from the ecological perspective is to "improve the goodness-of-fit between the client and others in the ecosystem, including the social worker" (Greene, 1991, p. 373). Social workers aim interventions at promoting personal competence or a sense of positive identity. Of equal concern is how a client may effect change in his or her environment. From an ecological viewpoint, clients are both the "products and producers of development" (Bronfenbrenner, 1989, p. 273). The social worker should encourage

> Interventions are aimed at improving goodness-of-fit.

the client to address goodness-of-fit with key aspects of his or her physical environment, including spatial or housing situations. For example, the practitioner must consider the stresses of unemployment and the relationship of goodness of person-environment fit with other socioeconomic factors. Furthermore, he or she should explore political factors related to the client as well as how institutions support and encourage social relationships.

Person-Level Interventions

Person-level interventions involve an ecological framework. In situations such as widowhood or widowerhood, the social worker may guide mental health services toward the bereavement process. Because the death of a spouse is a highly stressful

> Interventions at the personal level need to be congruent with the client's environmental and cultural context.

event, it is recommended that the practitioner include outreach and network supports as part of the interventions (Potocky, 1993).

Bicultural Interventions

Far too often, practitioners may perceive norms and cultural patterns that vary as cultural deficits rather than differences they need to understand. Practitioners who work in bicultural client-social worker relationships should perform the following six functions, according to de Anda (1984):

1. Determine areas in which two cultures merge that can serve as "doorways" between those cultures.
2. Note the major points of conflict between the two cultures and the negative consequences for the client.
3. Search out and provide translators, mediators, and models who can offer guidelines for dealing with such conflicts, and offer critical experiential information.
4. Arrange, when possible, for increased corrective feedback for the client in the environment.
5. Work to expand the client's repertoire of problem-solving skills, particularly those skills that are the least context-bound. Help to develop a larger repertoire of context-specific problem-solving skills.

6. Educate people of the majority culture about the significant charac-
    teristics, values, and needs of minority cultures, serving as an ad-
    vocate of greater flexibility and adjustment in the institutions of the
    mainstream culture (p. 107).

Interventions at Multiple Systems Levels

Interventions may be at any or all personal or systems levels and may
be directed toward anyone in any of the ecosystems. For example, according to Eisikovits and Edleson (1989) there are five levels of intervention
with men who batter: (1) the individual—intervention involves a one-to-
one process; (2) the couple—intervention encompasses conjoint couple
therapy and couple therapy groups;
(3) men's group—intervention addresses gender-role socialization and
sociocultural values on woman batter-
ing; (4) institution—intervention involves the use of educational programs on military bases and in educational systems; and (5) culture—
intervention involves examining and influencing the media and literature. Another example of intervention at several systems levels is Castex's
(1992) intervention strategies for school social workers who helped Soviet
refugee children and families. Among the interventions was an orientation and information session including questions ranging from microsystems to macrosystems (Table 3.4).

> Interventions may be directed at any aspect of the ecosystem.

Interventions may address either internal factors or any systems of any
size in the client's life space. Systemic change may also be a goal of
intervention, particularly in environments that clients perceive as oppressive or nonnutritive. Planning of interventions necessitates that the social
worker identify intersystemic relationships to optimize goodness-of-fit.
Just as in assessment, interventions from an ecological viewpoint encompass intrapsychic factors and emphasize self-efficacy, mastery, and competence; foster attachments; and promote natural helping systems. The
ecological perspective stresses empowerment and advocacy in seeking
resources for client enhancement. Therefore, empowerment techniques
and advocacy are key interventions.

Family Interventions

Many family interventions combine an ecological family-centered approach to problem-solving (Monahan, 1993). In ecological-family-
centered practice with dementia patients, for example, the practitioner
may deal with memory loss issues within the family as well engage the

Table 3.4. Questions to Determine Intervention Strategies at Several Systems Levels for School Social Workers

- What is the concept of public education in this country? What must be paid for? What is free?
  How does one choose a school to attend? What are the school districts, and what alternative options are available?
- How many hours are the school day, and how long is the school year?
- Who must attend school? Who should attend school?
- What constitutes an acceptable reason for being absent or tardy? What are the consequences of unsatisfactory absences or tardiness?
- How does the school deal with discipline issues? What is the philosophy behind these policies?
- What should the parent's involvement in discipline be, and to whom should they voice concerns?
- What are the roles and expectations appropriate of a teacher? An administrator? The support staff (including social workers)?
- What is the role of the parents in the schooling process? How do parents gain access to teachers?
- What issues are appropriate to discuss? How do parent-teacher conferences work, and what should their content be?
- What is the role of the Parents' Association or Parent-Teacher's Association?
- What curriculum options and expectations exist?
- What are the expectations regarding homework?
- How are grades determined?
- How are standardized tests important for people who have recently learned English?
- How will the child be fed? How much do meals cost? Are there other options?
- Does the school provide after-school care and at what price? If not, can the school provide referrals or suggest a resource?
- What extracurricular activities are available? When and how should students participate?

Source: Castex, G. M., Soviet refugee children: The dynamics of migration and school practice, *Social Work in Education, 14*(3), 141–151 (1992). Reprinted by permission.

family with the health care system and other formal and informal community services. Family interventions, however, need to be congruent with a family's form, including its cultural and normative traditions. For example, when providing social work services in the form of home care, it is critical that the practitioner ensure

> Family interventions must be harmonious with a family's cultural traditions.

that the home care is consistent with a cultural tradition that values that home and family (Cox, 1992). Beckett and Coley (1987) have contended that it is essential to understand black elderly clients within their context of the families' helping networks. To achieve this end, they suggested use of the ecomap to plot the parameters of the family network.

The nature of family interventions also is affected by changes in socially expected behavior and pressures resulting from political and economic transitions. The practitioner needs to be aware of how changing societal demands influence his or her long-standing assumptions about the family, and how these seeming contradictions in societal beliefs affect the family (Boss & Thorne, 1989; Sherman, 1976; Walsh & Scheinkman, 1989). For example, societal transitions have been particularly stressful for women who have increasingly entered the work force and tried to continue with household chores and child care.

Group Interventions

The *mutual aid approach* to groups—frequently discussed in the social work literature—is based on the idea that group members are a source of help to one another for coping with life stress, environmental pressures, or maladaptive interpersonal processes (Gitterman & Shulman, 1986). Social work with mutual aid groups also has roots in the ecological tradition (Coyle, 1930). The mutual aid approach may be used with naturally occurring neighborhood groups or with groups organized by the social worker (Gitterman & Shulman, 1986). In their study involving people with sickle cell disease, Kramer and Nash (1995) found that the "alternative social environment" of the group's social ecology helped members experience less isolation and find support for people affected by sickle cell disease (p. 61). In their discussion of mutual support group design, Slusher, Mayer, and Dunkle (1996) cited the group Gays and Lesbians Older and Wiser (GLOW), which was established in Ann Arbor, Michigan, as part of a university-based geriatric clinic. The authors cautioned that although older gay men and lesbians are a diverse population, support groups may allow them to safely meet and identify with one another. Strauss and McGann (1987) also described a group program that reflected an ecological design. The program, which was based on the view that a child's school is a naturally occurring network, involved a time-limited structured group for children of divorced parents. The intervention also combined workshops for teachers and the Parent-Teacher Association.

> Group interventions rely on the expertise of group members.

Interventions within the group must address the multiple issues of diversity—the patterns of oppression, discrimination, and privilege. Even groups that appear homogeneous will have differences on some diversity issues. Therefore, the social worker who is leading groups needs to understand how a person's behavior and perception of the group environment affects another. The group experience, then, becomes a microcosm for addressing issues of equity and social justice (Garvin & Reed, 1994).

Professional and Informal Helping

Ecological intervention involves both informal helping and professional strategies. *Informal helping* means that the social worker promotes interaction in social networks within a community context. The use of volunteers is inherent in the mutual aid approach. Wolf (1985) called for the use of volunteers in the design of services for inner-city elderly black residents in a Midwestern neighborhood. Transportation to shopping centers, telephone contacts, provision of light housekeeping, bathing, and

> Ecological interventions combine informal and professional helping strategies.

grooming help were some of the supports offered to neighbors. A study of the model revealed that most participants preferred acting as helping neighborhood friends than in a semistructured paraprofessional role.

Guided by the ecological view of human behavior, many social workers have learned to seek out natural helpers in their communities (Berthold, 1989; Kelley & Kelley, 1985). Mokuau (1990) described participation of indigenous people in education, economic, and health programs to implement culturally appropriate service delivery models. Such programs give attention to cultural change, historical perspectives, modernization, and issues such as epidemics, diet and nutrition, and consumption of alcohol and drugs. In addition, Olmstead (1983) suggested that outreach and adjunct services involve ministers and neighbors.

The extent to which natural helping networks are used versus professional social work services, or a combination of the two, has been debated (Auslander & Litwin, 1988). For example, in some cultures, such as the traditional Vietnamese culture, the concept of "social work" does not exist (Timberlake & Cook, 1984). Moreover, some agencies may develop services around formal and informal processes. Such a model was used in a crisis house for Northern Ontario Indian clients. Success of the model was attributed to the adoption of four ecological practice principles: (1) mutuality—the reduction of the power differences between the social worker and client; (2) the maximization of differences—the acknowledgment from the onset of the major cultural differences between social worker and client; (3) empowerment—the promotion of power among the agency clients, staff, and board; and (4) a structural approach, in which the agency worked to achieve change at all levels, including client, staff, agency, and wider community.

REFERENCES

Ackerman, N. ([1972] 1984). Family psychotherapy theory and practice. In G. D. Erikson and T. P. Hogan (Eds.), *Family therapy: An introduction to theory and technique.* Monterey, CA: Brooks/Cole.

Ainsworth, M. D., & Bell, S. M. (1974). Mother-infant interaction and the development of competence. In K. J. Connolly and J. Bruner (Eds.), *The growth of
competence.* New York: Academic Press.
Allen-Meares, P. (1985). Assessing behavior disorders in children: An eclectic
approach. *Social Work in Education, 7*(2), 100–113.
Allen-Meares, P., & Lane, B. A. (1983). Assessing the adaptive behavior of children
and youths. *Social Work, 28*(4),297–301.
Allen-Meares, P., & Lane, B. A. (1987). Grounding social work practice in theory:
Ecosystems. *Social Casework, 68*(9), 515–521.
Anderson, R., & Carter, I. (1990). *Human behavior in the social environment: A social
systems approach* (4th ed.). New York: Aldine de Gruyter.
Aponte, H. J. (1991). Training on the person of the therapist for work with poor
and minorities. *Family Systems Application to Social Work,* 23–39.
Applegate, J. S. (1990). Theory, culture, and behavior: Object Relations in context.
Child and Adolescent Social Work, 7(2)85–100.
Auslander, G. K., & Litwin, H. (1988). Social networks and the poor: Toward
effective policy and practice. *Social Work, 33*(3), 234–238.
Bandura, A. (1977). Self-efficacy: Toward a unifying theory of behavior change.
Psychology Review, 84, 191–215.
Bandura, A. (1986). *Social foundations of thought and action.* Englewood Cliffs, NJ:
Prentice-Hall.
Bauer, A. M., & Shea, T. M. (1987). An integrative perspective on adaptation to the
birth or diagnosis of an exceptional child. *Social Work in Education, 9*(4), 240–
252.
Beckett, J. O., & Coley, S. M. (1987). Ecological interventions with the elderly: A
case example. *Journal of Gerontological Social Work, 11*(1/2), 137–157.
Berthold, S.M. (1989). Spiritism as a form of psychotherapy: Implications for social
work practice. *Social Casework, 70*(8), 502–509.
Biegel, D. E., Shore, B. K., & Gordon, E. (1984). *Building support networks for the
elderly.* Beverly Hills: Sage.
Birren, J. E. (1969). The concept of functional age, theoretical background. *Human
Development, 12,* 214–215.
Blumer, H. ([1937] 1969). The methodological position of symbolic interactionism.
In E. P. Smidt (Ed.), *Man and society.* New York: Prentice-Hall.
Bosch, L. A. (1996). Needs of parents of young children with developmental delay:
Implications for social work practice. *Families in Society, 77*(8), 477–487.
Boss P. G., & Thorne, B. (1989). Family sociology and family therapy: A feminist
linkage. In M. McGoldrick, C. Anderson, and F. Walsh (Eds.), *Women in
families: A framework for family therapy* (pp. 78–96). New York: Norton.
Bowen, M. (1978). *Family therapy in clinical practice.* New York: Jason Aronson.
Bowlby, J. (1973). Affectional bonds: Their nature and origin. In R. S. Weiss (Ed.),
Loneliness: The experience of emotional and social isolation (pp. 38–52). Cam-
bridge, MA: MLT.
Brennan, E. M., & Rosenzweig, J. M. (1990). Women and work: Toward a new
developmental model. *Families in Society, 71*(9), 524–533.

3Bronfenbrenner, U. (1989). Ecological systems theory. *Annals of Child Development, 6,* 187–249.

Brooks, C. M. (1974). New mental health perspectives in the black community. *Social Casework, 55*(8), 489–496.

Bryant, C. (1980). Introducing students to the treatment of inner-city families. *Social Casework 61*(10), 629–636.

Bryant, C., & Zayas, L. H. (1986). Initial moves with school-family conflict: Entering, engaging and contracting. *Child and Adolescent Social Work, 3*(2), 87–100.

Burghardt, S. (1986). Marxist theory and social work. In F. J. Turner (Ed.), *Social work treatment: Interlocking theoretical approaches* (pp. 590–617). New York: Free Press.

Castex, G. M. (1992). Soviet refugee children: The dynamics of migration and school practice. *Social Work in Education, 14*(3), 141–151.

Child welfare league of America (1993). *Cultural competence self-assessment instrument.* Washington, DC: Author.

Comas-Diaz, L. (1996). Cultural considerations in diagnosis. In F. W. Kaslow (Ed.), *Handbook of relational diagnosis and dysfunctional family patterns* (pp. 152–168). New York: Wiley.

Congress, E. P. (1994). The use of culturagrams to assess and empower culturally diverse families. *Families in Society,* 531–538.

Cox, C. (1992). Expanding social work's role in home care: An ecological perspective. *Social Work, 37*(2), 179–183.

Coyle, G. L. (1930). *Social process in organized groups.* New York: Richard R. Smith.

de Anda, D. (1984). Bicultural socialization: factors affecting the minority experience. *Social Work, 29*(2), 101–107.

De La Rosa, M. (1988). Natural support systems of Puerto Ricans: A key dimension for well-being. *Health and Social Work, 13*(1), 181–189.

Doelker, R. E., & Lynett, P. A. (1983). Strategies in staff development: An ecological approach. *Social Work, 28*(6), 380–384.

Dore, M. M., & Dumois, A. O. (1990). Cultural differences in the meaning of adolescent pregnancy. *Families in Society, 71*(2), 93–101.

DuBois, W. E. B. (1969). *Darkwater voices from within the well.* New York: AMS.

Dworkin, J. (1990). Political, economic, and social aspects of professional authority. *Families in Society, 71*(9), 534–541.

Eisikovits, Z. C., & Edleson, J. L. (1989). Intervening with men who batter: A critical review of the literature. *Social Service Review, 63*(3), 385–414.

Ewalt, P. (1980). *NASW Conference Proceedings: Toward a Definition of Clinical Social Work.* Washington, DC: NASW Press.

Fandetti, D. V., & Goldmeier, J. (1988). Social workers as culture mediators in health care settings. *Health and Social Work, 13*(3), 171–179.

Garbarino, I. (1986). Where does social support fit into optimizing human development and preventing dysfunction? *British Journal of Social Work, 16(suppl.),* 23–27.

Garvin, C., & Reed, B. G. (1994). Small group theory and social work practice: Promoting diversity and social justice or recreating inequities. In R. R. Greene

(Ed.), *Human Behavior Theory: A Diversity Framework* (pp. 173–202). Hawthorne, NY: Aldine de Gruyter.

Germain, C. B. (1976). Time: an ecological variable in social work practice. *Social Casework, 57*(7), 419–426.

Germain, C. B. & Gitterman, A. (1995). Ecological perspective. In R. L. Edwards & J. G. Hopps (Eds.), *Encyclopedia of social work* (19th ed.) (816–824). Washington, DC: NASW Press.

Gitterman, A., & Germain, C. B. (1981). Education for practice: Teaching about the environment. *Journal of Education for Social Work, 17*(3), 4–51.

Gitterman, A., & Miller, I. (1989). The influence of the organization on clinical practice. *Clinical Social Work Journal, 17*(2), 151–164.

Gitterman, A. & Shulman, L. (1986). *Mutual aid groups and the life cycle.* Itasca, IL: F. E. Peacock.

Goldstein, E. G. (1986). Ego psychology. In F. J. Turner (Ed.), *Social work treatment,* pp. 375–406. New York: Free Press.

Greene, R. (1986). *Social work with the aged and their families.* Hawthorne, NY: Aldine de Gruyter.

Greene, R. R. (1991). The ecological perspective: An eclectic theoretical framework. In R. R. Greene and P. H. Ephross (Eds.), *Human behavior theory and social work practice* (pp. 261–296). Hawthorne, NY: Aldine de Gruyter.

Gutierrez, L. M. (1990). Working with women of color: An empowerment perspective. *Social Work, 35*(2), 149–153.

Gwynn, F. S., & Kilpatrick, A. C. (1981). Family therapy with low income Blacks: A tool or a turn-off? *Social Casework 62*(5), 259–266.

Hardy-Fanta, C. (1986). Social action in Hispanic groups. *Social Work, 31*(2), 119–123.

Hartman, A. (1978). Diagrammatic assessment of family relationships. *Social Casework, 59,* 465–476.

Hartman, A. (1979). The extended family. In C. G. Germain (Ed.), *Social work practice: People and environment* (pp. 282-302). New York: Columbia University Press.

Hasenfeld, Y. (1987). Power in social work practice. *Social Services Review, 61*(3), 469–483.

Ho, M. K. (1991). Use of Ethnic Sensitive Inventory to enhance practitioner skills with minorities. *Journal of Multicultural Social Work, 1,* 57–67.

Howard, T. U., & Johnson, F. C. An ecological approach to practice with single-parent families. *Social Casework, 66*(8), 483–489.

Johnson, L. C. (1986). *Social work practice.* Boston: Allyn & Bacon.

Joseph, M. V. & Conrad, A. P. (1980). A Parish neighborhood model for social work practice. *Social Casework, 61*(7), 423–432.

Karls, J. M., & Wandrei, K. E. (1994). *Person-in-environment system.* Washington, DC: NASW Press.

Kelley, P., & Kelly, V. R. (1985). Supporting natural helpers: A Cross-Cultural Study. *Social Casework, 66*(6), 358–366.

Kirschner, C. (1979). The aging family in crisis: A problem in living. *Social Casework, 60*(4), 209–216.

Kluckhohn, F., & Stodbeck, F. L. (1961). *Variation in value orientations.* Westport, CT: Greenwood.

Kramer, K. D., & Nash, K. B. (1995). The unique social ecology of groups: Findings from groups for African Americans affected by sickle cell disease. *Social Work with Groups 18*(1), 55–65.

Kropf, N. P., & Greene, R. R. (1993). Life review with families who care for developmentally disabled members: A model. *Journal of Gerontological Social Work, 21*(1/2), 25–40.

Land, H. M. (1986). Life stress and ecological status: Predictors of symptoms in schizophrenic veterans. *Health and Social Work, 11*(4), 254–264.

Lemann, N. (1986). The origins of the underclass. *Atlantic Monthly, 257*(June), 31–35.

Lewin, K. (1935). *A dynamic theory of personality.* New York: McGraw-Hill.

Litwak, E. (1985). *Helping the elderly.* New York: Guilford.

London, B., Bradley, D. S., & Hudson, J. R. (1980). Introduction: Approaches to inner-city revitalization. *Urban Affairs Quarterly, 15*(4), 373–380.

Longres, J. F. ([1900] 1990). *Human behavior in the social environment.* Itasca, IL: F. E. Peacock.

Maluccio, A. N. (1981). *Promoting competence in clients.* New York: Free Press.

Matsuoka, J. K. (1990). Differential acculturation among Vietnamese refugees. *Social Work, 35*(4), 341–345.

McAdoo, J. L. (1993). The roles of African-American fathers: An ecological perspective. *Families in Society, 74,* 28–35.

McGoldrick, M., Pearce, J. K., & Giordano, J. (1982). *Ethnicity and family therapy.* New York: Guilford.

McLain Park, K. (1996). The personal is ecological: Environmentalism of social work. *Social Work, 41*(3), 320–323.

McPhatter, A. R. (1991). Assessment revisited: A comprehensive approach to understanding family dynamics. *Families in Society, 72*(1), 11–21.

Mead, M. (1930). *Growing up in New Guinea.* New York: Mentor.

Meyer, C. (1987). Direct practice in social work: Overview. In A. Minahan et al. (Eds.), *Encyclopedia of social work* (18th ed.) (pp. 409–422). Silver Springs, MD: NASW Press.

Meyer, C. H. (1988). The eco-systems perspective. In R. A. Dorfman (Ed.), *Paradigms of clinical social work* (pp. 275–294). New York: Brunner/Mazel.

Miley, K. K., O'Melia, M., & DuBois, B. L. (1995). *Generalist social work practice: An empowering approach.* Boston: Allyn & Bacon.

Minuchin, S. (1974). *Families and family therapy.* Cambridge, MA: Harvard University Press.

Mokuau, N. (1990). A family-centered approach in native Hawaiian culture. *Families in Society, 71*(10), 607–613.

Monahan, D. J. (1993). Assessment of dementia patients and their families: An ecological approach. *Health and Social Work, 18*(2), 123–131.

Montalvo, B. (1974). Home-school conflict and the Puerto Rican child. *Social Casework, 55,* 100–110.

Murphy, G., & Jensen, F. (1932). *Approaches to personality*. New York: Coward McCann.

Olmstead, K. A. (1983). The influence of minority social work students on an agency's service methods. *Social Work, 28*(4), 308–312.

O'Neil, M. J. (1984). *The general method of social work practice*. Englewood Cliffs, NJ: Prentice-Hall.

Palmore, E. (1977). Facts on aging: A short quiz. *Gerontologist, 22,* 273–276.

Pearlin, L. I., & Schooler, C. (1978). The structure of coping. *Journal of Health and Social Behavior, 19,* 2–21.

Pennekamp, M., & Freeman, E. M. (1988). Toward a partnership perspective: Schools, families, and school social workers. *Social Work in Education, 10,* 246–259.

Potocky, M. (1993). Effective services for bereaved spouses: A content analysis of the empirical literature. *Health & Social Work, 18*(4), 288–301.

Red Horse, J. G., Lewis, R., Feit, M., & Decker, J. (1978). Family behavior of urban American Indians. *Social Casework, 59*(2), 68–72.

Searles, H. F. (1960). The nonhuman environment. New York: International Universities Press.

Selye, H. (1956). *The stress of life*. New York: McGraw-Hill.

Sherman, S. N. (1976). The therapist and changing sex roles. *Social Casework, 57*(2), 93–96.

Slusher, M. P., Mayer, C. J., & Dunkle, R. (1996). Gays and Lesbians older and wiser (GLOW): A support group for older gay people. *Gerontologist, 36*(1), 118–123.

Strauss, J. B. & McGann, J. (1987). Building a network for children of divorce. *Social Work in Education, 9*(2), 96–105.

Strean, H. S. (Ed.) (1971). *Social casework theories in action*. Metuchen, NJ: Scarecrow.

Swenson, C. (1979). Social networks, mutual aid and the life model of practice. In C. B. Germain (Ed.), *Social work practice: People and environments,* pp. 215–266. New York: Columbia University Press.

Tideiksaar, R. (1986). Preventing falls: Home hazard checklist to help older patients protect themselves. *Geriatrics, 41* (5) 26–28.

Timberlake, E. M., & Cook, K. O. (1984). Social work and the Vietnamese refugee. *Social Work, 29*(2), 108–113.

Tinetti, M. E., & Powell, L. (1993). Fear of falling and low self-efficacy: A cause of dependence in elderly persons. *Journals of Gerontology, 489*(Special Issue), 35–38.

Tran, T. V. (1993). Psychological traumas and depression in a sample of Vietnamese people in the United States. *Health and Social Work, 18*(3), 185–194.

Walsh, F., & Scheinkman, M. (1989). Fe(male): The hidden gender dimension in models of family therapy. In M. McGoldrick, C. Anderson, and F. Walsh (Eds.), *Women in families: A family therapy* (pp. 78–96). New York: Norton.

Wells, L. M., & Singer, C. (1985). A model for linking networks in social work practice with the institutionalized elderly. *Social Work, 30*(4), 318–322.

White, R. W. (1959). Motivation reconsidered: The concept of competence. *Psychological Review D, 66,* 297–331.

Wilson, J. W. (1985). Cycles of deprivation and the underclass debate. *Social Service Review, 59*(4), 541–559.

Wolf, J. H. (1985). "Professionalizing" volunteer work in a Black neighborhood. *Social Service Review, 59*(Sept.), 423–434.

4

Culturally Relevant Practice: Addressing the Psychosocial Dynamics of Oppression

REBECCA VAN VOORHIS

We must acknowledge that structures and behavior are inseparable, that institutions and values go hand in hand. How people act and live are shaped— though in no way dictated or determined—by the larger circumstances in which they find themselves.

—C. West, *Race Matters*

Since 1982, the Council on Social Work Education's (CSWE, 1982) curriculum policies have recognized the importance of content on the experiences and responses of people whose lives have been affected by institutionalized oppression. As a result of such awareness, social workers are challenged to be prepared to comprehend the complex functioning of clients who are members of oppressed population groups. To practice effectively with these clients, social workers must have a solid understanding of the effects of oppression on people's functioning. Practitioners must also be prepared to connect the experiences of clients in oppressed groups to the problems that are the presenting reasons for clients' needing help, such as substance abuse, depression, hunger, housing, or school failure. The risk for social workers who are unprepared to assess the complexity of a client's situation, including how the client's life experiences are affected by oppression, is that interventions may be simplistic and victim blaming.

The framework for culturally relevant practice enables social workers to prepare for practice that is relevant for clients from oppressed population groups. The framework is broad enough to apply to clients from population groups who have been oppressed and is not limited to any particular oppressed group. Most authors (e.g., Bell, 1981; Cass, 1979; Cross, 1991; Fanon, 1967) have focused on only one population group; however, to achieve a broad framework, the current author synthesized common, recurring themes from the literature on several oppressed population groups. Social workers can use the framework for culturally relevant practice to learn about each client's specific experiences with oppression. Also, the framework does not require that practitioners first learn all the types of oppressed groups and the forms of oppression that each group experiences.

Social workers may also use the framework to understand the *difference that difference makes* and to develop assessment and intervention skills that are sensitive to the client's *lived experiences* with oppression based on diversity. Thus, the framework prepares social workers to intervene to reduce client self-hatred and alienation that result from institutionalized oppression, to support the client to claim his or her full identity, and to seek change in oppressive conditions.

This chapter defines the concept of oppression and presents the literature that forms the foundation for the model. It describes the framework for culturally relevant practice with clients from oppressed population groups, including a discussion on the use of autobiographies, fiction, and case material to understand how to use the framework with clients. The chapter also gives a rationale for using the framework in practice.

OPPRESSION DEFINED

Being oppressed means the absence of choices.
    —b. hooks, *Feminist Theory: From Margin to Center*

Understanding oppression begins with an examination of the roots of oppression and the meaning of the concepts *oppressor* and *oppressed*. According to Suzanne Pharr (1988), oppression originates in and is maintained by the *normative group* through institutional and economic power and institutional and individual violence. The normative group need not represent a numerical majority. In the United States, the normative group is male, white, heterosexual, Christian, able-bodied, youthful, and has access to wealth and resources.

Although Pharr has identified the oppressor group as the normative group, hooks (1984) has referred to the oppressor group as *the center*.

Russell (1993) explained that this term refers to the center of political, economic, and social power and resources as well as cultural and linguistic dominance in a social structure. Those groups lacking power and resources are identified as *the margin*. In contrast to the center, "to be in the margin is to be part of the whole but outside the main body" (hooks, 1984, p. ix). hooks described her childhood experience of literally living in the margin of her small town. She reported how she could enter the world on the "other side of the tracks" to work in a service capacity, (e.g., a maid, janitor, or prostitute), but always had to return to the margin.

Practitioners must be prepared to understand the experience of oppression for people in the margin and privilege for those in the center. As hooks indicated, "Being oppressed means the absence of choices" (ibid., p. 5), which results from the normative group's control of societal institutions such as schools, banks, legislative bodies, and the military. Control of institutions permits the center to control all others and limit access to resources, mobility, jobs, and so forth. Furthermore, as Pharr (1988) pointed out, people on the margin are pitted against each other along lines of race, class, gender, sexual orientation, age, ability, and religion, whereas people in the center continue to reap huge profits and retain the power to make policies and establish norms.

FOUNDATIONS OF OPPRESSION

[Taking on the oppressor's culture] plunge[s] oneself into profound alienation in all its varieties and anguish.
—H. Bulhan, *Frantz Fanon and the Psychology of Oppression*

To make assessments and carry out interventions that are sensitive to clients' experiences living with oppression, the practitioner must establish a foundation of knowledge about the psychosocial effects of oppression for people in all marginalized groups. The knowledge base includes scholarship about oppression and alienation, identity formation, and coping responses. According to scholars on oppression (Bulhan, 1985; Fanon, 1967, 1968), alienation occurs when people are separated from their culture and inserted into another culture. Bulhan suggested that taking on the oppressor's culture "plunge[s] oneself into profound alienation in all its varieties and anguish" (p. 189). Alienation, in all its forms, represents the psychoaffective injuries associated with oppression.

In the process of forming an identity as a member of a marginalized group, oppressive conditions deter members from claiming and becoming proud of this aspect of their identity. Instead, oppression often leads to shame and alienation from the self and the "internalization of negative identities . . . [as] the oppressed . . . falls victim to the oppressor's damaging assaults and psychic mutilation" (Bulhan, 1985, p. 196). Collins (1986), Gould (1987), hooks (1983), and Smith (1986) have all identified the negative effects on identity and self-image for women, in general, and women of color, in particular, that result from societal attitudes and discriminatory treatment. Likewise, Tatum (Ayvazian & Tatum, 1994) pointed out that racism leads people of color to deny their own perceptions and experiences so that they may maintain their relationships with people in the center. Morris (1993) has asserted that disrespect and denigration "often lead to lower self-confidence and distorted self-images" among African-American women (p. 108). Thus, identity formation for members of marginalized groups is a developmental process that usually takes considerable time and requires a supportive environment. Morris (1993) regarded this process of self-definition as "an assertion of power" (p. 108) that is essential to self-esteem and a person's commitment to action. Several models of identity formation for African-American people, lesbians, and gay males have been synthesized into the knowledge base for the framework for culturally relevant practice described in this chapter (Bell, 1981; Bowles, 1988; Cass, 1979; Chestang, 1984; Coleman, 1981–1982; Cross, 1991; McNaught, 1988).

Scholarship about the major life patterns of responding to sustained oppression adds to the base for the framework. The models developed by Bulhan (1985) and Russell (1993) identify major patterns of coping with prolonged oppression. These patterns characterize a person's typical way of responding to oppression as a result of their membership in a marginalized population group. For example, in one pattern identified in both models, the person abandons his or her own distinctive identity and seeks to become like people in the center. In another response pattern, the person distances herself or himself from the oppressor group and seeks to have contact only with members of her or his own group.

FRAMEWORK FOR CULTURALLY RELEVANT
SOCIAL WORK PRACTICE

We are feeling what it's like to love ourselves—two brown women, born to an era that said we were all wrong. . . . It takes a long time for a brown woman to know that. . . . It takes hard work and self-permission and self-love.
—P. Raybon, *My First White Friend: Confessions on Race, Love, and Forgiveness*

The framework for culturally relevant practice integrates knowledge about the psychosocial effects of oppression with the skills of listening to clients' stories, assessing the psychosocial effects of oppression on clients, intervening to enhance identity and change oppressive social conditions, and evaluating practice interventions. The framework was developed to prepare social workers to connect with clients in the margin and to understand how oppression has affected client functioning. Practitioners may use the framework to understand their clients' experiences; validate their clients' aspirations, struggles, and experiences; and empower clients to fully claim their identity as members of oppressed groups.

Listening to Clients' Stories

To gather clients' experiences, social workers must develop interviewing skills to *listen* to what a client has to say and to refrain from interpreting a client's experiences from their own perspective. Like ethnographic interviewing, the goal should be to understand the client's life experiences as a member of an oppressed population group "from the native point of view" (Spradley, 1979, p. 3). Thus, social workers should carefully listen so they may understand the client's experience of oppression and then apply this knowledge in their interventions with the client.

To achieve such understanding, the social worker must be prepared to encourage the client to tell her or his story and then listen carefully to the client's words. It is particularly important for social workers to be skilled in drawing out clients who are members of oppressed groups (e.g., women, people of color, poor people, lesbians, and gay males). Fully listening to people in the margin is a revolutionary act, because their lives and

> Fully listening to clients in the margin is a revolutionary act, because typically the center has ignored the client's lives and experiences.

experiences have typically been ignored by people in the center. As Pharr (1988) pointed out, people in the center, including experts, often know little about the experiences of those in the margin. The result has been widespread interpretation by professionals of the lived experiences of people in the margin. Holbrook (1995) graphically showed the significance of such interpretation when she described the differences between the stories told by a mother receiving child welfare services and those told about her by her caseworker. For example, the case record stated, "This has always been a problem case. . . . Mrs. T has given birth to 12 children. She is a very poor housekeeper" (Holbrook, 1995, p. 748). In contrast, Mrs. T's diary recorded these entries:

> Well, I have Allen's lunch packed. Breakfast made, and have called Richard. So, [I] can sit down for a while before I start to wake up girls . . .
> Woke up at 3:55 a.m. Washed some slacks for Lisa and other clothes.
> Woke up at 5:30 this morning. Washed out socks, blouses and dried Andrew's pants that were already washed.

Thus the heart of effective multicultural practice is "listening carefully to that person's story and bringing to awareness the themes and values that the storyteller is using to give meaning to the events of personal experience" (Holland and Kilpatrick, 1993, p. 304).

Assessing the Psychosocial Effects of Oppression

As clients tell their stories, the listener can understand and assess how living with oppression has affected the client. Assessment involves attention to violations of the client's space, time, energy, mobility, bonding, and identity that have resulted from her or his membership in a marginalized population group. Assessment also addresses the client's alienation from self or others as a result of institutionalized oppression, the client's stage of identity formation as a member of a marginalized population group, and the client's primary pattern of coping with membership in a marginalized group. Attention to these areas should be an integral part of the assessment of each client, regardless of the reason for service.

Assessing Violations.   Assessing violations of the client's freedom and independence involves identifying ways in which the client experiences limitations as the result of his or her membership in a marginalized population group. For example, a client who is openly gay likely will be restricted from serving in the military or being ordained as a minister in most Christian denominations. Likewise, the assessment of space and mobility violations for people of color often reveals places that clients avoid because people in the center do not welcome the presence of people of color. Many clients' lived experiences with oppression have been captured by Bulhan (1985):

> Their bodily and psychological integrity are constantly violated. . . . The frequent comings and goings of landlords, police officers, social workers, and a host of others render their homes more like an inescapable . . . "trap" than a protective and protected "castle." (p. 259)

Likewise Patricia Raybon (1996), an African-American writer, reflected the violations experienced by many clients from oppressed population groups:

> White people controlled me. They were my masters—my neighbors, my bosses, my schoolmates, the store clerks, the doctors, the judges, the co-workers, . . . who, in their "whiteness," held over me a . . . power . . . to define and ascribe and legislate and subjugate. (p. 6)

Assessing the impact of such violations on clients will help social workers to identify the effects of oppression on client functioning, including the problems that necessitated social work intervention.

Assessing Alienation. This assessment involves an examination of the ways in which a client from a marginalized population group experiences a lack of synchrony between himself or herself and the wider society and, hence, does not experience the sense of acceptance and belonging that members of the population in the center enjoy. The social worker assesses the client's alienation from the client's self. This form of alienation results because the client has internalized the center's views of the margin. Consequently, the client develops a negative self-image and experiences a lack of connection to his or her own culture. The client also may have become alienated from significant others as they strive to fit into the center. Thus, the social worker assesses whether the client has distanced from family, friends, and other significant people in the oppressed group in order to be accepted by the population in the center. The social worker also examines the client's alienation from the general other, meaning the ways that the client is estranged from the oppressor group. Another form of alienation is a lack of connection to one's own culture. A client also may become alienated from the creative social praxis by becoming detached from organized activities of society, such as work or school.

Assessing the Client's Identity Formation. This assessment involves using a synthesis of identity formation models for people in marginalized population groups (Bell, 1981; Cass, 1979; Coleman, 1981–1982; Cross, 1991; McNaught, 1988). Because each of these models focuses on a specific marginalized population group, themes common to the identity formation process for clients from all marginalized groups were identified. To assess identity formation, the practitioner must determine the degree to which the client claims her or his identity as a member of a marginalized population group.

For members of oppressed groups, the four key stages of identity formation are (1) beginning, (2) adolescence, (3) identity pride, and (4) identity synthesis. In the beginning, the client barely acknowledges membership in a marginalized population group; has limited contact, if any, with others in her or his population group; and may conceal this aspect of identity and strive to "pass" as a member of the population in the center. In the adolescent stage, the client somewhat acknowledges his or her identity as a member of a marginalized group; discloses the identity in limited ways; has some contact with others in her or his population group; and still maintains some "passing" behaviors. During the identity pride stage, the client publicly reveals his or her identity in many ways, such as through dress, language, and activities; is immersed in her or his own group; and avoids contact with people in the population group at the center. In the identity synthesis stage, the client fully embraces his or her identity; comfortably interacts with members of both her or his own group and the oppressor group; and has internalized an identity as a member of a marginalized group and synthesized this identity as an important aspect of the client's total identity.

Assessing the Client's Primary Pattern of Coping with Oppression. This assessment involves determining how the client copes with oppression. Some clients may cope by capitulation, that is, they conform to the expectations of the population in the center and disconnect from experiences on the margin. Others follow a revitalization coping pattern in which they reject the center and its expectations and defend their own identity on the margin. Other clients may fall into a radicalization pattern, in which they claim their identity, *choose* to stand on the margin, and seek change in conditions that oppress (Bulhan, 1985; Russell, 1993). Seldom will an individual follow only one pattern. Instead, for most clients, one of the patterns will be dominant at a particular time and reflect their social milieu. Movement from one pattern to another usually occurs gradually as the conditions in a client's social environment change. Such changes often parallel the client's progress in claiming her or his identity as a member of a marginalized population group.

Intervening to Enhance Identity and Change
Oppressive Social Conditions

Assessing the client's alienation, identity as a member of a marginalized population group, and coping response to prolonged oppression

enables the social worker to plan culturally relevant interventions. The
framework also aids the practitioner
to make interventions that avoid Type
I clinical errors, which can occur
when the social worker assumes the
individual client's experiences are like
those of other members of the client's
oppressed population group (Nor-

> To assist clients in their transformation from oppressed people to agents who are active on their own behalf, social workers must engage in practice that is founded on an ethic of caring.

man & Wheeler, 1996). Intervention with clients from oppressed population groups might involve:

- empowering clients to define themselves and affirm their identity as
  a member of one or more marginalized population groups,
- supporting clients to develop identity pride and synthesize an identity that reflects all aspects of themselves,
- increasing clients' mutually empathic relationships,
- aiding clients to overcome alienation from significant others and the
  population in the center,
- engaging clients in seeking change in conditions that oppress and
  violate their freedom.

Defining themselves becomes a starting point for intervention with
many clients from oppressed population groups. The courageous act of
defining oneself is viewed by Patricia Collins (1986) as taking power
away from the oppressor: "Women who . . . choose to be self-defined and
self-evaluating are . . . retaining a grip over their definitions as subjects,
as full humans, and rejecting the definitions of themselves as the objec-
tified 'other'" (p. 24). Russell (1993) has maintained that people who
actively choose to claim their identity as members of a marginalized
group are showing that despite everything, they really would not want
another identity. Clients' defining themselves in ways that affirm their
identity is a vital antidote to the debilitating psychological consequences
of having internalized the oppressor's demeaning stereotypes of their
group (Bowles, 1988; Cass, 1979; Chestang, 1984; Cross, 1991). Morris
(1993) concluded that "the process of self-definition is viewed as an assertion of power, critical to the self-esteem and action orientation" (p. 108).
Furthermore, research has revealed that aiding clients to claim their personal power is vital to clients' mental health and social functioning (Garber & Seligman, 1980; Miller, 1976; Morris, 1989; Taylor, 1983).

Developing identity pride is vital for clients from all marginalized
groups. Social workers are encouraged to help their male and female
clients become a *womanist*, which is someone who loves themselves re-

gardless (Walker, 1983, p. xii). To achieve such self-love and overcome the internalized oppressor, practitioners must use interventions to aid clients to value their blackness, femaleness, blindness, gayness, Jewishness, gray hairs, or well-worn clothing. Practitioners should apply Raybon's (1996) keys to transforming such alienation: forgive yourself, stop hating yourself, and learn to love yourself as you are.

Mutually empathic relationships are fostered by social workers who validate their clients' experiences. Theorists from the Stone Center in Wellesley, Massachusetts, have viewed mutuality and empathy as central to therapeutic relationships (Jordan, Kaplan, Miller, Stiver, & Surrey, 1991). As reported by Tatum (Ayvazian & Tatum, 1994), people from marginalized population groups do not usually experience such mutually empathic relationships with those in the center. Therefore, clients often experience vital emotional growth from a social worker's validation. For the client in the margin, mutually empathic relationships lead to emotional wholeness because the client does not have to deny or separate from his or her own experiences to connect with the social worker (ibid.).

Overcoming alienation can be achieved by supporting clients to develop mutually empathic relationships in every area of their lives. When social workers have established such relationships with their clients, they then can encourage clients to develop similar relationships with others. Thus, practitioners can guide clients to seek relationships with others who will affirm their full identity. They also may aid clients to pursue change in relationships in which they have been unable to claim all parts of the self. For example, practitioners might encourage clients to stop "de-selfing" so they can reduce their alienation from the self and establish mutually empathic relationships with friends, family, and co-workers (Lerner, 1985, p. 20).

Seeking changes in oppressive conditions can be undertaken by clients after they have been supported to claim their identity as members of marginalized population groups. When clients become self-affirming, they can be transformed from people who exhibit "victim behavior" into agents who act on their own behalf. Victim thinking may be seen in clients who believe that they are helpless and feel that there is nothing that they can do to affect their lives because they are at the mercy of their environment. Thinking that others control the client's life leads to behaving passively and depending on others to take care of things instead of actively addressing the client's own problems. Lorde (1984) has asserted that such internalized patterns of oppression must be rooted out "if we are to move beyond the most superficial aspects of social change" (p. 122). Likewise, Paulo Freire (1970) claimed that the heart of revolutionary change is recognition of the oppressor rooted deep within each of us.

In his writings about this process of transforming despairing oppressed people into self-affirming agents of change, Cornel West (1993) proposed that love and affirmation are essential for this transformation. To aid clients to make such a transformation, social workers must engage in practice that is grounded in an ethic of caring. Noddings (1984) and Collins (1991) described this ethic of caring as a hallmark of both Afrocentric and feminist values and actions. This commitment to caring recognizes the long tradition among both women and African-Americans of expressiveness, empathy, and feelings. Shulman (1992) found that "understanding client's feelings" and "sharing worker's feelings" (p. 24) were two traits that clients viewed as essential for effective practice. Likewise, in her research on educators whose teaching is culturally relevant, Ladson-Billings (1994) found that each participant in her study exhibited the ethic of caring. Like listening to clients' lived realities, practice that reflects this ethic of caring is a revolutionary act. As described by Ladson-Billings, "The dispassionate, 'objective,' white male discourse" (p. 156), which was the clinical standard set by Freud, is displaced as social workers reach out to show clients from marginalized population groups that they care about what happens to their clients.

Evaluating Practice Interventions

Having carried out interventions to enhance the client's identity as a member of an oppressed group, strengthen mutually empathic relationships, and change oppressive conditions, the practitioner needs to evaluate outcomes to ascertain practice effectiveness. Through practice evaluation, the social worker monitors the client's progress in claiming his or her identity as a member of a marginalized population group, developing mutually empathic relationships with members of the client's marginalized group and the population group in the center, decreasing victim thinking and behavior, and increasing proactive behavior as a member of an oppressed group who seeks change in oppressive conditions. The practitioner should perform these outcome evaluations in addition to measuring outcomes related to the client's reason for seeking service.

Learning the Framework: Strategies

Practitioners may begin developing their skills in applying the framework for culturally relevant practice in work with individuals and families from oppressed population groups by using the framework to assess the psychosocial effects of oppression on people in short stories, autobiographies, biographies, and fiction. Autobiographies such as Patricia Raybon's (1996) *My First White Friend,* Paul Monette's (1992) *Becoming a Man,* and Robb Dew's (1994) *The Family Heart* provide compelling examples of the experiences of people in marginalized population groups. Likewise, social workers may study and use case examples to assess the psychosocial effects of living with prolonged oppression. They might also heighten their awareness of the effects of oppression by writing about their own experiences with stereotyping, victimization, or marginalization resulting from membership in an oppressed population group.

To use the framework in practice, social workers should follow four steps: (1) listen to client's experiences with institutionalized oppression; (2) assess the effects on clients of institutionalized oppression because of client's race, gender, sexual orientation, age, religion, class, or disability; (3) plan and carry out interventions with clients to reduce the negative effects of oppression; and (4) evaluate the outcomes of intervention.

Using the Framework: Rationale

There are advantages to incorporating the framework for culturally relevant practice into direct practice. For one, an understanding of the psychosocial effects of oppression provides essential knowledge because the traditional psychological theories and therapeutic modalities are comprised of European-American, white, male constructs that limit their usage in practice with oppressed population groups. As pointed out by several authors (Gould, 1984; Lowenstein, 1976; Saltman & Greene 1993; Tice, 1990; Wetzel, 1986), social work educators are concerned about the applicability of a theory to women and other oppressed population groups. Carol Tavris (1992), in *The Mismeasure of Woman,* suggested that the prevailing stage theories and constructs about human development were developed using subjects in the center and then generalized to those in the margin without attempting to determine the validity of such generalizations. Bulhan (1985) has critiqued the prevailing approaches to psychotherapy because they "spring from Eurocentric and class-specific values" (p. 271) that fail to address oppressive social conditions and they have "universally adopted the legacy of victim-blame" (p. 7). Bulhan indicated that such approaches lead practitioners to adjust clients to the status quo even when such action is intolerable and hostile to human needs. Thus, the framework encourages social workers to engage in interventions that empower clients and strengthen their

> Danger! Social workers who do not use the framework for culturally relevant practice may approach practice with only piecemeal knowledge about their clients from oppressed populations.

sense of esteem and worth as members of marginalized population groups. Furthermore, the framework aids practitioners to focus on solutions and avoid interventions that adjust clients to oppressive conditions or reinforce the client's sense of helplessness and victimhood.

In addition, including a framework for practice that is sensitive to a client's experiences in oppressed population groups is particularly important for social workers who believe themselves to be "color blind." Ladson-Billings (1994) regards such beliefs as a subtle form of racism because they ignore a significant feature of the person's identity. When people put energy into pretending that differences do not exist, they often come to view difference as deviance (Lorde, 1984). Thus, social workers must be prepared to recognize a person's color, sexual orientation, ethnicity, and so on, and understand that differences between groups of people do not mean that one group is inferior. The framework for culturally relevant practice prepares practitioners to understand Lorde's message:

> It is not the differences of race, age, and sex that separate us. It is rather our refusal to recognize those differences, and to examine the distortions which result from our misnaming them and their effects on human behavior and expectation. (ibid., p. 115)

Another advantage of incorporating the framework into practice is that it prepares social workers for culturally relevant practice that is not simply a "one-size-fits-all" approach. Chow (1994) described her experience attending a family therapy workshop in which a case study did not give attention to the client's race or poverty. She questioned how relevant the treatment approach was for the client when such significant factors were ignored. Similar concerns have led clinicians at the Stone Center to develop a *relational approach* to treatment with women instead of continuing to apply the traditional treatment approaches that were based on male development and then generalized to women (Jordan et al., 1991). Thus, the framework for culturally relevant practice prepares practitioners to think about complex functioning in a complex manner rather than engaging in superficial assessments and interventions.

A danger of not using the framework is that social workers may approach their practice with only fragmented knowledge about their clients from oppressed population groups. Thus, they would apply the dual perspective in practice with African-American clients and feminist approaches in practice with female clients, but not know how to apply their knowledge about the dual perspective or feminist practice in their work with clients from other oppressed population groups, such as gay males. An advantage of the framework for culturally relevant practice is that it has synthesized knowledge presented for specific population groups, such as African-Americans, lesbians, or Jews, into a meaningful whole that social workers can use for practice with clients from all oppressed population groups. This synthesis of common themes for people in oppressed population groups reflects Gould's (1987) call to educators and practitioners to recognize the similarity of experiences among members of various oppressed population groups.

Using the framework for culturally relevant practice aids social workers to avoid the objectification of clients that results from a homogenized approach to social work practice—a Type II clinical error (Norman & Wheeler, 1996). Social workers can use this comprehensive framework to make assessments and carry out interventions that recognize the client's life experiences with oppression based on gender, color, sexual orientation, class, physical or mental ability, age, and religion.

CONCLUSION

[Culturally relevant social work practice advances Russell's vision of the] transformed society of justice where . . . no one will . . . be marginalized.
—L. M. Russell, *Church in the Round: Feminist Interpretation of the Church*

The framework for culturally relevant practice prepares social workers to effectively assess the effects of institutionalized oppression on their clients, intervene to reduce the negative influence of sustained oppression, as well as empower clients to challenge the oppressive conditions. Far from being "color-blind," practitioners learn to regard the client's membership in a marginalized population group as an integral part of culturally relevant social work practice. Social workers must also develop mutually empathic relationships as the heart of their practice with clients so their actions will affirm each client's identity and culture. According to Holland and Kilpatrick (1993), "What clients often need is not so much expert advice, technical fixes, or precise data but rather . . . overt, caring encouragement to resume their roles as the authors of their own stories" (p. 304). Such support and affirmation fuels self-affirmation for clients who belong to oppressed population groups. Self-affirmation leads clients to be transformed from people exhibiting victim behavior into agents who act on their own behalf.

Culturally relevant social work practice also involves questioning the structural inequality and the injustices that exist in society. It means empowering clients to stand up to oppression in all its forms—racism, sexism, heterosexism, ageism, ableism, and classism. Culturally relevant practice aids clients who have been discounted and demeaned as members of marginalized population groups to fully claim their identity. Social

workers who are prepared for culturally relevant practice will be committed to work to transform the center and achieve Russell's vision of the
"transformed society of justice where . . . no one will . . . be marginalized" (1993, p. 193).

REFERENCES

Ayvazian, A., & Tatum, B. D. (1994). Women, race and racism: A dialogue in black
    and white. In *Work in Progress* (Stone Center Working Paper Series, Vol. 68).
    Wellesley, MA: Stone Center.
Bell, P. (1981). *Counseling the black client.* Minneapolis, MN: Hazelden.
Bowles, D. D. (1988). Development of an ethnic self-concept among blacks. In C.
    Jacobs & D. D. Bowles (Eds.), *Ethnicity & race: Critical concepts in social work*
    (pp. 103–113). Silver Spring, MD: NASW Press.
Bulhan, H. (1985). *Frantz Fanon and the psychology of oppression.* New York: Plenum.
Cass, V. (1979). Homosexual identity formation: A theoretical model. *Journal of
    Homosexuality, 4,* 219–235.
Chestang, L. (1984). Racial and personal identity in the black experience. In B. W.
    White (Ed.), *Color in a white society* (pp. 83–94). Silver Spring, MD: NASW
    Press.
Chow, C. S. (1994). Too great a price. *The Family Therapy Networker, 18*(4), 30–34.
Coleman, E. (1981–1982). Developmental stages of the coming out process. *Journal
    of Homosexuality, 7*(2/3), 31–43.
Collins, P. H. (1986). Learning from the outsider within: The sociological signifi-
    cance of black feminist thought. *Social Problems, 33*(6), S14–S32.
Collins, P. H. (1991). *Black feminist thought.* New York: Routledge & Kegan Paul.
Council on Social Work Education (1982). *Curriculum policy for the master's degree
    and baccalaureate degree programs in social work education.* New York: Author.
Cross, W. E. (1991). *Shades of black: Diversity in African-American identity.* Phila-
    delphia: Temple University Press.
Dew, R. F. (1994). *The family heart: A memoir of when our son came out.* New York:
    Ballantine.
Fanon, F. (1968). *The wretched of the earth* (C. Farrington, Trans.). New York: Grove.
Fanon, F. (1967). *Black skin, white masks* (C. L. Markmann, Trans.). New York:
    Grove.
Freire, P. (1970). *The pedagogy of the oppressed.* New York: Seabury.
Garber, J., & Seligman, M. (Eds.) (1980). *Human helplessness.* New York: Academic.
Gould, K. H. (1984). Original works of Freud on women: Social work references.
    Social Casework, 65(2), 94–101.
Gould, K. H. (1987). Feminist principles and minority concerns: Contributions,
    problems and solutions. *Affilia, 2*(3), 6–19.
Holbrook, T. L. (1995). Finding subjugated knowledge: Personal document re-
    search. *Social Work, 40,* 746–751.
Holland, T. P., & Kilpatrick, A C. (1993). Using narrative techniques to enhance
    multicultural practice. *Journal of Social Work Education, 29,* 302–308.
Hooks, B. (1983). Ain't I a woman: Black women and feminism. *Black Scholar, 14*(1),
    38–45.

Hooks, B. (1984). *Feminist theory: From margin to center.* Boston: South End.

Jordan, J. V., Kaplan, A. G., Miller, J. B., Stiver, I. P., & Surrey, J. L. (1991). *Women's growth in connection: Writings from the Stone Center.* New York: Guilford.

Ladson-Billings, G. (1994). *The dreamkeepers: Successful teachers of African American children.* San Francisco: Jossey-Bass.

Lerner, H. G. (1985). *The dance of anger.* New York: Harper & Row.

Lorde, A. (1984). *Sister outsider.* Freedom, CA: Crossing.

Lowenstein, S. F. (1976). Integrating content on feminism and racism into the social work curriculum. *Journal of Education for Social Work, 12*(1), 91–96.

McNaught, B. (1988). *On being gay.* New York: St. Martin's.

Miller, J. B. (1976). *Toward a new psychology of women.* Boston: Beacon.

Monette, P. (1992). *Becoming a man: Half a life story.* New York: Harcourt Brace Jovanovich.

Morris, J. K. (1989). *Patterns of acceptance among black mothers of mentally handicapped sons.* Unpublished doctoral dissertation, University of Chicago.

Morris, J. K. (1993). Interacting oppressions: Teaching social work content on women of color. *Journal of Social Work Education, 29,* 99–110.

Noddings, N. (1984). *Caring: A feminine approach to ethics and moral education.* Berkeley: University of California Press.

Norman, J., & Wheeler, B. (1996). Gender-sensitive social work practice: A model for education. *Journal of Social Work Education, 32,* 203–213.

Pharr, S. (1988). *Homophobia: A weapon of sexism.* Inverness, CA: Chardon.

Raybon, P. (1996). *My first white friend: Confessions on race, love, and forgiveness.* New York: Penguin.

Russell, L. M. (1993). *Church in the round: Feminist interpretation of the church.* Louisville, KY: Westminster/John Knox.

Saltman, J. E., & Greene, R. R. (1993). Social workers' perceived knowledge and use of human behavior theory. *Journal of Social Work Education, 29,* 88–98.

Shulman, L. (1992). *The skills of helping: Individuals, families, and groups* (3rd ed.). Itasca, IL: F.E. Peacock.

Smith, B. (1986). Some home truths on the contemporary black feminist movement. In N. Van Den Bergh & L. Cooper (Eds.), *Feminist visions for social work* (pp. 45–60). Silver Spring, MD: NASW Press.

Spradley, J. (1979). *The ethnographic interview.* New York: Holt, Rinehart & Winston.

Tavris, C. (1992). *The mismeasure of woman.* New York: Simon & Schuster.

Taylor, S. (1983). Adjustment to threatening life events. *American Psychologist, 38*(11), 1161–1173.

Tice, K. (1990). Gender and social work education: Directions for the 1990's. *Journal of Social Work Education, 26,* 134–144.

Walker, A. (1983). *In search of our mothers' gardens.* San Diego, CA: Harcourt Brace Jovanovich.

West, C. (1993). *Race matters.* New York: Vintage.

Wetzel, J. W. (1986). A feminist world view conceptual framework. *Social Casework, 67*(3), 166–173.

5

Children in the Child Welfare System:
An Ecological Approach

GAIL FOLARON and MARION WAGNER

The very concept of child maltreatment is socially and historically produced,
varying in its definition according to the ethnicity, sex, class, race, and age of
those who use the concept. We can assume that its shape and content will
continue to evolve as the surrounding society continues to change.
　　　　　　　—S. Kirsh and F. Maidman, "An Ecological Approach"

Child welfare practice focuses on the protection and welfare of children.
In the past, *protection* meant placing children in out-of-home placements
for extended periods and providing therapeutic interventions to the child.
The intent was to "rescue" the child from "bad" parents and caretakers, a
practice exacerbated by social workers' cultural and class bias (Gordon,
1985). The belief in child-saving was so deep that the focus of service was
entirely on the child's care and maintenance. There were few interventions with parents and little consideration given to maintaining contact
between the parent and the child.

　　In the 1970s, government-funded demonstration projects produced
findings that, when parents were included in social work interventions,
children could be permanently reunited with their families. Two landmark studies during the this era of change were the Oregon Project and
the Alameda Project. The Oregon Project was designed to establish permanent placements (adoptive families) for children in long-term foster
care. The project sample included families in which the parents were
considered unable or unwilling to reunify. When child welfare workers
contacted parents and asked them to relinquish their parental rights,
however, they found parents who were interested in reunifying with their

children and who had resolved some of the problems that had led to the original placement. The reason many of the parents had not sought to reunify earlier was because of a misunderstanding about the nature of their child's placement. Parents did not know that reunification was an option and did not know how to negotiate the child welfare system. In the end, 26% of the children involved in the Oregon Project were returned to their families of origin (Lahti, Green, Emlen, Zendry, Clarkson, Kuehnel, & Casciato, 1978).

The Alameda Project demonstrated that children could be reunified in a timely manner using interventions of intensive agency services, goal-oriented casework, deliberate case planning, focused decision-making, and outreach efforts (Stein, Gambrill, & Wiltse, 1974). Two years into the project, 41% of the families in the experimental unit, compared with 25% of the families in the control group, were reunified and their cases closed. In addition, 35% of the children in the experimental group and 15% of those children in the control group moved out of foster care into permanent living situations.

The findings from those studies directly contributed to the drafting and passage of the Adoption Assistance and Child Welfare Act of 1980, landmark legislation that redefined good child welfare practice from a focus on the child as the center of practice to family-centered practice. The act redefined child welfare philosophy with an emphasis on *permanency planning,*

> the systematic process of carrying out, within a brief time-limited period, a set of goal-directed activities designed to help children live in families that offer continuity of relationships with nurturing parents or caretakers and the opportunity to establish life-time relationships. (Maluccio & Fein, 1983, p. 197)

Child welfare practice continues to evolve. Good practice continues to be family centered but child welfare workers no longer view the family in isolation. Assessments and interventions are becoming more ecologically based, particularly as the result of an increase in awareness and sensitivity to diverse populations. Extended family and community supports are considered during assessment as are the child's interactions with the school and neighbors. Efforts are now on keeping children as close to their natural supports as possible when they must be removed from their families.

Today, risk to a child is no longer defined only as maltreatment from abuse or neglect; there is a greater understanding of the need for a child to maintain attachments. The essence of permanency planning is to provide stable and continuous relationships with a nurturing caretaker. It is believed that stability and continuity are necessary for a child to develop physically, socially, emotionally, intellectually, and morally. Before removing a child, social workers must weigh the risk of potential abuse or neglect against the harm that separation from family and friends may cause.

Good child welfare practice rests on an ecological framework of service delivery that promotes mutuality in social worker–client relationships. Successful programs use a team approach with parents, foster parents, social worker or caseworker, and service providers, who work together toward a common goal of permanency for the child (Ahart, Bruer, Rutsch, Schmidt, & Zaro, 1992).

Effective child welfare work requires a holistic view of people in their environment. Child welfare workers focus on both the individual interactions and attachments between the parent and child and the environmental barriers that interfere with safety in the home. With a knowledge of attachment and bonding theory, community resources, strategies for client advocacy, a variety of theoretical orientations to problem solving, and an understanding of cultural beliefs and child-rearing practices, child welfare workers can directly enhance client functioning by identifying and intervening in areas in which there is a poor interface between a parent and his or her environment.

Child welfare work is challenging. Many of the decisions made by child welfare workers have life-changing effects on children and families. The social worker cannot make decisions such as whether to remove a child from his or her parents, when to reunify, how often to allow parents and children to visit, and whether to seek permanent termination of parental rights lightly or in isolation. Child welfare workers must be trained in the principles of diversity and supported by a diverse team of professionals who can share responsibility for life-altering decisions and ensure that interventions are culturally sensitive.

ATTENTION TO DIVERSITY
IN CHILD WELFARE PRACTICE

Child welfare workers must constantly assess the goodness-of-fit or adaptive balance of the families with whom they are working and of each family's environment. To ensure that the .ssessments are factual and reliable, a child welfare worker must have a good understanding of the cultural and historical contexts that support or stress the families' interactions with their environment. Attention to diversity requires a knowledge base in a client's history, culture, traditions, customs, value orientations, and spiritual orientations. Child welfare workers must be knowledgeable

about the dynamics of oppression and how social problems affect different client groups. They must under-

> Social workers in child welfare
> must pay attention to the diversity
> of clients and client systems.

stand and be open to the diversity of
family structure and the functionality
of diverse family forms and child-
rearing practices. Furthermore, these social workers must be knowledgeable about concepts related to strengths and resilience that can be incorporated into explanations of behavior and approaches to intervention
(McPhatter, 1997).

There is often a cultural split between clients in the child welfare system and the various service providers. Social workers are often members
of urban, individualistic, middle-class, nuclear families that are usually
small, independent, and "semiclosed" (Laird, 1979). In contrast, children
living in poverty (Lindsey, 1991, 1994) and minority children of color are
disproportionately placed in out-of-home care. Nationally, 26% of the
children entering out-of-home care are African-American and 10% are
Latino (National Center on Child Abuse and Neglect, 1994). Child welfare
workers need to be aware of the importance of extended families, places
of worship, and neighborhoods to minority families so that they may
effectively mobilize informal supports (Devore & Schlesinger, 1987; Laird,
1979; Martin & Martin, 1985; McAdoo, 1978; Stack, 1974). Social workers
who understand the importance of the community and client's cultural
adaptive strategies before completing assessments or structuring intervention methods will be better able to intervene in maladaptive transactions between clients and their environments.

The investigative team of child welfare workers often works in a crisis
mode when protecting a child. When attention to diversity is viewed as
secondary to finding "any available placement" for the child, the results
can be disruptive to a healthy social and emotional development. The
case of Tonia, a child of mixed racial heritage, illustrates the effects of
culturally insensitive practice:

At the age of seven, Tonia was moved from her mother's home in a
metropolitan area and placed with a Caucasian foster family, in a rural
community in a neighboring county. When the placement was arranged,
the caseworker told the foster mother, "Although Tonia looks biracial, her
mother said she is really Italian." During the three years that Tonia remained in foster care, the foster mother put considerable effort into teaching her about the Italian culture.

Following her return home, Tonia was frequently abused by her mother's Caucasian boyfriend, cumulating in an attempted drowning. Tonia
was subsequently re-placed with her former foster family. At the time of
placement, the newly assigned caseworker told the foster parent that the

child had been frequently abused by her mother's boyfriend because of her race.

During the three years this family received services, neither the service providers nor the child's caseworkers discussed with either the child or her mother the question of the child's race and its effect on her treatment within the family. When the caseworker was asked about the child's racial background, she said, "I knew the child was biracial, but her mother said she was part Italian. As a caseworker, I have no business addressing this if the mother isn't interested."

> According to the foster parent, Tonia, now 10, is confused about her racial identity. She is glad to be back with the foster family she had known for three years, but feels isolated in a community that does not accept minorities and whose population contains no African-American role models or playmates. In fact, the census reports only 9 African-American citizens in the entire county. Tonia's foster mother says she doesn't know how to help her and doesn't have community support to which she can turn. She hopes the social worker at the local counseling center can help Tonia. (Folaron & Hess, 1993, p. 118)

SOCIAL WORKER BIAS AND CULTURAL DIFFERENCES

Culture, class, and gender differences between social workers and clients have affected child welfare practice from its inception in the 19th century until the present. Not only were families from the late 1800s until recently expected to adhere to middle-class values in child rearing, but they were also expected to follow accepted social patterns for the roles

> Social workers must develop and maintain self-awareness about their own biases.

of women and white, Anglo-Saxon, Protestant family structures (Gordon, 1985). Children were removed from the home because their parents did not fit the values of the social worker and white, middle-class society, although family-centered services may have prevented many painful separations and enabled children to maintain their attachments.

Often children were placed in families of different cultures. Festinger (1983) studied 277 former foster children who left their placements in 1975. She found that they were rarely given information about their originating cultures. Of the respondents, 50% expressed their right to know more about their ancestry and indicated that they felt they had no roots. "They emphasized that not only their own histories but 'the past history of one's people' were important information to impart" (p. 267).

Issues of culture also emerged in the Oregon Project, which focused on children whose parents were not considered a likely recourse. Among the children reunified was Chris, a 9-year-old boy who had been in placement for 7 years. His Japanese mother married Chris's father while he was stationed in Japan. The father sexually abused Chris and was imprisoned. The parents divorced and the mother remarried.

> Although [the mother] had been described as "apathetic," the project case-worker discovered that she had really not understood the juvenile court proceedings through which Chris had been placed in foster care, due to her poor grasp of the English language. She had accepted the decision, believing that planning by the "State" was not to be questioned or thwarted. (Pike, 1976, p. 24)

The caseworkers had misinterpreted the mother's language and cultural barriers as a lack of interest. Social workers and other observers may misinterpret cultural differences in child-rearing practices and family structures as child maltreatment. Such findings have enhanced a focus in child welfare practice on striving for cultural competence.

Cultural differences in the areas of race and ethnicity, which occasionally interact with issues of class, continue to be of concern in the practice of child welfare. Courtney, Barth, Berrick, Brooks, Needell, and Park (1996) reported on several studies that indicated that children of color are less likely to receive supportive services in child welfare cases than are Caucasian children. Child welfare agencies can work to decrease situations in which bias may potentially result in disparate treatment. One approach to increase social worker competence and reduce bias focuses social worker attention on attitudes, knowledge, and skills of both the social worker and the client system through all phases of the case: contact, problem identification and data collection, assessment, case planning, intervention, termination, and evaluation (Leung, Cheung, & Stevenson, 1994; Stevenson, Cheung, & Leung 1992). Agencies can assess their macro-environment for cultural competence by using tools such as the Child Welfare League of America's (1993) Cultural Competence Self-Assessment Instrument. This tool provides a mechanism for an agency to evaluate its documents, administrative and governing structures, program and policy development and delivery, and treatment of clients. By focusing on the macrosystem of the client as well as the microsystem, the ecological concerns are kept in focus.

Another area of bias among social workers is homophobia and heterosexism. A recent study of social workers found that 10% of respondents were homophobic and a majority were heterosexist (Berkman & Zinberg, 1997). Some social workers may consider families with gay or lesbian parents, especially those with two partners in addition to children, unsafe for children solely because of the parents' sexual orientation. Homophobic attitudes influence services to the biological family when parents are lesbians or gay, services to gay or lesbian adolescents, and the approval of lesbian or gay people as foster or adoptive parents. Sullivan (1994) found inflexible arrangements available to those older lesbian or gay children placed in foster families and group homes. Moreover, social workers and foster parents often lack the skills necessary to resolve conflicts that derive from the children's relationships with their families of origin as well as lack the information to develop supports in a community that will promote the foster parents' and social worker's empowerment and cushion them from homophobia. Child welfare agencies can work to alleviate the existence and effects of homophobia and heterosexism on lesbian and gay youths by hiring supportive staff, by increasing the visibility of an accepting attitude through literature and wall posters, and by providing ongoing staff development on these issues (Phillips, McMillen, Sparks, & Ueberle, 1997).

Gender issues are infrequently mentioned in considerations of social worker bias, although women compose the majority of parents in the child welfare system. Gordon (1985) pointed out that much of the bias of 19th-century social workers included stereotypes about the proper roles and domain of women. Although women have made professional and legal progress since, issues of gender continue to affect child welfare practice. In their 1985 study, Hartman and Vinokur-Kaplan found that women and men had differing concerns in the area of child welfare. A majority of women and few men considered concern about separation and loss, connectedness, and the maintenance of the family to be among the top priorities considered. Differing worldviews can influence decision-making in the child welfare arena, and thus should be considered. Differential treatment of children in child welfare based on gender has been a well-established practice. Differential treatment plans, rules, goals, and placements have been the norm. For example, girls are more likely to be placed in residential care for status offense[1] than boys. Furthermore, adoption of girls has been generally easier, because families did not have to deal, in a traditional sense, with adopting a boy "to carry on the family name."

Another area of bias is religion. Foster parents and foster children often have different religions, and attempts to convert foster children to the foster family's may exacerbate a child's low self-concept and weaken connections to her or his family of origin. Social workers need to work closely with foster parents regarding treating a child without religious prejudice.

Social worker bias also manifests in areas of identification and affiliation. Child welfare workers establish close, collaborative relationships with foster parents, working to create a team that is focused on the child's well-being. The strength of this relationship influences the social worker's interventions in situations in which the foster parent and biological parent disagree. Social workers must work to counteract any tendency to let such affiliations affect their decisions concerning visitations and placement, for example.

Awareness of the possibility of bias in these and other areas is a first step toward reducing the influence of bias. Social workers in child welfare should be encouraged to maintain a continual stance of self-assessment, with assistance from supervisor and peers. Agencies should establish an ongoing staff development agenda in the areas of cultural competence, diversity, and self-awareness and also provide for substantive staff involvement. Focusing on the different worldviews of diverse populations and ways the environment may affect them enhances the child welfare practitioners' ecological perspective.

SIGNIFICANT ATTACHMENTS

As increasing numbers of studies have reported the detrimental effects of disrupted attachments on healthy childhood development, the field of child welfare has moved toward measures to preserve families and decrease the number of out-of-home placements. This effort has required a shift from problem-based assessments, in which maltreated children are frequently removed from their families, to an ecologically oriented, strengths-based approach in which social workers recognize the interrelatedness of families in distress and their environment. Before removing children, social workers now assess the attachment and bonding within the parent-child relationship. Furthermore, they explore the social supports available in the family's natural environment to determine whether a child can remain home safely with additional support and advocacy from a professional social worker. When the child welfare investigator determines that the risks outweigh the family's ability to mobilize resources and protect the children from further maltreatment, then the children are removed and placed in substitute care. Once removed, the social workers then focus on helping the families improve their situations so that the children can be returned home expediently and severed attachments may be restored.

> Social workers must assess attachments and bonding within the parent-child relationship.

Attachment is an affectionate bond between two individuals that lasts through space and time and acts to bring them together emotionally

(Klaus & Kennell, 1976). The basic tenet of attachment theory, according to Bowlby (1980), is that individuals are profoundly motivated and affected by attachments and seek to maintain those attachments. Evidence of this motivation is often displayed in "acting out" behaviors by children in out-of-home placements as well as by the parents and siblings left behind when a child is removed.

A healthy infant can form attachments with any caregiver. The key factor seems to be the caregiver's sensitivity to the baby's signals. Bowlby (1969) reported that the speed and intensity with which a mother responds to an infant's crying and the extent to which the mother initiates interactions with the infant will determine the kind and degree of attachment that will develop between the two. Fahlberg (1991) graphically illustrated this interaction in an arousal-relaxation cycle (Figure 5.1). The arousal-relaxation cycle depicts successful care-providing interactions between the parent and child. The interactions begin when a child expresses a need. The child's need results in an expression of displeasure, such as crying, kicking, or squirming. The cycle is completed when the caregiver responds in a manner that fulfills the need. Then, a period in which the child is quiescent or content follows. Successful completion of this cycle over time helps infants develop trust, security, and attachment to their caregivers.

A children may attach to either a biological parent or a psychological parent, an adult who regularly meets the child's physical and emotional

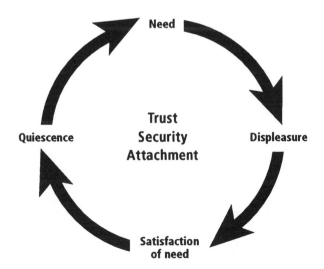

Figure 5.1. The arousal-relaxation cycle. Source: Fahlberg (1991, p. 33). Reprinted with permission.

needs, regardless of biological relationship (Goldstein, Freud, & Solnit, 1979). A child with an affectional bond to a parent values that relationship as a major source of his or her psychological identity and well-being (Wasserman & Rosenfeld, 1986).

Bowlby (1969) reported that, by 18 months, children ordinarily are attached to more than one individual, with fathers and siblings being the most common attachment figures besides mothers. Separations therefore affect the child's relationship with all family members and, if prolonged, can affect the child's sense of self and his or her self-esteem.

The effects of separating children from their families and primary care-givers, therefore, is extremely stressful and often traumatic. In an effort to decrease the number of long-term separations and to move children expe-ditiously into a permanent living situations, the Adoption Assistance and Child Welfare Act of 1980 mandated a double review system. Every 6 months, a court or administrative team must review each case. In addi-tion, every 18 months, a dispositional hearing by a court or sanctioned agent must occur. These reviews are designed to monitor the need and appropriateness of a child's placement. Over time, if parents do not make significant progress toward resolving their problems and reunifying with their children, then the court may move to terminate their parental rights and place their children into permanent living situations. Currently, some states, such as California and Illinois, allow parents 12 months to demon-strate significant change.

DISRUPTED ATTACHMENTS

Before parental rights are severed and a child is moved into an adop-tive home or transferred to a legal guardian, an ecologically oriented assessment is necessary to determine the likelihood that the new home will provide the child with a perma-nent family. Bowlby (1980) found that children suffered emotionally and of-ten physically when separated from the parents to whom they were attached. Regardless of how parents treat their children, most children remain attached to their biological parents and may be reluctant to attach to a new parenting figure (Wasserman & Rosenfeld, 1986).

> Social workers need to work to reduce the effects of disrupted attachments.

When the parent-child relationship is severed or the attachment pro-cess is disturbed, several problems may surface, such as reduced learning (Mosey, Foley, McCrae, & Evaul 1980), increased impulsiveness, and a lowered frustration tolerance (Fraiberg, 1977). As children grieve, they may engage in aggressive behaviors that result in visits to the community mental health center. Often these children are given a label of adjustment disorder, conduct disorder, or attention deficit disorder (ADD). A significantly higher proportion of children in out-of-home placements have a diagnosis of ADD than children in the population as a whole (Fahlberg, 1991). Children labeled as having ADD are often medicated. For grieving children, such medication may be inappropriate. Furthermore, labels such as conduct disorder or ADD may result in a change to special education classrooms, further severing connections and attachments to friends and affecting a child's social status.

Social workers need to understand that grieving behaviors are typical reactions to involuntary parent-child separations. Bowlby (1980) identified several features related to "normal" grieving, such as anger and the intense effort to recover and reproach the lost person or object:

> When confronted with a loss, all species have a tendency to seek to recover the lost object and then reproach it after recovery, apparently to decrease its likelihood of getting lost again. In his attempt to normalize the grief process. Bowlby suggested four phases of mourning:
>
> 1. numbing that usually lasts from a few hours to a week and may be interrupted by outbursts of extremely intense distress and/or anger
> 2. yearning and searching for the lost object, which can last for months and sometimes for years
> 3. disorganization and despair (p. 85)
> 4. reorganization. (Bowlby, cited in McNeil, 1995, p. 286)

A situation of prolonged stress is created when children actively grieve over a long period with little consolation. According to attachment theory, "prolonged stress together with ineffective coping and personal vulnerability, can lead to physiological, emotional, or social dysfunction" (ibid., p. 266). Common factors in health mourning include anger directed at third parties, the self, and sometimes the lost person. There is a tendency to search for the lost person in hopes of reunion. The angry behavior displayed by children in out-of-home placements often creates alarm in new foster parents and social workers who are unfamiliar with the grieving process, as the case of Merideth suggests:

> Merideth may have been told that the disruption was not her fault. However, she knew she had played a part in it, and rightly so. In the Norman home, this previously toilet trained child would pull down her panties and have a bowel movement on the carpet. She flushed her toys down the toilet, necessitating a call to a plumber. She scratched the neighbor's new car with a rock. And she clobbered the six-year-old already in the family with a toy, leading to an injury that required stitches. (Fahlberg, 1991, p. 152)

ESSENTIAL CONNECTIONS WITHIN MULTIPLE
LEVELS OF THE ENVIRONMENT

When children are removed from their biological families and placed in a new environment, their linkages to siblings, relatives, friends, school, and social organizations are disrupted, sometimes severing significant sources of support and self-esteem. Ecologically oriented social workers consider both the personal attachments children have with their families as well as the child's connections in the greater environment. Wasson (1989) identified nine areas of essential connections, or attachments, that are necessary for healthy, satisfying lives: connections to (1) information, (2) a significant person, (3) a group, (4) a meaningful role, (5) a means of support, (6) a source of joy, (7) a system of values and morals, (8) personal history, and (9) a place. These areas are described as follows, with considerations given for practice.

> Social workers must focus on the nine areas of essential connections.

Information. The information connection is a basic one that social workers often overlook. When children are removed from their families, both the child and family are left with information gaps that may result in inappropriate behaviors and unnecessary anxieties. The child needs information on the reasons for removal and the plan for his or her return. Parents need information about the processes and mores of the child welfare system, including client rights and possible outcomes (Wagner, 1992).

Children placed in new family environments are often confronted with family cultures that differ from the one in which they were raised. Cultural differences may include, but are not limited to, child-rearing practices, diet, language, religious practices, holiday traditions, and expectations of male-female relationships. Cross-cultural placements are especially common for African-American or mixed-race children. Placed children and their families need basic information on family rules, expectations, and patterns of living to interact successfully with their new environments.

Significant People. When removed, children are separated from the most significant person in their lives: their primary caregiver. Given the importance of continuity of attachments to healthy development, efforts must be directed at maintaining the parent-child bond while helping the child attach to his or her new caregiver. In neglect situations in which the primary caregiver was the child's sibling, the child's primary significant attachment may be with one or more siblings (Bank & Kahn, 1982, cited in Hegar, 1993). Child welfare workers should place siblings together and pay particular attention to situations in which the sibling was the primary caregiver. Social workers should also pay attention to the extended family, because many cultures with people of color define family as extended family.

Group Membership. Not only do children lose their group identity as members of their family of origin, but many lose their membership and status in school; among peers; and in athletic, social, and religious groups. On occasion, a group identity may be an essential component of the child's self-esteem and a bridge to healthy social and emotional development. Gay and lesbian adolescents, for example, who are at risk of violence, stigma, and other discriminatory behaviors, may find support in a group of other lesbian or gay adolescents. For other children and adolescents, participation in an athletic team or social club enhances their self-concept. In considering appropriate placements, the child welfare worker must assess the child's ability to continue in these or similar activities. The loss of group identity may lead to a sense of isolation and hopelessness.

Meaningful Roles. The social worker should also be aware of the effect of disconnecting family members from meaningful roles. A *meaningful role* is a meaningful function that is related to another person or group, such as "daddy's little girl, student, best friend." For children, roles are lost when they are integrated into a family in a new sibling order, when a caregiving role is eliminated by separation from parents or siblings, and when children are moved to a different school and neighborhood and must reestablish a new reputation among peers. For parents, a child's removal means they are no longer the parental authority in their child's life. The immediate affect of the loss of a role, status, and function may be a loss of identity and self-esteem. Longer term effects may increase feelings of incompetency and lead to a lack of motivation to succeed.

Source of Joy. Human beings develop various mechanisms through which they may find a source of joy, including rituals, holidays, vacations, and play activities. Families celebrate rituals in different manners, and children lose the certainty and comfort of familiar rituals. Sometimes children are placed in families who do not celebrate their holidays or who conduct unfamiliar rituals. In some foster homes, foster children are omitted from family rituals and vacations. Although a family travels out of state to vacation or visit with extended family, the foster child may be temporarily moved to the home of a respite care provider. Although such an action may provide a much needed break for the foster family, the message to the foster child is one of unworthiness and exclusion. Participation in family rituals and holidays provides a symbol of belonging.

Values and Morals. Every family has some mechanism of imparting a system of values and morals, often in the form of a particular religion, spirituality, or philosophy. Foster children may value a different system of values and morals than the families in which they are placed. Many foster parents become involved in the child welfare system in response to a religious calling. Religious differences and challenges to a child's established value system may lead to feelings of confusion for a child. Schatz and Horejsi (1996) described a former foster child who had lived in three foster families, each with a different religion. "She recounted with tears in her eyes how bad she remembers feeling when the foster mother told her she would not be okay until she was 'saved'" (p. 84). Children who have been accustomed to participating in religious services and who are placed in a foster family with different beliefs suffer both the loss of their familiar value system and the particular rituals with which they feel comfortable. Whenever possible, children in placement should be given the opportunity to continue membership in their family's religion and, if feasible, to attend the church, synagogue, or mosque with which they were affiliated.

Personal History.   In a study of 277 former foster children, 7 out of 10 adults interviewed said they wished they had known more about their biological family background during their placement and 50% reported they had felt they had no roots (Festinger, 1983):

> They spoke strongly about their right to know about their ancestry, their heritage, or their roots. "A person has a right to know early on about their own family or else they make up all kinds of things in their heads." They believed that "a lot of foster children wonder about where they came from" and that at the very least photographs should be provided. (p. 266)

To keep children connected to their families, their family-related roles, and their personal history, social workers often work with children on life storybooks or life books (Aust, 1981; Backhaus, 1984; Holody & Maher, 1996; Jewett, 1978; Wheeler, 1978). A *life book* is a collection of pictures, papers, stories, and other memorabilia that preserves a child's history. A child's personal history is an important source of pride, understanding, and comfort. The importance of preserving and discussing children's pasts is to help them understand who they are, the events and decisions that profoundly affected their lives, and to obtain the "facts" of significant life events such as abuse or removal from their homes. When children can openly discuss their own history, they may discard fantasies and reduce self-blame that may interfere with their abilities to prepare for the future.

Place.   People tend to identify with a particular geographical location, a city, a neighborhood, a particular house, or even a room. Removal from home means a loss of place for a foster child; their special place, such as a bedroom, is lost or, at the extreme, the child's removal suspends the family's eligibility for public assistance and ultimately leads to eviction from the family home.

Connections to some familiar place helps to maintain the child's sense of identity. The child welfare worker may help maintain a child's connection to a place by keeping pictures of the child's home, providing means of continuing affiliations to sports teams or other symbols of geographic identity, and working with the biological parents to keep some parts of the child's room and possessions the same as before placement.

Addressing essential connections from a ecological perspective enables a social worker to focus on ways to keep the identity of a child in placement intact. Parents and siblings are also affected when a child is removed from the home. The social worker can assist parents to work through their own sense of loss of connections, enabling them to focus on issues their children may have and to work toward successful reunification.

MAINTENANCE AND BUILDING OF ATTACHMENTS IN OUT-OF-HOME PLACEMENT

For optimal parent-child attachment to occur, continuity, stability, and mutuality in relationships must exist. *Continuity* refers to the parents' availability to the child during times of need (Fraiberg, 1977). *Stability* is the environment that supports the capacities of both the child and parent to engage in a bonding process. *Mutuality* refers to the interactions between parent and child that reinforce that each person is important to the other (Hess, 1981). To maintain an optimal

> Social workers should strive to maintain and build attachments for children in out-of-home placements.

parent-child attachment, the social worker should ensure that visits arranged between the parent and child will encourage continuity, stability, and mutuality of the parent-child relationship.

Hess and Proch (1988) suggested that visits be structured to best meet a child's needs and strengthen a biological parent and child's attachment. One approach to strengthening parent-child attachment is to structure the visits in a way that provides the parent with the opportunity to meet a child's need. With infants from birth to age 2 years, the parents may arrive at the foster home during mealtime or bathtime and take over the infant's care. Similarly, Hess and Proch proposed that children's developmental needs at all ages can be the basis for parent-child interaction. For example, children aged 2 to 4 years are developing small motor coordination. A parent may help a child with this skill development by drawing together or stringing beads. Hess and Proch further suggested that visits extend beyond the foster parent's home and into the child's environment. For example, early-school children aged 5 to 7 years are often transferred to a new school when placed in a foster home. Parents may take their children to the playground before the first day to introduce them to the school environment, take their children shopping for school clothes, or visit their children at school. These types of interactions meet a child's need and promote continuity of care and mutuality in the parent-child relationship as much as possible in an unnatural child caring arrangement. See Table 5.1 for other considerations for maintaining this relationship.

REUNIFYING FAMILIES

Foster care is only a temporary respite for children and families while social workers and parents work to improve environmental supports to the family and to resolve interpersonal problems that resulted in maltreatment of the child. As parents increase their coping skills, they are encouraged to commit to a permanent plan for their child. A permanent plan may be to reunify with their child or to help the child move into an adoptive setting. Most, but not all parents seek to reunify.

Families who reunify are challenged by the change in each family member. Children who reunify are different than they were when they left home. Frequently, they have grown and parents and siblings are confused by their developmental changes. Parental authority had been challenged by the child's removal and the reunifying family must struggle with power relationships. Often, the families themselves are changed by the addition or deletion of members through births, divorces, and new paramours. Stuart (1982) wrote:

> Social workers should consider interpersonal and environmental changes for families and children when planning for reunification.

When the child in substitute care is returned to the family of origin, it is, in every sense, a placement. The family system has readjusted and closed. It is not a matter of plugging the child back into the hole he/she left behind; there is no hole. The system has to open, readjust and close again. Since people do change, and since children do grow and develop, child and family are not the same people who lived together before; they may be as much strangers to each other as are the child and the foster family when they are brought together. Reunification is complicated by the fact that the emotional climate and the expectations of the child and family are different from the climate and expectations in foster placement. The expectations are

Table 5.1. Considerations for Maintaining Parent-Child Attachment

Social Worker Decision	*Considerations for Maintaining Attachments*

The risk of maltreatment outweighs the damage that may result from placement
Explore family and community options. For example, is there a relative or friend that can foster the child?

The child(ren) is removed
Arrange for contact between the child and parent as early as possible so the child can be reassured that he or she was not abandoned. If more than one child is removed all efforts should be made to keep the siblings together.

Child(ren) is put into a foster family
Efforts should be made to keep the child within close proximity to his/her old neighborhood and school district.

The child adjusts to his/her new environment
Frequent and meaningful visits should be arranged to enhance the parent-child connection and to keep the sibling relationship in tact.

The family is reunified
Aftercare services are needed to help the child reintegrate into the family and the larger community.

often that everyone will be as they were when the child left the family, and the emotional climate is clouded by a history of negative interactions, old angers, fears, and resentment. (p. 2)

The challenge for the social worker is not only to help the family find a balance but also to help each member build bridges to the community. Reunifying children are often emotionally and socially delayed as a result of the trauma of removal. Younger children are often clingy and afraid to leave their parents' sight (Folaron, 1992). Older children need help in reintegrating into their neighborhoods and schools (Folaron & Williamson, 1997). Parents often need supports that neighbors could provide, such as transportation and respite.

Ecologically oriented social workers target the problems resulting from the child's transition home and seek support from the environment to empower families to safely reunify and sustain a life-style free of abuse or neglect. This requires a partnership between the social worker and the family and support from the natural environment.

Working with children and families in the child welfare system requires a team effort on several levels. The parents need to be involved in the partnership and treated with respect. On the other hand, social workers also need the support of a informed community. To work effectively in this field, a social worker must have a knowledge of several systems, including child welfare, mental health, and juvenile justice; an under-standing of diverse life-styles and practices; knowledge of various prob-lems areas such as mental illness, substance abuse, and domestic violence; an understanding of the effects of poverty and oppression on daily life; an ability to advocate for a client within various systems; an understanding of diverse populations; and a knowledge of available community re-sources to support a client. Such extensive knowledge comes only with years of experience and adequate training. Therefore, it is critical that social workers network with other professionals to staff cases and build resources to ensure the best possible service to their clients.

CONCLUSIONS

Using an ecological perspective tied to an understanding of diversity enables a child welfare worker to develop comprehensive assessments and culturally sensitive interventions for children in jeopardy. Child wel-fare workers assess and intervene on multiple levels of the child's envi-ronment, including the parent-child relationship and broader community setting in which the child has status and support. The child welfare work-er's first goal is to preserve attachments and community connections while protecting a maltreated child. The effects of placement are traumat-ic for a child. Therefore, the social worker must make every effort to keep the child connected to their families, their supports, and their own per-sonal history. To intervene effectively, and with the least risk to the child, the social worker must have an understanding of diverse life-styles and cultures, a sensitivity to the goodness-of-fit between clients and the envi-ronment, and awareness of the stress resulting from life transitions and environmental pressures.

NOTE

1.   A status offender is a juvenile who is under the jurisdiction of a court for an offense that would not be a crime if committed by an adult. Some examples are runaways, truants, and minors in possession of alcohol.

REFERENCES

Ahart, A., Bruer, R., Rutsch, C., Schmidt, R., & Zaro, S. (1992). *Intensive foster care reunification programs* (Report). Washington, DC: U.S. Department of Health and Human Services.

Ainsworth, M., Blehar, M., Waters, E., & Wall, S. (1978). *Patterns of attachment: A psychological study of the strange situation.* Hillsdale, NJ: Erlbaum Associates.

Aust, P. (1981). Using the life story book in treatment of children in placement. *Child Welfare, 60,* 535–560.

Backhaus, K. A. (1984). Life books: Tool for working with children in placement. *Social Work, 29,* 551–554.

Bank, S. P., & Kahn, M. D. (1982). *The sibling bond.* New York: Basic Books.

Berkman, C. S., & Zinberg, G. (1997). Homophobia and heterosexism in social workers. *Social Work, 42,* 319–334.

Bowlby, J. (1969). *Attachment and loss.* Vol. 1: *Attachment.* New York: Basic Books.

Bowlby, J. (1980). *Attachment and loss.* Vol. 3: *Loss: Sadness and depression.* New York: Basic Books.

Child Welfare League of America (1993). *Cultural Competence Self-Assessment Instrument.* Washington, DC.: Author.

Courtney, M. E., Barth, R. P., Berrick, J. D., Brooks, D., Needell, R., & Park, L. (1996). Race and child welfare services: Past research and future directions. *Child Welfare, 74,* 99–137.

Devore, W., & Schlesinger, E. G. (1987). *Ethnic-sensitive social work practice* (2nd ed.). Columbus, OH: Merrill.

Fahlberg, V. I. (1991). *A child's journey through placement.* Indianapolis, IN: Perspectives.

Festinger, T. (1983). *No one ever asked us: A postscript to foster care.* New York: Columbia University Press.

Folaron, G. (1992). *The impact of family reunification: The experiences of four families.* Unpublished doctoral dissertation, University of Illinois, Champaign-Urbana.

Folaron, G., & Hess, P. (1993). Placement considerations for the child of mixed race parentage, *Child Welfare, 72,* 113–125.

Folaron, G., & Williamson, C. (1997). Preliminary report on the Intensive Reunification Project submitted to the Marion County Division of Children & Family Services and The Marion County Juvenile Court. Unpublished.

Fraiberg, S. (1977). *Every child's birthright: In defense of mothering.* New York: Basic Books.

Goldstein, J., Freud, A., & Solnit, A. (1979). *Beyond the best interests of the child.* New York: Free Press.

Gordon, L. (1985). Child abuse, gender, and the myth of family independence: A historical critique. *Child Welfare, 64,* 213–224.

Hartman, A., & Vinokur-Kaplan, D. (1985). Women and men working in child welfare: Different voices. *Child Welfare, 64,* 307–314.

Hegar, R. L. (1993). Attachment, permanence, and kinship in choosing permanent homes. *Child Welfare, 72,* 367–378.

Hess, P. M. (1981). *Working with birth and foster parents: Trainer's manual.* Knoxville: University of Tennessee School of Social Work.

Hess, P. M., & Proch, K. O. (1988). *Family visiting in out-of-home care: A guide to practice.* Washington, DC: Child Welfare League of America.

Holody, R., & Maher, S. (1996). Using lifebooks with children in family foster care: A here-and-now process model. *Child Welfare, 75,* 321–335.

Jewett, C. (1978). *Adopting the older child*. Boston: Harvard Common Press.

Kirsh, S., & Maidman, F. (1984). An ecological approach. In F. Maidman (Ed.), *Child welfare: A source book of knowledge and practice*, pp. 1–15. New York: Child Welfare League of America.

Klaus, M. H., & Kennell, J. H. (1976). *Maternal infant bonding*. St. Louis: C.V. Mosby Co.

Lahti, J., Green, K., Emlen, A., Zendry, J., Clarkson, Q. D., Kuehnel, M., & Casciato, J. (1978). *A follow-up study of the Oregon Project*. Portland, OR: Regional Research for Human Services, Portland State University.

Laird, J. (1979). An ecological approach to child welfare: Issues of family identity and continuity. In C. B. Germain (Ed.), *Social work practice: People and environments* (pp. 174–212). New York: Columbia University Press.

Leung, P., Cheung, K. M., & Stevenson, K. M. (1994). A strengths approach to ethnically sensitive practice for child protective service workers. *Child Welfare, 73,* 707–721.

Lindsey, D. (1991). Factors affecting the foster care placement decision: An analysis of national survey data. *American Journal of Orthopsychiatry, 61*(2), 272–281.

Lindsey, D. (1994). *The welfare of children*. New York: Oxford University Press.

Maluccio, A. N., & Fein, E. (1983). Permanency planning: A redefinition. *Child Welfare, 62,* 195–201.

Martin, J. M., & Martin, E. P. (1985). *The helping tradition in the black family and community*. Silver Spring, MD: NASW Press.

McAdoo, H. P. (1978). The impact of upward mobility on kin-help patterns and reciprocal obligations in Black families. *Journal of Marriage and the Family, 40,* 761–778.

McNeil, J. S. (1995). Bereavement and loss. In R. L. Edwards (Ed.-in-Chief), *Encyclopedia of social work* (19th ed., Vol. 1), pp. 284–291. Washington, DC.: NASW Press.

McPhatter, A. R. (1997). Cultural competence in child welfare: What is it? How do we achieve it? What happens without it? *Child Welfare, 76,* 255–278.

Mosey, A. C., Foley, G. M., McCrae, M., & Evaul, T. (1980). *Attachment-separation-individuation*. Philadelphia: Pennsylvania Dept of Education and Berks Intermediate Unit #14.

National Center on Child Abuse and Neglect (1994). *Child maltreatment 1992: Reports from the states to the National Center on Child Abuse and Neglect.* Washington, DC: U.S. Government Printing Office.

Phillips, S., McMillen, C., Sparks, J., & Ueberle, M. (1997). Concrete strategies for sensitizing youth-serving agencies to the needs of gay, lesbian, and other sexual minority youths. *Child Welfare, 76,* 393–409.

Pike, V. (1976). Permanent planning for foster children: The Oregon Project. *Children Today, 5,* 22–25, 41.

Schatz, M. S., & Horejsi, C. (1996). The importance of religious tolerance: A module for educating foster parents. *Child Welfare, 75,* 73–86.

Stack, C. B. (1974). *All our kin: Strategies for survival in a Black community*. New York: Harper & Row.

Stein, T. J., Gambrill, E. D., & Wiltse, K. T. (1974). Foster care: The use of contracts. *Public Welfare, 32*(4), 20–25.

Stevenson, K. M., Cheung, K. M., & Leung, P. (1992). A new approach to training child protective services workers for ethnically sensitive practice. *Child Welfare, 71,* 291–305.

Stuart, M. (1982). *Reunification.* Denver, CO: University of Denver: Graduate School of Social Work.

Sullivan, T. R. (1994). Obstacles to effective child welfare services with gay and lesbian youths. *Child Welfare, 73,* 291–304.

Wagner, M. (1992). *Information as power in personal social service transactions.* Unpublished doctoral dissertation, University of Illinois, Champaign-Urbana.

Wasserman, S., & Rosenfeld, A. (1986). Decision-making in child abuse and neglect. *Child Welfare, 65,* 515–529.

Wasson, D. L. (1989). *Fosterparentscope:A preservice training curriculum.* New York: New York State Child Welfare Training Institute.

Wheeler, C. (1978). *Where am I going?* Juneau, AK: Winking Owl.

6

Against All Odds:
An Ecological Approach to Developing
Resilience in Elementary School Children

GAYLE COX and GERALD T. POWERS

When spider webs unite, they can tie up a lion.
—Ethiopian Proverb

SIGNIFICANCE OF THE PROBLEM

There is nothing more important to the survival of a democracy than the education of children. Yet the problems associated with the achievement of this ideal are becoming more complex in the context of a rapidly changing society. An increasing number of teachers are faced with issues that go well beyond their capacity to cope. Many children come to school ill prepared to enjoy the excitement and challenge of learning. They are hungry and poorly clothed. They come from families who struggle with problems of health, housing, and unemployment. Indeed, they come from families for whom the ideal of a democracy is little more than a lost dream.

Many parents feel disenfranchised from the very schools their children attend. Their sense of helplessness and hopelessness reflects the marginal nature of their day-to-day existence—an existence that is preoccupied with what Maslow (1954) referred to as the struggle to meet basic survival needs. The relentless nature of this existence inevitably contributes to a loss of self-esteem and ultimately to a reactive rather than proactive posture to life. When a person's very existence depends on the responsiveness of an environment that is perceived as inherently threatening, it is not surprising that the self-actualizing nature of education has little meaning.

The primary focus of public education has always been the comprehensive educational development of the individual student. The desirability of this objective has never been a subject of serious debate. Few educators would disagree with the notion that it is virtually impossible for schools to maximize individual development in the absence of concerned participation of the community. This proposition, however, seems to be accepted more in principle than in practice.

To understand and appropriately address many of the learning difficulties encountered by children, especially those children from economically and politically oppressed neighborhoods, it is essential to attend to the culture of the environment in which they live—its values, conflicts, and potentialities. It is essential that school social workers not only strive to understand how parents come to feel disenfranchised from the schools that their children attend, but seek ways to empower parents in their efforts to take an active role in their children's education.

The concept of the school as a center of community activity is certainly not new. As early as 1902, John Dewey argued that, in its purist form, education was preparation for citizenship. He likened the role of the school to that of the early settlement houses. In reference to the Chicago-based Hull House, he suggested that schools should be viewed as centers of social activity charged with providing, at least in part, the training necessary to enable children and their families to adjust to a rapidly changing environment. "To extend the range and fullness of sharing in the intellectual and spiritual resources of the community is the very meaning of community" (Dewey, 1902, p. 175) and the essence of effective education.

Dewey suggested that no good school could stand apart from the life of the community because the two are inevitably woven together by human values and common interests. His vision foreshadowed the position taken by the American Association of School Administrators (1957), which asserted that "the school is no longer a thing *apart from* the community; it is *a part of* the community" (p. 168, italics added).

The ecological perspective of school social work proposed in this chapter concurs with Dewey's fundamental assumption that any comprehensive concern for the educational development of children must consider the social, psychological, physical, and environmental context of the realities in which children live. If one concedes that education should be concerned with the *whole person*, then it follows that professional personnel, both inside and outside the school, must work cooperatively to involve families, neighborhoods, and communities who give meaning and substance to the lives of the children they serve. The focus of this chapter, therefore, is to explore the means by which interested individuals and organizations can be brought together in a partnership within a school-community context so that, collectively, ideas, beliefs, and capacities can be shared in ways that will ultimately contribute to a deeper understanding and appreciation of how to address the complex human problems facing contemporary education. It proposes a model of social work practice in the schools that builds on people's strengths in ways that will empower them to become proactive participants in the cooperative enterprise of educating children.

RISK AND RESILIENCE

The issue of identifying the students who are "at risk" is controversial. Historically, these students have been identified as minorities of color, recent immigrants, and poor people. Terms such as *culturally disadvantaged* or *educationally disadvantaged* are often used to describe them. Their "deficiencies" are seen as emanating from personality flaws, dysfunctional families, and chaotic communities. Although somewhat diminished, the controversy and the debate continue and are reflected in the struggles among and between policymakers, educators, and human services providers. Not surprisingly, because the beliefs about who is at risk differ, the approaches to resolving risk vary accordingly and reflect the philosophical positions of their proponents.

> The school can be a focal point for empowering children who may be "at-risk."

Hixson and Tinzmann (1990) have identified three general approaches that have been used to define at-risk students. Each approach has both strengths and limitations. The *predictive approach* uses an actuarial methodology that compares individual students' characteristics, as derived from school and other agency records, with social and demographic variables that are known to correlate with academic achievement. As a speculative strategy, it lends itself well to interventive approaches that emphasize prevention. However, the underlying ideology adheres to a deficit model that focuses on the deficiencies of the students, their families, and the communities in which they live. As such, little attention is given to personal strengths and other systemic conditions or forces that may serve to positively shape the life circumstances of the subjects under consideration. This approach carries with it the potential danger of becoming a self-fulfilling prophecy as well as the tendency to deflect attention away from any changes that may need to occur from within the school system itself.

The descriptive approach uses a monitoring strategy as its primary mode of classifying students. As such, it represents a post hoc approach that attributes the status of being at risk only after a student has exhibited an identifiable problem. By the time the kinds of problems that warrant the at-risk label have been recognized, they may be so severe and well entrenched that remediation is the only plausible intervention available. Unfortunately, in such cases, the student may have fallen so far behind his or her peers academically that any form of remediation becomes extremely difficult, if not impossible. Even when problems and risk factors are identified early, the intervention usually results in the placement of the child in an ancillary program such as special education, or a "pull-out" program that may have the effect of negative labeling, pigeonholing, and isolating the student from others in the mainstream. Not infrequently, such experiences may also lead to the student's psychological withdrawal and failure.

The unilateral approach is based on a more egalitarian philosophy in that it views all students as being at risk in one way or another. Although it may have broad appeal for those people who are concerned with the disproportionate amount of attention paid to students who are not performing well, it, too, fails to examine any societal or structural impediments that may thwart the academic development of students experiencing the most difficulty in their efforts to succeed. Under the banner of being "nondiscriminatory," unscrupulous administrators may use the unilateral approach as a justification for the elimination of or failure to create programs for the students who are most in need.

What seems apparent in all three of these approaches is that the concept of risk can be and has been viewed in a variety of ways. Regardless of the orientation, however, more often than not the onus for educational failure seems to fall on the victim. Learning is a complex process that occurs both within and outside the school. The extent to which school social workers succeed or fail in their efforts to garner support for any particular pedagogical philosophy is similarly determined by forces both within and outside the school. In the eyes of many, the ecological perspective is likely to be perceived as one of the more radical philosophies. It espouses the notion that inadequacies, in any area of life—in the individual, within the family, in the school, or in the community—may contribute to academic failure when it is not compensated for in another arena. For example, children who suffer some form of physiological trauma that results in cognitive or emotional impairment are at risk, but the effects of that risk or the risk itself may be mitigated by a supportive family and community environment. It is this interactive, interdependent worldview that requires social workers to consider the less immediate and less apparent aspects of a person's life. What social workers often discover in the process is that their ability to separate cause and effect is not quite as simple as may have appeared when viewed within the context of a more linear model.

Poverty is often identified as a risk factor in that it circumscribes the resources available to families as they struggle to meet basic survival needs and access essential services, including adequate health care, housing, and transportation. In some instances, poverty becomes associated with dysfunctional and unsupportive family environments (Hart & Risley, 1995). In other situations, faced with a comparable set of circumstances, families react quite differently. The same factors that appear to immobilize the problem-solving capacities of some families seem to actualize the strengths and coping capacities of others, for whom adversity seems to present an opportunity for growth. Why it is that some families are able to develop ways to share resources, form common goals, and exhibit care and love for one another, whereas others are not? The answer remains a mystery. Differences can only be explained on the basis of the dynamic interplay among the complex set of variables that determines each family's unique life circumstances. Many children who have faced considerable adversity still manage to grow up to enjoy happy productive lives, suggesting that specific protective conditions may insulate some children from the risks associated with damaging life events (Garmezy, 1985; Rutter, 1987; Werner & Smith, 1992). Human services providers responsible for the delivery of services to children need to become familiar with the factors that have been found to support resiliency and, in doing so, work toward the creation and enhancement of those processes that protect children.

One of the first social scientists to discuss the concept of resiliency was Anthony (1974), who described what he called *psychologically invulnerable children,* that is, children who seem to be impervious to adversity. Anthony's conception of psychological invulnerability conveyed a "fixed" quality that was later challenged by Rutter (1979, 1985). Rutter viewed invulnerability as a more "relative" concept that he considered to be neither innate nor applicable to all risk circumstances. He was joined in this view by a number of other theorists, including Garmezy (1985), who advanced the premise that vulnerability varies over time and changes in response to life circumstances, a conception that may be more accurately captured in the notion of resilience than that of invulnerability. Rutter elaborated on this point:

> Protection does not reside in the psychological chemistry of the moment but in the ways in which people deal with life changes and in what they do about their stressful or disadvantageous circumstances. Particular attention needs to be paid to the mechanisms operating at these turning points in

people's lives when a risk trajectory may be redirected onto a more adaptive path. (Rutter, 1987, p. 329)

Among the most influential studies of resilience was a longitudinal study conducted by Werner and Smith (1982). In tracking a group of Hawaiian students from birth through their early thirties, they found that about one-third of the 225 identified high-risk children grew into competent, caring adults. A variety of risk factors were explored, including having been born into poverty, having experienced early biological perinatal stress, having experienced family instability, and having been exposed to chronic poverty. Despite these risk factors, the "resilient" group not only demonstrated more effective coping capacities, but seemed to thrive in the process. Werner and her colleagues discovered that the resilient children possessed a number of key characteristics that seemed to distinguish them from their counterparts. They were described as having been active, sociable infants; they had had at least one person in their lives who accepted them unconditionally; and they had subsequently developed skills that instilled in them a sense of pride and acceptance within their peer group.

The relevance of these same characteristics has been confirmed in a number of more recent research endeavors. Resilient children are typically identified as having been "easy babies" with happy temperaments who elicit positive responses from their caregivers (Brooks, 1994; Cowan, Wyman, Work, & Parker, 1990; Grizenko & Pawliuk, 1994). The studies are consistent with respect to the earlier cited finding concerning the importance of having at least one caring, accepting person in the child's life. The caregiver need not be the "natural" parent. Increasingly, grandparents and other kin are assuming caregiving roles and providing nurturance in the absence of parents. In the lives of some children, these roles may be assumed by a teacher, a neighbor, a church member, a human services worker, or a variety of other individuals who represent community-based organizations and agencies (Garmezy, 1985).

Resilient children tend to score higher on measures of self-esteem. It is difficult to sort out all the causal connections between self-esteem and the many variables with which it correlates. However, children who possess positive self-esteem are likely to feel better about themselves, including their ability to control the events that affect their lives. Similarly, high levels of self-esteem and self-acceptance have been found to correlate positively with prosocial behaviors among children, including their capacity to use appropriate assertiveness skills and their ability to cooperate and share with others (Brooks, 1994;

> School social workers' interventions are intended to enhance a child's resilience and promote his or her self-esteem.

Rutter, 1987; Werner, 1993). All of these variables seem to be associated with a child's capacity to earn the acceptance of peers (Taylor, 1991), a necessary ingredient in sustaining healthy relationships. It is probably reasonable to conclude that the development of self-esteem, coupled with the sense of personal empowerment it engenders, represents one of the most important protective factors to be developed in children.

Rutter (1987) has recommended the following four "protective processes" that appear to incorporate much of what is known about altering the risk factors that confront children.

Protective Processes

Reduce Negative Outcomes by Alternating the Risk or the Child's Exposure to the Risk. There are two different routes to achieving this objective. One alternative is to alter the meaning or danger of the risk to the child; the other is to alter the child's exposure to the risk. An example of altering the meaning or danger of risk is captured in the actions of a social worker who enables a child to see how the child may use conflict resolution as a means of resolving a dispute between two people and having them both emerge as winners. Altering exposure to risk is illustrated by the social worker who creates an opportunity for a child to participate in a group designed to provide the recognition and support the child needs and deserves as an alternative to gang membership involving antisocial or violent behavior.

Reduce a Negative Chain Reaction Following Risk Exposure. Despite exposure to potentially damaging risk factors, a child's own innate qualities may be drawn on to help offset or reduce the likelihood of a negative chain reaction. Painful life experiences may be viewed as inherently destructive or as opportunities for growth. For example, a child who experiences a significant loss may benefit from counseling that encourages the expression of feelings and the exploration of options for dealing with the loss. By encouraging a child to draw on his or her inner strengths—strengths the child may not even realize he or she possesses—the social worker affirms the child's capacity to cope with painful feelings and chaotic life experiences. In the process of attaining mastery over the immediate set of circumstances, the child becomes empowered to constructively handle the chain of events that will inevitably follow. Indeed, when handled effectively, painful experiences can be the occasion for children to strengthen their problem-solving capacities and grow as human beings. Without such help, they can easily become discouraged and disillusioned.

Establish and Maintain Self-Esteem and Self-Efficacy. This is perhaps the most critical of the protective processes. The development of self-esteem and self-efficacy does not occur in a vacuum. It is inextricably bound to the quality of the relationships people experience. For young children, self-esteem and self-efficacy require an enduring relationship with at least one responsible adult who possesses the ability to convey both a caring attitude and a genuine belief in the child's inherent worth. This means that adults need to maximize the opportunities for children to engage in growth-producing behaviors, particularly when they are exposed to the risks and hardships that will inevitably come their way (Brooks, 1991). Children develop and maintain self-esteem and self-efficacy when they are provided with opportunities to make meaningful decisions about matters that directly affect their lives.

Open Up Opportunities. By creating opportunities for children and encouraging their constructive involvement in the community-at-large, social workers can help them to experience life outside their families and their school in a supportive way—as an environment that not only meets their needs, but one in which they can contribute to others' needs. This is especially important for minority children for whom the larger sustaining environment provides fewer nurturing experiences than are available for children from the dominant culture. Opportunities for community involvement should provide constructive means for fostering an increased sense of responsibility in ways that encourage the acquisition of new skills as well as the sharing of skills already mastered.

In his discussion of the protective processes, Rutter (1987) contended that the goal of intervention should always be one of supporting children in the acquisition of a life with quality. To accomplish that goal, he argued that social workers must be prepared to move beyond the process of simply identifying risk factors and then engaging in remedial attempts to undo psychological dysfunction. Instead, he advocated a proactive and preventive strategy that relies heavily on the identification of the protective processes and mechanisms that minimize risks and foster resilience in the various systems in which children live. This represents a significant shift in ideology from a focus on illness to a focus on wellness. As the concept of resilience has gained prominence in the literature, it has provided the impetus for the development of an entirely new set of systemically based interventions. It allows for the opening up of options and opportunities to work within and across varying systems including the systems comprising the student and teacher, the home and school, and those people and organizations in the external environment.

Case Studies

The following cases suggest some of the challenges posed when developing resilience in elementary school-aged children.

The Case of J.R. J.R. was a short, overweight, 11-year-old fifth grader. He had been at his present school since the third grade. Before then, J,R.'s family had moved frequently, contributing to J.R.'s sporadic attendance record. Despite his marginal grades, J.R.'s test scores indicated that he was of "above average" intelligence. He lived with his single mother, two younger sisters, and a teenaged aunt. J.R. has not seen his father, who, according to school records, has been living "out West" since J.R. was 5 years old. After school each day, J.R. can be seen standing on a corner across from the school in the company of several older boys smoking. He was referred to the school social worker for smoking, and also because he was suspected of "extorting" lunch money from some of the younger students. He admitted to the social worker that he "smokes" but denied that he had ever taken money from the younger students. The social worker explored J.R.'s interests in an attempt to gear him to more constructive after school activities. Although he identified an interest in sports and other recreational activities, he balked at the notion of joining the neighborhood Boys' Club or the local YMCA, describing them as places for "chumps." In a conversation with his mother, the social worker learned that she was both frustrated and fearful of J.R.'s behavior and worried that he was going to wind up in some serious "trouble." J.R.'s mother was unable to persuade him to try out one of the community youth programs.

One day, while making a home visit, the social worker met a local police officer, a young man in his third year on the force. He expressed pleasure in being back in what had been his childhood community, but he was saddened by the self-destructive behavior that he observed among some of the young people. The social worker described her efforts with J.R. as well as her concern, and asked the officer for his suggestions. The officer expressed an interest in meeting J.R. He requested that he not be introduced as a police officer but rather as someone working with the youths in the community. J.R.'s mother approved the meeting, but expressed doubt that J.R. would be comfortable with a "cop." Nevertheless, her concern over J.R.'s growing interest in gangs made her anxious to try any option, especially one that might allow J.R. to have a positive male role model. As it turned out, the two hit it off on the first meeting. They shared not only many interests, but also some of the same life experiences. Officer Smith invited J.R. to join him and another young man, whom he had been mentoring for several years. This young man was close to completing high school, a goal that made his dreams of going into the military a realistic possibility.

Although somewhat serendipitous, this case is offered as an example of how often overlooked indigenous helpers can become allies in the intervention process. J.R.'s life was filled with risk factors: a single parent, poverty, poor school achievement, neighborhood gang activity, and so on, but his protective processes included a caring (if overwhelmed) parent, concerned school staff, J.R.'s basic intelligence, his ability to relate to peers, and an adult male who had taken an interest in him and his well-being. The protective processes, enhanced by the attention and encouragement that he received from Officer Smith, enhanced his self-esteem. Their friendship turned out to be a lasting one, and J.R. ended up with a big brother (the high school student) as well as a mentor. In school, J.R. still had to be prodded to do his school work but his interest increased and he began to work hard on becoming "physically fit" so that he could pass the tests to become a police officer. J.R. had gained a sense of hope and could see a future. Mentoring two young men from his community was a source of personal pride for Officer Smith, but it also enhanced and promoted the image of the police department. Here was a "good cop" in a community that was suspicious of law enforcement.

The Case of Mama Rose.   Jason was a quiet, rather somber 7 year old boy. He was very protective of his sister Corey, a happy, chatty kindergartner who sometimes rebelled against her older brother's tight reins on her. Their mother, Kimberly, had barely turned 15 years old when Jason was born and now, at age 21 years, she looked more like Jason's sister than his mother. It had not been easy for Kim to raise two children. Her mother had been a big help, and losing her to cancer during the past year created an enormous void in Kim's life. She and her mother talked to one another at least once a day. Her mother was a real source of support and encouragement, even during a stormy, though brief, marriage to the children's father, who was in Germany now. Although Kim received regular child support, she often felt that the challenge of raising the children alone was a "heavy burden." She loved her children, yet wondered what it would be like to be free of the responsibility of raising children. Some mornings she felt like sleeping in, which meant that the children were either late for school or did not show at all. It was Jason's absences that triggered a social work referral.

During visits to the home, it was clear to the social worker that his mother provided considerable nurturance for her children. However, she could be quite critical of Jason, whom she had nicknamed "Little Man." Jason was placed in charge of the apartment and took care of Corey when Kim was at work at the nursing home. She worked a 3-to-11 P.M. shift, which meant that the two children were latchkey kids. At first, being in charge had appealed to Jason, but as the months went by and nightfall came sooner, he wished that someone else could be at the apartment with him and Corey. Kim would call faithfully throughout the evening to see if they were okay and to see if Jason had done his chores. One night, a fire broke out in an adjacent apartment and the building had to be evacuated. Jason and Corey were standing out in the cold night air when Mama Rose, who lived two houses down the block, spotted the children and insisted that they come to her house to keep warm. Jason was reluctant and fearful that his mother would become angry with him because he had been instructed *not* to go into anyone's home.

Jason had met Mama Rose the preceding summer. He had been staring at her because "she walked funny." Mama Rose had noticed him staring, had invited him into her yard, and had given him a bag of apples from one of her trees. She explained that she had a disease called diabetes and that poor circulation had caused her to lose a foot, which was why she walked "funny." The two became fast friends and Jason looked forward to helping her with yard work and running short errands. He was rewarded for his thoughtfulness with "pocket change" and home-baked cookies. He helped to fill some lonely summer afternoons for Mama Rose, reminding her of her son when he was Jason's age.

Mama Rose had Jason call his mother to let her know what had happened. Kim was very upset when she heard about the fire but relieved to know that the children were all right and safe with Mama Rose. The next day, Jason shared the story of the fire in great detail with the social worker. Because of all of the excitement the children had overslept and did not arrive at the school until 11 A.M. Kim called to explain the children's tardiness. She seemed a bit on edge and asked if she could come in and talk. During her visit, the social worker asked if she was worried or frightened about something. Tearfully, Kim described how frightened she was about the fire and her fear of continuing to leave the children alone. She indicated that she needed the job and that, with a little more seniority, she could secure better hours. However, in the meantime, she could not come up with a plan that would enable her to afford child care. The afterschool programs only ran until early evening.

Given Jason's fondness for Mama Rose, the social worker wondered if she might be a resource for child care. Kim felt that Mama Rose would probably not want to have small children underfoot but agreed to give it some thought and to make some inquiries. The social worker shared the information that Mama Rose had worked in food service at the school for many years before her retirement. The children and the staff at the school all thought highly of her. She had lived alone since her husband died about 2 years ago. Mama Rose did agree to care for Jason and Corey. Although she did not want to accept payment for her services, saying that the company of the children would be more than adequate compensation, Kim insisted.

Mama Rose cared for the children for 6 months until Kim was assigned to a shift that closely corresponded to the children's school schedule. Kim and Mama Rose became close. Kim valued Mama Rose's wisdom, even though at times she thought she was a bit "nosy." Mama Rose enjoyed the children, who she said kept her feeling young and kept her mind off her worries. The children enjoyed the nurturing of the older woman who helped their mother learn patience and how to plan. Jason was becoming more spontaneous and was able to be more like a little boy and less like the "little man" of the house.

Jason's case epitomizes how exposure to certain of the risk factors can set the stage for a "negative chain reaction." At such a young age he had already experienced multiple and significant losses in his life. The loss of a father (through divorce); the loss of a grandmother with whom he had a close relationship (through death); and the psychological and emotional loss of his mother, which resulted from her preoccupation with her own grief and the survival needs of her family. While Jason's self-esteem and self-efficacy was probably bolstered by his being "placed in charge" and given adult roles, such responsibilities would appear to be inordinate given his age and developmental needs. At this stage, children are moving toward greater self-sufficiency and have a need to be productive, but they also have a need for nurturance and to be able to depend upon an adult. The impact of these risk conditions could be seen in Jason's emotional detachment from much of his world.

The social worker's intervention focused on Jason's mother and included being available, providing her with support, and enabling her to begin to define and address the problems facing the family. As was true in the earlier case, Jason and his family were not the only beneficiaries in the outcome. In any analysis of an ecological system, there emerges an appreciation for the fact that people reciprocally influence each other. Mama Rose benefited from feeling needed. Being needed afforded her an opportunity, often missing in the lives of the elderly, to pass along knowledge, which assures a living legacy.

Both of these case examples illustrate well how a school social worker can draw on the client's personal strengths, as well as existing environmental resources to create protective buffers against the kinds of factors that place children at risk. In developing their interventive strategy, it is apparent that the social workers in both case studies were aware of the interdependent and reciprocal nature of people's needs. By viewing the problems systemically, they were able to exploit existing opportunities to meet the normal developmental needs of the clients. The social workers appealed to the "healthy" aspects of each person and, in so doing, were able to simultaneously reduce the risk factors for one client while strengthening the resilience of another. They could not have accomplished this goal had they not been sensitive to the unique developmental needs of each client.

Influence of Race, Culture, and Class on Risk Factors

Developmental theorists seem to agree that childhood is one of the most critical phases in the life cycle. Although children in general tend to follow certain predictable developmental patterns, there are important individual differences that can only be explained in terms of each child's unique life experiences. In his epigenetic theory of psychosocial devel-

> A child's sense of competence is learned within the context of the dual perspective.

opment, Erikson (1950) maintained that the central crisis facing school-aged children may be characterized as one of industry versus inferiority. During this critical period (from age six to twelve years), children need to feel that they are productive and successful, especially when they engage in activities involving the mastery of academic skills and the formation of interpersonal relationships with peers. Erikson contended that a child's personal sense of competence depends in large part on his or her ability to resolve this important developmental crisis.

Other developmental theorists such as Sullivan (1953) and White (1960) have extended and modified Erikson's framework. Sullivan emphasized the importance of experiences outside the family. He suggested that the limitations and peculiarities of a child's home could be remedied or at least mollified by virtue of the child's accomplishments at school and in the broader community. For example, a child from a troubled home might find social approval and self-esteem through successes in the classroom or in recreational activities. Conversely, a child from a secure family might suffer a corresponding loss of self-esteem when faced with the harsh realities of a competitive and unnurturing world outside the home. In an effort to build on Erikson's concept of competence, White coined the term *effectance motivation* to describe the child's need to gain a feeling of mastery over the environment. According to White, *competence* includes all the kinds of learned behaviors that enable a child to deal effectively with the social and physical environments in which he or she lives.

Children are differentially affected by the unique configuration of risk factors they encounter during their developmental journey. Although all children are exposed to risk factors, the incidence, magnitude, and types of risks encountered vary widely with respect to race, culture, and class. An added risk factor for poor or minority children in schools is the lack of a goodness-of-fit. Schools have tended to ignore or reject different cultural expressions of development that, although "normal," do not fit the established models on which school skills and knowledge are built (Bowman, 1997). As a result, children from poor and minority families are typically judged as inadequate.

Before ever entering school, children have learned a great deal. They have attained what Bowman (1997) has referred to as "developmental competence" and "maturity," that is, a stage in their development that indicates they have achieved the normative learning benchmarks of their community in which they have been socialized. These benchmarks typically include a beginning mastery of their native language, a capacity to establish and maintain positive social relationships with their families and neighbors, and some ability to organize and regulate their own behavior in situations with which they are familiar. Notwithstanding the rigor of such expectations, some children who demonstrate developmental competence within the context of their home environments are unable to adapt to a school environment and succeed at the academic tasks subscribed to and valued by the teacher.

When the school misinterprets cultural differences, such misinterpretations may lead to the placing of children who are developmentally "normal" into special education and low-ability remediation groups. For example, African-American children, particularly those from low-income families, may display behavioral and language patterns that differ in significant ways from those of white, middle-class families (Hale-Benson, 1986). African-American children have higher rates of motor activity, more expressive social-interpersonal styles, and may use nonstandard English (ibid.). Children who are taught to view the world, the qualities of interpersonal relationships, and appropriate standards of behavior in ways that differ from those promulgated by the school are placed at risk. The risk is present even when the family and the school share a common set of values and agree on the competencies that need to be acquired, if there is some variance as to how such values and competencies are to be expressed. When culture is not respected or is devalued by schools, children are faced with the difficult dilemma: Should they identify with the values they learned from their family, friends, and community, or those espoused by the school?

Although ethnic minorities are inevitably faced with being a part of two cultures, and so develop bicultural competence, a minority child cannot have a bicultural self-identification (Ho, 1992). Minority children are forced to develop and differentiate between a personal identity and an ethnic or racial identity to form a cohesive sense of self. Children can be protected from this risk factor by being helped to develop bicultural competence. In their studies of Hispanic children (Buriel, Calzada, & Vasquez, 1982) found that bicultural competence resulted when the children were helped to maintain a "footing" in their traditional culture, while simultaneously adopting Anglo cultural patterns. Maintaining a footing in traditional cultural patterns served to counteract any negative messages or images to which the children might have been exposed.

Although it appears that some children who develop bicultural competence do well in areas such as self-esteem and are high academic
achievers, others are overwhelmed as they attempt to relate to the vari-
ances between their two conflicting worlds (Ho, 1992).

EMERGENCE OF AN ECOLOGICAL PERSPECTIVE

The major tenets of an ecological perspective for social work practice in
the schools began to appear in the literature as early as the 1980s, following the publication of Bronfenbrenner's (1979) classic treatise, *The Ecology
of Human Development*. Winters and Easton (1983) proposed a view of
school social work that challenged conventional thinking regarding the
prevailing service models that, for the most part, focused on the "psychosocial deficits of students" and relied almost exclusively on the provision
of traditional casework services. They envisioned the school as an ecological unit in which school social workers served as catalysts in facilitating
transactions between and among various subsystems, including students
and teachers, home and school, and teachers and administrators. This
position has subsequently been reinforced and refined in the extensive
literature that has followed (Constable, Flynn, & McDonald, 1991; Early,
1992; Germain, 1987; Levine, Allen-Meares, & Easton, 1987; Pennekamp,
& Freeman, 1988; Winters & Maluccio, 1988).

The emergence of an ecological perspective for school social work
coincided with the publication of *A Nation at Risk* (National Commission
on Excellence in Education, 1983), a document that generated a national
public debate concerning the overall quality of education in the United
States. The political furor surrounding this debate served as a catalyst for
an educational summit in which U.S. governors and the president joined
for the first time in an effort to set a national educational agenda. Both of
these events, together with the enactment of the Hawkins-Stafford Elementary and Secondary School Improvement Amendments of 1988 [P.L.
No 100-297; 102 Stat. 130, (1988)], helped to heighten public awareness
concerning some of the more endemic issues facing contemporary education in America (1994). The insights gained from these earlier initiatives
were later echoed in the so-called Goals 2000 legislative package [Goals
2000: Educate America Act of 1994, P.L. No. 103-227, 108 Stat. 125, (1994)],
which in essence espoused the philosophy that education works best
when parents, educators, and the public decide to make their schools
better.

A number of the themes that emerged as part of this continuing debate
had long been espoused within the social work profession. What had

been obvious to most social workers for many years was finally being recognized and championed by politicians and the general public alike, that is, the problems that children exhibit in school do not occur in a vacuum. More often than not, these problems are the product of a complicated set of environmental circumstances over which the child has little or no control (Hixson & Tinzmann, 1990). The origins of many of these problems go well beyond the school walls and may be traced to the social, economic, and political inequities of society itself. A growing body of research has clearly indicated that most of the barriers to learning are the result of problems that have their origins outside the classroom, including factors such as poverty, unemployment, inadequate housing, substance abuse, discrimination, and violence (Hilliard, 1989; Letgers, McDill, & McPartland, 1993). It is obvious that children do not choose the circumstances in which they live, nor do they possess the power to change them. Hixson (1993) captured the essence of this point in his reminder that "Students are not 'at-risk,' but are placed at risk by adults" (p. 3). Unfortunately, in systems that fail to recognize this reality, there is a propensity to "blame the victim."

The ecological perspective provides a conceptual framework within which it is possible to shift the primary locus of the change effort away from the child by focusing attention on the appropriate environmental conditions. Rather than defining problems in terms of individual deficits, it attempts to build on personal strengths by exploiting the opportunities that either exist, or can be developed, within and among the systems that define the child's life space. In technical terms, Bronfenbrenner (1979) referred to these various systems as the *microsystem,* the *mesosystem,* the *exosystem,* and the *macrosystem.* In the present context, these four system levels parallel the family, school, community, and nation, as reflected in prevailing values, priorities, legislation, policies, and funding patterns (Winters & Maluccio, 1988).

The ecological perspective is based on the assumption that there is no quick fix that will significantly improve the lives of at-risk school children and their families. Although the adversities with which many children struggle are often exhibited in the classroom in the form of academic failure, disruptive behavior, truancy, and the like, such manifestations are almost always symptomatic of a much deeper and more complex set of systemic issues. Persistent inadequacies or limitations in any area of a child's life, whether they originate in the school, home, or community, are likely to contribute to academic difficulties in one form or another. The nature and scope of the issues that need to be addressed are far too complex to be handled adequately within the context of the traditional clinical paradigm, or by any single profession for that matter. Attempts to do so run the real risk of stigmatizing the child and deflecting attention from more important systemic issues.

With its eclectic focus on the dynamic interplay among the social, psychological, political, and economic determinants of human behavior, an ecological perspective helps bring into sharper relief the inherent inequities that are woven into the fabric of society itself. It provides a constructivist worldview that enables practitioners to understand the meaning of behavior within the context of the racial, cultural, and ethnic value systems of the clients they serve. It attempts to empower rather than blame, focuses on strengths rather than deficits, and emphasizes cooperation rather than conflict. All of these elements are entirely consistent with the most cherished values of the social work profession.

CHILD-CENTERED, FAMILY-FOCUSED, COMMUNITY-BASED PARTNERSHIPS

The ecological approach is grounded in a holistic philosophy that "emphasizes the need to address child and family problems and opportunities on a multi-institutional and multiprofessional basis" (Sugarman, 1993, p. 2). Implicit in this view is the notion that what goes on in school is inextricably bound to what goes on outside school. Social workers who view education in ecological terms understand that the opportunities for learning that exist at school are only

> School social work interventions range from prevention to system reform and are embedded in the community.

part of a much larger social milieu that both shapes and is shaped by the other social systems in which a child lives. For many children, especially children at risk, the existing social arrangements just do not seem to work to their advantage. Social workers are familiar with the various environments that form a child's ecosystem (i.e., the school, family, and community), and are uniquely positioned to facilitate the kinds of collaborative efforts between and among them that are necessary to bring about meaningful change.

Fostering School-Family Partnerships

A substantial body of research (Epstein, 1988; Henderson & Berla, 1994; Olmstead & Rubin, 1983) has indicated that children whose parents are actively involved in their education tend to demonstrate higher academic achievement and more positive attitudes toward school. Parental involvement has also been found to correlate positively with increased attendance, a reduction in discipline problems, and higher academic aspirations. As parental involvement increases, parents' perceptions of the school's effectiveness are more positive (Caplan, Choy, & Whitmore, 1992).

School-family partnerships work best when they get off to a positive start. Unfortunately, the first encounter that many parents have with the school is when their child experiences a difficulty. Ortner (1994) found that parents who received a visit from a "school welcoming committee" comprising a parent and a staff member from the school were more likely to attend parent-teacher conferences and increase their volunteer efforts on behalf of the school. This finding was supported by a similar study by Powers, Cox, and Minton (1996), who found that, not only were parents and their children's attitudes positively affected by home visits, but so were the attitudes of teachers and social workers when they served as visitation team members. Because most of the teachers do not live in the same neighborhoods as the children they teach, such visits serve to sensitize teachers to the environmental circumstances from which their students come. The philosophy behind this strategy is simple. It is designed to begin the process of empowering parents by conveying the message that education begins at home and that parents are valued members of their child's educational team. Establishing a positive relationship with the family on their own turf not only serves to minimize future problems, but also lays the foundation for constructive problem solving if a problem occurs later.

It is essential that school administrators, teachers, and other professional staff create an atmosphere of trust from the outset, one that conveys a consistent message that school staff genuinely value and enthusiastically encourage parental involvement (Dauber & Epstein, 1989). This is especially true with respect to minority families who, for various reasons, often feel disenfranchised from the very schools their children are required to attend. Ritter, Mont-Reynaud, and Dornbusch (1993) found that many factors contribute to the parents' perceptions of schools as well as the level of their willingness to get involved in school-related activities. Some parents have had a long history of negative encounters with schools. For many parents of minority children, life experiences have provided little reason to trust social institutions in general. The school system is just one of many institutions that may have failed them in the past. If they have personally experienced school as part of a larger sustaining environment that has not been responsive to their own needs, it is not surprising that they may be skeptical about the school's ability to meet their children's needs. Given this frame of reference, parents may

perceive teachers' questions as displays of disrespect. Language difficulties may also exacerbate the problem for some minority cultures,
whereas for others the traditional deferential view of education sometimes inhibits interaction with school officials. The danger is that school
personnel may view any one factor or a combination of these factors as a
lack of caring or indifference on the part of parents about their children's
education (North Central Regional Education Laboratory, 1997). Bridging
the gap between these conflicting realities poses a major challenge in
efforts to establish viable home-school partnerships.

Facilitating School-Community Partnerships

While the school-family partnership is essential, it represents only one
aspect of a larger community context within which children live and
learn. Education does not take place in a sociopolitical vacuum. Whether
schools like it or not, the nature of community life largely determines
what goes on in school. In fact, it has long and persuasively been argued
(Conant, 1961; Dewey, 1915; Kilpatrick, 1935; Mead, 1961; Olson, 1951)
that only when public schools consider the diversity of interest and experiences that characterize the community can they hope to meet their responsibility to children and their families. Schools cannot afford to carry
on their work with an insular detachment from the life of the community
if they hope to realize the democratic ideal on which they were founded.
"The schools of any free nation will fail their primary function unless they
consciously promote social progress in the future as well as they preserve
the culture of the past and prepare the individual for effective participation in the present" (Olson, 1954, p. 8).

This ecological perspective requires that education be viewed as a total
community process. It is based on the central notion that the child is a
whole being who is educated by his or her total life experience—not just
by what happens in the school. Children are molded in their knowledge,
skills, attitudes, and values by the forces in the communities that bear
directly on their development. Washburne (1962) captured this notion
well more than a half-century ago when he cautioned, "Children who
come into the schoolhouse to learn must leave the schoolhouse to learn—
they must find in the outside world the stuff that makes education real"
(p. 113). Despite what a child may learn in school, the community plays a
significant role in shaping important attitudes about the realities of life,
including attitudes that speak to issues of fairness, respect, morality, and
responsibility. If the values espoused in school are not reinforced in the
community, and vice versa, the child can easily become confused and
disillusioned. When this occurs, the child is placed in the untenable posi-

tion of having to choose between conflicting value systems, a dilemma that is difficult or impossible for most children to resolve.

The role of the school social worker is to help facilitate the bridging process so that the school and the community see themselves as partners in the educational enterprise. When this occurs, the community becomes an educational resource for the school and the school becomes an educational resource for the community. Together they become partners in the education of children and their families, including the enhancement of community life. The concept of "community" encompasses more than just people. It includes the network of relationships and social structures that characterize the social environment in which they live.

Unfortunately, it is not as easy as it once was to define the community boundaries for what used to be thought of as the "neighborhood school." With the onset of mandated busing, the consolidation of school corporations, the development of magnet schools, and the like, the geographical boundaries for many schools are often uncertain and elusive at best. For this reason, it is all the more important that the school become the focal point for school-community partnerships. The school is the only social institution capable of holding the various components of a community together, regardless of how amorphous the structure of that entity might be. To accomplish this end, the school social worker must think inclusively and as creatively as possible in an effort mobilize the full range of available community services on behalf of the school and the families it serves—including parent/teachers organizations, neighborhood groups, social services, health providers, government agencies, law enforcement, businesses and industries, churches, recreational programs, community service organizations, and funding sources. Of course, the reverse of this is also true. The school must make itself available to the community in ways that contribute to the general commonweal. This reciprocal relationship may sometimes be facilitated by the collocation of community services in the school and/or the extension of off-campus educational programs offered throughout the community. The ultimate goal is to create an education-centered community with a social orientation that recognizes and accepts its collective responsibility for the educational welfare of its children. The attainment of this ideal is not an easy task, but it is helpful to keep in mind that, in a democracy, agreement is not necessary—but participation is.

School-community partnerships redefine the way schools do business. They are based on a unique set of assumptions regarding the nature of the educational enterprise—assumptions that inevitably lead to new working relationships among the participants. Partnerships succeed to the extent to which they are able to arrive at a functional division of labor and resolve related issues of power and control. Because each community is unique, the process of developing a partnership will vary from school to school. Although there is no blueprint to assure success, there are a number of components that may help facilitate the development process and increase the likelihood that collaborative efforts will lead to quality services that help children and also support their families realize their potential.

Organizational Commitment. The development of the School-community partnership concept requires a fundamental commitment on the part of a school's administration and faculty to an ideology of teamwork and collaboration that includes representation from a diverse professional community. This ideology is based on the assumption that the nature and scope of the barriers facing at-risk children as they attempt to maximize personal and academic success within the public school system are exceedingly complex and multidimensional in nature. As such, the model uses an interdisciplinary approach that attempts to effectively mobilize available community resources to create dynamic partnerships to serve the needs of the educational community.

Community-Based Planning. To ensure local ownership of the model, key community leaders including parents collaborate with school representatives to form a steering committee, whose responsibility it is to develop a plan of action and establish policies that reflect the idiosyncratic needs and culture of the particular school community it serves. Although advisory in nature, this committee serves an essential function in shaping the mission, goals, and objectives of the model in ways that legitimately reflect the vested interests and concerns of those people it is intended to serve.

Needs Assessment. School-based social workers, serving in the role of team coordinators, are responsible for gathering baseline data and conducting initial assessments of the students and families identified as being in need of service. The goal of the assessment is to provide the service partners with a profile of the risk and protective factors to which students are exposed. Emphasis is on a strengths-based process targeted around a student-centered, family-focused, neighborhood-based perspective designed to identify existing barriers and opportunities for personal and academic success.

Service Planning. The needs assessment serves two important functions: (1) it creates a general database built around the kind of information concerning existing risk or protective factors that are necessary to plan appropriate prevention programs, and (2) it provides the specific information needed to develop a coordinated service delivery plan tailored to the needs and strengths of each student and his or her family. The plan generally includes a combination of operationally defined short- and long-term goals that draw on resources both within and outside the school, including resources available through the broader community service network.

Service Implementation.   The members of the school-community partnership work together to provide a range of remedial and preventive services designed to address the factors that have been identified as barriers to personal and academic success. It is the responsibility of each member of the partnership to ensure that the specific components of the overall service delivery plan for which they are personally responsible are implemented in a coordinated manner.

Prevention.   The model views each student's functioning from a person-in-environment strengths perspective. As such, it is designed to provide preventive as well as remedial services. It attempts to address the broader public issues that are manifest in the more obvious private problems that children and their families typically encounter in their efforts to negotiate the complexities of the various systems of which they are a part.

Brokering.   It is the responsibility of the school social worker to link identified students and their families to needed services that cannot be provided by the school. The social worker draws on the array of health and human services available within the community service network. Brokering includes not only referral, but also the identification, coordination, and management of services provided by appropriate external service providers. The brokering role anchors the services to the school and provides families with a readily available reference person on whom they can rely for accurate and timely information relative to the larger intervention plan.

Advocacy.   Many of the difficulties encountered by at-risk students and their families involve one or more issues related to employment, health care, financial assistance, legal services, housing, and the like. The school social worker serves as an advocate for students and their families by helping to mediate student-family communications within and outside the school as they attempt to negotiate the many different bureaucracies involved in the service delivery process.

Parent Involvement.   School-community partnerships succeed to the extent to which parents become actively involved in the collaborative process. By definition, school-community partnerships function as systems, on behalf of systems. The single most important system in a child's life is her or his family—the one essential system that must be meaningfully involved if lasting changes are to occur. For such involvement to happen, parents must be accepted as full partners in the change process, not only with respect to issues concerning their own children, but also with respect to the kinds of school-related activities that serve to enfranchise and empower them as responsible and effective partners in the educational process.

Program Monitoring.   The quality of services delivered to students and their families depends in large part on the ability of the members of the school-community partnership to monitor the services provided and track students' performance and emerging needs. With an ongoing accountability system in place, members of the partnership can make adjustments and document program milestones as circumstances dictate. The emphasis during program monitoring is on issues related to process rather than outcome. The focus is on intensive designs of evaluation that attempt to track the efficacy of the services provided to specific students and their families, including services provided by organizations outside the school.

Program Evaluation and Dissemination.   To survive over the long haul, school-community partnerships need to be able to demonstrate the effectiveness and efficiency of the services they provide. Such information is considered essential, not only because politicians and funders demand it, but more important, because the ongoing viability of the program requires it. The ultimate efficacy of programmatic initiatives requires some form of outcome-based evaluation that compares actual performance with stated goals. Because of the underlying philosophy of collaboration, school-community partnerships can provide exciting natural laboratories for conducting research that contributes to the ongoing development and refinement of the services provided.

Interprofessional Staff Development.   In the final analysis, the survival of any school-community partnership depends on the ability of the participating members to work together in an intelligent and coordinated manner. All members of the immediate and extended group must share a common philosophy regarding the nature of the services being provided, as well as a clear understanding of the complementary role that each must play to effectively operationalize that philosophy. Therefore, opportunities for ongoing staff development are critical, especially opportunities that enable the participants to communicate about issues that directly or indirectly affect their ability to carry out the responsibilities associated with their respective roles.

EVALUATION OF THE ECOLOGICAL APPROACH
TO SCHOOL SOCIAL WORK

Improvement in the quality of school social work will depend inevitably on the quality of the research that accompanies it. Unfortunately, the evaluation of school social work within an ecological framework is difficult and often ambiguous at best for several reasons. Collaborative intervention initiatives do not easily lend themselves to the more conventional experimental research designs. Such models require the cooperative participation of a number of different constituencies, each of which brings to the table a unique contribution. Because such arrangements typically involve dynamic interactions within and across a variety of different systems (i.e., the individual, family, school, and community), it is virtually impossible to sort out the relative contribution at any given level. An action by any one part of the collaborative arrangement in and of itself is likely to explain little with respect to any given outcome measure. Each component of the model is considered to be a necessary but insufficient part of the larger whole. Theoretically, it is the synergistic effect of the interaction among the various components of the model that makes the difference. The efficacy of any of the partners (e.g., social workers) working in isolation is likely to be quite limited.

Because of the phenomenological nature of the ecological perspective, midcourse corrections are not only considered necessary, but inevitable. Hence, it is virtually impossible to isolate and control the shifting nature of the independent variables. There is and ought to be a constant flow of information among the participants. As this occurs, intervention strategies change accordingly. Therefore, it is difficulty to establish clear-cut cause and effect relationships, at least in any linear sense. For this same reason, and because each school and neighborhood are unique, comparisons between similar interventions at different schools are risky at best. Attempts to establish control groups from among at-risk children attending the same school raise a number of ethical and legal concerns. The random assignment of students to comparable treatment and control groups results in the systematic withholding of services from similarly situated students. That poses a serious problem in public school systems that espouse equal opportunities for all students.

One of the major difficulties in trying to evaluate the effects of an ecological approach to social work in the schools is that it takes time. There are no quick fixes. Given the highly politicized atmosphere of many school systems, the demand by politicians and funders to demonstrate measurable outcomes in relatively short periods can be counterproductive. The evolution of functional partnerships does not occur overnight. There are likely to be a number of aborted efforts before the level of understanding and trust necessary to produce meaningful change comes to fruition. For this reason, Young, Gardner, Coley, Schorr, and Bruner (1994) have proposed a developmental approach to evaluation that is sensitive to the evolutionary nature of the collaborative process. It is built around a six-level framework that starts with the assessment of family-social worker-level interactions and systematically moves toward the evaluation of community-level effects. The six levels are as follows:

1. *Service penetration:* This is essentially a needs assessment phase that explores the characteristics, needs, and service penetration rates of the families most likely to benefit from the proposed program of services.

2. *Family engagement:* The focus at the family engagement stage of evaluation is on determining the extent to which the families targeted for service are willing to participate in a partnership with the school and on trying to understand the factors that serve to facilitate or inhibit the attachment process.

3. *Family growth:* During this phase, there is an attempt to understand the nature and extent of growth that occurs among families who participate in the intervention strategy and also to determine whether it is possible to attribute the observed changes to programmatic initiatives.

4. *Community embeddedness:* The scope of the evaluation broadens during this phase to include the exploration of issues having to do with community awareness of and willingness to participate in the collaborative effort.

5. *System response, climate for reform, and change:* This phase attempts to assess the effectiveness of efforts to advocate on behalf of children and their families. In essence, the goal is to determine the extent to which other service delivery systems have responded to efforts to involve them and the community (e.g., business, industry, and funders) in the school-community partnership.

6. *Community-wide family well-being:* This phase in the evaluation process addresses the more traditional questions concerning outcome. It focuses on broader indicators of family well-being that are attributable to programmatic initiatives, particularly those that relate to school performance criteria such as academic achievement, absenteeism, and the incidence of behavior problems.

There is a tendency among many school administrators to place primary importance on the remediation of the most pressing and perceptually public problems. Children who act out or perform poorly in class are the most likely candidates to be referred for immediate "treatment." Although it is essential that school social workers provide remedial services to children and their families when they experience difficulties, there is often a failure to recognize that behind virtually every personal problem are a number of important public issues that must be addressed. There is even less awareness of the need to develop and assess the kinds of preventive measures required to address these broader societal issues. When the value of prevention programs is acknowledged, the patience of politicians and funders often runs out long before such programs can reasonably be expected to work.

Therefore, when developing an evaluation strategy, it is important that the major stakeholders appreciate that meaningful change in terms of the more politically expedient goals (e.g., improved performance on standardized tests, reductions in absenteeism, and declines in the incidence of disruptive behavior) take time and require the full participation and cooperation of all the partners involved in the change process. This means that, initially at least, the stakeholders must be patient enough to judge progress in relation to a number of less exotic interim goals, the attainment of which represents necessary benchmarks in the development of a viable infrastructure for long-term meaningful change of the type most often discussed in the local media.

As a general framework for the evaluation of school-based social work practiced from an ecological perspective, the authors support the approach proposed by Hawkins and Catalano (1993). The philosophy behind their risk-focused prevention strategy is based on the premise that the key to the achievement of far-reaching and lasting solutions is to intervene in the cycle of events *before* problems occur. In their words, "to prevent a problem from happening, we need to identify the factors that increase the risk of that problem developing and then find ways to reduce the risks in ways that enhance protective or resiliency factors" (p. 4). The concepts of risk and resiliency are central to the notion of the strengths-based model of school social work that are proposed in this chapter and, as such, provide the primary foci of evaluative efforts.

Hawkins and Catalano (1993) have argued that there is a compelling literature that identifies the major risk factors associated with the kinds of social or psychological problems typically encountered by children. They classified these risk factors in four general categories that closely parallel the four systems composing the ecological model: (1) individual or peer risk factors, (2) familial risk factors, (3) school risk factors, and (4) community risk factors. The first step in developing an effective service delivery strategy is to identify the major risk factors that are prevalent in each of the four systems that compose the ecosystem within which children live. Obviously, the constellation of these risk factors will tend to vary to some degree from school to school. Once the risk factors have been identified, it is possible to create "buffers" against them by either "reducing the impact of the risks or by changing the way a person responds to the risks" (ibid., p. 9). These buffers are referred to as *protective factors*, that is, factors that serve to "promote positive behavior, health, well-being and personal success" (ibid., p. 11). Some of the protective factors are best provided through remedial services, whereas others can only be addressed through long-term prevention efforts.

The ultimate measure of a successful intervention program is the extent to which risk factors are counterbalanced by protective factors that enhance the resiliency of children and their families. As mentioned previously, Rutter (1987) recommended four protective processes as a means of fostering resilience in children, all of which are supported by an impressive body of research. If resilience is identified as a primary dependent variable in relation to which the success of school social work is to be measured, then it makes sense to follow the suggestion of Winfield (1991): Conduct in-depth evaluations and inventories of each child's personal strengths, including their interests and learning styles. By doing so, school social workers will not only learn more about each student's personal strengths and needs but, in the process, begin to understand why some children are able to succeed despite the negative influences that so often block academic achievement. Information of this type not only provides useful baseline data against which to measure progress, but also serves as an early warning system for the identification of potential problems before they become manifest.

With resilience as an organizing concept around which evaluation is conducted, it is possible to draw on an extensive literature to identify the specific variables that correlate with a child's capacity to handle the factors that put that child at risk. For example, Werner and Smith (1982) found that the single most important factor differentiating children who succeed in school and those who are identified as being at-risk is the influence of a "caring adult." If true, then this finding suggests that one component of a comprehensive school-based social work program might be the creation of parent effectiveness and mentoring programs (Flaxman, 1992) that promote caring relationships between children and responsible adults. To the extent to which such programs are made available to students, it should be possible, as part of the evaluation design, to demonstrate that children who have access to such relationships will be better equipped to handle stress and adversity in their lives, and thus encounter fewer school-related problems.

The evaluation model proposed in this chapter includes the use of qualitative as well as quantitative measures. Although it is essential that school social workers be able to demonstrate the attainment of clearly articulated and operationally defined interim and long-term goals, much of the information needed to make informed decisions about the ongoing development and efficacy of programmatic initiatives can only be obtained through the use of more constructivist research strategies (see Chapter 12).

Ecologically grounded social work practice suggests that many of the complexities of human behavior with which school social workers must deal on a daily basis may not be easily explained by existing theory. By exploring issues solely within the context of prevailing behavioral paradigms, social workers may inadvertently cut themselves off from important insights concerning the human condition, especially as it experienced by the clients they are trying to understand and help.

The evaluation strategies used to assess the efficacy of social work interventions should reflect the eclectic nature of the ecological orientation on which they are based. It should include all parties involved in the partnership and should be flexible enough to provide the kinds of information necessary to make appropriate midcourse corrections as well as informed judgments about the effectiveness and efficiency of programmatic initiatives.

CONCLUSION

Meeting the needs of at-risk children represents one of the greatest challenges facing the nation as we approach the 21st century. Schools continue to struggle in their efforts to educate children whose daily existence mirrors the inadequate resources and limited opportunities available in the communities from which they come. It is not unusual for such children to be raised by parents whose educational, economic, psychological, and social resources are equally strained. Under such circumstances, both the communities and the families residing within them typically experience a persistent sense of powerlessness—the inevitable forerunner of hopelessness. The debilitating nature of such feelings is dramatically evidenced in the faces of a growing number of children for whom the vision of a promising future no longer exists. The inevitable result is the devaluation of education and, indeed, life itself.

Apart from their immediate families, most children spend more time in school than in any other social system. The school is a natural and important part of every child's life. It is not surprising, therefore, that the personal difficulties children experience often surface at school and affect their ability to function appropriately in the student role. For these same reasons, the school can be seen as the ideal environment within which to mobilize the resources necessary to achieve meaningful change in the lives of children. This ideal, however, can only be realized in an environment that values diversity and encourages cooperation.

Attempts to help these children and their families often fall short of our best intentions because of the complex nature of the issues and the piecemeal fashion in which services are delivered. The school, as a central component in the lives of children, offers the greatest potential for not only providing and enhancing the quality of learning, but also the quality of living for children, their families, and the communities in which they reside.

REFERENCES

American Association of School Administrators (1957). Stockpile of human resources. In E. G. Olson (Ed.), *The school and community reader: Education in perspective* (pp. 168–169). New York: Macmillan.

Anthony, E. J. (1974). The syndrome of the psychologically invulnerable child. In E. J. Anthony and C. Koupernik (Eds.), *Vulnerable children* (pp. 3–15). New York: Wiley.

Bowman, B. T. (1997). *Cultural diversity and academic achievement.* Oak Brook, IL: North Central Regional Educational Laboratory.

Bronfenbrenner, U. (1979). *The ecology of human development.* Cambridge, MA: Harvard University Press.

Brooks, R. (1991). *The self-esteem teacher.* Circle Pines, MN: American Guidance Service.

Brooks, R. (1994). Children at risk, fostering resilience and hope. *American Journal of Orthopsychiatry, 64,* 545–553.

Buriel, R., L., Calzada, S., & Vasquez, R. (1982). Relationships of traditional Mexican-American culture to adjustment and delinquency among three generations of Mexican-American male adolescents. *Hispanic Journal of Behavioral Sciences, 4,* 41–55.

Caplan, N., Choy, M., & Whitmore, J. K. (1992). Indochinese refugee families and academic achievement. *Scientific American, 2,* 36–42.

Conant, J. B. (1961). Community and school are inseparable. In J. B. Conant (Ed.), *Slums and suburbs* (pp. 3–21). New York: McGraw-Hill.

Constable, R., Flynn, J. P., & McDonald, S. (Eds.) (1991). *School social work: Practice and research perspectives.* Chicago: Lyceum.

Cowan, E., Wyman, P., Work, W., & Parker, G. (1990). The Rochester child resilient project: Overview and summary of first year findings. *Development and Psychopathology, 2,* 193–212.

Dauber, S. L., & Epstein, J. L. (1989). Parents' attitudes and practices of involvement in inner-city elementary and middle schools. In N. Chavkin (Ed.), *Families and schools in a pluralistic society* (pp. 53–71). Albany: State University of New York Press.

Dewey, J. (1902). The school as a social center. In E. G. Olson (Ed.), *The school and community reader: Education in perspective* (pp. 175–176). New York: Macmillan.

Dewey, J. (1915). *School and society* (rev. ed.). Chicago: University of Chicago Press.

Early, B. P. (1992). An ecological-exchange model of social work consultation within the workgroup of the school. *Social Work in Education, 14,* 207–214.

Epstein, J. L. (1988). How do we improve programs for parent involvement? *Educational Horizons, 66* (2), 58–62.

Erikson, E. H. (1950). *Childhood and society.* New York: W.W. Norton.

Flaxman, E. (1992). *Evaluating mentoring programs.* New York: Institute for Urban and Minority Education, Teachers College, Columbia University.

Garmezy, N. (1985). Stress resistant children: the search for protective factors. In J. Stevenson (Ed.), *Recent research in developmental psychopathology* (pp. 213–233). Tarrytown, NY: Pergamon.

Germain, C. B. (1987). Review of social work services in schools. *Social Casework, 68,* 510–511.

Grizenko, N., & Pawliuk, N. (1994). Risk and protective factors for psychopathology in children. *Canadian Journal of Psychiatry, 37,* 711–721.

Hale-Benson, J. (1986). *Black children: their roles, culture and learning styles.* Baltimore: Johns Hopkins University Press.

Hart, B., & Risley, T. (1995). *Meaning differences in the everyday experience of young American children* Baltimore: Paul H. Brooks.

Hawkins, J. D., & Catalano, R. F. (1993). *Communities that care.* Seattle: University of Washington Press.

Henderson, A. T., & Berla, N. (1994). *A new generation of evidence: The family is critical to student achievement.* St. Louis, MO: Danforth Foundation, and Flint, MI: Mott (C.S.) Foundation.

Hilliard, A. (1989). Teachers and cultural styles in a pluralistic society. *NEA Today, 7*(6), 65–69.

Hixson, J. (1993). *Redefining the issues: Who's at risk and why?* Revision of a paper originally presented in 1983 at "Reducing the Risks," a workshop presented by the Midwest Regional Center for Drug-Free Schools and Communities (unpublished manuscript).

Hixson, J., & Tinzmann, M. B. (1990). *Who are the "at-risk" students of the 1990's?* Oak Brook: IL: North Central Regional Educational Laboratory.

Ho, M. K. (1992). *Minority children and adolescents in therapy.* Newbury Park, CA: Sage.

Kilpatrick, W. H. (1935). Visions of the best education. In National Education Association (Ed.), *Socializing experiences in elementary schools: Fourteenth yearbook* (pp. 534–543). Washington, DC: National Education Association.

Letgers, N., McDill, E., & McPartland, J. (1993). Section II: Rising to the challenge: Emerging strategies for educational students at risk. In N. Letgers, E. McDill, and J. McPartland (Eds.), *Educational reforms and students at risk: A review of the current state of the art* (pp. 47–92). Washington, DC: U.S. Department of Education, Office of Educational Research and Improvement. Available on-line: http://www.ed.gov/pubs/edreformstudies/edreforms/chapt6a.html.

Levine, R. S., Allen-Meares, P., & Easton, F. (1987). Primary prevention and the educational preparation of school social workers. *Social Work in Education, 9,* 145–157.

Maslow, A. H. (1954). *Motivation and personality.* New York: Harper.

Mead, M. (1961). Radical changes within education itself. *National Education Association Journal, 50,* 11–13.

National Commission on Excellence in Education (1983). *A nation at risk: The imperative for educational reform.* Washington, DC: U.S. Government Printing Office.

North Central Regional Education Laboratory (1997). *School-family partnership: A literature review.* Oak Brook, IL: Author. Available on-line: http://www.ncrel.org.

Olmstead, P. P., & Rubin, R. I. (1983). Linking parent behaviors to child achievement: Four evaluation studies from the parent education follow-through programs. *Studies in Educational Evaluation, 8,* 317–325.

Olson, E. G. (1951). Community foundations for teacher education. *Journal of Teacher Education, 2,* 126–132.

Olson, E. G. (1954). Relating our schools to life. In E. G. Olson (Ed.), *The school and communityreader: Education in perspective* (pp. 1, 7–11, 13–20, 477–480). Englewood Cliffs, NJ: Prentice-Hall.

Ortner, M. L. (1994). *An alternative approach to increase parent involvement among culturally diverse families* (practicum report). Nova University, Miami, Florida.

Pennekamp, M., & Freeman, E. M. (1988). Toward a partnership perspective: Schools, families, and school social workers. *Social Work in Education, 10,* 246–259.

Powers G. T., Cox, G., & Minton, M. D. (1996). *An evaluation of the Indiana University School of Social Work school/community partnership program* (unpublished manuscript). Indiana University School of Social Work, Indianapolis.

Ritter, P. L., Mont-Reynaud, R., & Dornbusch, S. M. (1993). Minority parents and their youth: Concern, encouragement, and support for school achievement. In N. Chavkin (Ed.), *Families and schools in a pluralistic society* (pp.107–119). Albany: State University of New York Press.

Rutter, M. (1979). Protective factors in children's responses to stress and disadvantage. In M. Kent and J. Rolf (Eds.), *Primary prevention and psychopathology* (pp. 49–74). Hanover, NH: University Press of New England.

Rutter, M. (1985). Resilience in the face of adversity: Protective factors and resistance to psychiatric disorder. *British Journal of Psychiatry, 147,* 598–611.

Rutter, M. (1987). Psychosocial resilience and protective mechanisms. *American Journal of Orthopsychiatry, 57,* 316–331.

Sugarman, J. M. (1993). Integrating community services for young children and their families. In *NCREL's Policy Briefs* (Report No.3). Oak Brook, IL: North Central Regional Education Laboratory.

Sullivan, H. S. (1953). *The interpersonal theory of psychiatry.* New York: Norton.

Taylor, A. R. (1991). Social competence and the early school transition: Risks and protective factors for African-American children. *Education and Urban Society, 24,* 15–26.

Washburne, C. (1962). Pulsing life of humanity. In E. G. Olson (Ed.), *The school and* communityreader: Education in perspective (pp. 113–114). New York: Macmillan.

Werner, E. (1993). Risk, resilience and recovery: Perspectives from the Kauai longitudinal study. Development and Psychopathology, 5, 503–515.

Werner, E., & Smith, R. (1982). Vulnerable but invincible: A longitudinal study of resilient children and youth. New York: McGraw-Hill.

Werner, E., & Smith, R. (1992). Overcoming the odds: High risk children from birth to adulthood. Ithaca, NY: Cornell University.

White, R. N. (1960). Competence and the psychosexual stages of development. In M. Jones (Ed.), Nebraska symposium on motivation (pp. 97–141). Lincoln: University of Nebraska Press.

Winfield, L. A. (1991). Resilience, schooling, and development in African-American youth. Education and Urban Society, 24, 11–18.

Winters, W. F., & Easton, F. (1983). The practice of social work in schools: An ecological perspective. New York: Free Press.

Winters, W., & Maluccio, A. (1988). School, family, and community: Working together to promote competence. Social Work in Education, 10, 207–217.

Young, N., Gardner, S., Coley, S., Schorr, L., & Bruner, C. (1994). Making a difference: Moving to outcome-based accountability for comprehensive service reforms. Falls Church, VA: National Center for Service Integration.

7

Youth Development Principles and Field Practicum Opportunities

MARIE WATKINS and ELSA IVERSON

Children's development cannot be understood independent of the multiple and diverse context or ecologies in which they reside. While context is critical across the life span, links between contexts may be particularly important when considering children's development. Children are imbedded in families, which are themselves influenced by their community.
—J. Brooks-Gunn, "Big-City Kids and Their Families: Integration of Research and Practices"

The most compelling theories in child development scholarship that define and describe children's and adolescents' developmental stages advance knowledge and practice models beyond the traditional cultural (Colls, 1992) and gender-limited (Gilligan, 1987; Miller, 1986), individually focused (Archer, 1992; Patterson, Sochting, & Marcia, 1992), deficit (Spencer & Markstrom-Adams, 1990) models. A conceptualization that offers a broader scope in which to understand and apply child development concepts is the ecological systems model. The ecological systems model acknowledges the interrelatedness between youths and their environment, which consists of the different contexts and networks in which children and youths grow and learn and the interactional systems of family, kin, peers, school, neighborhood, and community, which are important contributors to healthy development (Bronfenbrenner, 1979). In addition, the ecological perspective proposes that the process of transitioning from childhood to adulthood involves an interchange between individuals and systems rather than an unidimensional analysis of a child's personality characteristics (Steinberg, Dornbusch, & Brown, 1992).

The ecological perspective of social work practice with a diverse population of youths considers the daily realities of living for youths and the adaptive competencies this population brings to cope with, influence, and excel within their environment.

This chapter discusses the interconnections between ecological, diversity, and youth development principles. Youth development principles incorporate the multiple systems interactional model of ecological social work practice and a holistic conceptualization of child growth and development. Using these principles, the social worker builds youths' assets and capacity through self-esteem-enhancing and empowerment-focused strategies. Youth development principles framed by an ecological perspective of social work are illustrated in this chapter through a discussion of a community/youth development approach to youth issues, community-based youth organizations, and the application of youth development in social work field education. The chapter also discusses how the social worker can enhance a youngster's sense of competency, power, belongingness, and usefulness to build the goodness-of-fit (Lerner, 1983) between a youngster and his or her environment within these contexts. In addition, the chapter highlights risk and protective factors within a child's environment that the social worker may address.

COMPELLING YOUTH ISSUES

The lives of children and adolescents cannot be put on hold until the larger social, economic and political problems are solved. American youth are entitled to health-enhancing action now. To safeguard their health is not an act of charity. It is a reaffirmation of a humane society and an investment in the nation's future.
        —F. Hechinger, *Fateful Choices: Healthy Youth for the 21st Century*

Youth issues are typically described in terms of social problems: teenage school dropout rates, drug use, pregnancy, and juvenile crime. When social workers examine these circumstances and the opportunities available to develop youths, they often become discouraged. Young people today, who must deal with violence, acquired immune deficiency syndrome (AIDS), drugs, poverty, and lack of opportunity, are at far greater risk for developing difficulties than previous generations (Carnegie Council on Adolescent Development, Task Force on Youth Development and Community Programs, 1995; Annie Casey Foundation and the Center for the Study of Social Policy, 1992). National trends have identified emerging patterns that influence young people's behavior, health, and education and the requisite skills for preparation for adulthood (Brooks-Gunn, 1996; Dryfoos, 1990; Schoor, 1988). Poverty, poor health, and minimal educational preparation for the 21st century are the reasons an increasing number of youths are living in "at-risk" circumstances (Annie Casey Foundation, 1997). Demographic forecasters have predicted a larger population of youths who will be increasingly likely to live in poverty. For example, according to Scales (1991), these trends will increase the probability that the youth cohort of the 1990s will have one of the highest age group chances of being victimized by poverty, crime, abuse, health problems, and lack of relevant educational and employment opportunities. The effects of political, social, cultural, and demographic realities have become evident as the resources needed for youths to grow up in families, neighborhoods, and communities become more limited and stressed (Coles, 1968; Coulton, 1996; Watkins, 1995). To compound the challenge of social work practice with youths—given the trends that indicate increased risk to personal, physical, and psychological well-being—data also have indicated that a greater proportion of young people will not have access to adequate physical and mental health services (Carnegie Council on Adolescent Development, 1995). These realities of minimal resources affect the nature of a child's transition from childhood to adulthood.

Given the distressing indication that social environments are becoming more limited in their capacity to support youths, a growing number of scholars and social work practitioners have been increasing their efforts to examine the capacities and resources of youths to grow and develop within their social contexts. The current dialogue about youth potential and resilience (Bernard, 1992) has challenged the previous deficit, medical model that pathologizes youth behavior and identifies youths as "at-risk." Youth advocates are promoting the enhancement of the social and economic capital to rebuild the resources and infrastructures of families, agencies, and communities (Brown, 1993). According to recent studies (Chaskin & Ogletree, 1993; Merry, Berg, Baker, & Wynn, 1995; Wynn, Costello, Halpern, & Richman, 1994; Rosewater, 1992), the enhancement of these resources would foster holistic mastery-building and relationship-enhancing opportunities to increase the number of positive youth outcomes and hence minimize the "rotten outcomes" (Dryfoos, 1990) society has come to expect. *Positive youth outcomes* have been defined as psychosocial and competency-based outcomes (Academy for Educational Development/Center for Youth Development and Policy Research, 1996; Pittman, 1993). Psychosocial outcomes include a sense of safety and protection, a sense of self-worth or positive self-concept, mastery, autonomy, a sense of belonging, and spirituality and self-awareness. Competency-based outcomes include personal competency or efficacy, physical health, mental health, cultural and social competence, and employability. However, to create opportunities for the achievement of positive youth outcomes, it is necessary to explore and assess critical components of sufficient nutrients and environmental supports.

EXAMINING YOUTH ISSUES
FROM AN ECOLOGICAL PERSPECTIVE

The ecological perspective . . . maintains that unbalance and conflict may arise from any focus in the interlocking transactional systems, ranging from microsystems of the individual, family and the school to the macrosystem of governmental social and economic policies. The level of emphasis upon each of these systems, in turn, depends on the specific nature of the child's problem.
—M. K. Ho, *Minority Children and Adolescents in Therapy*

The ecological perspective, as an organizing framework, can assist the social worker to understand and assess youth issues and intervene from a broader political, educational, social, or educational context. This wider-based taxonomy is vital: ecological theorists have suggested that the historically and socially varied contextual environments that create social redefinition and changing expectations of society influence a child's development (Sisson, Hersen, & Van Hasselt, 1987). The child is faced with the consequences of rapidly changing socialization pressures and behavioral expectations, as well as shifting interpersonal, economic, and legal contexts (Markstrom-Adams, 1992).

> Family and community resources are essential to build youth competencies.

This process of influence becomes a circular one in which the child acts as both the initiator and responder to his or her development within the context of his or her environment (Bronfenbrenner, 1979). Elder's (1975) research indicated that youths experience society and its values directly as those values are presented through the youth's actual participation in the school and family settings and with peers. According to Konopka (1976), "It is quite clear that creation of conditions that facilitate healthy (youth) development begins with the encouragement of equal and responsible participation by youth in the family or other societal units" (p. 12). The overarching theme points to the interface between person and environment: conditions for healthy *youth development*—the enhancement of a youth's sense of belonging, competency, power, and usefulness through the intentional design, implementation, and evaluation of programs and services—are interdependent on conditions for healthy fami-

The Social Contexts of Youth Experience

Figure 7.1. A framework for understanding youth outcomes in the context of development. Source: Leffert et al. (1996, p. 3). Reprinted with permission.

lies, schools, neighborhoods, and communities. Therefore, the goodness-of-fit between expectations of a youngster's particular social context and his or her maturational course are important variables in the youth's psychosocial developmental outcomes (Lerner, 1983, 1991; Figure 7.1).

Another ecological principle pertinent to youth development is the effect of unfavorable factors in the communities. Lack of nutrition; racial, class, and gender discrimination; inadequate housing; and poverty can present obstacles to the progression of normal development. Other risk factors that persist over generations include violation of a youth's self-respect by the adult world, youth's prolonged economic dependence, limited outlet for experimentation by youth, influences that encourage youth egocentricity, lack of opportunities for moral development, society's belief that family is the only place for a youth, dominance of youth organizations by adults, denial of equal participation to youths, and uneven laws pertaining to youths (Konopka, 1976). Recent ethnographic studies have provided vivid descriptions of the circular interactions among children, their development, and the multiple levels of systems in their lives. The stories of children growing up in the barrio of the South Bronx (Kozol, 1995), a housing project unit on the South Side of Chicago (Kotlowitz, 1991), or the working poor Appalachian neighborhoods of Indianapolis (Watkins, 1995) reveal similar themes of the effects of youngsters' living environment on their psychosocial development. Issues of fear for personal safety, minimal support services, and physical deteriora-

tion of the neighborhood are on the minds of children across the nation.
As one early adolescent female explained,

> It's hard (growing up . . .) my mother never lets me go outside 'cause she
> was scared that I was gonna get shot or something or somebody might run
> me over. She don't want us running the streets 'cause it will be a lot of
> drunk people out in front of our house . . . fighting, drinking beer . . . be
> cocaine people smoking . . . it gets scary for me and makes me mad that I
> can't go out when I want. (ibid., p. 296)

Ecological theorists have argued that the responsiveness of societal
institutions is critical to personal development. The 1995 Carnegie Council on Adolescent Development report, which cited the lack of responsiveness of families, schools, communities, health systems, and the public
media in contributing to healthy youth development opportunities, underscores the depth of the challenge to provide a prosperous healthy
environment in which youths may achieve positive outcomes. The importance of active positive involvement in the lives of children also necessitates an ecological multisystemic level of engagement and participation
(Carnegie Council on Adolescent Development, 1992, 1995; Committee on
Economic Development, Research and Policy, 1987; Connell, Aber, &
Walker, 1995; Heath & McLaughlin, 1993; Ho, 1992; Lerner, 1991, 1995).
Thus, it becomes obvious that family and community resources are vital
components in the investment in and building of youth competencies
(Academy for Educational Development/Center for Youth Development,
1996; Pittman, 1996). A fundamental comprehensive approach that acti-
vates a long-term view of change with a sustained commitment by all
stakeholders—youth, parents, service providers, and funders—is a critical beginning. Specific recommendations include the following:

> Increase supports to families with teenagers, increase parental involve-
> ment in school-time and after-school activities, create family-friendly em-
> ployment policies, and offer child care tax credits.
> Strengthen communities and increase opportunities for young adoles-
> cents such as safe and growth-promoting out-of-school leisure time. Youth
> organizations need to expand beyond traditional services.
> Create schools for adolescents that respond to their biopsychosocial de-
> velopmental needs and create cooperative learning environments that are
> safe, intellectually stimulating, and that promote relationships.
> Increase the level of media promotion and advertisements of the con-
> structive healthy lifestyles geared toward youths.
> Create strategies for health promotion to instill values, skills, and knowl-
> edge for youths to avoid and change risk-taking behaviors. (Carnegie Coun-
> cil on Adolescent Development, 1995)

These recommendations reinforce the ecological design in which practitioners work interdependently within and among different spheres of influences in a youngster's life. Pittman (1996) has pointed out that "development requires engagement. It is fostered through relationships, influenced by environments, and triggered by participation" (p. 6). Furthermore, the social worker should realize that young people grow in families and communities and not in social services programs; any one program cannot significantly resolve society's youth-related problems (Pittman, 1996).

Social workers also need to appreciate the ecological connectedness among the different sources of environmental systems and supports. The level of effectiveness of one source of support is altered by the quality of other dimensions in young people's lives, such as the interconnectedness among children's families, schools, neighborhoods, and peer groups, as well as the physical characteristics of their environment (Hughes, 1994). For example, recent research has indicated that the shift from elementary school to middle school dramatically influences the psychosocial effects on youths, particularly early adolescent females (Brown & Gilligan, 1992; Simmons, Garlton-Ford & Blyth, 1987; Steinberg, 1985; Ward, 1989). One 12-year-old African-American girl's explanation of her transfer to a new school demonstrates the effects of peer relations on academic achievement and self-esteem. She described the harassment of her classmates as follows:

> [T]he kids treat each other badly . . . especially the dudes, everybody talk about everybody and everybody punked everybody. I hate it. I want to make my straight A's and leave it at that. I'll stay by myself and then come home and be by myself for a long time until I find the right crowd. I want to go to a quiet little school where nobody will mess with me. (Watkins, 1995, p. 298)

Studies have shown a decrease in academic motivation and academic performance (Greenberg-Lake Analysis Group, Inc., 1991) and loss of self-esteem (Brown & Gilligan, 1992; Simmons et al., 1987) during this transition. Furthermore, given that making well-thought out choices for the next 4 years in school is vital, the lack of responsiveness of educational systems to early and midadolescent girls' needs can be disastrous (Fine, 1987; Fine & Zane, 1989; Sadker & Sadker, 1993, 1994). Although school and teachers have the potential to influence self-esteem and aspirations, research has indicated that these potential support systems are limited in their reach to provide girls with the skills, role models, and self-confidence needed to compete in today's society (Sadker & Sadker, 1993). The essence of this invisibility and marginalization leads to a "hidden curriculum" (Sadker & Sadker, 1994), through which girls receive a different quality of education and experience different relationships with their teachers than their male peers. This challenge for girls was expressed by a 12-year-old female who participated regularly in leadership programs at a Boys and Girls Club and experienced success because of her verbal skills and her demonstrated ability to "take charge" in large group settings. However, her behavior in one setting, which encouraged active involvement and use of her "voice," created problems for her at school:

> The teachers are all mean to you. . . . They yell at you, put you out in the hall. I've been yelled at for talking. The teacher said to be quiet, or she'd send me to the principal. . . . So I be quiet. You don't want to go nowhere near our principal cause he's got a paddle. . . . I hear it could leave blisters on your heiny [sic]. (Watkins, 1995, p. 276)

This youngster's experience is an example of the interconnections among systems in which social workers intervene. A part of the strategic assessment and intervention of an ecologically sound practice is to strive for a goodness-of-fit among the mission or purpose, the styles of relationship-building, and the strategies of intervention based on the values and beliefs of the different systems. For example, extracurricular activities in community-based youth organizations provide opportunities for constructive use of leisure time, leadership and civic development, and self-esteem enhancement. Staff, programs, and activities can demonstrate a constructive effect on youths' lives (Public/Private Ventures, 1995; Pope, Bynum, Greene, & Feyerherm, 1995; Schinke, Cole, & Orlandi, 1991), through the types of positive experiences for development that are different than families or schools. Whereas the achievement of a child's psychosocial outcomes may be enhanced in one environment with specific types of supports, services, and relationships, the same level of opportunity may not occur in another environment (Konopka, 1974, 1976). One adolescent member described the difference between the types of relationships found in a youth organization and her school:

> [We are like one big family at the youth organization]. . . . Like if one person get in trouble, it'll be thousands of 'em saying "I did it," but they didn't do it. They just be tryin' to be on that person's side and let them know. Up here at the club they treat each other nice . . . at school they treat each other real mean. (Watkins, 1995, p. 301)

The ecological perspective allows the social worker to see that the child's behavior is influenced by a unitary system of connections among social networks. Therefore, if one part of the social network system changes, for example, a youngster moves into a new neighborhood, changes schools, and is unable to continue membership in his or her Scout troop, there will be a shift in dynamics among the child, his or her family members, peer groups, and school environment (Bronfenbrenner, 1979; Lerner, 1991). This dynamic has been called the "co-influence of the external assets of the community with the internal assets of youth" (Search Institute, 1996).

Therefore, the social worker's role is expanded beyond interpersonal interventions with young people. An integral role for the ecologically minded social worker is to explore and advocate for the quality supports that a youth-centered community can offer its young people. According to recent work on youth outcomes (Center for Youth Development and Policy Research, 1994; Connell et al., 1995; Pittman, 1996), when a caring community provides safe places to go, access to structured activities, opportunities to learn, and adequate access to health care, and also engages youths in decision-making, it will achieve positive results. Positive outcomes also may depend on the ability of a community to celebrate youths' community service; perceive young people positively; vote for necessary resources; create effective youth services; and increase the number of positive, youth-related media stories and messages.

EXAMINATION OF YOUTH ISSUES
WITHIN A DIVERSITY PERSPECTIVE

By the 1990's, nothing about ethnicity or gender in the identity of inner city youth went down smoothly or in predictable ways. The United States . . . had a love/hate relationship with cultural diversity . . . in institutions from schools and to public arts. . . . The public seemed to want to discern and label any possible source of ethnicity or cultural diversity while on the other hand to claim to promote integration and cultural homogenization to deny differences.
—S. Heath and M. McLaughlin, *Identity and Inner-City Youth*

The ecological premise of circularity between the child as participant and his or her environment is especially evident in an examination of the effects of diversity—gender, race, and class, and sexual or affectional orientation—on youths' experiences. The ecological framework, therefore, creates a foundation on which to examine multicontextual levels of influence on the conditions for healthy youth development. Components of a youth-centered community that focuses on the development of positive, healthy youth outcomes include opportunities for youths to participate in

> Ecologically framed and diversity-sound practice requires an understanding of the many levels of power and the structural inequities in the lives of youth.

building positive relationships
building self-acceptance
building active minds
building character and spirit
building a healthy body
building a caring community
building creativity and joy
building economic independence
building a global perspective
building a humane environment [Indiana Youth Institute (IYI), 1995]

Conditions needed to achieve the healthy development of youths are related to specific attributes of the context in which children learn, develop, and live. In addition to the physical environments—social networks and institutions that play a vital role in the development of children—there are key components in the valuation of the cultural characteristics of contexts in which youths grow. These components include an appreciation of pluralism, an acceptance of differences, the opportunity for participatory democracy, attention to human rights, participation in economic growth, and a general climate conducive to growth and learning (Konopka, 1976).

A reexamination of the Anglocentric dominant cultural views of healthy youth development is warranted by the social worker who practices from an ecologically framed, diversity-sensitive perspective. The variables of race, gender, class, and sexual or affectional orientation have been traditionally marginalized by researchers who have used predetermined categories and parameters of white, male populations and have extrapolated findings from this group onto other racial and ethnic groups (Cannon, Higginbotham, & Leung, 1991; Reid, 1991). Thus, it is important for the social worker to recognize that practice models may be based upon research and human behavior theories that promote a model of development that fits the values, beliefs, and daily realities of heterosexual male adolescents from mainly two-parent, Caucasian, middle- and upper-middle-income families (Beck, 1987; Dornbusch, Petersen, & Hetherington, 1991; Spencer & Dornbusch, 1990; Steinberg, 1985). Because of the limitations of the scholarship upon which the practice models are derived, these models are not inclusive (Acker, Barry, & Esseveld, 1990; Belenky, Clinchy, Goldberger, & Tartule, 1986; Gilligan, 1982; Landrine, Klonoff, & Brown-Collins, 1992). Moreover, the lived experiences and the biopsychosocial development of females, gay males and lesbians, African-Americans, Latin-Americans, American Indians, and Asian-Americans are not fully represented in the models because of the paucity of research relative to those specific groups of youths. According to Lam (1997), there is a "danger inherent in . . . the tendency [of existing theories] to modify diverse populations in the direction of the Western ideal" (p. 97), which minimizes the cultural specific needs of youths. Lam offered as an example of the "Western ideal" autonomy and sense of individualized self as primary tasks of adolescence (Erickson, 1968). The conceptualization of these adolescent tasks is in complete contradiction to Chinese cultural values of familism and interpersonal relationships.

Other examples of conflicting values between dominant belief systems and cultural group members may be found in Steinitz and Solomon's (1986) study of working-class youths in a northeastern urban city and Ladner's (1971) study of urban, low-income, African-American girls. Steinitz and Solomon's study examined the struggles of students from blue-collar families. They reported on the conflict youths experience when they move beyond the community and their families into a world of the materially successful middle and affluent classes. Ladner's research on what approaching womanhood meant to urban, low-income, African-American girls vividly described the sociohistorical forces of the cycle of poverty. Ladner suggested these forces are the impetus for the development of practical and positive adaptive skills that enable youths to survive in difficult environmental conditions, but at the social expense of being excluded from schools and job opportunities. Heath and McLaughlin's (1993) research indicated that, as youths' neighborhoods change, they receive conflicting messages about concepts of gender and identity based on the demographic, political, and economic conditions.

It is important for social workers to recognize that identification of the variables of race, gender, and class is usually within the context of the social definitions of "at-risk" youths. "At-risk" research approaches information about diverse populations of youths (particularly adolescents) from a "deviant" or "deficit" model (Reid, 1991). Spencer and Markstrom-Adams (1990) have challenged this process, calling instead for a "multi-faceted theoretical formulation for understanding the developmental processes for minority status youth" (p. 295) rather than formulations that are based on deviance and deficiency models. As social workers come to recognize the limitations of traditional human behavior theories and practice models, the intersection of the ecological and diversity perspectives will afford practitioners with a model that integrates theories and skills grounded in the reality of the client.

Social workers in effective practice with youths from diverse populations learn to modify traditional techniques and skills and develop strategies that reflect culturally specific interventions. This ability to stay "grounded with the youth's perspective" requires the social worker to:

- be aware of his or her own ethnocentric biases and personal internalization of the dominant values systems;
- be aware of his or her own biases related to the concept of youth;
- be aware of preconceived notions of the capacity and ability of diverse populations of youths;
- be in tune with his or her own styles and patterns of verbal and nonverbal communication;
- explore his or her idea of "appropriate" and "inappropriate" codes of behavior, dress, language, and other methods of youth expression;
- recognize and articulate his or her fears and concerns for personal safety and well-being;
- accept that the social worker is the learner and the youths are the teachers of their own successes and failures;
- learn humility and acceptance because youths act on their own sense of power;
- recognize the importance of interpersonal relationship-building so that he or she may negotiate and establish guidelines, limits, and mutually agreed on goals and interventions.

In addition to the ability to be self-aware, cognizant of their own interpersonal communication skills, and proficient in individual and group social work practice, social workers in ecologically framed, diversity-sound practice must understand the multiple levels of power and structural inequities in youths' lives. Therefore, practice also involves empowerment and advocacy to change destructive social conditions that present barriers to the youth's growth and development.

> Effective diversity-sensitive practice requires recognition of one's biases toward youth from diverse populations.

YOUTH DEVELOPMENT MODELS: APPLYING
THE ECOLOGICAL AND DIVERSITY PERSPECTIVES

Promoting positive youth development is an excellent investment in the future of our nation that can be postponed only at a great cost to society.
—K. Bogenschneider, "An Ecological Risk/Protective Theory for Building Prevention Programs, Policies and Community Capacity to Support Youth"

An ecological framework with a diversity perspective that promotes positive growth and development of youths is vital for relevant social work practice in the 21st century. This approach is critical, given that an examination of social work practice literature has suggested that social workers' methodology still predominantly maintains a clinical treatment focus (Morrison, Alcorn, & Nelums, 1997). More needs to be done to interest social workers in youth development strategies that are based on a developmental approach, and that emphasize asset-building, focus on preparation for adulthood, build youth capacity through relationships, as well as foster skill-development and interconnectedness with the youths' environment.

There is no one definition of youth development, nor can one conceptual model fully respond to the vastly increasing individual, family, and community challenges of youth development. As with other populations in social work practice, the effectiveness of types of services for youths are being examined to determine what works best with whom under which circumstances. Over the past two decades, social workers increasingly have used two prevention models: the risk-focused model (Hawkins, 1989; Hawkins & Catalano, 1992; Hawkins, Catalano, & Miller, 1992) and the resiliency of protective process approach (Bernard, 1993a, 1993b, 1993c; Rutter, 1987). The risk-focused model promotes prevention by identifying community, family, school, individual, and peer risk factors that increase the probability of youth-related problems. Risk factors

> exist in multiple domains
> are greater when more risk factors are present
> predict diverse behavior problems
> show much consistency in effects across different races cultures and classes
> may be buffered by factors that prevent risk exposure.
> (Hawkins et al., and the William T. Grant Foundation Consortium on the School-Based Promotion of Social Competence, 1992)

The resiliency of protective process approach moves beyond a focus on risks to an examination of conditions that facilitate youth's healthy development. The resiliency model emphasizes children's resiliency characteristics and circumstances that foster health and promote competencies and positive behaviors within different environments. The protective processes are seen as individual or environmental deterrents or safety nets that enhance youngsters' capacity to withstand stressful situations.

Bogenschneider (1996) has proposed that both prevention models are key components in creating conditions that facilitate youth development. She promoted an ecological risk-protective theory that combines the ecological and developmental frameworks. Ecological theory draws social workers' attention to the risk and protective processes at different levels of the human ecology, that is, individual, family, peer, school, work, and community settings. Simultaneously, the developmental context approach focuses on how the ecological environment may shift as youths mature and settings vary. Bogenschneider argued that the ecological risk-protective theory promotes working on both fronts to help bolster protective processes that assist youths to negotiate risky environments and to reduce the number of risks to which youths are exposed. There is growing recognition that identification of risk and protective factors provide a needed articulation of the multitude of factors that affect youths. On the other hand, social workers need to be aware that

> we must change how we look at youth and expect young people to be "not just problem free, but fully prepared." To be fully prepared, young people need people, places, possibilities, preparation, practice, participation, permission, promotion, and perspective. And that equals power. (Pittman, 1996, p. 7)

Many researchers, youth advocates, and practitioners are urging greater investment in a move beyond problem-focused interventions. That is, the best practices in services to youths are slowly evolving from the "fix a child" remedial interventions to a "prepare a child" developmental paradigm. This paradigmatic shift advocates channeling energies from prevention or treatment services into policies, programs, and relationships that build on youth competencies and prepare children for adulthood (Carnegie Council on Adolescent Development, 1992, 1995; Center for Youth Development and Policy Research, 1994; Pittman, 1993; Pittman & Fleming, 1991). In essence, the challenge of preparing children for adulthood moves social workers beyond a problem-focused to an asset-building approach (Blyth & Roehlkepartain, 1993; IYI, 1993, 1995).

The asset-building approach differentiates between problem-based social problems and the asset-building capacities of youths. Inherent in this youth development model are critical components related to meeting young people's basic needs. These components include a sense of safety and structure, belonging and membership, self-worth and an ability to contribute, independence and control over one's life, closeness and several good relationships, and competence and mastery. In addition to the basic needs of young people, the model addresses other areas considered crucial to building youth competencies such as adequate attitudes, skills, and behaviors. Among these ares are health, personal and social skills, reasoning, knowledge and creativity, vocational awareness, and citizenship (Pittman, 1993; Pittman & Fleming, 1991). In keeping with an ecological perspective, this asset-building approach to youth development not only focuses on individual youths, or a single aspect of a youth's behavior, but advocates for the design of multiple strategies that encompass an individual youth's social context (Barton, Watkins, & Jajoura, 1997).

A recent report of the Carnegie Council on Adolescent Development (1995) parallels Pittman's (1993) identification of critical components of youth development. The report suggested essential requirements to shift the paradigm from one of fixing youth problems to one that identifies key developmental characteristics for healthy adolescence. This broader, holistic framework of youth development, which is based on theory and research of the biopsychosocial needs of youths, suggests that the achievement of key human needs is the foundation for healthy adult lives. Incorporated into this framework are components of youth development that are integral to an ecological perspective of social work practice with diverse youth populations. Although each component is socially constructed, there is a recognition of the universality of children and youths' needs. Youths' increased sense of belonging, usefulness, competency, and power can be achieved through the following opportunities:

- Learn how to form close, durable human relationships.
- Find a valued place in a constructive group.
- Feel a sense of worth as a person.
- Achieve a reliable basis for making informed choices.
- Know how to use the available support systems.
- Express constructive curiosity and exploratory behavior.
- Find ways of being useful to others.
- Believe in a promising future with real opportunities (Carnegie Council on Adolescent Development, 1992, 1995; Center for Youth Development and Policy Research, 1994; Pittman, 1993; Pittman & Fleming, 1991).

COMMUNITY YOUTH DEVELOPMENT: AN ECOLOGICAL APPROACH FOR COMMUNITY AND YOUTH GROWTH AND CONNECTION

Community youth development . . . is a philosophy that moves beyond programs, services and treatment. At its core are a set of principles that require orienting ourselves to thinking about youth development and community responsibility in a way that demands that all youth, especially those who are trouble and in trouble, be given the opportunity to finish the business of growing up.
—D. Hughes, "Community Youth Development"

Youth development, as with any ecologically based approach to social work practice, does not occur in a vacuum. The reciprocity between the goodness-of-fit of the environmental conditions in which youths make the transition into adulthood has been the primary treatise of this chapter. Taking the concept of goodness-of-fit one step forward, one realizes that not only do healthy communities con-

> Healthy youth development focuses on a strengths-based, empowerment model of social work practice with youth.

tribute to the well-being of their youths, but healthy, prosperous youths can also simultaneously make a difference within their own community. Therein lies the mutuality between the concepts of youth development and community development. Through community/youth development, youths engage in roles of leadership and partnership for the common good of the community, which in turn enhances their sense of mastery, self-esteem, and empowerment. When youths experience increased involvement in responsible actions that are vital for the good of their community, they are better prepared to be active participants in their community. Characteristics of successful youth-adult leadership and partnership programs include the following:

> Young people take the lead in community action that meets a real need.
> Young people work in collaborative relationships with peers and adults.
> Young people take a share in planning and decision-making that affects themselves and others.
> Young people take the time to reflect on the consequences of their own actions and decisions, with guidance from adults. (IYI, 1993)

Possession of these characteristics may deter youths from feeling alienated, acting recklessly, or engaging in other destructive behaviors. Therefore, community/youth development may be a mechanism to respond to the basic social, recreational, leadership, and civic development needs of youths in rural, suburban, and urban communities. In addition, there is congruence between the purpose of community development and youth development. Both forms of development focus on common goals of increased economic and social investment; focus on basic functions of health, citizenship, and family; occur within the broader political context; and celebrate cultural identity (Boyte & Kari, 1996; Pittman, 1996).

There is much concern about people, particularly young people, losing a vital sense of community. However, therein lies the challenge and the promise: "Amid the growing discussion in this country about the need to reweave our social fabric, a critical strand often is oddly overlooked: young people" (Kressley & Skelton, 1996, p. 6). One approach to community/youth development is through civic engagement to integrate the concepts of youth development with the tasks of public works (Kressley & Skelton, 1996). This integration offers opportunities for youths to become productive citizens, and to create youth-adult relationships based on mutual concerns for the public good (Boyte & Kari, 1996). When implementing the community/youth development model, social workers would advocate with different systems (e.g., schools, families, community organizations, the United Way, and foundation boards) so that youths are provided a key role in program planning, decision-making, and governance. Such an effort signals respect for a youth's talent and experiences and fosters a youth's skills development through public works.

COMMUNITY-BASED YOUTH DEVELOPMENT SERVICES

Fortunately, there are a wide variety of organizations that provide basic supports—sustained adult attention and guidance and a variety of positive activities. Big Brothers/Big Sisters, Boys' & Girls Clubs, Y's, local organizations like Brooklyn's El Puente—these and others have, over the past 25 years, not pursued the problem-oriented, quick-fix programming of public policy, but stuck to the basics.

—G. Walker, "Back to Basics: A New/Old Direction for Youth Policy"

More than 400 national, nonprofit, adult-sponsored youth organizations provide services and programs based on the youth development strategies. Organizations such as Scouts, Boys and Girls Clubs, YMCAs, Campfire, Inc., PAL Clubs, 4-H programs, and Girls, Inc., have as their sole mission the provision of relevant social, recreational, physical, and educational services to enhance youths' skills and preparation for adulthood. The following Girls, Inc., and Big

> Youth development organizations provide safe and supportive environments, structured recreational and educational activities to meet youths' developmental needs.

Brothers and Big Sisters of America mission statements illustrate the application of the ecological, diversity, and youth development principles. Within these mission statements, the concepts of person-environment, appreciation of the uniqueness of each child, and capacity-building are evident. For example, the mission statement for Girls, Inc., is as follows:

The purpose of Girls, Incorporated is to meet the needs of girls in their communities, in helping girls and young women overcome the effects of discrimination and to develop their capacity to be self-sufficient, responsible citizens and to serve vigorous advocates for girls, focusing attention on their special needs. (Girls, Incorporated, 1992, p. 1)

The mission statement of Big Brothers and Big Sisters of America is:

The mission of Big Brothers and Big Sisters of America is to make a positive

> The mission of Big Brothers and Big Sisters of America is to make a positive difference in the lives of children and youth, primarily through a professionally supported, one-to-one relationship with a caring adult, and to assist them in achieving their highest potential as they grow to become responsible men and women by providing committed volunteers, national leadership and standards of excellence. (Big Brothers/Big Sisters, 1996, p. 2)

Recent studies have documented the positive outcomes of healthy development of youth members of youth services agencies (Schinke et al., 1991; Public/Private Ventures, 1995; Tierney, Baldwin, & Resch, 1995) and specific programs (Girls, Incorporated, 1991; Pope et al., 1995). That the environment of these youth-focused safe havens is supportive is clearly expressed by two members of Boys and Girls Club:

> It's a club and we do things and they serve food here. I always feel happy here because there's just a lot of kids here that I can have fun with. I feel good about myself because I have friends and they help me with things I need help with.
>   At the club, I play pool. We chase each other, we go swimming, play basketball, get in different activities. I just have fun. I join stuff. I mean like a cooking club, we used to go in there and bake cookies. . . . What makes the club fun is that I didn't have to worry about nobody else but myself when I was in there and having fun and I was doing what I wanted to do. (Watkins, 1995, 278)

In addition to having "fun" and "things to do," these organizations also provide positive relationships with professionally trained adult youth workers and social workers. Because parents, schools, and communities are less frequently available to fulfill their roles in nurturing the healthy development of youths (Hechinger, 1992), these relationships are critical given the reality that such agencies are increasingly providing psychosocial support and supervision to more children and adolescents (Carnegie Council on Adolescent Development, 1995; DeWitt-Wallace Reader's Digest Fund, 1996). That the importance of the professionally trained youth work staff is critical in providing safe, nurturing relationships is evident in the words of this 13-year-old member:

> Like if a little kid gets hurt or something, Keith or Mike or one of them [staff] will help them out and punish the person who did it. Make them sit down or go home. Keep them away from the person that they hurt. . . . The club's important to me. So's the staff important to me too. It means that I know there is somebody there who will help you with your problems and stuff. (Watkins, 1995, p. 281)

The number of youths involved and the amount of time youths spend in these agencies ranks second only to the number and time spent in the public schools (Carnegie Council on Adolescent Development, 1995). Recent research has documented that, although youth development programs cannot fill the void of generations of poverty, inadequate housing, unemployment, and inadequate health care, they do offer opportunities for young people to experience success, positive and meaningful relationships, self-initiative, leadership and conflict resolution skills, and a sense of belonging (Quinn, 1995; Smith, 1991). At the same time, the programming and staffing capacity of youth-serving agencies are unable to maintain the pace of increased demands (Carnegie Council on Adolescent Development, 1995; DeWitt-Wallace Reader's Digest Fund, 1996). Although the numbers of youths nationally indicate a grave need for such services, funding is decreasing and youth development activities are in short supply in many neighborhoods. Recent policy papers have indicated a growing need for youth development services; however, agency resources and the ability of youth development agencies to maintain programs and hire well-prepared staff are diminishing (Carnegie Council on Adolescent Development, 1995; DeWitt-Wallace Reader's Digest Fund, 1996). Compounding this problem of limited resources is the paucity of literature and empirical data to substantiate the merit and practice effectiveness of youth development agencies (Girls, Incorporated, 1992), which would aid agencies in their bid for dwindling philanthropic dollars.

COMMUNITY-UNIVERSITY COLLABORATION: YOUTH DEVELOPMENT INTENSIVE FIELD UNIT

[Field practicum involves] structured learning opportunities that enable students to compare their practice experiences, integrate knowledge acquired in the classroom, and expand knowledge beyond the scope of the practicum setting.
—Council on Social Work Education, *Accreditation Standards and Self-Study Guide*

Across hundreds of campuses nationwide, universities are attempting to define meaningful collaborative roles for helping to restore urban communities (Harkavy & Puckett, 1994). Social work students and faculty are increasingly being called on to advance knowledge-building and to build productive partnerships between researchers and practitioners (Hess and Mullen, 1995). This section describes a pilot project to develop a Youth Development Intensive Field Unit with two youth development agencies: a direct-services agency and an intermediary indirect-services agency.

The purpose was to expand the traditional field placement to provide
intensive education in youth services

> Schools of social work more
> frequently are being requested to
> build productive partnerships
> between researchers and
> practitioners.

through school of social work–
community agency collaboration
(Boyer, 1996; Rice, 1996). Youth development agencies provide a practicum
with a mix of service delivery efforts
focused on youth empowerment, issue advocacy, and community involvement (Jarman-Rohde, McFall, Kolar, & Strom, 1997).

The Intensive Youth Development Field Unit field practicum model
was initiated to meet service needs of youth development agencies while
achieving the academic and field placement requirements of students.
Social work field practicum students, who were selected for their interest
in a social work career with youth, focused their required educational
experiences to respond to the agency's youth-community-civic development missions. In addition, the Youth Development Intensive Field Unit
matched a faculty liaison's service, research, and teaching interests with
the needs and organizational capacities of the community-based youth-
serving agencies.

Currently the two agencies partners of the Field Unit are the Boys and
Girls Clubs of Indianapolis and the Indiana Youth Institute. The Boys and
Girls Clubs of Indianapolis's mission is to "promote and enhance development of youth of all backgrounds with special attention to youngsters
ages 6–17 years from disadvantaged backgrounds and communities."
The Boys and Girls Club conducts its individual, small group, and large
structured youth programs at its five clubhouse facilities located within
economically stressed Indianapolis neighborhoods. Two clubhouses are
located in working-poor and poor African-American neighborhoods, two
clubhouses are located in working-poor and poor Caucasian neighborhoods with a heavy influence of Appalachian culture, and a new influx of
Hispanic immigrants. Another clubhouse is located in a working-poor
and poor African-American and Caucasian neighborhood. Two of the
clubhouses are adjacent to Indianapolis Housing Authority housing projects. The organization has more than 8,000 youths; the daily average
attendance is 178 youths at any one time. The membership demographics
are as follows: 41% of the members are girls and 59% are boys; 54% of the
youths are African-American; 7% Latino and 39% are Caucasian. Of the
youths, 96% are eligible for the federally paid school lunch program and
85% reside in female-headed, single-parent households.

The IYI is an intermediary organization dedicated to promoting and
supporting staff who work with youths. The IYI is actively involved in the
generation and dissemination of research in the areas of policy initiatives,
program development, and program evaluation. Moreover, IYI conducts

staff training for youth-serving agencies throughout Indiana. Staff from the Boys and Girls Club and IYI have co-created positive working relationships through collaboration on projects designed to enhance services to Boys and Girls Club members and to promote positive youth development in central Indiana.

Building on the previously established relationships between the staff of the field department and the Boys and Girls Club, the faculty member who serves as the field liaison for the club, as well as her relationships with the staff from the two agencies, the youth development field unit was developed. Relationships are currently being developed with staff from other youth development agencies, such as the Indiana Youth Group, which provides support and advocacy services to gay male, lesbian, bisexual, and transgender youths, to expand the Field Unit.

A primary goal of the Youth Development Intensive Field Unit was to enhance the bachelor of social work (BSW), master of social work (MSW), and PhD students in the area of youth development. Such improved preparation is critical given the need for staff who can assist with the rising social, economic, and professional demands of youth development organizations. Another goal of the Youth Development Intensive Field Unit was to apply best practices—in this case, ecological and diversity principles—to the application of youth development principles in two distinct agency settings. Ongoing BSW and MSW student evaluations were also a key component of the assessment and evaluation of the field unit's design.

One male BSW student, who is employed full-time and attends school full-time, expresses his appreciation for the opportunity for input into the design and time frames of student learning responsibilities:

> I especially appreciated the approach which Marie [field liaison], Beth and Lisa [peer group facilitator] took, viewing placement as a fluid experience open to revision and change as we [the students] moved through the semester, encountering challenges and opportunities rather than a narrower approach which views placement as "an extension of the classroom" governed by an inflexible set of rules and prescribed learning experiences. (MSW student, cited in Watkins & Muelhausen, 1997d)

Curriculum to increase knowledge and skills related to the ecological contexts of youths' everyday life experiences was developed by an advisory committee and taught to social work students by the field liaison, the peer group facilitators, and the on-site task instructors. The curriculum included information on the biopsychosocial developmental stages of youths aged 6 to 16 years and how developmental tasks might be affected by race, class, gender, or sexual or affectional orientation. The curriculum also examined how to achieve gender equity within a mixed-gender setting of the Boys and Girls Club. In-depth attention to generalist social work practice principles, specifically individuals, groups, and community practice, was intended to increase understanding of ecological thinking—in this case, the intersection of youth, community, and civic development. In addition, the curriculum addressed how youth development related to the principles of program planning, implementation and evaluation, the development of youth-centered outcome measures, and policy and legislative analysis and decision-making.

Social work services were implemented to meet the physical, emotional, social, educational, and civic development needs of youths within the context of their families, schools, neighborhoods, and Boys and Girls Club. Examples of direct youth development social work services activities include facilitation of social skills; development of group clubs; creation of ongoing networks between schools, families, and youths; facilitation of civic development or service learning opportunities for youths; and brokering between social services agencies. Indirect social work service activities, which often included youths, encompassed community mapping, program needs assessments, and programmatic evaluations. These ecological practice learning activities provided youths with opportunities to collaborate with social work students in planning, implementing, and evaluating their own group activities, as well as community service projects. Youths and social work students involved in the pilot project also participated in community councils, youth services committees, and neighborhood advisory councils.

Key to increasing students' knowledge, skills, and attitudes from an ecological perspective were the formal and informal opportunities for students to experience self-awareness and the ethical use of self in social work practice with youths from diverse backgrounds. These learning experiences, a dominant emphasis throughout the duration of placement, served as catalysts for lively discussions and personal reflection during weekly peer group meetings, monthly educational seminars, and weekly supervision with the social work students by on-site instructors.

The first two weeks of placement focused on a "personal inventory" of students' assumptions, fears, stereotypes, and skills level. Students were required to complete three projects designed to help them articulate their understanding of personal and professional boundaries, biases, and belief systems. The first project was a narrative paper that described students' assumptions (Watkins & Muelhausen, 1997a) about the agencies and its constituents; their understanding of youth development principles; and their concerns, fears, and personal strengths. Students shared their concerns about "being in that neighborhood after dark," "will the kids like me," and "will I stand out because I am the only [white/black] person there."

The students also completed a process recording of a "walk-in-the-hood" (Watkins & Muelhausen, 1997b) taken with their instructor or an older youth member through the neighborhoods adjacent to the Boys and Girls Club facility. The intent of this activity was to enhance students' understanding of the concept of the sustaining and nurturing environments articulated in the dual-perspective concept. Students were also asked to reflect on the similarities and differences between the neighborhoods where the Boys and Girls Club members resided and their own experiences growing up in their own neighborhood. One Caucasian male MSW student documented his reactions to a racially integrated, working-poor neighborhood:

> I saw trash everywhere and graffiti. The only bus stop I saw was at the edge of the neighborhood. I saw a lot of churches—some were kept nice and others were run down and converted from a house. One church had a liquor store next to it. [Within a 3-square mile radius] there were five taverns in the neighborhood, two schools, one multiservice center, one Boys and Girls Club, no large supermarkets or hospitals. These people are living in very poor conditions, some have dirt floors in their house. . . . I could not believe that people live in such poor conditions. I would see the world as a place where I had to struggle to survive. I would see an unfair and unjust world. . . . At first I thought these people were lazy. After thinking about the neighborhood, I decided that this was due to a sense of no one cares (including the city administration), or lack of ownership, instead of laziness. (MSW student, cited in Watkins & Muelhausen, 1997d)

In addition, students completed a participant observation exercise (Watkins & Muelhausen, 1997c), in which they visit each Boys and Girls Club unit located in various neighborhoods. Students were asked to reflect on what they "see, hear, think, feel, and react to" after their first 90-minute visit to each of the clubhouses. One Caucasian female MSW student demonstrated the power of the activity through her articulation of her feelings of racial isolation during her observation of activities at a clubhouse that served predominantly African-American youths from economically stressed families and neighborhoods. She observed,

> I see: Many black people, only one other white person in the whole building, teens co-mingling: more teens here than other clubs I've been to, a young pregnant girl, two guys cutting kids' hair, posters on the wall about AIDS and not doing drugs.
> I hear: Basketball, a lot of screaming and yelling, unusual names (to me), it quieted down after 7:45 P.M. when the kids 12 and under go home.
> I think: That the kids are not going to want to hang out with me—that they will wonder why I am there, that I stick out like a sore thumb.
> I feel: Nervous at first, REALLY uncomfortable. I feel invasive—scared

to go into the gym or other rooms because I feel nervous that the kids will wonder why I am there. I feel like I don't fit in, overwhelmed for a while, great for the last 10 minutes when I talked with Joe [staff member] and some of the kids.

I react to: My own fears keep me from approaching anyone. I seem to just try to get out of everyone's way. (MSW student, cited in Watkins & Muelhausen, 1997d)

These activities facilitated skills for self-awareness and an introduction to key issues related to ecologically framed social work practice with diverse populations of youths. Other components of the intensive field unit included a pretest and posttest of knowledge of youth development, generalist practice, and group work skills. In addition, student portfolios document achievement of learning objectives.

Finally, there was a capstone paper in which students discussed key areas of personal and professional growth. The following questions guided the students' introspection related to issues of diversity and social and economic justice:

• Describe your initial reaction to the setting.

—What dimensions of diversity reflected by the population served by the agency are similar or dissimilar to your own background?
—Ride around the neighborhood of the agency, and observe how this neighborhood may be similar or dissimilar to your own.
—What are some of the assumptions that you have about people at this setting, and the way you will interact with them? Or they will interact with you?
—What are your fears, strengths, and areas of comfort?

• Describe and demonstrate your own understanding of your values and beliefs and their implications for relationships with people from other backgrounds.

—How are your values a help or a hindrance to build relationships with others?
—What do you notice about the diversity of interpersonal communication styles? Body language? Spatial differences? About the interaction between boys and girls and different racial groups?
—What is surprising to you about your initial assumptions about your interaction with people and their interaction with you?

• Describe your understanding, appreciation, and personal sensitivity to the unique life-styles, customs, value systems, aspirations, and experiences of the youths with whom you have come into contact at the agency.

• Discuss how issues of inequality are a part of the everyday lives of youths served by the Boys and Girls Club.

—What have you learned about the strengths of youngsters?

—What is surprising to you about your initial assumptions about your interaction with youths and their interaction with you?

—What was the greatest lesson that you learned about yourself? About social work practice with youths? About the concept of youth development? (MSW student, cited in Watkins & Muelhausen, 1997d)

As one student gauged his semester's learning process, he articulated his ability to confront his initial biases about the qualities of the children, their behavior, and his understanding of his role as a social worker:

> In my assumption paper, I wrote that I heard that the kids were "holy terrors". . . . When I wrote my assumption paper, I documented my assumptions as if they were negatives and I would dislike the placement. The kids are difficult at times . . . yet I have enjoyed the kids, and most of all have enjoyed the feeling that I am being pushed to stretch and grow. . . . I will smile at the times that I was encouraged to grow beyond my complacency. I assumed that all of the kids in the club would use foul language as a routine means of communication. This belief was based upon my assumption that all kids from the inner-city cussed. . . . I have not heard it at the club and although cussing is frowned upon at the club, it is not written anywhere that it is strictly forbidden which leads me to believe that my assumption is incorrect. What I hear are voices competing to be heard. . . . Not being heard could be devastating for these kids as being heard is synonymous with being recognized and having at least a chance of getting their needs met. I see this in relation to issues of race, gender and oppression of the kids. . . . Gender equity is especially important in Boys and Girls Club because most of the kids are still in the process of learning the "rules of the game." As a social worker, it is extremely important for me to be aware of the dysfunctional ways in which gender inequity is supported through [club] practices. (BSW junior, spring 1997)

Effective ecologically framed social work practice with diverse populations of youths can be readily promoted through the integration and application of youth development and community youth development principles. While social workers have major roles in the intervention of the multiple systems that impact upon the lives of children, it is critical that the first step to develop a diversity-sensitive practice be the social worker's awareness of their own prejudices and stereotypes.

A final, yet most vital, step for the social worker is to remain a humble learner:

The kids in my group clubs taught me more than anything—they want to be seen, heard, respected, and given the nurturing and attention they deserve. They have also taught me that it doesn't take a rocket scientist to deliver these things—only a person to be compassionate and nurturing, but also someone who is willing to get out of the way of their process. Kids are much smarter and capable than any of us give them credit for. (BSW junior)

REFERENCES

Academy for Educational Development/Center for Youth Development (1996). *Youth program/community outcomes.* Washington, DC: Author.

Acker, J., Barry, K., & Esseveld, J. (1990). Objectivity and truth: Problems in doing feminist research. In M. M. Fonow & J. A. Cook (Eds.), *Beyond methodology: Feminist scholarship as lived research* (pp. 133–154). Bloomington: Indiana University Press.

Annie Casey Foundation (1997). *City kids count: Data on the well-being of children in large cities.* Baltimore: Author.

Annie Casey Foundation and the Center for the Study of Social Policy (1992). *1992 kids count data book: State profiles of child well-being* Washington, DC: Center for the Study of Social Policy.

Archer, S. L. (1992). A feminist approach to identity research. In G. Adams, T. Gullotta, & R. Montemayor (Eds.), *Adolescent identity formation* (pp. 25–49). Newbury Park, CA: Sage.

Barton, W., Watkins, M., & Jajoura, R. (1997). Youth and communities: Towards comprehensive strategies for youth development. *Social Work, 42*(5), 483–493.

Beck, S. (1987). Research Issues. In V. Van Hasselt & M. Hersen (Eds.), *Handbook of Adolescent Psychology* (pp. 227–244). New York: Pergamon.

Belenky, M., Clinchy, B., Goldberger, N., & Tartule, J. (1986). *Women's ways of knowing: the development of self, voice and mind.* New York: Basic Press.

Bernard, B. (1992). *Fostering resiliency in kids: Protective factors in the family, school and community.* Portland, OR: Western Center for Drug-Free Schools and Communities.

Bernard, B. (1993a). Fostering resiliency in kids. *Educational Leadership, 51*(3), 44–48.

Bernard, B. (1993b). Resiliency paradigm validates craft knowledge. *Western Center News, 6*(4), 6–7.

Bernard, B. (1993c). Resiliency requires changing hearts and minds. *Western Center News, 6*(2), 4–5.

Big Brothers/Big Sisters (1996). *Annual report.* New York: Author.

Blyth, D., & Roehlkepartain, E. (1993). *Healthy communities, healthy youth: How communities contribute to positive youth development.* Minneapolis: Search Institute.

Bogenschneider, K. (1996). An ecological risk/protective theory for building prevention programs, policies and community capacity to support youth. *Family Relations, 45,* 127–138.

Boyer, E. (1996). The scholarship of engagement. *Journal of Public Service and Outreach, 1*(1), 11–20.

Boys and Girls Clubs of Indianapolis (1996). *Annual report.* Indianapolis: Author.

Boyte, H., & Kari, N. (1996). Young people and public work. *Wingspread Journal, 18*(4), 4–5.

Bronfenbrenner, U. (1979). *The ecology of human development.* Cambridge, MA: Harvard University Press.

Brooks-Gunn, J. (1996). Big-city kids and their families: Integration of research and practices. In A. Kahn and S. Kamerman (Eds.), *Children & their families in big cities: Strategies for service reform* (pp. 261–280). New York: Columbia University School of Social Work, Cross National Research Studies Program.

Brown, L., & Gilligan, C. (1992). *Meeting at the crossroads: Women's psychology and girls' development.* Cambridge, MA: Harvard University Press.

Brown, P. (1993). *Comprehensive neighborhood-based initiatives: Implications for urban policy.* Chicago: University of Chicago, Chapin Hall Center for Children.

Cannon, L., Higginbotham, E., & Leung, M. (1991). Race and class bias in qualitative research for women. In M. Fonow and J. Cook (Eds.), *Beyond methodology: Feminist scholarship as lived research* (pp. 107–118). Bloomington: Indiana University Press.

Carnegie Council on Adolescent Development (1995). *Great transitions: Preparing adolescents for a new century* (Executive Summary). New York: Carnegie Corporation of New York.

Carnegie Council on Adolescent Development, Task Force on Youth Development and Community Programs (1992). *A matter of time: Risk and opportunity in the nonschool hours.* New York: Carnegie Corporation of New York.

Center for Youth Development and Policy Research. (1994). *Enriching local planning for youth development: A mobilization agenda.* Washington, DC: Center for Youth Development and Policy Research/Academy for Educational Development.

Chaskin, R., & Ogletree, R. (1993). *The Ford Foundation's Neighborhood and Family Initiative (NFI)—Building collaboration: An interim report.* Chicago: University of Chicago, Chapin Hall Center for Children.

Coles, R. (1968). *Children of crisis: A study of courage and fear.* New York: Dell.

Colls, C. (1992). *Cultural diversity: Implication for theory and practice* (The Stone Center Colloquium Series). Wellesley College, MA: Stone Center.

Committee for Economic Development, Research and Policy. (1987). *Children in need: Investment strategies for the educationally disadvantaged.* New York: Author.

Connell, J., Aber, J., & Walker, G. (1995). How do urban communities affect youth? Using social science research to inform the design and evaluation of comprehensive community initiatives. In J. Connell, A. Kubisch, L. Schoor, and C. Weiss (Eds.), *New approaches to evaluating community initiatives: Concepts, methods, and contexts* (pp. 93–125). Washington, DC: Aspen Institute.

Coulton, C. (1996). Effects of neighborhoods on families and children: Implications for services. In A. Kahn and S. Kamerman (Eds.), *Children and their families in big cities: Strategies for Service Reform* (pp. 87–120). New York: Columbia University School of Social Work, Cross National Research Studies Program.

Council on Social Work Education (1995). *Accreditation standards and self-study guide*. Alexandria, VA: Author.

DeWitt-Wallace Reader's Digest Fund (1996). *Strengthening the youth work profession: An analysis of and lessons learned from grantmaking by the DeWitt-Wallace Reader's Digest Fund*. New York: Author.

Dornbusch, S., Petersen, A., & Hetherington, E. (1991). Projecting the future of research on adolescence. *Journal of Research on Adolescence, 1*(1), 7–17.

Dryfoos, J. (1990). *Adolescents at risk: Prevalence and prevention*. New York: Oxford University Press.

Elder, G. (1975). Adolescence in the life cycle: An introduction. In S. Dragastin and G. Elder, Jr. (Eds.), *Adolescence in the life cycle: Psychological change and social context* (pp. 1–22). Washington, DC: Halsted.

Erickson, E. (1968). *Identity: Youth and crisis*. New York: W.W. Norton.

Fine, M. (1987). Silencing in public schools. *Language Arts, 64*(2), 157–174.

Fine, M., & Zane, N. (1989). Being wrapped too tight: when low income drop out of high school. In L. Weis, E. Farrar, and H. Petrie (Eds.), *Dropouts from school*. Albany, NY: SUNY Press.

Gilligan, C. (1982). What do we know about girls? In Girls Clubs of America (Ed.), *Seminar proceedings*. Indianapolis, IN: Girls, Inc., National Resource Center.

Gilligan, C. (1987). Women's place in a man's life cycle. In S. Harding (Ed.), *Feminism and Methodology* (pp. 57–73). Bloomington: Indiana University Press.

Girls, Incorporated (1991). *Truth, trust, and technology: New research on preventing adolescent pregnancy*. Indianapolis, IN: Girls, Inc., National Resource Center

Girls, Incorporated (1992). *Gender issues in youth development programs*. Indianapolis, IN: Girls, Inc., National Resource Center.

Greenberg-Lake Analysis Group, Inc. (1991). *Shortchanging girls, shortchanging America: A nationwide poll to assess self-esteem, educational experience, interest in math and science and career aspirations of girls and boys ages 9–15*. Washington, DC: American Association of University Women.

Harkavy, I. & Puckett, J. (1994). Lessons from the Hull House. *Social Service Review*, 299–321.

Hawkins, J. D. (1989). *Risk-focused prevention: Prospects and strategies*. Lecture presented at the Coordinating Council on Juvenile Justice and Delinquency Prevention, Washington, DC.

Hawkins, J. D., & Catalano, R. (1992). *Communities that care: Action for drug abuse prevention*. San Francisco: Jossey-Bass.

Hawkins, J. D., Catalano, R. F., Barnard, K. E., Gottfredson, C. D., Holmes, A. B., IV, Miller, J. Y., and the William T. Grant Foundation Consortium on the School-Based Promotion of Social Competence. (1992). *Communities that care: Action for drug abuse prevention*. San Francisco: Jossey-Bass.

Hawkins, J. D., Catalano, R., & Miller, J. (1992). Risk and protective factors for alcohol and other drug problems in adolescence and early adulthood: Implications for substance abuse prevention. *Psychological Bulletin, 112*, 64–105.

Heath, S., & McLaughlin, M. (1993). *Identity and inner-city youth*. New York: Teachers College, Columbia University.

Hechinger, F. (1992). *Fateful choices: Healthy youth for the 21st century* (executive summary). New York: Carnegie Corporation of New York.

Hess, P., & Mullen, E. (1995). *Practitioner-researcher partnerships: Building knowledge from, in, and for practice.* Washington, DC: NASW Press.

Ho, M. K. (1992). *Minority children and adolescents in therapy.* Newbury, CA: Sage.

Hughes, D. (1994, Winter). Community youth development. *New Designs for Youth Development,* 3–5.

Indiana Youth Institute (1993). *Youth/adult partnerships.* Indianapolis, IN: Author.

Indiana Youth Institute (1995). *Blueprint for healthy development.* Indianapolis, IN: Author.

Jarman-Rohde, L., McFall, J., Kolar, P., & Strom, G. (1997). The changing context of social work practice: Implications and recommendations for social work educators. *Journal of Social Work Education, 33*(1), 29–46.

Konopka, G. (1973). *Requirements of healthy development of adolescent youth.* Washington, DC: Office of Child Development of the Department of Health, Education, and Welfare.

Konopka, G. (1974). *Adolescent girls in conflict.* Englewood Cliffs, NJ: Prentice-Hall.

Konopka, G. (1976). *Young girls: A portrait of adolescence.* Englewood Cliffs, NJ: Prentice-Hall.

Kotlowitz, A. (1991). *There are no children here: The story of two boys growing up in the other America.* New York: Doubleday.

Kozol, J. (1995). *Amazing grace: The lives of children and the conscience of a nation.* New York: Harper-Collins.

Kressley, K., & Skelton, N. (1996). Fully prepared: Weaving the work of youth and civic development. *Wingspread Journal, 18*(4), 4–5.

Ladner, J. (1971). *Tomorrow's tomorrow: The black woman.* New York: Doubleday.

Lam, C. (1997). A cultural perspective on the study of Chinese adolescent development. *Child and Adolescent Social Work Journal, 14*(2), 95–113.

Landrine, H., Klonoff, E., & Brown-Collins, A. (1992). Cultural diversity and methodology in feminist psychology: Critique, proposal, empirical example. *Psychology of Women Quarterly, 16,* 977–992.

Lerner, R. M. (1983). Children and adolescents are producers of their own development. *Developmental Review, 2,* 342–370.

Lerner, R. M. (1991). Changing organism-context relations as the basic process of development: A developmental contextual perspective. *Developmental Psychology, 27,* 27–32.

Lerner, R. M. (1995). *America's youth in crisis: Challenges and choices for programs and policies.* Thousand Oaks, CA: Sage.

Markstrom-Adams, C. (1992). A consideration of intervening factors in adolescent identity formation (pp. 173–192). In G. Adamson, T. Gullotta, and R. Montemayor (Eds.), *Adolescent identity formation.* Newbury Park, CA: Sage.

Merry, S., Berg, P., Baker, S., & Wynn, J. (1995). *The children, youth and families initiatives: Annual report.* Chicago: University of Chicago, Chapin Hall Center for Children.

Miller, J. B. (1986). *Toward a new psychology of women* (2nd ed.). Boston: Beacon.

Montemayor, R., Adams, G., and Gullotta, T. (1989). *From childhood to adolescence: A transitional period.* Newbury Park, CA: Sage.

Morrison, J., Alcorn, S., & Nelums, M. (1997). Empowering community-based programs for youth development. *Journal of Social Work Education, 33*(2), 321–331.

Patterson, S., Sochting, I., & Marcia, J. (1992). The inner space and beyond: Women and identity. In G. Adams, T. Gullotta, and R. Montemayor (Eds.), *Adolescent Identity Formation* (pp. 9–24). Newbury Park: Sage.

Pittman, K. (1993). *Stronger staff, stronger youth conference, October, 1992: Summary report.* Washington, DC: Center for Youth Development and Policy Research.

Pittman, K. (1996, Winter). Community youth development: Three goals in search of connection. *New Designs for Youth Development,* 4–8.

Pittman, K., & Fleming, W. (1991). *A new vision: Promoting youth development.* Washington, DC: Center for Youth Development and Policy Research/ Academy for Educational Development.

Pope, C., Bynum, T., Greene, J., & Feyerherm, W. (1995). *Boys and Girls Clubs in public housing.* Rockville, MD: National Criminal Justice Reference Service.

Public / Private Ventures (1993). *Community change for youth development: Establishing long-term supports in communities for the growth and development of young people.* Philadelphia: Author.

Public / Private Ventures (1995). *Research on voluntary youth serving organizations: Developmental opportunities.* Philadelphia: Author

Quinn, J. (1995). Positive effects of participating in youth organizations. In M. Rutter (Ed.), *Psychosocial disturbances in young people: Challenges for prevention* (pp. 115–228). New York: Cambridge University Press.

Reid, P. (1991). Socialization of black female children. In P. Berman and E. Ramsey (Eds.), *Encyclopedia of adolescence: A developmental perspective* (pp. 85–87). New York: Garland.

Rice, E. (1996). *Making a place for the new American scholar.* Paper presented at the American Association for Higher Education Conference on Faculty Roles and Rewards, Atlanta.

Rosewater, A. (1992). *Comprehensive approaches for children and families: A philanthropic perspective.* Washington, DC: Grantsmaker for Children, Youth and Families.

Rutter, M. (1987). Psychosocial resilience and protective mechanisms. *American Journal of Orthopsychiatry, 57,* 316–331.

Sadker, M., & Sadker, D. (1993). Fair and square: Creating a nonsexist classroom. *Instructor, 102,* 44–46, 67–68.

Sadker, M., & Sadker, D. (1994). *Failing at fairness: How America's schools cheat girls.* New York: Scribner.

Scales, P. (1991). *A portrait of young adolescents in the 1990's: Implications for promoting healthy growth and development.* Carrsboro, NC: Center for Early Adolescence.

Schinke, S., Cole, K., & Orlandi, M. (1991). *Executive summary and final research report: The effects of Boys and Girls Clubs on alcohol and other drug use and related problems in public housing.* Atlanta: Boys and Girls Clubs of America.

Schoor, L. (1988). *Within our reach: Breaking the cycle of the disadvantage.* New York: Anchor Press, Doubleday.

Simmons, R., Garlton-Ford, S., & Blyth, D. (1987). Predicting how a child will cope with the transition to junior high school. In R. Lerner and T. Fochs (Eds.), *Biological-psychosocial interactions in early adolescence* (pp. 75–98). Hillsdale, NJ: Erlbaum Associates.

Sisson, L., Hersen, M., & Van Hasselt, V. (1987). Historical perspectives. In V. Van Hasselt and M. Hersen (Eds.), *Handbook of adolescent psychology* (pp. 3–12). New York: Pergamon.

Smith, C. (1991). *Overview of youth recreation programs in the United States.* Unpublished manuscript, Carnegie Council on Adolescent Development, Washington, D.C.

Spencer, M., & Dornbusch, S. (1990). Challenges in studying minority youth. In S. Felman and G. R. Elliot (Eds.), *At the threshold: The developing adolescent* (pp. 123–146). Cambridge, MA: Harvard University Press.

Spencer, M., & Markstrom-Adams, C. (1990). Identity processes among racial and ethnic children in America. *Child Development, 61,* 290–310.

Steinberg, L. (1985). *Adolescence.* New York: Knopf.

Steinberg, L., Dornbusch, S., & Brown, B. (1992). Ethnic difference in adolescent achievement: An ecological perspective. *American Psychologist, 47*(6), 723–729.

Steinitz, V. & Solomon, E. (1986). *Starting out: Class and community in the lives of workingclass youth.* Philadelphia: Temple University Press.

Tierney, J., Baldwin, J., & Resch, N. (1995). *Making a difference: An impact study of Big Brothers and Big Sisters.* Philadelphia: Public/Private Ventures.

Walker, G. (1996). Back to basics: A new/old direction for youth policy. *Public/Private Ventures News, 11*(2), 1–6.

Ward, J. (1989). Racial identity, formation and transformation. In C. Gilligan, N. Lyons, and T. Hanmer (Eds.), *Making the connections: The relational worlds of adolescent girls at Emma Willard School* (pp. 215–232). Cambridge, MA: Harvard University Press.

Watkins, M. (1995). *Where are the girls? A study of the relational experiences of early adolescent girls considered to be at-risk.* Unpublished doctoral dissertation, Syracuse University, Syracuse, New York.

Watkins, M., & Muelhausen, B. (1997a). *Methods to complete an assumption paper: Youth development intensive field unit workbook.* Unpublished manuscript.

Watkins, M., & Muelhausen, B. (1997b). *Methods to complete a participant observation: Youth development intensive field unit workbook.* Unpublished manuscript.

Watkins, M., & Muelhausen, B. (1997c). *Methods to complete a "walk-in-the-hood": Youth development intensive field unit workbook.* Unpublished manuscript.

Watkins, M., & Muelhausen, B. (1997d). *Methods to complete a capstone paper: Youth development intensive field unit workbook.* Unpublished manuscript.

Wynn, J., Costello, J., Halpern, R., & Richman, H. (1994). *Children, families and communities: A new approach to social services.* Chicago: University of Chicago, Chapin Hall Center for Children.

8

Provision of Services to Older Adults within an Ecological Perspective

IRENE QUEIRO-TAJALLI and LINDA SMITH

*An ecological view provides an integrative framework for social work practice
[with the elderly client population]. . . . Ecology provides an appropriate
metaphor for taking a holistic view of people and environments as a unit in
which neither can be fully understood except in the context of its relationship to
the other.*
—J. A. B. Lee, *The Empowerment Approach to Social Work Practice*

For several decades now, scholars have alerted practitioners and policy-makers to the graying of the U.S. population and its implications on the family, work force, education, delivery of human services, and social policies, to mention just a few (Katz Olson, 1994; Rieske & Holstege, 1996; Rubinstein, Kilbride, & Nagy, 1992). Population data have indicated that the United States, along with several European countries, has a relatively high proportion of people aged 65 years and older compared with other countries (Atchley, 1996). In 1990 there were 31.1 million older adults in the United States, 12.5% of the population. By 2020, the elderly population will reach 52 million, and it is projected that by 2050, there will be 68.5 million older people, raising the percentage of older adults in the total population to 22.9% (Atchley, 1996; U.S. Senate Special Committee on Aging et al., 1991).

Although the current percentage of nonwhite older adults is 14% of the older population, by 2020, 22% of the older population is projected to be nonwhite, and by 2050, 36% will be nonwhite (Hooyman & Kiyak, 1996). African-Americans and Latinos are the two largest groups among non-white older adults. In 1992, an estimated 8% of the African-American population was aged 65 years and older, and only 5% of the Latino population was aged 65 years and older. However, the United States will experience a tremendous increase in the older population of these two groups. It is expected that between 1990 and 2030, the older African-American population and people of other races will grow by 247%, and the older Hispanic population will grow by 395% (U.S. Senate Special Committee on Aging et al., 1991).

In addition, the life expectancy at birth for African-Americans fell slightly, to age 69.4 years from 69.7 years between 1984 and 1987. Although the gap in life expectancy at birth between whites and blacks was 5.6 years in 1984, it increased to 6.2 years in 1987 (ibid.). However, after age 65 years, life expectancy differences by race are smaller. In 1987, at age 65 years, African-Americans could expect to live 15.4 more years, compared with 17 more years for whites at that age. The well-known crossover effect at around age 80 years in the African-American population indicates that, for reasons that are not well understood, the life expectancy for this group begins to exceed that of whites.

Furthermore, elderly people are more likely to be poor than other adults. In 1989, 11.4% of people aged 65 years and older were below the poverty level compared with 10.2% of those aged 18 years to 64 years, and 13.0% of all people younger than age 65 years (ibid.). These figures shrink when the older adults live alone and reside in rural areas. Although 26% of the elderly living in suburban areas have incomes below 125% of the poverty threshold, 37% of those in central cities are poor or near-poor, and an alarming 44.6% of people living in rural areas have incomes below 125% of poverty (ibid.). Older African-Americans and Hispanics living alone have even higher percentages of poverty. That is, 72% of older African-Americans and 60% of Hispanics who live alone have incomes below 125 percent of poverty. Among older whites living alone, 32% have incomes below 125% of poverty (ibid.).

It is within the ramifications of these demographic characteristics that fundamental issues at the individual, family, community, and societal levels need to be addressed. This significant population, with its rich diversity, will challenge the validity of current helping paradigms, social policies—and probably most important—our philosophical approach to aging.

ECOLOGICAL PERSPECTIVE

The ecological perspective provides a holistic view of the person in constant interaction with his or her environment (Zastrow & Kirst-

Ashman). This perspective is useful in addressing the profession's dual commitment to assist individuals to develop their maximum potential and to achieve social and economic justice.

Although some of the terminology used in explaining the ecological perspective, such as *adaptation, interdependence,* and *maladaptive interpersonal processes,* may indicate a rather pathological orientation, this perception may be deceiving. The ecological perspective views the person as a dynamic entity in constant interaction with the environment. Although accommodation may occur in this process, changes also may occur both in the individual and the environment.

> Social workers in gerontological practice that arises from an ecological perspective focus on the coping mechanisms of the older person and the quality of her or his environment.

The interaction between person and milieu is viewed as complementary and essential for growth and well-being. The attention of the perspective to the environment gives the social worker the opportunity to use liberating and empowering approaches. *Liberating* and *empowering approaches* are those that awake the conscience within the client system about the nature and causes of its oppression and enhance capacity of the client system to act individually or as a group to eliminate the oppressive conditions.

Furthermore, one distinguishing characteristic of the ecological approach is "namely the requirement that the person, the environment, and the relations between them be conceptualized in terms of systems, and subsystems within systems" (Bronfenbrenner, 1975, p. 10). Fundamental to the field of gerontology is the conceptualization in the ecological perspective of the foci of attention as being problems resulting from stressful life transitions, maladaptive interpersonal processes, and unresponsive environmental processes (Germain & Gitterman, 1980). In gerontological practice that arises from an ecological perspective, the professional is concerned with the coping mechanisms of the older person and the quality of her or his environment. Although life transitions occur all throughout life, the coping mechanisms and the resources available to the person may vary at different stages in life. For example, older adults experience high levels of poverty, which result in a decreased capacity to buy services and address certain personal needs.

The practitioner also needs to be familiar with the quality of the environment impinging on the older adult and assess the effects of the environment on the individual. *Environment* includes family, friends, community, social policies, services, and so on. The professional must clearly understand the interdependence and reciprocal obligations of the person and her or his environment. The ecological perspective challenges the monolithic view of aging by reminding us that aging itself is a diverse process and that the aged population is a diverse cohort.

ECOLOGICAL PERSPECTIVE AND AGE
AS A STAGE OF DEVELOPMENT

The concept of life course [rather than life cycle stages] is concerned with the timing of life events in relation to the social structures and historical changes affecting them. It thus takes into account the synchronization of individual life transitions with collective family configurations under changing social conditions.

—T. L. Hareven, "The Life Course and Aging in Historical Perspective"

An understanding of the experience of aging is fundamental to research, policy, and practice in the field of aging. At present, life period or life span approaches to aging are prevalent; the Eriksonian model of psychosocial development remains highly influential. Life span theorists have challenged the intense focus on early development of earlier models of human growth and development; they also have identified developmental issues across the life span (Erikson, 1964; Hansen Lemme, 1995; Havighurst, 1953; Levinson, Darrow, Klein, Levinson, & McKee, 1978). Erikson identified eight stages of psychosocial development and distinguished developmental tasks and basic conflicts associated with each

A model where stages are mastered in a linear sequence does not consider cultural variations in behavior, whereas the study of the life course addresses human behavior within changing cultural, social, and political eras. In addition, practice frameworks grounded in the ecological perspective (i.e., empowerment practice, the strengths perspective, and cultural competence) clarify the need to address issues of social justice throughout the life span.

stage. Stage 8 is: Maturity lasts from age 65 years to death. The basic conflict at this stage of development is one of ego integrity versus despair. The essential task is reflection on the meaning of a person's life. When the individual has successfully negotiated this stage, he or she gains a sense of acceptance, a strong sense of self, and a feeling of fulfillment (Erikson, 1950). Erikson recognized the influence of culture and the environment primarily on the rituals through which life tasks are recognized and expressed. Neither the tasks nor the stages themselves are viewed as altered by transactions with variables such as class, culture, gender, or ethnicity. In Erikson's model, as with other life stage models, the essential tasks, conflicts, and stages of development are seen as fixed and universal.

Using the ecological perspective as a lens, particularly as it influences concepts of diversity, the limitations of life span models become apparent. The ecological perspective has a nonlinear base with person-environment transactions looping continuously (Germain & Gitterman, 1987). This view offers a fundamental challenge to the notion that human development moves in a predictable line from birth to death. In their review of trends in human behavior theory, Lyons, Wodarski, and Feit (1988) indicated that life span models have also been criticized for ignoring the effects of time, place, gender and sexual identity formation, racial discrimination, and culture on human development, and for being grounded in stereotypical white, male, middle-class assumptions.

Sociodemographic trends related to grandparenting in the African-American community underscore the necessity for the holistic view of development offered by the ecological perspective. A combination of factors, including an increase in the rate of adolescent pregnancy, in the number of single mothers, in the incarceration of African-American males, and in addiction and substance abuse, have contributed to the increase in parenting grandparents in the African-American community. Aged African-American women are finding themselves parenting grandchildren, and former teenage parents are finding themselves grandparenting prematurely. The following two case examples taken from the authors' clinical experience illustrate this point:

> Mrs. Satterwhite came to the Stuyvesant mental health clinic because "her nerves [were] bad." She was having trouble sleeping, and had experienced loss of appetite. She was taking time off from work because of family demands and was concerned about losing her job. The family's income was limited. In addition, drug traffic in the neighborhood had increased and the family was feeling unsafe. Mrs. Satterwhite was divorced and the only wage earner in the family. Her eldest daughter, aged 15 years, and her daughter's 9-month-old son were living in the household. Mrs. Satterwhite shared caretaking responsibility for the baby in the evening so that her daughter could complete her homework. Mrs. Satterwhite had two younger children, aged 7 and 9 years, who seemed to demand more attention since the birth of her grandson. At age 32 Mrs. S. felt "old" and resented the lack of time she had for herself. This was not what she expected at this stage of her life.

> "Ma Bennett," as she was known throughout the neighborhood, came to the agency for "whatever help" she could get to help her cope with raising her grandchildren aged 8 and 12 years. Ma Bennett's daughter died 6 years earlier from the effects of alcoholism. The children's father sent money and visited intermittently, but was not in a position to care for the children full-time. Ma Bennett, aged 67 years, and her husband, aged 68 years, found themselves parenting during what was to be their retirement.

> Ma Bennett described her situation as a mixed blessing. On the one hand, the children kept her young and up on events she might have otherwise ignored. They made her feel closer to the daughter she had lost and were a painful reminder of that loss. Neither she nor her husband could even think about dying until the children had at least graduated from high school. On the other hand, both of them were "permanently tired" and worried about

the effects of exhaustion on their health. They were living on Social Security and a small pension and had to be very careful with money. Ma Bennett would have liked to have moved out of the neighborhood to give her grandchildren a better chance than her daughter had had, but her ties there were strong and she could not afford it. Like Mrs. S., this is not what Ma Bennett had been planning to do at this age.

At age 32 years, Mrs. Satterwhite would be classified as a young adult in an Eriksonian model of development. Early grandparenting, coupled with parenting young children, altered her view of herself as well as the life tasks at center stage. According to the life span model, Ma Bennett should have been reviewing her life and coming to terms with her successes and failures instead of focusing on preparing another generation. Both clients share devalued status as low-income, African-American women. Because of that status, their limited access to resources and opportunities and the nonnutritive nature of their environments each contributed to altered roles and life tasks. Interventions grounded in the assumption that certain tasks indicate optimal development clearly would be inadequate. When the effects of transactions with the environment have not been considered, the difficulties of members of devalued group members are erroneously interpreted as originating from failures in personal development. This deficit perspective is inconsistent with the values of belief in human dignity, human worth, and social justice (Miley, O'Melia, & Dubois, 1995).

The life model approach to practice (Germain & Gitterman, 1980, 1987) applies ecological principles to human growth and development in a way that is consistent with the values and ethics of the profession. The life model approach directs attention to three interdependent realms that compose the life space of the individual: life transitions, interpersonal processes, and environmental processes. Conceptualizing life transitions as significant events over the life span allows for the dynamism and diversity of the aging experience, and focusing on the play between interpersonal and environmental processes directs social worker's attention to macro- and microconcerns. Although the life model approach recognizes culture as significant, culture is viewed as one of many variables within interpersonal and environmental processes; culture provides the context of transactions, including developmental transactions.

The following are selected ecological principles presented to examine older adults' strengths and challenges in a world enriched by new technological advances but also impoverished by a growing gap between "the haves" and "the have nots." Factors contributing to this impoverishment include the international trend to support neoliberal policies that call for privatization of the welfare state, deindustralization, unemployment, and loyalty to few multinational corporations.

CULTURAL ECOLOGY AND SERVICES
TO THE AGED POPULATION

Adaption is the central action-oriented concept of an ecological framework.
—J. A. B. Lee, *The Empowerment Approach to Social Work Practice*

*Cultural ecology provides a framework for broadening our conceptions of
environmental influences on competencies and their acquisition.*
—J. Ogbu, "Origins of Human Competence:
A Cultural Ecological Perspective"

Concepts from cultural anthropology (LeVine, 1967; Ogbu, 1981) grounded in the ecological perspective such as culture add to our understanding of human development and aging in a way that can enhance service. *Culture* has been defined as a "cognitive map" of a self-identified group (Spradley, 1979), and as the prescribed norms of conduct, beliefs, values, and skills of a given society.

Ogbu (1981) theorized that the obtaining, perfecting, and passing on of "instrumental competencies" constitute an organizing concept in human growth and development, and that instrumental competencies are culturally bound. *Instrumental competence,* which is similar to operative intelligence, is the ability to apply what is known rather than merely knowing (ibid., p. 414). Furthermore, subsistence is a primary driving force behind instrumental competencies. Instrumental competencies develop out of a cultural ecology. Within a cultural ecology, transactions between a specific population, the population's environmental influences, its cultural values, and social organizations strongly influence the growth and development, personal attributes, and behaviors of group members. This process is grounded in the concept of adaptedness in the ecological perspective. According to Germain and Gitterman (1987), in adaptedness,

> The concept of competence is understood in the context of individual agency, group identity, group processes, and that of indigenous theories of success.

> biological, cognitive, emotional and social adaptations are active efforts to effect personal change in order to meet environmental demands and take advantage of environmental opportunities or to effect environmental change so that social and physical environments will be more responsive to people's needs, rights, and goals. (p. 489)

Ogbu's concept of cultural ecology takes the notions of competence and adaptiveness still further by placing greater emphasis on group identity, group processes, and the quest for group survival. A final guiding concept of cultural ecology is that of indigenous theories of success. Every group has a theory of success, which develops out of cultural tasks, rewards in society, and consideration of costs. In other words, a folk theory of success will reflect the values of the group and its instrumental competencies. Using this framework, the practitioner can expect that the process and meaning of aging will be different for members of different groups, as will the interpretation of aging successfully. For example, in African-American churches, the role of "church mother" is accorded to older black women who are highly respected and receive recognition from the community for their nurturing role (the passing on of competencies) and deep spirituality. The following passage from the Wilson and Mulally (1983) collection of narratives from older black women in the South depicts this model of successful aging:

> Let God fight the battle, and He will face it. When you think nothing's coming your way, He'll just move in so nice. And that's the reason I serve the Lord. I get a blessing. Every day. Not one day, but every day. I get my blessing. I'm seventy-five years old. And so young people call and ask me and say, "Mrs. Roundtree, such and such-a thing." I say, "Hold your peace, honey. Let God fight the battle." (p. 8)

In the traditional Hispanic culture, older adults are respected and venerated; they keep the family together and teach cultural norms and behaviors to younger generations. Similarly to the older woman in the black community, the Latina older woman plays an important role within the family and the community. The following excerpt from *Mi Abuela Fumaba Puros* (*My Grandma Smoked Cigars*) by Sabine R. Ulibarri (1977) illustrates some of the rich dimensions of the Latina older woman:

> The years went by. I was now a professor. One day we returned to visit the grandmother. . . . With the death of my father, my grandmother got rid of all the stock. The ranch hands disappeared with the stock . . .
> When we left the highway and took the little used and much abused road full of the accustomed ruts, the old memories took possession of us. Suddenly we saw a column of black smoke rising beyond the hill. My sister shouted. "Grandma's house" . . .
> When we came out of the pine grove, we saw that only ruins remained of the house of the grandmother. . . . We found her surrounded by the few things that were saved. Surrounded also by the neighbors of all the ranches in the region who rushed to help when they saw the smoke. I don't know what I expected but it did not surprise me to find her directing all the activities, giving orders. No tears, no whimpers, no laments. "God gives and God takes away, my son. Blessed be His Holy Name". . . . After supper my

grandmother disappeared. I looked for her apprehensively. I found her where I could very well have suspected. At the top of the hill. Profiled by the moon. The wind in her face. Her skirt flapping in the wind. I saw her grow. And she was what she had always been: straight, tall and slender. I saw the ash of her cigar light up. She was with my grandfather, the wicked one, the bold one, the quarrelsome one. Now the decisions would be made, the positions would be taken. She was regaining her spiritual strength. Tomorrow would be another day, but my grandmother would continue being the same one. And I was happy. (pp. 27, 29)

As these vignettes illustrate, the ecological perspective as reflected in the concept of cultural ecology can be used to help practitioners recognize the strengths of older clients. However, social workers need to critically analyze culture, searching for those cultural aspects that are oppressive to its own members, in this case, to older people in general and older women in particular. Some historians have pointed out that older adults have not always been treated with respect and fairness (Fischer, 1978). Stereotypes that depict older adults as feeble, old-fashioned, and incapable of understanding new trends diminish their "value" as contributors to society. Feminist theories such as cultural and ecofeminist theories, lesbian feminist theory, postmodern feminist theory, womanism, and global feminism (Flynn Saulnier, 1996) are some of the alternative conceptual feminist frameworks that can assist the practitioner to understand older women within the context of women's present realities.

Practitioners should be aware that aging might present less dramatic life changes for members of devalued groups than it does for members of privileged groups. The challenges of racism persist across the life span. To be aged and black suggests mastery over the instrumental competencies associated with subsistence, with fewer opportunities, with illness, and so on. Along with confronting the obstacles faced by all elderly members of society, elderly members of minority (*minority* refers to a power differential) groups experience a sense of triumph at having survived at all. Services directed at older members of minority groups are frequently justified by research that has compared statistics of their socioeconomic status to that of members of the dominant group in society. The statistics are cited so frequently that they become the basis of research-generated stereotypes of elderly people (Stoller & Gibson, 1994). The stereotypes, in turn, begin to influence social workers' perception of clients and also direct interventions. The unintentional result is a deficit model of practice with the elderly population. The ecological perspective reminds us that the unique coping responses of the elderly population are as significant as the social problems they may experience. Ecologically based services for aged people maintain a dual focus on fostering client competence and confronting oppression, both of which involve recognition and use of those cultural traits that are empowering to the individual.

EMPOWERMENT, THE STRENGTHS PERSPECTIVE, AND SERVICES TO THE AGED POPULATION

Intrinsic to the ecological theory of the strengths model of practice is a dual commitment to deliver services in collaboration with clients and to confront dysfunctional service and support systems that thwart client development.
—C. J. Tice and K. Perkins, *Mental Health Issues and Aging—Building on the Strengths of Older Persons*

The ecological perspective laid the groundwork for two practice frameworks aimed at confronting oppression: the empowerment approach and the strengths perspective.

Empowerment Approach

The empowerment approach to practice is aimed at reducing the powerlessness of members of stigmatized groups on personal, collective, and sociopolitical levels (Lee, 1994; Solomon, 1976). Empowerment involves using culturally determined strategies to mobilize a range of resources (Pinderhughes, 1989; Simon, 1990). There are several challenges in using an empowerment approach to services for aged people. Empowerment emphasizes self-determination and working collaboratively with clients. The stereotype of aged people as frail and incompetent coupled with the reality of increasing health concerns affect the social worker's perception of the aged client's decision-making ability and ability to work collaboratively. To sort these issues of empowerment, the social worker must be willing to explore her or his own assumptions about aging in relation to the client's situation at hand through the process of critical consciousness. *Critical consciousness* is a nondeterministic way of thinking, that "always submits causality to analysis" (Lee, 1994, p. 116). From this perspective, it is impossible to rely on labels such as dementia to determine if collaboration with an elderly client is possible. Instead, the door to collaboration is opened to the greatest extent possible at a given moment in time.

The suspension of disbelief on the part of the practitioner is another requirement of the empowerment approach that presents demands in delivering services to the elderly. *Suspension of disbelief* refers to a profound level of respect for the integrity of the client's story (Green, 1995;

Lee, 1994; Lum, 1996; Pinderhughes, 1989). Society patronizes the elderly population. The practitioner must be careful not to dismiss communications from elderly clients or to frame those communications in terms of loss of memory or dementia.

Empowerment also must include assisting people in overcoming blocks to resources and opportunities. Although aging may be associated with disengagement from society, this is a highly individualized, non-linear process. Examples of political activism among the elderly population abound (Nelson Mandela, the American Association of Retired Persons, the Grey Panthers, and so forth), but aside from voter registration efforts, the literature reflects a lack of attention to organizing older members of minority groups to achieve political goals. Empowerment-based services to minority aged clients should include information about resources and opportunities as well as assistance in mobilizing seniors for political action.

Strengths Perspective

The strengths perspective takes the people and environment principle from the ecological perspective and places goodness-of-fit between person-environment transactions at its center (Tice & Perkins, 1996). The strengths perspective acknowledges obstacles to power, resources, and opportunities for the aged population but maintains that the change process stems from the strengths embedded in people and their environments (Saleebey, 1992).

> Consequently, micro social work intervention combines with macro practice as the client begins to place demands on the larger society for change and support. The strengths model engages social workers and clients in forms of empowerment by undermining the notion that people at various levels of income or retired from employment must settle for less than desirable benefits or conditions. (Tice & Perkins, 1996, p. 23)

The strengths perspective assists practitioners and older clients in distinguishing the differences between acceptance, which is often a healthy appropriate stage of aging, and internalizing oppression, which is not. Additional features of the strengths perspective include a holistic viewpoint, an emphasis on collaboration with clients, an approach to the environment as an "oasis of resources," the reframing of problems in terms of client wants, and a restriction on the use of labels and diagnostic categories (Cowger, 1992; Lum, 1996; Tice & Perkins, 1996). The strengths perspective demands that practitioners look past the losses associated with aging (e.g., income, status, and relationships) to the aged client's coping capacities. The strengths assessment is a tool to help social worker and client identify the specific, culturally bound capacities of the elderly population. Using a strengths assessment, the social worker and client collaborate to identify current client wants and needs in specific life domains or environments. In contrast, a diagnostic assessment is aimed at identifying pathology and other problem behaviors (Tice & Perkins, 1996, p. 38).

The *process* of conducting a strengths assessment as well as the outcomes are intended to be liberating and healing. The present focus of the strengths assessment means it must be continuously revised throughout the social worker–client relationship (Weick, Rapp, Sullivan, & Kisthardt, 1989). Cowger (1992) identified the following domains of client strength: cognition, emotion, motivation, coping, and interpersonal. Openness to the other viewpoints is a cognitive strength, whereas a repertoire of problem-solving skills is a coping strength. In addition to these person-centered strengths, strengths exist in environments or life domains, such as financial, education, and leisure and recreation. These domains also provide the structure for the identification of client goals (Tice & Perkins, 1996, pp. 36–37). Aged members of stigmatized groups have a wealth of untapped knowledge and experience that, when accessed through the strengths assessment, can be used as a resource for social change as well as personal change.

Environment

Social workers in the field of aging combine a strengths assessment with an assessment of the client's environment. The quality of the environment as reflected in the family, social supports, and so forth is an indicator of the extent to which the older person will succeed in accomplishing those tasks specific to this stage of life.

The Family.   Beginning with the immediate environment, the family is a source of emotional and—many times—financial support. However, the family itself is under a great deal of pressure; therefore, when assessing the role of the family the practitioner needs to decode or separate the myths from the realities surrounding the role of the family in the life of elderly clients. Among people aged 65 years and older, 31% live alone, and only 15% reside with children, relatives, or friends (U.S. Senate Special Committee on Aging et al., 1991). Contrary to common thinking, the proportion of older African-Americans living alone is slightly higher (33%) than that of older whites (31%). The proportion of older Latinos living alone is 22% (U.S. Bureau of the Census, 1990). Those older adults living alone are at a higher risk of being poor. At the same time, nearly 80% of those who live by themselves are women (Crispell & Frey, 1995);

this figure will increase to 85% by 2020. Some of the reasons for this phenomenon are that widowed or divorced men are more likely to remarry, and women in general have a longer life expectancy and tend to marry men several years older than themselves. Quite often, these women believe their economic status is diminished by partners' costly illnesses and decrease in earnings. The oldest old women are at a higher incidence of risk as a result of not having much in terms of personal supports and economic reserves.

Although a large number of elderly people live alone, they receive care from the family. Within the family, it is unquestionable that women have been and still are the main caregivers for their elderly relatives. According to U.S. Bureau of the Census (1993), families, especially adult daughters and daughters-in-law, provide care and perform a series of tasks— transportation, household tasks, shopping, and so forth—to help maintain the older person's independence. Even though caregiving can result in feelings of self-worth and personal satisfaction (Foster & Brizins, 1993), women also pay a dear price in terms of their own well-being. Elaine Brody (1990) mentioned several manifestations in female caregivers including emotional exhaustion, demoralization, sleeplessness, guilt, and frustration. Another negative affect of caregiving on women is that they may need to decrease their working hours and in many instances, quit their jobs to take care of a frail relative. Women spend an average of 11 years out of the work force to take care of offspring and elderly parents, compared with 1.3 years for men (U.S. House of Representatives, Select Committee on Aging, 1990). Obviously, a decrease in earnings has a negative impact on a woman's current as well as future economic situation.

It is romanticized in the literature that minority families take care of their own seniors. Although many cultural groups do respect and value their older family members, the reality is that most of these groups are poor. Consequently, it is difficult for them to shelter an older person in already crowded quarters and to share with her or him the scarce resources much needed for the younger generations. In addition, there may be magical thinking that once a person reaches a certain age (e.g., 55, 62, or 65 years) unsolved family conflicts will disappear and the older person will live happily ever after in the nucleus of the family. Such a fantasy may prove productive for literature books, but not for practitioners who need to be prepared to work with those conflicts in their daily practice. Sexual orientation is a painful issue for many families. It is well documented that many older lesbian and gay people have been marginalized all of their lives by both their families and society (Hooyman & Kiyak, 1996), making it difficult for older lesbians and gays to perceive the family as a support system. In general, there may exist numerous reasons why a "good fit" does not exist between older persons and their families. For example, relatives who rejected a lesbian aunt all along will not openly entertain the idea of moving her into their home. Well-to-do relatives may feel embarrassed in the presence of an uneducated older relative. A daughter or a son may be reluctant to have to take care of an uncaring, unloving, and abusive parent. It is within the dilemmas of these possible scenarios that the practitioner needs to assess with the older person the goodness-of-fit between her or him and the family.

Given these realities then, the quality of the home environment becomes essential to assess older persons' probability to succeed in that environment. For many elderly people, the home is a symbol of independence (Rubinstein et al., 1992). Thus, using an ecological approach, the practitioner needs to be attuned to the fine line between the meaning of independence as desired by the elderly person and the critical concept of interdependence as described by the ecological perspective.

The Geographical Community. As the ecological perspective encompasses the community, the practitioner needs to assess the qualities of the community where the older person lives. It is probably in thinking "community" that the ecological perspective can help the practitioner the most. *Community* may be classified as geographical and functional: *geographical community* refers to those communities where people's interactions are based, among others, on customs, norms, and shared history within a given geographical location, such as neighborhoods, or rural communities; *functional community* refers to people's interactions based on a common characteristic or common interest regardless of geographical location, such as the Latino community or the aging community. In terms of geographical communities, the practitioner needs to assess a number of variables, for example, the physical aspects of the neighborhood (housing conditions; streets that are safe, clean, well lighted, free of health hazards; availability of green spaces); communication patterns among neighbors; styles of community leadership; and the degree of involvement exercised by the community in deciding its own destiny, degree of security, transportation, recreational facilities, and other types of relevant services to elderly citizens offered by community agencies. It is through the assessment of these and other community variables that the practitioner can understand the areas in which there is a goodness-of-fit as well as a "lack of fit" between the older person and her or his environment. It is also within the context of the environment that connections occur.

Functional Communities. Most older adults today grew up in geographical communities where their most important relations developed and blossomed. They experienced firsthand the community functions as described by Warren (1973): socialization, mutual support, social participation, production-distribution-consumption, and social control. It is not uncommon for older adults to reminisce about the goodness of the geographical communities where they lived most of their lives. However, as structural changes occur in society, the geographical community has lost some of its meaning for community residents and, as a result, many older adults have found refuge in functional communities. Functional communities may reduce the sense of isolation that many older adults experience in their residential areas. This is illustrated in the following case vignette taken from the authors' social work experience:

> This is the case of Mr. Lee who lives in a low-income community of south Chicago. A native of the area, he clearly remembers the stories his grandparents used to tell him about their immigration to this country and how they raised his father in an atmosphere hostile to Asians. To survive, his family always had to depend on their own people regardless of where they lived. For Mr. Lee this is also a reality. His economic and emotional supports stem from his Asian-American friends living in different areas of the state and much less from his actual geographical community. When cultural festivals, poetry reading nights, and other events are organized by the Asian-American community, he forgets about his aches and pains and attends them regardless of the location. On one occasion, he admitted that, thanks to this community, he was able to confront some difficult economic times.

Certainly, Mr. Lee's linkages with his functional community strengthened his individual functioning and provided him with a sense of well-being and control over his social relationships.

Connections. *Connections,* as understood by the authors of this chapter, are those meaningful ties a person has with a partner, relatives, friends, neighbors, networks, agencies, and other significant systems. Furthermore, these connections may be nurtured by direct or face-to-face interaction, or indirect interactions by way of correspondence, telecommunication, mail, or e-mail. Older immigrants have typically relied on indirect interactions as seen in another vignette.

> This is the case of Ms. Khanum who came to the U.S. with her husband and two sons 20 years ago. Her oldest daughter, married to a successful lawyer, stayed in the old country. At the beginning, Ms. Khanum used to travel to her country to visit with her family, friends, and neighbors; however, after her husband died and her income was considerably reduced, she stopped traveling. Since then, mail has special meaning for her. Her connections with her loved ones, even with one of the sons who moved to California, is by mail. Through her only granddaughter in town, she has become familiar with e-mail and the Internet, and now has decided to attend a short summer training on the use of the Internet at one of the high schools within walking distance from her home. She feels delighted to know that soon she will be

communicating daily with her daughter and grandchildren. As she was telling the news to her Medicaid worker her face brightened in anticipation of this new way of keeping in touch with her family, and she added, "My body may be weak to travel long distances but my mind can do the job."

Some futurists have predicted that, as the information tools of the interactive society are made more available, people will become more connected to others (Eder, 1997). Although there is concern that this new wave of connections may also bring isolation, the benefits to older adults promise to be far more important than the drawbacks. Overall, the quality and array of connections in the life of an older person will determine the extent to which that person feels physically or psychologically isolated.

Community Services.   Although services are part of the community, they are discussed separately, given their importance in the life of elderly people. Older adults' independent living is closely related to the type of services offered by the community, such as transportation, shopping centers, recreational facilities, entertainment facilities, and libraries, in general, and human services, in particular. As with younger people, older adults need quality community services. In some ways, as people grow older and become less mobile, the availability of those services in the community becomes primordial. Human services are pivotal in the life of older adults. Not only should these services be present in the community but they should also be sensitive to older adults' needs. How many of those agencies have programs geared to the elderly population? How well trained are the staff to work with older adults? How inviting is the agency atmosphere to older adults? Are the agency and its services sensitive to ethnic or racial older groups? Do older adults have a voice in the agency? These are just some of the questions that the practitioner needs to address to determine the quality of the human services delivery system in the community. By asking herself similar questions, Ms. Pastorini's social worker began to understand why her client did not want to attend any functions at the nearby community center:

Ms. Pastorini immigrated from Bolivia when she was 46 years old and worked in domestic services until age 65 years. The social worker from the area council on aging worked with Ms. Pastorini in a number of areas, one being Ms. Pastorini's need for socialization with other community members. At the beginning of their professional relationship, she urged Ms. Pastorini to attend the senior activities at the local community center. Ms. Pastorini would say yes but would not attend. When asked if she had gone, she would respond that she was busy for that type of activity or would ignore the question. Confronted one day by the social worker, Ms. Pastorini said "You do not understand. . . . You do not understand." The social worker wanted to ask Ms. Pastorini what she meant, but felt she was unprepared to pursue the issue.

From that time on, the social worker began to familiarize herself about Bolivia using books at the library and surfing the Internet. She also began to ask Ms. Pastorini about Bolivia to take on the role of the learner (Green, 1995). Also, she began to assess the community center approach to serving older adults, specifically those who were not Anglo. To her surprise, she found little in terms of symbols related to older adults and ethnic minorities. Most posters and photographs from center activities related to younger, fair-skinned, blue-eyed people. Also, she learned that the board of directors was formed primarily by middle-age community representatives, with a youth representative, but no senior representative. As the social worker felt more comfortable with diversity issues and began to understand some of the barriers at the community center, she asked Ms. Pastorini what is it that she did not understand about Ms. Pastorini attending the center. In her usual broken English and with a smile on her face, Ms. Pastorini responded, "Well, my friend, I think by now you can answer that question yourself. What you did not understand is that the community center people do not resemble my own people; they look more like my past employers than my friends. But most important, I am fearful of not being understood. I have not socialized much with Americans outside my work. How about if my behavior does not meet their approval? Once I went there, but I felt I was not welcome. I have a few Latin American friends and they feel the same way. One of them told me that the meals for seniors were no way similar to ours. . . . See, why go there? I had seen discrimination in my early days in this country. At that time, I had to stand it for my own survival, but now I am economically independent and I don't need that treatment." In a few words, Ms. Pastorini explained the lack of ethnic sensitivity of that agency that took the social worker so many months to comprehend.

The following case example based on the authors' experiences illustrates how one agency with an ecologically based approach to services to aged clients operationalized concepts related to strengths and empowerment theory:

Elder Family Service (EFS) is a private not-for-profit organization that provides case management and counseling services to aged clients, their families, and caregivers. Case management services included budgeting, arranging for home care, providing assistance with Medicaid and Medicare applications, offering assistance in obtaining legal services, and helping with travel arrangements. The agency's holistic approach to service required intense involvement with whatever systems affected each client's life. Although some clients were seen in the agency, many clients were routinely seen at home, at senior citizens centers, or in residential care agencies. Seeing clients on their home turf prevented some of the transportation problems faced by aged clients, provided relief for overburdened caregivers, and made it easier for social workers and clients to explore and recognize environmental resources. Social worker familiarity with family, neighbors, friends, and local organizations also facilitated resolution of crises when they arose. EFS used a team approach: clients had access to a psychologist, psychiatrists, social workers with a master of social work degree, and a creative arts therapist. The EFS referral network included physicians, physical therapists, and lawyers, all specializing in practice with the aged population. Increasing access to resources and opportunities was part of the agency's effort to participate in the empowerment of clients.

The case example of Mrs. Torrez illustrates EFS in action:

Mrs. Torrez, a 78-year-old Black Hispanic widow, was originally from Panama. She had been living in her Brooklyn neighborhood for nearly half a century. Mrs. Torrez had been a neighborhood fixture. She had known all the small business owners, cared for neighborhood children, and maintained deep ties with her neighbors. The neighborhood had changed. Many of her neighbors had either moved or died. Her son had moved to a neighboring state, and her daughter lived two and a half hours away. Both children had offered to take Mrs. Torrez in, but she valued her independence and thought she would be unable to get used to a new environment. Mrs. Torrez's daughter was her primary caregiver. She came to Brooklyn on a regular basis to buy food for her mother, but found that this was becoming a considerable strain. As a result, she contacted EFS. In addition, Mrs. Torrez had begun to insist that a mysterious man was coming in and stealing food from the refrigerator. A team from EFS arranged a visit to Mrs. Torrez's home while her daughter was present to develop a service plan. Mrs. Torrez felt "stuck" (in her own words). She realized that she could not bring back the life she had led in the neighborhood, but she did not know how to move forward. Among the many strengths identified were her ability to form deep friendship and kinship ties, her bi-lingualism, a history of political involvement as a member of the "Democratic Club," and strong spiritual beliefs.

During the initial team visit, a psychiatrist made an evaluation and a social worker began the process of helping Mrs. Torrez apply for Medicaid. Medicaid would pay for a home attendant who could shop for groceries and do some of the other tasks currently being done by Mrs. Torrez's daughter. The social worker continued to make home visits around case management needs and to work on the steps they had identified to help Mrs. Torrez "move forward." Despite these intensive services, food was still disappearing from Mrs. Torrez's refrigerator. Rather than dismiss this claim as a lie or a product of memory loss, the social worker continued to explore the issue with Mrs. Torrez. Because of the ecological base of EFS's approach to service, the social worker sought the involvement of neighbors and friends, including the building superintendent who had been close to the family, to help resolve the issue of the missing food. The superintendent eventually observed Mrs. Torrez throwing food out of her back window. Mrs. Torrez reasoned that older people are overlooked unless they were in crisis. She had looked forward to her home visits and enjoyed the increase in attention from her remaining neighbors and family. Older people in Panama were treated with more respect. This opened the door to more honest discussion about her anger and fear of abandonment. Rather than viewing her action as evidence of psychopathology, the social worker and Mrs. Torrez explored how she could put her obvious problem-solving skills to better use. As Mrs. Torrez's daughter's caregiver responsibilities lessened, she realized she had been treating her mother primarily as a burden. She then was willing to allow Mrs. Torrez to play a more active role as a grandparent and most trusted advisor. (Smith, 1991)

This case example demonstrates the complexity of providing ecologically based services to the aged population. The ecological perspective leads to an intensive form of service around the client's socioeconomic, psychological, and physical needs.

IMPLICATIONS FOR SOCIAL POLICIES AND SERVICES

There have been significant gains in the policy arena for older Americans, but many challenges remain. The recent changes in social security eligibility requirements, which, as of this writing, exclude legal, noncitizen immigrants as beneficiaries, unfairly target the elderly population. Elderly legal immigrants may find themselves without income, health insurance, or food stamps. This measure reflects popular sentiment against elderly immigrants "swelling the welfare rolls" (as in *Latino Link* and ACLU publications). Whether this measure remains in place, it alerts social workers to a combination of generational tension and ageism that is likely to influence future policies. In addition, as low-income families attempt to move from Temporary Assistance to Needy Families to work, their ability to play a supportive role with elderly family members is likely to be diminished.

Current changes in the welfare system place holistic services to the aged population in jeopardy. For example, the time the social worker in the case example spent interacting with neighbors was not covered by insurance, nor would it be covered under Medicaid. Social workers and their allies must lobby for third-party payment for the extensive case management services that evolve from the ecological perspective, to ensure these services will remain a reality. As the philosophy, goals, and expected outcomes of these policies are translated into programs and services, the social worker needs to be involved in this process to ensure that older adults' dignity and well-being are not sacrificed in pursuit of less sensitive programs oriented to older adults.

The authors of this chapter recognize that the social services delivery system is in need of reform; however, this reform should be based on the knowledge, information, and experience accumulated throughout the 20th century. Services to the elderly population should be the result of combining the concepts of the ecological perspective, empowerment perspective, strengths perspective, and feminist thinking within the broader concept of social and economic justice. The continuum of services to older adults should have the mark of sensitivity toward ethnic, racial, gender, sexual orientation, physical and mental abilities, and other dimensions included in the aging community. Aging is not a static and monolithic concept, rather, it is a combination of individual and social characteristics in constant interaction with each other to form that precious person called the older adult.

REFERENCES

Atchley, R. C. (1996). *Social forces and aging. An introduction to social gerontology* (8th ed.). Belmont, CA: Wadsworth.

Brody, E. M. (1990). *Women in the middle: Their parent-care years.* New York: Springer.

Bronfenbrenner, U. (1975, July). *The ecology of human development in retrospect and prospect.* Paper presented at the Conference on Ecological Factors in Human Development held by the International Society for the Study of Behavioral Development, University of Surrey, Guildford, England.

Cowger, C. D. (1992). Assessment of client strengths. In D. Saleebey (Ed.), *The strengths perspective in social work practice* (pp. 139–147). New York: Longman.

Crispell, D., & Frey, W. H. (1995). America maturity. In H. Cox (Ed.), *Aging* (10th ed.) (pp. 119–125). Guilford, CT: Dushkin.

Eder, P. F. (1997). The emerging interactive society. *Futurist, 31*(3), 43–46.

Erikson, E. H. (1950). *Childhood and society* (1st ed.). New York: W. W. Norton.

Erikson, E. H. (1964). *Childhood and society* (2nd ed.). New York: W. W. Norton.

Fischer, D. H. (1978). *Growing old in America.* New York: Oxford University Press.

Flynn Saulnier, C. (1996). *Feminist theories and social work.* Binghamton, NY: Haworth.

Foster, S. E., & Brizins, J. A. (1993). Caring too much? American women and the nation's caregiving crisis. In J. Allen and A. Pifer, *Women on the front lines: Meeting the challenge of an aging America.* Washington DC: Urban Institute Press.

Germain, C. B., & Gitterman, A. (1980). *The life model of social work practice.* New York: Columbia University Press.

Germain, C. B., & Gitterman, A. (1987). Ecological perspectives. In A. Minahan (Editor-in-Chief), *Encyclopedia of Social Work* (18th ed.) (pp. 488–499). Silver Spring, MD: NASW Press.

Green, J. W. (1995). *Cultural awareness in the human services. A multi-ethnic approach* (2nd ed.). Boston: Allyn & Bacon.

Hansen Lemme, B. (1995). *Development in adulthood.* Boston: Allyn & Bacon.

Hareven, T. L. (1981). The life course and aging in historical perspective. In T. K. Hareven and K. J. Adams (Eds.), *Aging and life course transitions: An interdisciplinary perspective,* pp. 1–26. New York: Guilford.

Havighurst, R. (1953). *Human development and education.* New York: Longmans, Green.

Hooyman, N., & Kiyak, H. A. (1996). *Social gerontology: A multidisciplinary perspective* (4th ed.). Boston: Allyn & Bacon.

Katz Olson, L. (Ed.) (1994). *The graying of the world. Who will care for the frail elderly?* New York: Haworth.

Lee, J. A. B. (1994). *The empowerment approach to social work practice.* New York: Columbia University Press.

LeVine, R. W. (1967). *Dreams and deeds: Achievement motivation in Nigeria.* Chicago: University of Chicago Press.

Levinson, D. J., Darrow, C. M., Klein, E. B., Levinson, M. H., & McKee, B. (1978). *The seasons of a man's life.* New York: Knopf.

Lum, D. (Ed.) (1996). *Social work practice and people of color: A process-stage approach.* Pacific Grove, CA: Brooks/Cole.

Lyons, P. W., Wodarski, J. S., & Feit, M. D. (1998). Human behavior theory: Emerging trends and issues. *Journal of Human Behavior in the Social Environment, 1*(1), 1–21.

Miley, K. M., O'Melia, M., & Dubois, B. L. (1995). *Generalist social work practice: An empowering approach.* Boston: Allyn & Bacon.

Ogbu, J. (1981). Origins of human competence: A cultural ecological perspective. *Child Development, 52,* 413–429.

Pinderhughes, E. (1989). *Understanding race, ethnicity and power: The key to efficacy in clinical practice.* New York: Free Press.

Riekse, R. J., & Holstege, H. (1996). *Growing older in America.* New York: McGraw-Hill.

Rubinstein, R. L., Kilbride, J. C., & Nagy, S. (1992). *Elders living alone: Frailty and the perception of choice.* Hawthorne, NY: Aldine de Gruyter.

Saleebey, D. (Ed.) (1992). *The strengths perspective in social work practice.* New York: Longman.

Simon, B. L. (1990). Rethinking empowerment. *Journal of Progressive Human Services, 1*(1), 27–39.

Smith, L. A. (1991). Elder family services: A holistic approach to service delivery. *Center for Aging Research and Educational Services Report, 3*(1).

Solomon, B. (1976). *Black empowerment: Social work in oppressed communities.* New York: Columbia University Press.

Spradley, J. F. (1979). *The ethnographic interview.* New York: Holt, Rinehart and Winston.

Stoller, E. P., & Gibson, R. C. (Eds.) (1994). *Worlds of difference: Inequality in the aging experience.* Thousands Oaks, CA: Pine Forge.

Tice, C. J., & Perkins, K. (1996). *Mental health issues and aging—Building on the strengths of older persons.* Pacific Grove, CA: Brooks/Cole.

U.S. House of Representatives, Select Committee on Aging (1990). *Women, caregiving, and poverty: Options to improve social security.* Washington, DC: U.S. Government Printing Office.

U.S. Senate Special Committee on Aging et al. (1991). *Aging America: Trends and projections* [DHHS Publication No. (FcoA) 91-28001]. Washington, DC: U.S. Department of Health and Human Services.

U.S. Bureau of the Census (1990). *Marital status and living arrangements: 1989.* In *Current population reports* (Series P-20, No. 445). Washington, DC: U.S. Department of Commerce.

U.S. Bureau of the Census (1993). *Current population reports* (Special Studies, pp. 23–178 R V), *Sixty-Five Plus in America* (May). Washington, DC: U.S. Department of Commerce.

Ulibarri, S. R. (1977). *Mi abuela fumaba puros y otros cuentos de Tierra Amarilla.* [My grandma smoked cigars and other stories of Tierra Amarilla.] Berkeley, CA: Quinto Sol.

Warren, R. L. (Ed.) (1973). *Perspectives on the American community: A book of readings* (2nd ed.). Chicago: Rand McNally.

Weick, A., Rapp, C., Sullivan, W. P., & Kisthardt, W. (1989). A strengths perspective for social work practice. *Social Work, 34,* 350–354.

Wilson, E. H., & Mulally, S. (1983). *Hope and dignity: Older black women of the South.* Philadelphia: Temple University Press.

Zastrow, C., & Kirst-Ashman, K. K. (1997). *Understanding human behavior and the social environment* (4th ed.). Chicago: Nelson-Hall.

9

Culturally Sound Mental Health Services: Ecological Interventions

W. PATRICK SULLIVAN

The time has come for a bold new approach. . . . I am convinced that, if we apply our medical knowledge and social insights fully, all but a small portion of the mentally ill can eventually achieve a wholesome and constructive social adjustment.

—President John F. Kennedy, 88th Congress 1st Session,
House of Representatives document 58, February, 1963

One of the central values of the community mental health movement in the early 1960s was that quality prevention and treatment services should be readily accessible for all Americans living in the U.S. Moving services to the local level, in small, less imposing clinics was one step toward increased accessibility for citizens. Nonetheless, by the 1970s critics claimed that many local mental health centers lacked responsiveness and were not relevant to the needs of the nearby populace (Foley & Sharfstein, 1983). In response, new amendments to the original 1963 act were introduced that required the existence of a local board to oversee the operations of each center.

Much has changed in the U.S. over the past 35 years. The country continues to become more diverse, and there is increased sensitivity to the needs and issues faced by diverse populations. Mental health services, like most American institutions, tend to reflect the worldview of the dominant culture and, at times, do so in a way that is hidden from and outside the consciousness of those people responsible for day-to-day operations.

This chapter examines various aspects of mental health services, from the assessment process to the overarching paradigm that shapes service delivery. Using an ecological framework, new ways of understanding mental illness and helping services are examined with respect to the challenge of providing effective services for all. This chapter also devotes attention to an important special population: those people who face the most serious and disabling conditions: what mental health professionals tend to call severe and persistent mental illness. The public mental health system increasingly is focusing on the care of this identified subpopulation, consisting of a segment of services heavily staffed by social workers.

However, it is not the position of this chapter that *mental illness* is fictional. The preponderance of evidence points to very real neurobiological involvement in human conditions that are labeled in a variety of ways worldwide. Thus, these conditions require attention and care, and this care extends beyond the identified individual to include family and community.

Severe mental illnesses, like schizophrenia, are unique with respect to other health conditions. Whereas disease states often vary by race, culture, or location, there is an amazing universality to severe mental illness, and prevalence rates vary little worldwide. It is this commonality that provides evidence for biophysical involvement, even though the exact cause(s) of illnesses such as schizophrenia remains a subject of much research and debate. This is not to suggest, however, that cultural or environmental forces have no bearing on the course of these illnesses. Indeed, it is a key position of this chapter that such forces have a major impact on the recovery process.

DIAGNOSIS AND ASSESSMENT
OF SEVERE MENTAL ILLNESS

The diagnosis of mental illness stops largely where the diagnosis of other illnesses are just beginning: with the expression of symptoms. Culture affects the manner in which clients express and professionals interpret symptoms. Obviously, use of the term *diagnosis* also indicates a specific overarching orientation. Although there have been consistent criticisms of diagnostic and labeling schematas, in practice the process of identifying and naming a phenomenon ultimately lays the foundation on which interventions proceed. This entire process is culture bound, both in the manner in which the practitioner conducts an assessment, and in the way the professional understands and explains the illness or condition. Disjunctures between the professional and the individual, family, and community can occur at any point in this process.

Comas-Diaz (1996) has commented that

culture provides an all-encompassing, pervasive context that infuses meaning to behavior. Because human behavior is expressed in a context, diagnostic practices that focus solely on individual and biologic forces are constricted. Relational variables such as family, group, community, minority group membership, and sociopolitical realties are central to the lives of many people of color. (p. 163)

Much of the Western orientation is based on the notion of the primacy of the individual; thus, the orientation is egocentric. Within this belief system are firm boundaries between self and others, and strict laws and codes of conduct to reinforce these mores. In such a society, illness is personal; thus, it is "my illness" and, as is true in the process of stigmatization, the total being becomes merged with the illness. Hence, a person no longer has schizophrenia or struggles with alcohol but instead is a schizophrenic or an alcoholic. The illness is located within the person, and the treatment is to eradicate the offending party from the system. At times, this treatment requires an identification and removal process, for example, involuntary psychiatric hospitalization.

However, many cultures, both within and outside Western society, do not draw such firm lines between themselves and others, or even between the material and nonmaterial world. Rather, they have adopted a sociocentric worldview that values group cohesiveness and interdependence. This orientation results in an entirely different view of illness such as schizophrenia.

The basic orientation of an individual or family must be considered on initial contact with the mental health system. For example, cultures define family composition differently. Many African-Americans rely greatly on extended family support, as well as the church, and close friends become fictive kin. Among Asian-Americans, the family is often considered three or four generations deep, a far different orientation than the notion of the nuclear family. In many ways, the same situation holds true for Italian-American families, who operationalize the value that multiple generations should be involved in important decisions that an individual faces (Finley, 1997).

The broad overall worldview held by an individual or family (i.e., sociocentric versus egocentric), the conceptualization of the family, and the structure of society influence the manner in which professionals understand mental illnesses and ultimately deal with them. Consider a culture that adopts an egocentric worldview, draws firms distinctions between self and others, and is oriented around the nuclear family. It is easy to see how, in this context, the professional might view mental illness as an individual problem and the affected person as deviant. Not surprisingly, the conflux of these forces creates an impulse to exclude the deviant literally, as is the case with psychiatric hospitalization, or socially by way of stigma and discrimination. It is equally easy to see how the burden of care largely falls on a small family unit until their ability to cope is exhausted.

A sociocentric orientation, in contrast, supports a permeable definition of the self. This definition leaves open the possibility that illnesses like schizophrenia are less permanent and are not just an individual matter but rather an issue the family or total community should handle. The impulse is to include, not exclude, and the care of the affected person is widely shared.

Although broad brush views of the general orientation to life held by different cultures are instructive, each practitioner holds unique views about all manner of phenomena, and we all forge our own accommodation with the world in our daily effort to thrive. The world may seem organized and predictable or, at the other extreme, marked by randomness and chaos. We each try to struggle and cope with adversities we face. Thus, social workers need a broad understanding of differing worldviews and also must reckon with the specific way individuals relate to their culture of origin and to the dominant culture.

For this reason culturally relevant assessments focus on both context and the multiple forces that influence people (Comas-Diaz, 1996). Such a process should also focus on the strengths present in person, family, and community. An assessment process that is only concerned with illness and pathology is largely reductionistic. It is as if the illness were the central nucleus around which all behavior and life events revolve. A holistic assessment process that includes strengths is more expansive, provides a more balanced view of the person, and supports an ecological understanding of human behavior.

Comas-Diaz (1996) argued for the adoption of a relational basis for diagnostic practice in mental health, suggesting that a strictly biological and individualistic approach to this process is ineffective in addressing the needs of many culturally diverse clients. Such an approach is consistent with the self-in-relation model proffered by feminist writers, and with ecological principles.

Cowger (1997) proposed that the assessment process—and all social work practice—is political, and saw particular danger in deficit and pathology-based assessment models. He suggested that

> diagnostic and assessment metaphors and taxonomies that stress individual deficiencies and sickness reinforce the political status-quo in a manner that is incongruent with a practice that attempts to promote social and economic justice. (p. 61)

Strengths-based practice, according to Cowger, is also political "in that its thrust is the development of client power and the more equitable distribution of societal resources, those resources that underlie the development of personal resources" (p. 62).

A strengths-based assessment process should ideally emphasize the uniqueness of each individual—something that standard, medically based diagnosis does not. McQuaide and Ehrenreich (1997) have proffered that strength is also a culturally laden concept because "events may be viewed as normal or unusual, depending on the cultural context" (p. 204). An assessment process that is culturally sensitive is not one that simply affirms the consumer's cultural identity, but also explores his or her *ethnocultural heritage,* the level of identification of the person with his or her culture of origin, and how the person's unique culture is positioned within the community of reference. In this respect, such an assessment has the opportunity to truly reflect the diversity of all people and rejects the tendency to view all people of a certain color, cultural orientation, or sexual orientation as the same.

Cowger (1997) has commented that "blame is the first cousin of deficit models of practice" (p. 65); there is perhaps no better example of this blame than what families of people with mental illness have faced. From the double-bind theory to the notions of the schizophrenigenic mother, families have been routinely blamed for their children's mental illness. As a result of mental illness in their midst, families must cope with both objective and subjective burdens (Marsh et al., 1996). The *subjective burden* is the load that comes from grief and mourning—the real pain of dealing with the realities of mental illness on a daily basis. The *objective burdens* are those tangible issues that families also face, such as the cost of care, the necessity to provide supervision, and daily alterations in life plans.

Time after time, researchers have confirmed the family experience of burden, but have devoted less attention to the flip side: the evidence of family resilience (Marsh et al., 1996). Marsh and associates, commenting on the evidence of resilience, suggested that "families have their own restorative powers, often surviving their crises and meeting their challenges with mastery, dignity, and empathy" (p. 4). Consistent with a strengths orientation, the concept of resilience underscores the capacity of people and communities to deal successfully with adversity, both as a result of their will and also family and community support.

Robinson (1993) noted that families often cope with chronic illness by constructing a normalization story, a strategy far different from a medicalized or deviance model. In a similar fashion, others have noted that the use of indigenous labels also helps families cope with troubling situations (Guarnaccia, Parra, Deschamps, Milstein, & Argiles, 1992; Swerdlow,

1992). Robinson (1993) observed that professionals are often counterproductive when they insist on introducing a problem-saturated perspective, noting that these professionals insist on "servicing the illness" as opposed to providing the help an individual needs for "getting on with your life" (p. 20).

Obviously, a professional should be held to a standard greater than "first, do no harm." Marsh and associates (1996) suggested that practitioners should direct interventions to help alleviate family burden and promote resilience as well. The first step in this process is to explore family strengths and to remain sensitive to the nuances of culture and diversity in this process. For example, many professionals may look askance at family reliance on prayer or spiritual support when confronted by mental illness. This reaction ignores a potential source of strength to a family and fails to recognize what is often a culturally validated response to a troubling situation. Similarly, professionals often view lesbian and gay male couples as enmeshed when there is a limited appreciation of cultural context. Considering the lack of culturally sanctioned support structures or, worse, the open hostility these couples face in a heterosexist world, the notion of enmeshment loses relevance.

Practitioners must also assess large extrafamilial, or macroforces with a keen eye toward the influence of such forces on individual behavior. For example, many minorities live in a bifurcated world: their culture of origin and the dominant culture in which they are nested. Considering other areas of diversity such as sexual orientation or physical or mental challenges, the layers of cultural influence and areas of negotiation become even more complex, an indication that "maintaining a bicultural or biracial identity, may itself be a strength" (McQuaide & Ehrenreich, 1997, p. 204).

Freeman (1990) has argued that assessment processes must consider the life cycle of the African-American family. In particular, professionals must acknowledge the experiences of racism, oppression, and economic deprivation, and recognize the functional adaptations to these negative forces. One example of such an adaptation is reflected in the fluidity of roles. The use of kith and kin in areas of child rearing and functional support is woven into the fabric of the African-American community. This fluidity of roles is also displayed in the care of mentally ill relatives. Guarnaccia and Parra (1996) reported that the concept of family burden has far less relevance in African-American and Latino families in which care for an ill relative at home and the provision of the necessary emotional and instrumental support are accepted as normal family responsibilities. Indeed, for many in this exploratory study, the caretaking role, although certainly fraught with challenges, was viewed as rewarding.

Baker (1994) has argued that clinicians often fail to capture the unique personal histories of individuals and families, proposing that a life-course assessment, which incorporates aspects of a life review, is particularly relevant in the treatment of African-American elders. This life review can capture relevant historical events that influenced entire groups of citizens as well as the specific effects of such events on the individual. Baker suggested that a reminiscence approach is useful in determining the consumer's coping capacities and resources. This exercise can help underscore why some individuals distrust some professionals, perhaps the response is based on actual experiences and is not merely an expression of paranoia.

Finley (1997) pointed out that each group present in this nation has a history of oppression and discrimination and thus holds both positive and negative attitudes toward its heritage. However, group membership also provides a psychological buffer and a sense of belonging, all of which may be a great source of strength. It stands to reason, therefore, that

> when families are facing stress, crisis, loss, or disability, they will rely inherently on those strengths, coping skills, and solutions that have been learned in the family and cultural context. (p. 498)

Tools common to social work, such as genograms and ecomaps may be useful to capture the range of forces that influence individual and family functioning. When working with diverse populations, it may be first necessary to assess the degree of cultural assimilation and identity and the effects on individuals and generations within a family. Freeman (1990) observed that African-Americans must often strive to maintain a positive racial identity and meet the expectations of the dominant culture. The ability to maintain a "dual perspective" is not easy: as Freeman has observed, attending only to the dominant culture will lead to alienation from one's racial group, whereas the reverse—tending only to one's group or cultural immersion—may limit the ability to function in the larger society. Logan (1990) has designed a model of family assessment that examines the structure and functions of African-American families and explores both family history and the environmental context in which life transitions must be negotiated.

Much of the previous discussion merely points to the reality that practitioners cannot understand individual behavior without an accounting of individual, family, and community forces. Furthermore, the manner in which practitioners address these specific domains must be sensitive to cultural traditions and history. Obviously, these are basic tenets of good social work practice.

However, there are times when the practitioner may view the assessment process as an end in itself, separating it from the interventions or treatments that follow. That is, once the practitioner has identified the

malady, the care and treatment then rest in the hands of "experts." In this
model, the consumer, family, and community are relegated to the role of
passive bystander, and what was once an effort to gain a holistic understanding of person-in-situation slowly becomes decontextualized. A person suffering from mental illness, a faulty gallbladder, or marital problem
then becomes like any other individual with a similar affliction. If the
ecological model can serve as a foundation for social work practice, it
must guide all phases of the helping experience.

EFFECTIVE MENTAL HEALTH SERVICES:
ADVANCING RECOVERY

There are no cures at this time for severe and persistent mental
illnesses—and recovery should not be mistaken for cure. However, the
concept of recovery provides a valuable guiding vision for services to
people who face severe and persistent mental illnesses. Anthony (1993)
viewed recovery as "a way of living a satisfying, hopeful, and contributing life even with the limitations caused by illness" (p. 15).

Kleinman (1980) has drawn a useful distinction between the terms
disease and illness: a distinction that has relevance for understanding the
recovery process from illnesses like schizophrenia. Disease, according to
Kleinman is the actual underlying pathology that accounts for a disorder.
In the area of severe mental illness,
disease would entail the actual neurobiological forces that account for
problematic cognitions and behavior.

> Advancing recovery is a healing
> and helping process that is strongly
> influenced by cultural factors.

Illness, on the other hand, reflects psychosocial processes, and is shaped
by personal, social, and cultural reaction to disease. Marsella (1988) has
observed that, "even in the most severe neurological diseases and disorders, cultural influence still occurs since the individual's interpretation
and experience of the disorder, its behavioral referents, and the social
response to these referents, is strongly influenced by culture" (pp. 10–11).
Certainly, a problem is only elevated to the status of a social problem
when there is broad general agreement that it is one. Similarly, a person is
only deemed disabled in the presence of another who is different.

It is Kleinman's (1980) contention that the Western approach to medicine is unnecessarily reductionist and relies too heavily on biotechnical
intervention, even when the problems of concern may be social in nature.
This paradigm, according to Kleinman, limits the inputs of the social
sciences in areas of medicine and psychiatry. Healing and helping is more
than an interpersonal episode that occurs between a professional and

consumer—it is a cultural phenomenon, because, as Kleinman recognized "the system as a whole, not just the healer, heals" (p. 72).

Those people affected by mental illness from all cultures must confront marginality, discrimination, and stigma from society. The process of ostracism often leaves them separated emotionally and physically from mainstream life. Furthermore,

> consumers and families from different cultures in the public care system may be caught in the "victim system." They come for services with their unique sociocultural histories, sometimes viewing the world as a hostile, dangerous, and unpredictable place. Suspicious of providers and lacking familiarity with dominant cultural institutions, they may be wary of receiving help form "outsiders." (Finley, 1997, p. 498)

Clearly, diverse populations face a host of barriers in the quest to receive effective mental health services. These barriers are present throughout the continuum of the helping process. To this end, there have been a variety of attempts over time to explore ways to fashion mental health services to increase their attractiveness to diverse populations. These efforts usually have resulted in alterations of operational aspects of the mental health service delivery system. Mental health services may devote more attention to the diversity of staff in place to offer services, may attempt to decentralize services and open offices in diverse neighborhoods, or may even focus on aggressive outreach.

However, a radical approach may be required: one that reexamines the entire mental health paradigm. One promising strategy is to work from what mental health professionals know thus far about the recovery process and to shape services in a manner consistent with this mission. The challenge is to develop a framework that truly affirms diversity and that includes the differences among people *within* groups as well as *between* groups.

To begin the process of building effective mental health services, it is appropriate to learn from diverse populations and cultures about what has worked both within and outside the system. Indeed, instead of simply trying to lure people into existing services it is likely that mainstream services have something to learn from the experience of consumers from diverse backgrounds. Years of research by the World Health Organization (WHO) has indicated that the Western world can learn much about recovery from schizophrenia from other cultures as well as benefit from understanding the actual experience of consumers of services.

The striking finding from a host of cross-cultural studies on the course of schizophrenia is that, on average, those people residing in the developing world have better outcomes than those from more developed, industrialized nations: a finding that is counterintuitive. Given the state of our knowledge about the true causes of schizophrenia, it is certainly plausible that future information may help explain this disparity. Nonetheless, Lin and Kleinman (1988) have argued that the reports of differential outcomes have received the most consistent support and may be the single most important finding in cross-cultural psychiatry.

Explaining the evidence for more positive outcomes for schizophrenia in the developing world is, at this time, an act of conjecture. Yet, there seems to be a host of important ingredients to be gleaned from cross-cultural studies, all of which can help us reexamine the state of mental health services in the United States and the predominant community response to such conditions. For example, some cross-cultural research has suggested that fundamental differences in the conceptualization of the self and the relationship of the self to family and community—issues at the very core of a given culture—may play a role in the recovery from mental illness. In societies characterized by a sociocentric orientation, there are rules, norms, and conventions that value group cohesiveness. These same rules extend to those individuals with obvious differences and disabilities. Therefore, as Warner (1983) suggested, dealing with those individuals "is very much a community phenomenon, tending not only to reintegrate the deviant individual into the group but also to reaffirm the solidarity of the community" (p. 209).

A similar theme emerges when one considers vocational activity, a long-standing staple in rehabilitation programs in the United States. Work is central to the self-esteem and personal identification of most people. People who face severe and persistent mental illness consistently speak of a desire to participate in either paid or volunteer work. Waters (1992) has spoken eloquently on the importance of work for individuals who face severe and persistent mental illness:

> Work puts us in a unique relationship with other human beings so that the opportunity to form meaningful relationships is readily available to us. Work also allows us to feel a common bond with the larger community and gives us a better picture of what our lives will be in the future. All people benefit from work . . . but in many ways, given the isolation and confusion that so often accompanies mental illness, people with psychiatric disorders may benefit most of all. (p. 40)

Yet, there are barriers to work, including the inherent disincentives embedded in a host of important financial aid programs and vocational rehabilitation services. However, some of the barriers rest with the very structure of Western society. Perhaps the greatest liability a person with mental illness presents is the lack of predictability brought on by the variable course of the illness. Industrial and postindustrial society is based on routinization, punctuality, and regimentation, which result in a poor match with those individuals with mental illness.

In contrast, many developing nations are marked by a subsistence economy in which any contribution of the individual is needed and appreciated. There is greater inherent flexibility in the work performed and the jobs do not require a great deal of training or expertise. In this context a natural accommodation process is present.

Although the picture has improved in Western society to some degree, historically there has been little accommodation at the work site or in the general cultural milieu for people with mental illness. In part, this situation also reflects an egocentric orientation. A review of most individual treatment plans for individuals with mental illness reveals that the theme of self-sufficiency is omnipresent. Although there is nothing inherently wrong with such goals, it must be recognized that many of the barriers that consumers face in accomplishing goals are socially constructed. In the effort to ensure reasonable accommodations for people with varying challenges, those individuals with mental illness have been among the least understood and appreciated.

In much of the developing world, the permeable lines between self and community, and even self and the spirit world, can reduce the burden on both the individual and the family. Mental illness can be traced to the spirit world or even the ill will of another person. In such cases, the illness is not viewed as a character flaw of the individual or as the result of the family's negligence. When the self is viewed as permeable and subject to outside influence, mental illness is viewed as a less permanent situation: one that may only intermittently affect the individual. This perspective is reflected in the normalized labels family members often use to describe their loved one's condition.

The egocentric orientation present in Western society has direct ramifications for those family members charged with the care of loved ones. In the Western world, the notions of autonomy and individual control abound. Thus, there is a greater tendency to assign blame for mental illness and to view such conditions as permanent. This tendency plus the general structure of Western society have dire consequences for the family. The presence of stigma for both the affected individual and family leaves them isolated and alone. Furthermore, given the mobility of much of the populace and the predominance of the nuclear family in some quarters, there is little formal and informal support available to them. In the absence of formal or informal community supports available to families, the burden will be great. Families' emotional and financial burden, particularly in the early days of the community mental health movement, left them little choice but to seek inpatient care for loved ones.

It is instructive to compare the preceding issues with consumers' reports about those areas they viewed as essential to their recovery process. In an exploratory study, current and former consumers of mental health services identified a host of important factors in their recovery (Sullivan, 1994). These factors reflected key aspects of the recovery paradigm and illustrated the distinction between disease and illness as presented by Kleinman (1980).

The consumers in the study, most of whom had faced multiple psychiatric hospitalizations, knew full well that they had a serious condition to confront. This recognition is reflected in their reports that medication was the single most important factor in their ability to surmount the effects of mental illness. Many of the consumers discussed how they learned about the illness over time, subsequently taking active steps to monitor their stress, diets, sleep, and other aspects of their life to compensate. The consumers also learned to identify personal signs when they were slipping, and even drew on their own will to struggle through. Therefore, there was no attempt to deny the reality that a "disease" process was present.

Other factors represent the combined efforts of the individual and other concerned people in the lives of these consumers. Consider the second highest factor noted by consumers, case managers, and community support programs. Without question, these programs and people represent an extrafamilial-dominated support network that has become at least a temporary necessity, given the realities of modern life.

Case managers, in the study, were not primarily valued for their technical expertise but rather for the friendship and guidance they offered. Consumers reported that these key people treated them like a friend and with respect. Likewise, consumers viewed community support programs as places where they felt safe and wanted. Informants who lived in a mental health–sponsored apartment program also expressed a similar view. Clearly residents looked after one another. Mutual support groups and supportive friends, also mentioned as important by consumers, provided a level of comfort and security, and the sense that at least one group truly understood the consumers' struggles and affirmed each consumer as a valuable person. At the most intimate level, consumers spoke of significant others: those romantic involvements that offered the support they needed to deal with the normal travails of life and the especially difficult times brought on by mental illness. Other areas mentioned as critical by consumers cover key areas mentioned previously. Vocational activity provided a sense of accomplishment and an opportunity to make a contribution to society, an area of extreme importance to many who face mental illness. Work also provided necessary structure and created a diversion from the daily grind of dealing with personal problems. Many also found solace in prayer and spiritual activities, suggesting a level of social support that can come from tangible (places of worship or congregation) and less tangible sources. Consumers reported the periods when they have felt their deepest despair, in psychiatric hospitals or when troubled by voices, and how prayer and faith saw them through. Such reports may make some professionals uncomfortable, but if the mission is recovery, it is important that consumers draw on any resource that helps them in daily life.

This brief review of the consumers' self-reports and cross-cultural research underscores key principles of the ecological model, that is, that behavior is a function of the interaction of person and environment. In the case of those people with severe mental illness, adjustments on the part of the individual and environment are needed for the person to thrive. This interaction may create a context for recovery or may lead to physical and emotional exclusion from social life. What can social workers take from these studies to aid in the development of effective mental health services?

STRENGTHS, NICHES, AND RECOVERY
FROM MENTAL ILLNESS

The forerunner of strengths-based practice is White's (1959) pioneering work in the area of competence. The concept of competence reflects the facility with which an individual is able to effectively deal with the environments he or she encounters. This is a conceptualization of human beings as actors: individuals who are goal driven and who actively seek to enlarge their ability and influence. Brower (1988), in a similar fashion, viewed the person-environment interaction as one of accommodation, a

> Recovery from mental illness is enhanced when practitioners build on clients' strengths and involve extended family and community support.

process effected by decision-making, past experiences, and beliefs about the future. In both cases, ecological principles are considered key in human development and behavior, because as Brower commented, "It makes no sense to think of individuals separate from their immediate environments, or to think of environments separate from the individuals that inhabit them" (p. 413).

The end result of this accommodation process is the creation of a *niche*, "the unique place within which one 'fits' into the environment, the workplace or the community" (ibid., p. 412). Taylor (1997) also recognized the use of the ecological model in social work practice but suggested that Brower's (1988) concept of niche draws too heavily on emotional or cognitive processes. Taylor observed that many people occupy a niche that they did not choose.

Taylor (1997) melded biological and social sciences, by offering the concept of *social niche*, "the environmental habitat of a category of persons, including the resources they utilize and the other category of persons they associate with" (p. 219). To illustrate the power of the concept, Taylor proposed two idealized types of social niche: entrapping and enabling. This discussion is particularly cogent when considering mental health services, because frequently those people with severe disorders find themselves in entrapping niches.

Individuals who occupy *entrapping niches* generally have limited economic resources; are treated as outcasts by others and, hence, must turn to their own kind for affiliation; have few opportunities to learn the skills necessary for escape; receive little reality feedback; experience few opportunities to gain rewards or improve their status; and have little incentive to set long-term goals (ibid., p. 221).

Clearly, people with mental illness often find themselves in an entrapped niche, the result of natural or willful exclusionary forces in the surrounding environment. Natural exclusionary forces include the stigma and discrimination that many people with mental illness face; when coupled with poverty, a concomitant condition—homelessness and disaffiliation—follows. Other exclusionary forces reflect actual policies and practices, such as incarceration both in jails and prisons as well as forced treatment in psychiatric hospitals, because as Scull (1977) commented, institutions remain a convenient way to deal with inconvenient people. In many respects diverse populations have faced the same process, particularly as they venture into the dominant social order. Not only do many of these people face daily hostility and discrimination, but they also are impoverished and are disproportionately represented among the poor population and in the census of jails and psychiatric hospitals. In mental health services, these constricted opportunities hinder the recovery process because as Taylor (1997) observed, "We do not have to assume that entrapping niches cause pathology in order to claim that they influence recovery from pathology" (p. 222).

At the opposite end of the spectrum are *enabling niches*, whose characteristics are the mirror image of entrapping niches. In enabling niches, people are included in social process and have access to resources and opportunity. These forces allow an individual to set long-term goals and hold a hopeful view of the future, even in the face of personal difficulty.

The previous review of cross-cultural research has indicated that in some parts of the developing world there is a ready-made or natural enabling niche available to people with serious mental illness. In such situations, there is a natural inclusionary process marked by extended family and community support, and there are opportunities to work and contribute to the collective. With this context as a basic starting point, the recovery process is augmented.

Furthermore, the previous discussions have focused some attention on the differences between the industrial, or developed, world, and the developing world, which comprises what is often called traditional societies. Indeed, even within industrial and postindustrial societies are enclaves that resemble, in structure and function, developing societies.

The very existence of social workers and other professional helpers is a response to modern society. Despite the romantic cries for volunteerism and community involvement, the human problems and needs that face communities far outstrip the resources of concerned townspeople. On the other hand, the reports of family members, diverse population groups, and consumers point to basic inadequacies in the current system of care. Certainly, there has been a decline in popular support for social programs, resulting in the restriction of the level of formal resources available to address these human needs. Yet services can be revamped to provide more effective services to all constituents.

In the absence of naturally occurring niches for people with severe and persistent mental illness, effective and culturally sensitive mental health services should be designed to reflect those factors that seem to abet the recovery process. To draw from the parlance of the previous section, efforts must be extended to create enabling niches, or what Taylor (1997) has tentatively labeled "support pods."

The importance of a strengths approach has been discussed throughout this chapter. To some, the use of a strengths approach with people with the most serious of mental illness seems ludicrous. However, the use of a strengths approach is particularly critical given the reality that the most serious mental illness are beyond cure and that there are a range of psychosocial challenges that arise when confronted by illness like schizophrenia. The necessary accommodations needed to advance the recovery process require that the individual, family, and community strengths be activated.

If family, individual, and community strengths are essential building blocks in the recovery from mental illness, all parties must first recognize them. Several strengths assessment tools have been developed since the pioneering work of Rapp and Chamberlain (1985). Recent examples of strengths assessment include Cowger's (1997) attempt to draw on both personal and environmental strengths and a more intrapersonally focused instrument developed by McQuaide and Ehrenreich (1997).

Choosing the right tools does not guarantee success. A consistent theme in this chapter has underscored the importance of gaining an appreciation of the culture, worldview, and values of the consumer and families. Without this understanding, important areas of strengths may be missed or, worse, considered pathological. For example, a practitioner may consider a family's spiritual beliefs and use of clergy as resistance to professional help or ignorance. By assessing in this manner, the practitioner may ignore potential resources.

Furthermore, stylistic considerations are important to making a strengths assessment work, such as suggesting that the actual process of conducting the assessment is as important as the product. Cowger (1997) has offered several important guidelines for consideration when conducting a strengths assessment, including believing the consumer and discovering what she or he wants, using language the consumer can understand, making the process mutual, and using the process to discover uniqueness. It is also important to avoid diagnosing and engaging in excessive cause-and-effect thinking. This process is designed to recognize, celebrate, and activate or reactivate consumer strengths. The overall model begins with an expectation that the consumer plays an active role in his or her recovery process.

In similar fashion, when appropriate, the consumer's family should play an active role. After all, families have served as the primary case manager for years. The process of joining with the family, however defined, is critical for culturally sensitive practice. This mission is best accomplished in the consumer's natural environment or on neutral turf. Obviously, if it is possible to match the professional's background with the background of the consumer, some barriers and translation problems likely will be reduced.

In terms of the danger of separating the assessment process from the helping phase consider that severe and persistent mental illnesses impacts people in a multiplicity of ways. Accordingly, the interventions that follow must be multidimensional. The previously described consumer reports underscored the importance of psychotropic medication in their recovery. Good medication management must consider differential response by persons of color. To illustrate, nonwhites suffer much higher rates of tardive dyskinesia than do white subjects, which suggests the possibility of differing biophysical reactions to medication or different prescribing practices by doctors (Glazer, Morgenstern, & Doucette, 1994).

Recovery is a psychosocial process. The difficulty to confront is that people with mental illness face pervasive discrimination and stigmatization, which is more severe for people of color. Very often, mental health services are viewed as an interpersonal endeavor and, even more narrowly, particularly in the psychodynamic tradition, an intrapersonal process. When professionals accept recovery as the guiding mission for mental health services, the scope of the work at hand becomes enlarged.

Effective practice must move beyond traditional services to include community development and organization and must also embrace a human rights paradigm.

Treatment for people with severe mental illness was relatively straightforward in the days before the community mental health movement. When individuals became too difficult for family to care for, they were labeled and excluded from society. Such a "solution" is unacceptable in light of recent advances in psychopharmacology and community services. Today, a new host of community-based services hold great promise to aid the recovery process. Many of these models, like strengths-based case management, boldly assert that advocacy is a prime activity for case managers.

Any accounting of the goals mental health consumers have for their lives indicates they desire the same things as all people: a nice place to live, meaningful work, friends, and family. A host of new community programs, consistent with the recovery paradigm, have altered the manner in which the challenge at hand is viewed. From a strict medical orientation, people with severe mental illness have a disease; a linear model holds that the disease should be cured before the consumer moves forward with his or her life. Unfortunately, this cure may never come.

In recent years, it has been recognized that it is the absence of supports, not the illness, that impedes the likelihood that consumers will reach their goals. These models of helping, under the choose-get-keep paradigm, affirm consumer choice and ability. In speaking of the supported employment model, for example, Anthony and Blanch (1987) opined that "all people—regardless of the severity of their disability—can do meaningful, productive work in normal settings, if that is what they chose to do, and if they are given the necessary supports" (p. 7). Contrast this approach with models anchored by inpatient psychiatric care. Similar programs, all emphasizing the importance of support, have arisen in the areas of education and housing. In all cases, a legion of helpers, from job coaches, peer support, active case managers, and involved community members, have been enlisted to provide the support needed for the person to be successful. This is a level of accommodation necessary for the creation of an enabling niche.

Additional evidence for the evolution of mental health services has been the emergence of peer support, self-advocacy, and consumer-run programming. Consistent with an emphasis on empowerment, consumers and former consumers are using their firsthand experience and expertise to help others. Consumers now have more direct involvement on the boards of community mental health centers and state offices as they try to help shape the system in a positive manner. Similar to other professionals, the act of helping also helps them. It is hoped that future developments will result in the emergence of more consumer-run programs that serve diverse populations.

At times, it is useful to take a step back to gain perspective on current issues and problems. The community treatment movement in the U.S. is still in its infancy. By the 1980s, it was clear that people with the most severe mental illness were not being adequately served, and the needs of families and consumers were largely ignored. From the nascent stages of the early community support programs, social workers have seen a constant evolution in community-based services—and there has been progress. The challenge into the next century is to assess the effectiveness of mental health services with the wide range of people who need and seek services.

REFERENCES

Anthony, W. A. (1993). Recovery from mental illness: The guiding vision of the mental health system in the 1990's. *Psychosocial Rehabilitation Journal, 16*(4), 11–23.

Anthony, W., & Blanch, A. (1987). Supported employment for persons who are psychiatrically disabled: An historical and conceptual perspective. *Psychosocial Rehabilitation Journal, 11*(2), 5–23.

Baker, F. M. (1994). Psychiatric treatment of older African Americans. *Hospital & Community Psychiatry, 45*(1), 32–37.

Brower, A. M. (1988). Can the ecological model guide social work practice? *Social Service Review, 62*(3), 411–429.

Comas-Diaz, L. (1996). Cultural considerations in diagnosis. In F. W. Kaslow (Ed.), *Handbook of relational diagnosis and dysfunctional family patters* (pp. 152–168). New York: Wiley.

Cowger, C. (1997). Assessing client strengths: Assessment for client empowerment. In D. Saleebey (Ed.), *The strengths perspective in social work practice* (2nd. ed.) (pp. 59–73). New York: Longman.

Finley, L. (1997). The multiple effects of culture and ethnicity on psychiatric disability. In L. Spaniol, C. Gagne, and M. Koehler (Eds.), *Psychological and social aspects of psychiatric disability* (pp. 497–510). Boston: Center for Psychiatric Rehabilitation.

Foley, H., & Sharfstein, S. (1983). *Madness and government*. Washington DC: American Psychiatric Press.

Freeman, E. (1990). The black family's life cycle: Operationalizing a strengths perspective. In S. Logan, E. Freeman, and R. McRoy (Eds.), *Social work practice with black families* (pp. 55–72). New York: Longman.

Glazer, W., Morgenstern, H., & Doucette, J. (1994). Race and tardive dyskinesia among outpatients at a CMHC. *Hospital & Community Psychiatry, 45*(1), 38–42.

Guarnaccia, P., & Parra, P. (1996). Ethnicity, social status, and families' experiences of caring for a mentally ill family member. *Community Mental Health Journal, 32*(3), 243–260.

Guarnaccia, P., Parra, P., Deschamps, A., Milstein, G., & Argiles, N. (1992). Si Dios quiere: Hispanic families' experience of caring for a seriously mentally ill family member. *Culture, Medicine, and Psychiatry, 16*(2), 187–215.

Kleinman, A. (1980). *Patients and healers in the context of culture.* Berkeley, CA: University of California Press.

Lin, K., & Kleinman, A. (1988). Psychopathology and clinical course of schizophrenia: A cross-cultural perspective. *Schizophrenia Bulletin, 14*(4), 555–567.

Logan, S. (1990). Diversity among black families: Assessing structure and function. In S. Logan, E., Freeman, & R. McRoy (Eds.), *Social work practice with black families* (pp. 73–96). New York: Longman.

Marsella, A. (1988). Cross-cultural research on severe mental disorders: Issues and findings. *Acta Psychiatrica Scandinavica, 78,* Suppl. 344, 7–22.

Marsh, D., Lefley, H., Evans-Rhodes, D., Ansell, V., Doerzbacher, B., Labarbera, L., & Paluzzi, J. (1996). The family experience of mental illness: Evidence for resilience. *Psychiatric Rehabilitation Journal, 20*(2), 3–12.

McQuaide, S., & Ehrenreich, J. (1997). Assessing client strengths. *Families in Society, 78*(2), 201–212.

Rapp, C., & Chamberlain, R. (1985). Case management services to the chronically mentally ill. *Social Work, 30*(5), 417–422.

Robinson, C. (1993). Managing life with a chronic condition: The story of normalization. *Qualitative Health Research, 3*(1), 6–28.

Scull, A. (1977). *Decarceration: Community treatment and the deviant—a radical view.* Englewood Cliffs, NJ: Prentice Hall.

Sullivan, W. P. (1994). Recovery from schizophrenia: What we can learn from the developing nations. *Innovations and Research, 3*(2), 7–15.

Swerdlow, M. (1992). "Chronicity," "nervios," and community care: A case study of Puerto Rican psychiatric patients in New York City. *Culture, Medicine, and Psychiatry, 16*(2), 217–235.

Taylor, J. (1997). Niches and practice: Extending the ecological perspective. In D. Saleebey (Ed.), *The strengths perspective in social work practice* (2nd ed.) (pp. 217–227). New York: Longman.

Warner, R. (1983). Recovery from schizophrenia in the Third World. *Psychiatry, 46*(3), 197–212.

Waters, B. (1992). The work unit: The heart of the clubhouse. *Psychosocial Rehabilitation Journal, 16*(2), 41–48.

White, R. (1959). Motivation reconsidered: The concept of competence. *Psychological Review, 66*(5), 297–333.

10

Marriage Enrichment Programs for African-Americans

LORRAINE C. BLACKMAN

[The couples reported] that during the [marriage enrichment] program they had felt much closer to one another because they were spending a large amount of time together focusing on their relationship, observing other relationships, and forming friendships with other couples.

—D. S. R. Garland, *Working with Couples for Marriage Enrichment*

According to national statistics, across U.S. ethnic groups whose members are aged 15 years and older, African-Americans have the second highest divorce rate (10%; U.S. Bureau of the Census, 1990; Table 10.1), compared with the more than 17% of all Americans who are divorced (U.S. Bureau of the Census, 1990). These statistics imply that an enormous number of adults, their children, and communities are affected by the social and economic consequences of divorce (Norton & Miller, 1992). As a result of disrupted marriages large numbers of children and adults are stressed by the enormous responsibility of having to head families as single parents or having to integrate members into remarried families. Another implication is the frequent occurrence of psychological and psychosomatic disorders precipitated by marital disharmony or disruption. These problems often result in intentional injury and death resulting from child abuse, domestic partner abuse, suicide, or homicide (Blackman, 1995a, 1995b, in press; Blackman and Smith, 1994; Branic, 1995; Chang, 1994, 1996; Evans, Evans, Croom, Berryman-Gilliam, and Davis, 1981; Gentry, 1978; Korbin, 1981).

All too often, the outcomes of divorce are costly mental or physical health interventions. In addition, an undetermined number of individuals

Table 10.1. U. S. Divorce Rates among Citizens by Ethnic Group, Ages 15 Years and Older

Ethnic Group	Divorced (%)
All Americans	17.7
Native Americans	11.5
African-Americans	10.0
White, not Hispanic	8.5
Hispanic	7.4
Asian-Americans/Pacific Islander Americans	3.9

Source: U.S. Bureau of the Census (1990, pp. 45–47).

are similarly affected by marital strife and separation. An estimated 25 to 54% of married couples are dissatisfied with their relationships (Azrin, Naster, & Jones, 1973; LoPiccolo & Miller, 1975; Markman, Floyd, & Dickson-Markman, 1986). In addition, women tend to be more dissatisfied with their marriages than men (Bernard, 1982; Billingsley, 1992; Staples, 1986). This gender difference is related to lower levels of instrumental and expressive support husbands give to wives than vice versa. Moreover, African-American wives tend to be more dissatisfied with their marriages than white American wives (Billingsley, 1992; Staples, 1986). The gender differences in marital partners' support is confounded by the effects of racism in the larger society.

For couples further strained by lower socioeconomic class struggles, marital satisfaction can be elusive even though marital stability typically is commonplace (Blackman, 1992). When men and women are able to develop and sustain functional, satisfying leadership partnerships within their families, they then are best able to socialize their children to become empowered societal members (Blackman, in press; Norton & Miller, 1992). Ethnic- and gender-sensitive solutions are needed to enable African-Americans to act in greater unity within marital and family relationships.

Marital disillusionment, dissatisfaction, and dissolution clearly are major social problems, particularly for African-Americans, and also for women. They are problems with which social workers grapple routinely. However, little theoretical or empirical research is available to guide social workers in designing ethnic- and gender-sensitive primary or secondary prevention interventions for African-Americans.

Marital enrichment programs, a form of primary or secondary prevention, encompass a concern for a wide range of ecological factors (Blackman, 1992, 1995a; Denton, 1986a, 1986b). Although greater emphasis is placed on environmental factors than on individual persons, groups, or communities, prevention is concerned with total at-risk populations and with decreasing new cases of physical, social, or mental disorders (Bloom, 1981, 1987; Markman et al., 1982). Social work prevention methods focus on eliminating or reducing causative factors at their source, in addition to treating problems already manifested. Causative factors in physical, social, and mental disorders include biological, material environmental factors, and "particularly those [factors] associated with institutional racism and discrimination, and their concomitant effects on people of color" (Miller, 1982). A value position of a prevention approach is that it is better to prevent human suffering and the related social problems than to treat them after they occur. This chapter connects the literature on African-American marital disillusionment and divorce to the design of ethnic- and gender-sensitive marriage enrichment practice models. It specifically discusses the marriage enrichment model developed and evaluated by Blackman (1992).

DEMOGRAPHIC DIVERSITY AMONG AFRICAN-AMERICANS

I want to suggest that in reality all these words of identification are a shorthand, even a fiction. Race, ethnicity, and language associated with them are constructs that we use for social convenience. They suggest a simple, neat, orderly world where everyone is slotted into their proper place.
—J. Green, *Cultural Awareness in the Human Services: A Multi-Ethnic Approach*

Cultural Heritage

The diversity among African-Americans intersects with every social institution in society (i.e., family structure, educational achievement, economic factors, and political and religious orientations; Billingsley, 1992). Therefore, designers of marriage enrichment programs for African-American couples must factor into the curricula the rich ethnic diversity among African-Americans. More than 32 million African-Americans compose approximately 12.5% of the U.S. population (National Urban League, 1995). More than 90% of them are descendants of Africans brought to this country as slave laborers (Allen & Turner, 1988). The remaining 10% are Cape Verdean Islanders, West Indians (e.g., Jamaican, Puerto Rican, Haitian), and recently immigrated East and West Africans (ibid.) who have ancestral roots in Africa, but have different migration, settlement, and cultural histories. Nonetheless, they are included in the U.S. census statistics as "blacks."

Geography

Another aspect of African-American diversity to be considered in marriage enrichment curriculum design is geographic diversity. In 1992,

Table 10.2. Distribution of African-American
Population by Region

Region	Distribution (%)
United States	100.0
South	54.8
Northeast	16.5
Midwest	20.5
West	8.1

Source: U. S. Bureau of the Census (1993, Tables 1 and 8).

African-Americans were dispersed across all regions of the United States (Table 10.2). The majority lived along the eastern seaboard, in the former southern slave states, and in the Florida peninsula. This is important information for social work practitioners, because those African-Americans living in urban, industrial areas outside the "old South" have migration, settlement, and cultural histories that vary from those whose roots are largely southern and agrarian:

> Between 1980 and 1992 the number of suburbanites increased nearly twice as fast for the Black population as for persons of all races (64% versus 35%). In 1992, however, only 30% of the Black population, compared with 49% of the entire U.S. population, lived in metropolitan suburbs. (McAdoo, 1997, p. 122)

Furthermore, although all African-Americans have histories of oppression (e.g., racism, sexism, and classism), they also vary in their awareness of and specific experiences with it (Davis, 1981). Therefore, social workers in marriage enrichment practice should assume geographic diversity among their audiences and encourage them to voice their varying life experiences accordingly (hooks, 1994).

Interracial Couples

Households headed by interracial married couples represent still another facet of African-American demographic diversity. In addition to families that identified themselves as "black," there were 827,000 African-American/white American interracial married couples (U.S. Bureau of the Census, 1990). The census report did not delineate interracial marriages among African-Americans and other white-American racial or ethnic groups. Given the escalation in interracial relationships (Billingsley, 1992), marriage enrichment practitioners will need to incorporate the strengths and strains within such relationships in a U.S. cultural context:

Interracial marriages are most likely to occur where white and black persons have sustained patterns of personal interactions; where the white partner takes the initiative; among middle- and upper-class individuals; in urban rather than rural communities; and in the North and West rather than the South—among persons in an age range from young to middle age and, more frequently, involving black males. In short, interracial marriage is just one more adaptation to the pushes and pulls of a changing society. (ibid., p. 255)

Unfortunately, given the psychological impact of racism, interracial partners are more than three times less likely than intraracial partners to have stable marriages, with "black husband-white wife" pairs more stable than "white husband-black wife" pairs (Billingsley, 1992; McAdoo, 1997; Mehta, 1978). Social workers designing and leading marriage enrichment programs must be knowledgeable of and recognize the effects of changing mate selection criteria on African-American marital dynamics.

Family Structure

The stereotype of African-American families is that they are headed by females, for whom marriage is nonexistent or uncommon (Billingsley, 1992; McAdoo, 1997):

Too many discussions of African-American families focus exclusively on single-parent families or on the underclass . . . as if these phenomena were characteristic of African-American families. Inadvertently, they contribute to stereotypical thinking that sets these families apart from other American families. The result is an absurd and counterproductive tendency to see African-American families in isolation, out of the context of their communities and the larger society. (Billingsley, 1992, p. 27)

In contrast to this stereotype, 47% of African-American families in 1993 were headed by married couples (U.S. Bureau of the Census, 1993).

Social workers must acknowledge the wide variety of family structures when working to empower African-Americans (Table 10.3). It is the historical ability to adapt family structure to environmental demands (e.g., poverty, or economic crisis) that accounts for African-American resilience (Hill, 1972, 1994). Practitioners must remember, though, that

none of the types of structures that have evolved are exclusive to the African-American people. Because these structures are driven by larger forces which affect the entire population, they appear in other groups as well. . . . If [white Americans] are more resistant to the destructive forces of society it is because they are more privileged and protected. (Billingsley, 1992, p. 45)

Table 10.3. Types of African-American Family Structures

Nuclear family
        Incipient nuclear family: Husband and wife only
        Simple nuclear family: Husband, wife, and children
        Attenuated nuclear family: Single parent and children

Extended family
        Incipient extended family: Husband, wife, and other relatives
        Simple extended family: Husband, wife, children, and other relatives
        Attenuated extended family: Single parent, children, and other
        relatives

Augmented family
        Incipient augmented family: Husband, wife, and nonrelatives
        Incipient extended augmented family: Husband, wife, other relatives,
        and nonrelatives
        Nuclear augmented family: Husband, wife, children, and nonrelatives
        Nuclear extended augmented family: Husband, wife, children, other
        relatives, and nonrelatives
        Attenuated augmented family: Single parent, children, and
        nonrelatives
        Attenuated extended augmented family: Single parent, children, other
        relatives, and nonrelatives

Source: Billingsley (1968, 1992).

ATTITUDES TOWARD MARRIAGE

*[Any comprehensive theory of ideal marriage cannot omit intimacy] a process in
which two caring people share as freely as possible in the exchange of feelings,
thoughts, and actions . . . [It is] marked by a mutual sense of acceptance,
commitment, tenderness, and trust.*
—W. Masters, V. Johnson, and R. Kolodny, *Masters and Johnson
on Sex and Human Loving*

Regardless of marital status or social class, African-Americans value marriage as the preferred means of marshaling the resources necessary to meet the needs of adults and children (Billingsley, 1992). Of the traditional six functions of marriage—child rearing, companionship, sustained love life/sex life, safety for women, help with housework, and the provision of financial security—African-Americans valued three functions most highly and consistently: Across social class, they valued child raising, companionship, and financial security (Billingsley, 1992). However, Billingsley found that, "at the same time, those from middle- and upper-income families tend to give higher value to having a marital partner for love life (sex) and companionship than those in low-income families" (ibid., p. 222). Nonetheless, Billingsley (1992) also noted that the belief in marriage is still so strong that a major-ity of African-American youths and

> Of the traditional functions of marriage, African-Americans value child-rearing, companionship, and the provision of financial security the most.

adults say they want to be married. Even when one marriage is dissolved by separation or divorce, a majority seek still another and continue to believe that marriage is preferable.

Despite their stated value of marriage, African-Americans' behaviors and values may contrast. For example, although both genders value mar-riage, men value marriage more than women, and married men value it more than never-married men (Billingsley, 1992). In addition, despite their stated esteem for the institution of marriage, African-Americans, like other Americans, appear to be abandoning or avoiding marriage (Bill-ingsley, 1992; Staples, 1986; Taylor & Marienau, 1995):

> In the past, black women have married later than White women but have eventually had similar proportions ever married by the time both groups reached their forties and fifties. . . . In 1990, the percent for White women 30–34 had fallen to 86 percent while the percent for black women 30 to 34 had plummeted to 61 percent. Further, only 75 percent of black women in their late thirties had ever married by June 1990, compared with 91 percent of White women in their late thirties. (Norton & Miller, 1992, p. 4)

One of the important consequences of these demographic changes is that a larger proportion women will remain unmarried during their principal child-bearing years, and thus may be more likely to become a one-parent family.

These demographic data indicate that marriage enrichment programs for African-Americans must be adaptable to the varied needs, experience, and meanings among men and women in this population. The construc-tion of curriculum materials, program format, use of time, staffing, and site selection will determine the accessibility of the model to African-American men *and* women with varied psychosocial characteristics.

CAUSES OF MARITAL DISILLUSIONMENT
AND DIVORCE AMONG AFRICAN-AMERICANS

Disillusionment and conflict arise in marriage as romantic love and expectations
do not correspond to the realities of marriage. . . . Men often come to resent
marriage for its economic responsibilities, sexual restrictions, and the surrender
. . . of the prerogative of the provider role.

—J. Bernard, *The Future of Marriage*

Programming for marriage enrichment groups encompasses a range of ecological issues. When framed within an ecological or person-in-environment perspective, the myriad causes of marital disillusionment and divorce (Blackman, 1995a, 1995b) can be see clearly at all levels of the social structure, from the individual to interpersonal relationships to the societal institutions, norms, and values, as well as global international relations. For instance, at the individual level, conflicts among African-American males and females are often related to issues of trust, sexual infidelity, and economic ability. Marriage enrichment program interventions with African-Americans desirous of satisfying marriages must also consider the issue of mate selection, or who is deemed to be marriageable. Differences in partners' biological features, such as sexual function and sleep patterns, can lead to disillusionment and conflict.

Chestang's (1984) *dual perspective,* as well as Pinderhughes's (1978) discussion of African-American mental health issues, have explicated the psychological effects of racial oppression on African-Americans. With self-actualization impeded by institutionalized racism throughout the society, individual self-concept, self-esteem, and hope for achieving the American dream are threatened, if not eroded (Blackman, 1996). These cognitive perceptions, assumptions, attributions, and predictions can lead to mistrust, jealousy, rage, and even violence within the marriage, and are critical factors for discussion in enrichment groups (Baucom & Epstein, 1990; Chang, 1994, 1996).

Another area of interpersonal conflict to be addressed in marriage enrichment groups involves incongruent moral/spiritual beliefs, such as religious ideologies. If not addressed, attitudes toward work or work ethic may also dissipate positive marital energies. Other incongruences in standards and values, such as those related to the use of leisure time and relationships with extended family and friends child rearing, can similarly lead to conflict and subsequent erosion of marital quality. Leaders of marriage enrichment groups can guide group members in identifying which specific conflicts or issues they want to address.

Family-level issues also are encompassed in marriage enrichment group discussions. It is important for social workers to examine what psychological factors may potentially rupture the intimate partnership and the partners' ability to perform the requisite family leadership functions. Another important social work role is exploring differing or negative role models from the partners' families of origin who may contribute to distorted expectations for marriage. Social workers also should examine stresses related to the normal developmental transitions of family life; for example, acquiring and expending money or balancing two careers can frequently threaten the viability of a relationship, particularly if the transitions are unanticipated (Subria, 1994). Family difficulties may be compounded when family members also lack effective parenting and conflict resolution skills. In addition, detrimental experiences with previous intimate partners can create conflicting expectations and assumptions in subsequent attempts at family life, thus affecting levels of trust, empathy, and commitment (Baucom & Epstein, 1990; Subria, 1994). Family life relationship skills to enhance compatibility in these areas can be encompassed in marriage enrichment group curricula.

Social workers also must be cognizant of the various forms of oppression at the societal level (e.g., racism, sexism, and social classism) that may frustrate individual aspirations and interfere with marital function (Chang, 1996; Patton, 1995; Pinderhughes, 1978; Turner, Singleton, & Musick, 1984; Villarosa, 1994). Inequitably restricted access to valued societal resources such as wealth, power, prestige-conferring roles, material goods, education, and occupational opportunities impedes African-Americans, both male and female, in their efforts to self-actualize and to perform their family leadership functions (Blackman, 1992, in press). Moreover, societal norms that value romantic love as the basis for mate selection or materialism that emphasizes the acquisition of "things" over nurturing relationships add to the confusion within individuals and their intimate relationships.

Similarly, global international relationships affect available employment opportunities and wage levels, often having a negative effect on the African-American family. For example, global conflicts such as wars involving the U.S. armed forces create disproportionate numbers of casualties among poor, African-American males. The number of available mates and, thereby mate selection processes, are thus affected. Certainly, national defense fiscal policies are the largest competitors for resources that might otherwise be invested in improving family and community life (Armstead, 1994).

Elements of Optimal Marriages

As with the causes of marital problems, optimal marriages also find their origins throughout the social structure, from individual to societal levels (Blackman, 1992). For instance, at the individual level, ideally each partner should be a self-actualizing person (Maslow, 1970) in the process of maximizing his or her individual potential, rather than being focused solely on meeting basic needs. More-over, each must be mentally flexible enough to adapt to inevitable developmental and situational changes that occur in family life. Job dislocations, births, illnesses and disabilities, the launching of children into adulthood, and career advancements all require psychological adjustments. Mentally inflexible individuals will find optimal intimacy elusive. Instead, such individuals can face their disillusionment and conflict with members of marriage enrichment groups who often are experiencing the same difficulties. Other critical individual-level variables in satisfying relationships that marriage enrichment group leaders should foster include self-respect, respect for one's partner, honesty, and empathy.

> Marriage enrichment group leaders should encourage individuals to embrace self-resect, respect for their partner, honesty, and empathy—factors that contribute to satisfying relationships.

At the interpersonal level, consensus on gender roles and the division of labor is the single most important variable for social workers to consider in harmonious family leadership subsystems. The marriage enrichment group can provide the basis for achieving such consensus through an enhancement of effective communication skills, particularly conflict resolution skills.

However, optimal relationships also require that, at the societal level, social institutions and organizations permit African-Americans, both females and males, equitable access to economic, educational, health, spiritual, and political resources. Without these requisite resources, intimate relationships will continue to be strained inordinately by frustrated, resentful, and often enraged individuals who are ineffectually attempting to engage in intimate relationships and to lead their families.

MARRIAGE ENRICHMENT PROGRAMS

The Negro, like other Americans, has accepted the belief . . . that individuals succeed or fail solely as a result of their individual effort. . . . [This] acceptance . . . has worked to his detriment—for it has operated to sustain a delusion in the face of contradicting reality.
—A. F. Poussaint, "The Psychology of a Minority Group with Implications for Social Action"

Philosophical Assumptions

Happiness versus Empowerment. The underlying assumption of most marriage enrichment programs is that couples can achieve relationships in which they are consistently happy. However, sociological studies have revealed that marital happiness varies with day-to-day life stressors, family developmental stages such as the birth or launching of children, and life crises such as financial crises or death. Furthermore, couples become "habituated" in their relationships over time (Pietropinto & Simenauer, 1979; Schwartz, 1989a, 1989b). For example, in a study of a random sample of the American population ($n = 3,880$), the authors (Pietropinto & Simenauer, 1979) found that couples—including cohabiting couples and divorced individuals who had remarried—became complacent with their marital relationships, including sexual component, despite creative strategies to make the relationships more exciting.

Given these realities of marriage and family life then, it is unlikely that marriage enrichment or any other current technology can give couples skills or knowledge to create relationships that will be invariably new, different, exciting, challenging, romantic, or stimulating. It seems more logical to empower couples by teaching them the requisite information and relationship skills (i.e., cognitive and behavioral) that will enable them to create relationships that are, on the average, satisfying. *Empowerment* is defined, then, as

> the process and outcome of helping [people] to increase their personal, interpersonal, and political power so that they can exert greater control and influence in their personal and [public] lives. . . . [It explicitly involves] . . . attempting changes in structural resources and opportunities, or . . . organizing people for collective action and increasing their political power. (Simon, 1994, p. x)

Because empowerment is the goal of marriage enrichment for African-American couples, the philosophy underpinning the curriculum design process should advance the goal (see Table 10.4 for the steps in the curriculum design process). Because racism, sexism, and classism severely restrict opportunities for creating and maintaining optimal marriages, social workers in this field should empower couples by teaching them the requisite information and relationship skills that will enable them to create satisfying relationships (Blackman, 1992, 1996, in press).

The curriculum design process also must help increase the opportunities for men and women to access the necessary resources for self-actualization and transcendence. It must be explicitly aimed at increasing their political power through collective action (Aschenbrenner, 1973; Bill

Table 10.4.   Designing a Curriculum for Marriage Enrichment Program

1. Clearly state the curriculum rationale and philosophy.
2. Clearly delineate the curriculum goals.
The first set of goals are general program goals and areas of study. For example, in the African American Marriage Enrichment (AAME) program (Blackman, 1992), one of the major goals was to increase marital satisfaction.

3. Clearly define the goal.
> For example, *marital satisfaction* was defined as
>> the subjective appraisal of the extent to which the relationship with one's spouse meets his or instrumental (e.g., material goods, direct services, information useful for daily living) and expressive (e.g., self-worth, intimacy, nurturance, emotional assurance) needs, as well as the extent of conflict (i.e., power struggles) within the married couple's interactions. Such appraisals are seen along a continuum from high levels of satisfaction to distress. (Blackman, 1992, p. 75)

4. Enumerate precise and measurable goals or objectives for an instructional course study.
> For example, the precise and measurable goals or mastery objectives for AAME were as follows:
>> By the end of the training program, each participant will demonstrate knowledge of 1) elements of optimal marriages and causes of marital disillusionment and distress among African American couples; 2) how gender identity and values are formed, 3) how gender identity and values create conflict in marital relationships; and 4) effects of racism and sexism on African American marriages. (Blackman, 1992, p. 280).

5. Create specific lesson plans to guide the adult student's day-to-day behavioral changes.
> The plans should be tailored to the teacher's style, abilities, and strengths as well as students' learning styles and abilities. For each week of the 7-week AAME program, a lesson plan was prescribed to include time allotment; lesson objectives; illustrations to be used (e.g., handouts, videotapes, demonstrations); procedures, lesson summary; weekly evaluation plan; and homework assignments.

6. Establish the instructional program.
> At this point, it is critical that the group leader have an understanding of the group member's ethnicity and gender history, language, customs, world view, and values. In the intimate, democratic, androgynous group, the social worker's knowledge and comfort with the student population is apparent.

ingsley, 1992; Chestang, 1986; King, 1964, 1981; Kunjufu, 1993; McAdoo, 1997; Stack, 1975). Therefore, marriage enrichment programs for African-American men and women should intentionally set both knowledge and political action as explicit program objectives. Because they are already extensively involved in empowering individuals and families, social workers are in a pivotal position to lead in the dissemination of marriage enrichment services to the African-American population.

Companionate Marriages.   In contrast to marriages based on romantic love, *companionate love* is an emotion characterized as intimate, emotionally and sexually gratifying to both partners, supportive of individual self-actualization, liberating versus possessive, steadfast, affectionate, and sustained by self-respect and continuous effort (Masters et al., 1986; Murstein, 1974). A fundamental element of companionate marriages is "true male and female equalitarianism" (Fitzpatrick, 1988, p. 91).

General Program Features

Program Components.   Marriage enrichment programs generally encompass cognitive, affective, and behavioral components. Although there is no comprehensive theory of satisfying marriage, cognitive variables such as positive perceptions and feelings about one's spouse and the relationship (Johnson, White, Edwards, & Booth, 1986; Lauer & Lauer, 1986), sexual knowledge (Fields, 1983; Sager, 1981), and affective variables such as affectionate feelings and emotional empathy (Baucom & Epstein, 1990; Dinkmeyer & Carlson, 1984; Marable, 1986; Staples, 1986) are viewed as the most critical ones to marital satisfaction (Garland, 1983; Hof & Miller, 1981).

Behavioral variables are factors in optimal marriages as well (Baucom & Epstein, 1990). These variables include effective conflict resolution skills (Johnson et al., 1986; Lauer & Lauer, 1986; Masters et al., 1986), communication and negotiation skills (Braithwaite, 1981; Lauer & Lauer, 1986; Masters et al., 1986), possession of adequate economic resources (Browne & Gary, 1985; Jacobson, 1981; Lauer & Lauer, 1986), consensus on the division of labor and gender roles (Asante, 1981; Jacobson, 1981; Marable, 1986; Masters et al., 1986), and joint participation of spouses in activities (e.g., meals, shopping, visiting, household projects, recreation; Johnson et al., 1986; Spanier & Lewis, 1980).

Class Style.   Marriage enrichment groups follow a curriculum design process for adult learners (Verduin, 1980). An adult learning style embodied in an andragogical model of teaching is considered an appropriate philosophy for teaching African-American adults to increase the control over their personal and public lives (Knowles et al. 1984; Taylor & Marienau, 1995). "Andragogy promotes an organizational climate of openness, collaboration, inquiry, creativity, competence, and ultimately success" (Bard, 1984, p. xi).

> Marriage enrichment groups using an andragogical approach to teaching promote an environment of democracy, openness, respect, and success, among other positive attributes.

This approach is particularly appropriate for women, other oppressed populations, and people aged 25–49 years old (hooks, 1994; Taylor & Marienau, 1995). People in this age range often reflect the global and national social and economic upheaval from the 1940s to the 1970s. They are members of the "Me generation," the television, video, and "instant everything" generation. Their previous educational experience often has stifled their creativity, their ability to analyze, organize, and synthesize data, as well as their participation in the civil exchange of ideas in the classroom or collaborative work groups. The result may be less than optimal academic achievement and a sense of powerlessness to change the conditions of their lives.

A group conducted in the style of the andragogical classroom fosters a climate of democracy, openness, respect, inquiry, creativity, competence, shared teaching and learning, as well as success (Bard, 1984; hooks, 1994). In such an environment, learning new marriage skills is fun, because it incorporates humor and laughter freely. Furthermore, group members' life experiences are valued, and group leaders actively solicit and welcome members' input. There is overt discussion of political standpoints, including the politics of racism, sexism, and heterosexism (hooks, 1994). Diverse opinions, then, are expected and respected by group leaders and members alike. All members of the group community feel safe to confront and express ideas and fears without being judged as intellectually or morally inadequate. Furthermore, social workers honor the need of group members to be self-directed as well as responsible for their own learning. This attitude creates a group climate in which a sense of competence and confidence does not solely depend on group leaders (Bard, 1984; hooks, 1994).

Program Goal. Marriage and family enrichment are in consonance with the emphasis on primary and secondary prevention in the field of physical and mental health (Guerney, 1987; L'Abate, 1981; Mace & Mace, 1975). The goal of marriage enrichment programs is to help couples "discover their strengths and enhance these before reaching the clinical stage" (Denton, 1986b, p. 3). These programs are formulated to address the types of relationship problems that plague American couples, including African-American couples: communication and negotiation difficulties, gender role conflicts, issues involving earning and controlling money, power inequities, and sexual skills, attitudes, and child rearing.

Target Population. The target population is heterosexual, married couples who enroll voluntarily because they desire greater marital satisfaction, but do not identify themselves as needing therapy. Typically, the wives are most often "draggers" and husbands are "draggees" to marriage enrichment programs (Mace & Mace, 1975). Unmarried cohabitating couples in intimate relationships are more likely to be welcomed in secular programs, but generally not in parochial programs (Blackman, 1989).

Although marriage enrichment programs are typically targeted toward nonclinical couples, maritally distressed couples also have found improvement with structured marriage enrichment programs (Blackman, 1992; Collins, 1987; Guerney, 1987). Both research and clinical findings have indicated that the programs are highly beneficial for distressed couples, particularly as a prelude or adjunct to formal marital or sex therapy. Larger positive effect sizes are frequently achieved by the most maritally distressed participants (Blackman, 1992).

Interventions. Structured as psychoeducational interventions, programs are designed to guide spouses in examining their expectations and attitudes regarding marriage, gender roles, and sexuality, or to teach specific interpersonal relationship skills such as communication, conflict resolution, or sexual techniques (Glisson 1976; Gurman & Kniskern, 1981; Witkin, Edelson, Rose, & Hall, 1983). In addition, a few models of sexual enhancement focus on "enhancing and enriching the sexual relationship of normal, nondysfunctional couples" (LoPiccolo & Miller, 1975, p. 41).

Formats. Program formats vary from couple-centered programs, which focus primarily on unmonitored couple interactions (Mace & Mace, 1986; Smith & Smith, 1976), to highly structured, behaviorally oriented models (Harrell & Guerney, 1976; Rose, 1974). They also vary from weekend retreats (Bosco, 1976; Hof & Miller, 1981) to multiweek programs (i.e., from 3 to 16 weeks; (Blackman, 1992; Dinkmeyer and Carlson, 1984; Gordon, 1988). Multiweek programs allow participants to learn over an extended period, incorporating new information and skills into their repertoire. Consequently, these programs tend to be more effective than weekend retreats, which serve primarily to improve participants' perceptions of each other and the marriage (Hof & Miller, 1981).

Settings. Marriage enrichment programs typically are offered in settings within target populations' natural helping networks (e.g., churches, community centers, and retreat complexes). Such settings are important in attracting voluntary participants from oppressed groups, such as African-Americans (Chestang, 1984; Sue, 1981). People are most likely to seek help for personal and family problems within their natural helping network. They generally mistrust formal helping structures, particularly those geographically located on unfamiliar turf or staffed by personnel who are unfamiliar with their culture and struggles against oppression. It is critical to avoid the social stigma associated with formal helping settings, especially mental health settings.

Practitioner Competence. Marriage enrichment programs require that social workers achieve competence in such areas such as psychosocial assessment, human growth and behavior across the life span, human sexuality, various marriage and family structures along with associated dynamics and transitions, and group facilitation skills, as well as be aware of the effects the social environment has on the growth and development of humans, particularly members of oppressed populations (e.g., African-Americans, women, older adults, people with disabilities, or people with inadequate incomes; Blackman, 1992). Social workers also must have knowledge concerning behavior change techniques, ethics, and adult education. The National Council on Family Relations (NCFR) requires competence in these areas for certification in the encompassing field of family life education (Bredehoft, 1995).

Currently, no formal training in marriage enrichment exists at the university level, and, according to NCFR (Dawn Cassidy, personal communication, 1997), only three universities provide accredited family life education programs at the baccalaureate level. Therefore, social workers interested in marriage enrichment practice must learn the methodology by self study, participation in model-specific training, or the few university-based programs available.

Program Outcomes

Although more than 100,000 couples have participated in Marriage Encounter programs alone (Hof & Miller, 1981), the literature has not indicated that African-American couples receive marriage enrichment services on a broad scale. Therefore, research is needed to determine what types of content, structure, leadership, and time frames are most appropriate for which segments of the African-American married population.

According to the literature, wives typically begin marriage enrichment programs with significantly better communication, negotiation, and empathy skills than men (Blackman, 1992; Hof & Miller, 1981). In addition, wives have higher scores at termination and follow-up than husbands on both observational and self-report measures (Hof and Miller, 1981). Both behavioral and subjective dimensions of client issues have followed this pattern. Nonetheless, husbands have tended to demonstrate more improvement from pretest to posttest or follow-up than wives, which demonstrates that men can achieve the cognitive and behavioral goals of marriage enrichment programs.

Although most models have not been empirically validated, models that include skills training (e.g., communication or behavioral exchange), attitudinal change (e.g., gender roles), or knowledge building (e.g., human sexuality) seem to produce more durable changes in behavior and in reported levels of marital satisfaction than models that simply raise the participants' consciousness (Garland, 1983; Hof & Miller, 1981). Furthermore, there is some evidence that "structured experiences have been reported to lead to greater group cohesiveness, greater involvement of participants in group activities, . . . and participants' self-report of greater learning from the group experiences" (Hof & Miller, 1981, p. 79). More specifically, a combination of communication training and behavior exchange seems to lead to greater change than either component alone (Hof & Miller, 1981; Witkin, 1977, 1997).

Approximately 40 studies have suggested that marriage enrichment is an effective technology for improving cognitive and behavioral elements of marital satisfaction or marital adjustment. However, more research needs to be done before a definitive statement can be made about the effectiveness of marriage enrichment and its universal application to American married couples or to African-American couples, in particular.

REFERENCES

Allen, J., & Turner, E. (1988). People of African origin. In *We the people: An atlas of America's diversity* (pp. 143–151). New York: MacMillan.

Armstead, R. (1994). *War trauma and urban violence: Linking veterans' issues and community research.* Paper presented at a conference entitled "What works?: Synthesizing effective biomedical and psychosocial strategies for healthy families in the 21st century," Indiana University, School of Social Work, Indianapolis.

Asante, M.A. (1981). Black male and female relationships: An Afrocentric context. In L. E. Gary (Ed.). Black men. Beverly Hills, CA: Sage.

Aschenbrenner, J. (1973). Extended families among Black Americans. *Journal of Comparative Family Studies, 4*(2), 257–268.

Azrin, N., Naster, B., & Jones, R. (1973). Reciprocity counseling: A rapid learning-based procedure for marital counseling. *Behavior Research and Therapy, 11,* 365–382.

Bard, R. (1984). Foreword. In M. S. Knowles (Ed.), *Andragogy in action* (p. x). San Francisco, CA: Jossey-Bass.

Baucom, D., & Epstein, N. (1990). *Cognitive-behavioral marital therapy.* New York: Brunner/Mazel.

Bernard, J. (1982). *The future of marriage* (2nd ed.). New Haven, CT: Yale University Press.

Billingsley, A. (1968). *Black families in white America.* Englewood Cliffs, NJ: Prentice Hall.

Billingsley, A. (1986). The changing American family. Paper presented at the 1986 Annual meeting of the Council of Foundations. Kansas City, MO: April.

Billingsley, A. (1992). *Climbing Jacob's ladder.* New York: Simon & Schuster.

Blackman, L.C. (1989). Marital enrichment and African American couples: A specialization paper. Unpublished manuscript. Tallahassee: Florida State University.

Blackman, L. (1992). *The effect of a marriage enrichment program on marital satisfaction and gender role attitudes among African American couples.* Unpublished manuscript, Florida State University, Tallahassee.

Blackman, L. (1995a). Marriage enrichment: A potential strategy for promoting marital satisfaction and stability among African Americans. *Black Caucus,* 2(1), 21–30.

Blackman, L. (1995b). What's love got to do with it? Violence in African American marriage. In A. Rodgers (Ed.), *Violence and the black family: Implications for health, education, domestic relations, criminal justice, workplace, child welfare, and human services* (pp. 52–70). Columbia: College of Social Work, University of South Carolina.

Blackman, L. (1996). *Correlated or predictive factors of African American success and health despite adverse psychosocial environmental origins.* Indianapolis: Indiana State Department of Health.

Blackman, L. (in press). The UMOJA principle in action: African American men and women pulling together to forge 21st century families. *Journal of African American Men.*Blackman, L., and Smith, L. (Speakers) (1994). *The real deal: Child abuse prevention in the African American community* (Audiocassette, Recording No. 1). Indianapolis: Indiana Chapter of the National Committee for the Prevention of Child Abuse.

Bloom, M. (1981). A working definition of primary prevention related to social concerns. In M. Nobel (Ed.), *Primary prevention in mental health and social work* (pp. 64–72). New York: Council on Social Work Education.

Bloom, M. (1987). Prevention. In A. Minahan (Editor-in-Chief), *Encyclopedia of social work* (18th ed.) (pp. 303–315). Silver Spring, MD: NASW Press.

Bosco, A. (1976). Marriage Encounter: An ecumenical enrichment program. In H. A. Otto (Ed.), *Marriage and family enrichment: New perspectives and programs* (pp. 94–100) Nashville, TN: Abingdon.

Branic, G. (1995). Violence and the black family: Where we are, where we want to be, and how we get there. In A. Rodgers (Ed.), *Violence and the black family: Implications for health, education, domestic relations, criminal justice, workplace, child welfare, and human services* (pp. 32–38). Columbia: College of Social Work, University of South Carolina.

Braithwaite, R. L. (1981). Interpersonal relations between Black males and Black females. In L. E. Gary (Ed.), *Black men* (pp. 83–99. Beverly Hills, CA: Sage.

Bredehoft, D. (Ed.) (1995). *Family life education curriculum guidelines* (2nd ed.). Minneapolis, MN: National Council on Family Relations.

Browne, D. R., & Gary, L. E. (1985). Social support network differentials among married and non-married Black females. *Psychology of Women Quarterly 9*(2), 229–241.

Chang, V. N. (1994). Connections between psychological abuse of women and physical and mental illness. In L. C. Blackman (Ed.), *What works? Synthesizing effective biomedical and psychosocial strategies for healthy families in the 21st century* (pp. 101–108). Indianapolis: Indiana University School of Social Work.

Chang, V. N. (1996). *I just lost myself: Psychological abuse of women in marriage.* Westport, CT: Praeger.

Chestang, L. (1984). Racial and personal identity in the black experience. In B. W. White (Ed.), *Color in a White Society* (pp. 83–94). Silver Spring, MD: NASW Press.

Collins, J. D. (1987). Experimental evaluation of a six-month conjugal therapy and relationship enhancement program. In B. G. Guerney, *Relationship enhancement* (pp. 192-226). San Francisco, CA: Jossey-Bass.

Davis, A. (1981). *Women, race and class.* New York: Random House.

Denton, W. (1986a). Starting a local marriage enrichment group. *Journal of Psychotherapy and the Family, 2,* 69–77.

Denton, W. (1986b). Introduction to marriage and family enrichment: A shift in the paradigm. *Journal of Psychotherapy and the Family* 2(1), 3–6.

Dinkmeyer, D. & Carlson, J. (1984). *TIME for a Better Marriage.* Circle Pines, MN: American Guidance Service.

Evans, H., Evans, R., Croom, G., Berryman-Gilliam, B., & Davis, B. (1995). Stress management for children who have witnessed violence. In A. Rodgers (Ed.), *Violence and the black family: Implications for health, education, domestic relations, criminal justice, workplace, child welfare, and human services* (pp. 117–131). Columbia: College of Social Work, University of South Carolina.

Fields, N. S. (1983). Satisfaction in long-term marriages. *Social Work, 28*(1), 37–31.

Fitzpatrick, M. (1988). *Between Husbands and Wives: Communication in Marriage.* Newbury Park, CA: Sage.

Garland, D. S. R. (1983). *Working with couples for marriage enrichment.* San Francisco: Jossey Bass.

Gentry, C. (1978). Incestuous abuse of children: The need for an objective view. *Child Welfare, 57*(6), 355–364.

Glisson, D. H. (1976). A comparison of reciprocity counseling and communication training in the treatment of marital discord. Ph.D. dissertation. Washington University. Dissertation Abstracts International, 37/12. 7973A.

Gordon, L. H. (1988). *PAIRS: Beyond survival.* Paper presented at American Association for Marriage and Family Therapy Conference, New Orleans, October.

Green, J. W. (1995). *Cultural awareness in the human services: a multi-ethnic approach* (2nd ed.). Needham Heights, MA: Allyn & Bacon.

Guerney, B. G. (1987). *Relationship enhancement.* San Francisco, CA: Jossey-Bass.

Gurman, A. S., & Kniskern, D. P. (Eds.). (1981). *Handbook of family therapy.* New York: Brunner/Mazel.

Harrell, J., & Guerney, B. (1976). Training married couples in conflict negotiation skills. In D. H. Olson (Ed.), *Treating Relationships.* Lake Mills, IA: Graphic.

Hill, R. B. (1972). *The strengths of black families.* New York: Emerson Hall.

Hill, R. B. (1994). *The strengths of families of color* (Videotape). Indianapolis: Indiana University School of Social Work.

Hof, L., & Miller, W. (1981). *Marriage enrichment: Philosophy, process, and program.* Bowie, MD: Robert J. Brady.

hooks, b. (1994). *Teaching to transgress: Education as the practice of freedom.* New York: Routledge.

Jacobson, N. S. (1981). Behavioral marital therapy. In A. S. Gurman & D. P. Kniskern (Eds.), *Handbook of family therapy* (pp. 631–661). New York: Brunner/Mazel.

Johnson, D., White, L., Edwards, J., & Booth, A. (1986). Dimensions of marital quality. *Journal of Family Issues, 7*(1), 31–49.

King, M. L., Jr. (1964). *Why we can't wait.* New York: Mentor.

King, M. L., Jr. (1981). *Strength to love.* Philadelphia, PA: Fortress.

Knowles, M. S., and Associates. (1984). *Andragogy in action.* San Francisco, CA: Jossey-Bass.

Korbin, J. (1981). *Child abuse and neglect: Cross-cultural perspectives.* Los Angeles: University of California Press.

Kunjufu, J. (1979). Not allowed to be friends and / or lovers. *Black Male/Female Relationships, 2*(1), 58–60.

Kunjufu, J. (1993). *The power, passion & pain of Black love.* Chicago, IL: African American Images.

L'Abate, L. (1981). Skill training programs for couples and families. In A. S. Gurman & D. P. Kniskern (Eds.), *Handbook of family therapy* (pp. 631–661). New York: Brunner / Mazel.

Lauer, R. H., & Lauer, J. C. (1986). Factors in long-term marriages. *Journal of Family Issues, 7*(4), 382–390.

LoPiccolo, J., & Miller, V. (1975). A program for enhancing the sexual relationship of normal couples. *Counseling Psychologist, 5*(1), 41–45.

Mace, D., & Mace, V. (1975). Marriage enrichment: Wave of the future. *Family Coordinator, 24*(2), 131–135.

Mace, D., & Mace, V. (1986). The history and present status of the marriage and family enrichment movement. *Journal of Psychotherapy & the Family, 2*(1), 7–18.

Marable, A. (1986). The Black male: Searching beyond stereotypes. In R. Staples (Ed.), *The Black family* (pp. 64–69). Belmont, CA: Wadsworth.

Markman, H., Floyd, F., & Dickson-Markman, F. (1982). Towards a model for the prediction and primary prevention of marital and family distress and dissolution. In S. Duck (Ed.), *Personal relationships* (pp. 173–195). New York: Guilford.

Maslow, A. (1970). *Motivation and Personality* (2nd ed.). New York: Harper & Row.

Masters, W., Johnson, V., & Kolodny, R. (1986). *Masters and Johnson on sex and human loving.* Boston, MA: Little, Brown.

McAdoo, H. (Ed.) (1997). *Black families* (3rd ed.). Thousand Oaks, CA: Sage.

Mehta, S. (1978). The stability of black-white vs. racially homogeneous marriages in the United States, 1960–1970. *Journal of Social and Behavioral Science, 24,* 133.

Miller, S. (1982). Themes and models in primary prevention with minority populations. In S. O. Miller, G. S. O'Neal, and C. A. Scott (Eds.), *Primary prevention approaches to the development of mental health services for ethnic minorities: A challenge to social work education and practice* (pp. 110–130). New York: Council on Social Work Education.

Murstein, B. (1974). *Love, sex and marriage through the ages.* New York: Springer.

National Urban League (1995). African Americans then and now: A statistical overview. In *The state of Black America* (pp. 289–315). New York: Author.

Norton, A., & Miller, L. (1992). *Marriage, divorce and remarriage in the 1990's* (Series 23–180). Washington, DC: U.S. Bureau of the Census.

Patton, J. M. (1995). The education of African American males: Frameworks for developing authenticity. *Journal of African American Men, 1*(1), 5–28.

Pietropinto, A., & Simenauer, J. (1979). *Husbands and wives.* New York: Times Books.

Poussaint, A. F. (1969). The psychology of a minority group with implications for social action. In C. U. Daly (Ed.), *Urban violence.* Chicago: University of Chicago Press.

Rose, S. D. (1974). *Treating children in groups.* San Francisco, CA: Jossey-Bass.

Sager, C. J. (1981). Couples therapy and marriage contracts. In A. S. Gurman & D. P. Kniskern (Eds.), *Handbook of family therapy* (pp. 85–132). New York: Brunner/Mazel.

Schwartz, P. (1989a, February). *Sex, power and gender in intimate relationships.* Paper presented at Annual Conference of the Alliance for Marriage and Family Therapy of Florida State University, Tallahassee.

Schwartz, P. (1989b, February). *Sexual issues in the 1980's and the predictions for the 1990's.* Paper presented at Annual Conference of the Alliance for Marriage and Family Therapy of Florida State University, Tallahassee.

Simon, B. L. (1994). *The empowerment tradition in American social work: A history.* New York, NY: Columbia University Press.

Smith, L. & Smith, A. (1976). Developing a national marriage communication lab training program. In H. A. Otto (Ed.), *Marriage and family enrichment: new perspectives and programs* (pp. 241–253). Nashville, TN: Abingdon.

Spanier, G. B., & Lewis, R. A. (1980). Marital quality: A review of the seventies. *Journal of Marriage and the Family, 42,* 825–839.

Stack, C. B. (1975). *All our kin: Strategies for survival in a Black community.* New York: Harper & Row.

Staples, R. (1986). Beyond the black family: The trend toward singlehood. In R. Staples (Ed.), *The black family* (3rd ed.) (pp. 99–106). Belmont, CA: Wadsworth.

Subria, G. (1994). *Money issues in black male-female relationships.* Newark, NJ: Very Serious Business Enterprises.

Sue, D. W. (1981). *Counseling the culturally different: Theory and practice.* New York: Wiley.

Taylor, K., and Marienau, C. (1995). Bridging practice and theory for women's adult development. In R. G. Brockett (Series Ed.), *New directions for adult and continuing Education,* Vol. 65, Learning environments for women's adult development: Bridges toward change (K. Taylor and C. Marienau, Vol. Eds.) (pp. 5–12). San Francisco, CA: Jossey-Bass.

Turner, J., Singleton, R., & Musick, D. (1984). *Oppression: A socio-history of black-white relations in America.* Chicago: Nelson-Hall.

U.S. Bureau of the Census (1990). General population characteristics. In *Census of Population.* Washington, DC: Superintendent of Documents.

U.S. Bureau of the Census (1993). Household and family characteristics: March, 1992. In *Current population reports* (Series P-20, No. 467). Washington, DC: U.S. Government Printing Office.

Verduin, J., Jr. (1980). *Curriculum building for adult learning.* Carbondale: Southern Illinois Press.

Villarosa, L. (Ed.) (1994). *Body & soul: The Black women's guide to physical health and emotional well-being.* New York: Harper-Collins.

Witkin, S. (1989). Responding to sexism in marital research and therapy: Is awareness enough? *Journal of Family Psychology, 3,* 82–85.
Witkin, S., Edelson, J., Rose, S., & Hall, J. (1983). Group training in marital communication: A comparative study. *Journal of Marriage and the Family,* 661–666.
Witkin, S., & Rose, S. (1997). Group training in communication skills for couples: A
preliminary report. *International Journal of Family Counseling, 6*(2), 32–35.

11

Individuals with Developmental Disabilities

NANCY P. KROPF

Across the life span, people with developmental disabilities (DD) often require support and services from social workers. Unfortunately, many social work students and practitioners have limited understanding about the experiences and needs of this client group (DePoy & Miller, 1996; DeWeaver & Kropf, 1992; Mackelprang & Salsgiver, 1996). Using an ecological framework, this chapter presents information about people with DD and their families and addresses service issues related to this population. The goal is to sensitize students to crucial issues that people with DD and their families face and to promote a more effective way of providing services to these clients.

OVERVIEW OF DEVELOPMENTAL DISABILITIES

The lives of [people] with mental retardation are highly varied, and if we are to understand them as people, we must recognize that in many ways each one of them is quite different from any other. . . . No single set of services, no simple drafting of policies can begin to serve the needs of these many individuals, either now or in the future.
—R. B. Edgerton and M. A. Gaston, *"I've Seen It All": Lives of Older Persons with Mental Retardation in the Community*

Diversity Perspective

Practice with people who have DD is most often considered through a biomedical or behavioral perspective. In a biomedical framework, people with DD are evaluated based on their physical status or function, such as having a certain type of syndrome or condition (e.g., Down syndrome or autism), or their requirement of certain environmental conditions (e.g., use of a wheelchair or need for a barrier-free environment). A behavioral perspective focuses on the management of problematic conditions such as self-stimulation or hyperactivity or skills acquisition, for example, using token economies or reinforcement schedules. Both perspectives emphasize the deficiencies or problem aspects of having a disability.

A rival framework—and one that is integrated into this chapter—is a diversity perspective. A diversity perspective differs from the other perspectives because the focus is on the social barriers experienced by people with DD rather than on their physical or social deficits. A diversity perspective has been previously used to argue that many of the problems people with disabilities face result from the social barriers that prohibit full participation in society (Beck, 1994; Kropf & DeWeaver, 1996). Like other groups that have experienced social devaluation (e.g., older adults, people of color, gay males and lesbians), people with DD do not receive equal social status in social roles. Many of the problems people with DD bring to social workers are a consequence of the disadvantaged social position they hold in our society.

Definition of DD

Like the other groups discussed in this book, people with DD are a heterogeneous segment of the population. Several different diagnostic categories are included in the definition of a developmental disability, but the four major conditions are (1) mental retardation, (2) cerebral palsy, (3) epilepsy, and (4) autism. Other early onset, lifelong impairments are also considered "development disabilities": spinal bifida, deafness, learning disabilities, and blindness, among others. The Developmental Disabilities Assistance and Bill of Rights Act of 1990 (P.L. 101-496 104 Stat. 1191) has defined a *developmental disability* as a severe, chronic disability of a person aged 5 years or older that has the following characteristics:

- is attributable to a mental or physical impairment, or a combination,
- is manifested before age 22 years
- is likely to continue indefinitely
- results from functional limitations in three or more of the following areas of major life activities: self-care, receptive/expressive language, learning, mobility, self-direction, capacity for independent living, economic self-sufficiency,

- reflects the person's need for a combination and sequence of special interdisciplinary, or generic, care or treatment, or other services that are of life-long or extended duration and are individually planned and coordinated.

Although the criteria specifically address children older than age 5 years, infants and young children are also addressed in the act. The criteria may be applied to younger children if they have a substantial developmental delay or a specific congenital or acquired condition with a high probability that the condition will result in a developmental disability if services are not provided.

The term *developmental disability* is a recent one, originating in the late 1960s and initially defined in the Developmental Disabilities Services and Facilities Construction Act of 1970 (P.L. No. 91-57, 84 Stat. 1316) (DeWeaver, 1995). The earliest definitions mainly addressed cognitive impairment as displayed in subaverage intelligence. Although mental retardation is still the predominant category, individuals with other forms of DD may have average or above average intelligence.

Incidence and Prevalence

The incidence of a developmental disability has been estimated across the different categories of disabilities. McLaughlin and Wehmann (1996) offered the following estimates for the four major developmental disabilities: 0.2% for cerebral palsy, 0.15% for autism, 0.4% for epilepsy, and 3% for mental retardation. However, several factors have made estimates difficult to gauge accurately. One is the use of a functional definition in which someone can be evaluated as having DD at one time, but at a later period, the person may have gained skills and competencies and would no longer be considered to have DD.

Another difficulty in estimating prevalence is that, across the life span, the rates of disability can vary within the overall population. Some types of DD are associated with higher infant mortality rates, such as Down syndrome. In addition, people with some types of disability, e.g., cerebral palsy, have shorter life expectancies (Turk & Machemer, 1993). For these reasons, the concept of late life has been operationalized differently than for the general population: People with DD are commonly considered "elderly" about 10 years earlier than their nondisabled cohorts (Seltzer & Krauss, 1987).

In addition, many individuals have multiple disabilities. In the population of people with DD, for example, the rate of epilepsy has been estimated to range from 20 to 40%, which is much higher than the rate in the general population. In addition, epilepsy has a higher prevalence in people who have an IQ below 50 and affects about 50% of people with DD who also have cerebral palsy (Baribeault, 1996).

AN ECOLOGICAL FRAMEWORK APPLIED
TO PEOPLE WITH DD

Families and their social environment form a complex and dynamic system with multiple factors that influence how families adjust to rearing a child with disabilities.

—J. Rogers-Dulan and J. Blacher, "African American Families, Religion, and Disability: A Conceptual Framework"

An ecological framework has been used extensively to examine experiences and service issues for various groups of clients. For people with DD, this perspective has been the framework to explore psychosocial issues of late-life parenting experiences (Kropf & Greene, 1993), an infusion model for social work education (Kropf, 1996), an intervention model for domestic violence for women (Carlson, 1997), and a treatment model for working with criminal offenders who have mental retardation (Demetral, 1994). At the microsystem level, a life span perspective is used to examine issues that involve the individual with DD and his or her family system. The mesosystem level explores the relationship between the family and environmental supports including friendships, labor force issues, and the formal services system. Relationships between systems are examined at the exosystem level. The macrosystem includes cultural values and beliefs that influence the experiences of people with DD and their family and the political environment through laws and policies. Attention to both the individual and family and the broader social context promotes a goodness-of-fit perspective to guide social work practice with this client population.

Microsystem

Childhood and Adolescence. A diagnosis of a developmental disability, as defined, can be made at multiple points during development from the prenatal phase until age 22 years. The issues that parents face in assimilating this diagnosis depend on the point at which it was made. For example, a woman who learns of a disability

> Families with children with DD must make adjustments to balance the many demands within the family system.

during pregnancy may face risks in carrying the baby to full term, a decision about whether to terminate the pregnancy, and questions about the effects of the child's condition on the family's quality of life. These issues differ from those confronting parents of a child whose disability is a result of an accident or illness. Although the diagnosis is a stressful experience in either situation, social work interventions vary because of the different periods in the family life cycle.

Being a care provider for any child can be challenging, but a child with a disability may present particular demands for a family. Parents have reported that they require ongoing emotional support, support with the financial obligations of caregiving, support dealing with crisis situations, support handling difficult behavioral problems, and assistance in securing respite care (Kropf, 1991). Gallimore, Weisner, Bernheimer, Guthrie, and Nihara (1993) studied family responses to raising young children with DD from an ecocultural theory perspective. This framework proposes that families with children with DD must engage in accommodations to balance multiple demands within the family system. Although all families make accommodations for their children, those families who have a person with DD have unique issues that require attention and energy. For example, the situation of one family in the study illustrated that point: "We're going to be looking for a house pretty soon, and kind of in the back of our mind, we're thinking, 'we've got to keep it near where her therapy is at, because it's got to be within driving distance twice a week'" (ibid., p. 185). Those parents were faced with the usual decisions about moving to a new location, but also had to consider how the move would influence their child's ability to access needed services.

The presence of a child with DD can also affect relationships within the family system. One subsystem is the relationship between siblings. Brothers and sisters of children with DD have expressed both negative and positive effects of their family situation (Wilson, Blacher, & Baker, 1989). Research on sibling relationships has suggested that offspring are often expected to assume some caregiving responsibility for their brother or sister (Stoneman, Brody, Davis, & Crapps, 1989). In addition, many parents may assume that nondisabled children will become the primary care provider of their brother or sister at some point. However, siblings also benefit from having a brother or sister with DD in that they may become more accepting of others, may learn patience, and may become more responsible.

Adulthood. As the child matures, families must deal with adult issues of caring for a person with DD. One of the most difficult issues for parents is the sexuality of their child. Although people with DD have lower cognitive or physical function, they do have desires to have sexual relations, marriages or partnerships, and, sometimes, children of their own. However, people with DD encounter numerous barriers related to sexual function including a lack of information, and lack of opportunities; in addition they are a high-risk group for abuse (Furey, 1994; Sundrum & Stavis, 1994).

Although social and physical factors may prevent many adults with DD from having children, some do become parents. The intellectual disability of a parent in terms of its effects on a child's welfare as well as on parenting skills has been a concern. Some research has suggested that children who are raised by parents who have mental retardation evidence developmental delays and that these parents experience difficulties in their caregiving roles (Feldman, Case, Towns, & Betel, 1985; Keltner, 1994; Unger & Howes, 1988). Social workers can provide support, education, and information about resources to assist parents with DD in their performance as parents.

One primary role during adulthood is as a worker. For adults with DD, few options exist in the labor force, and people with disabilities are the poorest and least educated minority group in the U.S. (Kopels, 1995). Often, adults with DD attend segregated workplaces such as sheltered workshops or day activity centers. These programs provide work-related training with the goal of integration into the community. However, few participants make the transition into more independent positions. A different model that begins with community integration is supported employment, which enables the worker to receive intensive on-the-job training by a job coach. This model allows a person with DD to be involved in "real jobs" in the community and provide an additional labor source in difficult market segments, such as minimum wage positions. An analysis of wage earners in supported employment positions has suggested that both personal and environmental factors are predictors of higher salaries. Those workers receiving greater wages were those with higher IQs and worked in businesses in which the employer received a federal subsidy for hiring workers with disabilities (Rusch, Heal, & Cimera, 1997).

Late Life. During late adulthood, older parents and adults with DD must handle several significant issues. The most difficult task for older parents is deciding on future care plans for their son or daughter. The process of future care planning is so emotionally difficult that many parents avoid this painful task, which results in a crisis situation when a parental health problem or death does occur (Kaufman, Adams, & Campbell, 1991; Smith & Tobin, 1993). In a study on the future plans of older families, researchers found that only 50% of their sample (mean parent age was 68 years) had residential plans for their son or daughter with DD

(Freedman, Krauss, & Seltzer, 1997). One mother described her "future care plan" for her son who has mental retardation as hoping that her son would die one minute after she does (Jacobson, Stoneman, & Kropf, 1995). This desire might minimize her emotional discomfort in the short term, but it would leave her son in a vulnerable situation if a crisis should occur.

In late life, many older adults experience one or more chronic health conditions. For older adults with DD, many geriatric conditions occur earlier than in the general population. For this reason, Seltzer and Krauss (1987) have argued that the term *elderly person* should be defined 10 years earlier in the population with DD at age 55 years. Some of the conditions that appear earlier in the population with DD are cardiac problems, musculoskeletal problems, and dementia. Certain types of problems result from the particular physiological condition that causes the disability, such as the early onset of Alzheimer's disease in people with Down syndrome. However, other conditions are a result of poor health practices with this population, lack of access to appropriate health care resources, and the lack of health care personnel who are trained to work with people who have DD.

Mesosystem

The mesosystem level involves the linkages between the individual and his or her family and other systems in the environment. These linkages include formalized services such as school, employment setting, and DD service programs, and informal connections such as friendship and voluntary associations.

Informal Supports. The responsibility for raising a son or daughter with a disability affects the family's informal support system. In trying to juggle the multiple demands of child rearing, holding a job, and other aspects of family life such as maintaining marital quality, little time is left for pursuing extrafamily involvement such as friendships. Social support networks of families with a son or daughter who has DD include fewer outside supports than families who have nondisabled children, which can lead to parental feelings of isolation and alienation (Kropf, 1991).

Another source of support for families is labor force participation. For parents, their job is a source of identity and provides an opportunity to make social connections. Parents of children with disabilities often have to make difficult choices between their jobs and their family situations (Gallimore et al., 1993). For example, service options for people with disabilities dramatically vary geographically. Parents may have to forgo advancements, relocations, or other job changes if the child's service eligibilities could suffer, for instance, if the family should move to a new community with fewer DD program options.

Formal Services.   The mesosystem also encompasses those relationships between families and formalized services. The current service model, one of collaboration between families and formal service providers, emphasizes person-centered planning, a model that involves identifying the goals, wishes, and desires of individuals with DD and their families. For many families, especially those in later life, this model is a radical change from the predominant one

> The service model in which families and formal service providers collaborate emphasizes person-centered planning.

that existed until recently. Previously, families had little role in decision-making about service options—that was the function of the professional provider. For older families, the experience with professionals (e.g., physicians) who *instructed them* to place their child in an institution or some other residential placement may have left them wary of formalized service providers. These past experiences need to be understood in appreciating the current relationships between families and formalized services (Kelly & Kropf, 1995; Kropf, 1997).

Another service issue is the uneven quality of services among various locations. Urban locations, for example, may offer an array of options: residential, vocational, transportation, and respite care. However, other locations may have little to provide families, who are then left to care for the son or daughter with DD without the benefit of any formal care resources. In addition, differences among geographic locations also have consequences for family function. Some states have closed all of the institutions for people with disabilities, whereas other states have continued to house people with disabilities in institutional facilities. Likewise, community resources also vary in the type and amount that families can receive. In Michigan, for example, families with children who have DD receive family support payments that allow families the flexibility of purchasing needed resources. Families can use the funds to purchase a variety of services to allow their son or daughter to remain in the family home (Herman, 1994).

Exosystem Level

On the exosystem level, system-level relationships are highlighted. For people with DD, these relationships involve the linkages among various service networks. People with DD who live in community settings instead of in institutions will need to access community-based health and social services. Unfortunately, many service providers do not have the expertise to effectively work with people with disabilities, especially if those people have a cognitive disability such as mental retardation. Coordination among different service networks must occur across the life span, including school-to-work transition, and DD and mental health services. The following are examples of inclusion of people with DD in addiction and aging services.

Addictions. One of the fallouts of community integration is an increased incidence of people with DD who engage in negative life-style habits of the general population. One such habit is substance abuse. One estimate on the incidence of addiction among the DD population has suggested it is higher than that in the general population (Westermeyer, Phaobtong, & Neidor, 1988). Several reasons might account for this statistic: people with DD may be trying to achieve social acceptance, they may lack awareness of harmful effects of alcohol and drugs, or they may show poor problem-solving and judgment that increases their vulnerability.

People with intellectual disabilities may not benefit from the addiction models that are based on problem solving and insight orientation. Unfortunately, few addiction programs are specifically structured for people with DD, providing the type of interventions that are necessary for this population. Hodermarska, Sherman, and Spiegel (1997) offered an example of a man with mental retardation who attended Alcoholics Anonymous meetings for his alcoholism. During the meetings, participants stressed that the man should get "tools" to be able to deal with the pressures of substance abuse in his life. During one meeting, the man was provided a certificate to commemorate an anniversary of his sobriety. He became agitated and hostile. He had worked to achieve this goal, expecting that his reward would be a box of work tools and all he received was a piece of paper. In this example, the abstract way in which the nondisabled participants discussed coping was totally misconstrued by the participant with mental retardation who was processing the information on a concrete level.

Aging. As in the general population, people with DD are living longer lives; the life expectancy rates have increased for this group. In 1929, for example, the average life expectancy for people with Down syndrome, the most common genetic form of mental retardation, was 9 years. Although infant mortality among the population with Down syndrome continues to be higher than in the general population, children with Down syndrome who live through childhood can expect to live into their sixties (Hand, 1993; Rasmussen & Sobsey, 1994). As the DD population ages, greater linkages between DD and aging networks is required.

Older people with DD can benefit from services that are provided to the older population in general. Retirement for people with DD has been a relatively new concept; these adults may need assistance in choosing activities and adapting to a leisure-based model. Programs that are part of the aging network, such as arts and recreation options, may be preferable for older adults with DD than continuing in their employment or day activity during late life. Practice models exist that promote integration of older adults with DD in community-based programs (Clements, 1994; Wilhite, Keller, & Nicholson, 1990).

Several initiatives have been implemented to link aging and DD services more closely. One early initiative was the Wingspread Conference, which brought together service providers in both of these networks to build more effective mechanisms for serving older people with DD (Ansello & Rose, 1989). The inclusive service delivery model has become part of the national agenda. The Older Americans Act of 1987 (P.L. No., 99-269, 100 Stat. 78) includes amendments that enable older people with DD to be served within community services provided in the act. Other changes have been mandated through this legislation, including establishing cooperation between state divisions of aging and local mental retardation or mental health agencies, and providing additional support to home-based caregivers who care for older adults with DD (Janicki, 1994). A recent evaluation of workshops to promote collaboration between service providers demonstrated that some successes have been achieved in bridging the networks, but community entities such as formalized coalitions are needed to maintain coordination between service sectors (Sutherland, Thyer, Clements, & Kropf, 1997).

Macrosystem Level

The macrosystem includes both the informal and formal social structures that affect the experiences of people with DD. On an informal level, cultural issues influence how people with DD and their families function. The formalized system includes the laws, policies, and service structures that regulate how people with DD fit into the larger social system.

Cultural Issues.   People with DD are members of families and communities that operate within cultural value systems and norms. Behaviors and decisions of people with DD need to be understood from within these cultural bases. Cultural factors include being a member of a particular racial or ethnic group, holding certain religious and life-style values, and being part of a particular cohort group.

Although people with DD are found in all races and ethnic groups, the patterns of care vary for families of different ethnicities. Ito and Nihira (1997) compared Euro-American and Japanese-American families who were caregivers of children with DD in southern California. Their findings suggested differences between the groups in both family orientation to care and interaction with service system. In the Euro-American families, caregiving was shared between the parents more than in the Japanese-American families, in which the mother assumed a majority of responsibility. In addition, the Japanese-American families were less likely to be involved in their child's school activities than the Euro-American families. The researchers provided cultural insight into the later findings, suggesting that the Japanese-American mothers believed that the school personnel have expertise in the education of their child and the parent should not intrude. This value is different than the Euro-American mothers, who believed that parents have the right and responsibility to give input into the educational experience of their child.

Studies also have focused on Latino families who are raising sons or daughters with DD. A study that analyzed maternal depression for Latina mothers found that those parents experienced elevated depression scores (Blacher, Shapiro, Lopez, Diaz, & Fusco, 1997). The strongest predictor of material depression was disruptions in family function. In Latino families, relationships and ties have strong cultural meanings (Zuniga, 1992). Raising a child with DD may disrupt family cohesion or generate conflict, which in turn may negatively affect the mother's well-being. In addition, other research has compared the experience of Latino families with those of Euro-Americans (Heller, Markwardt, Rowitz, & Farber, 1994). Latino parents were more likely to report problems with accessing services for their child. Other differences were found between the two ethnic groups, for example, Latino families were more religious and reported that caring for their family member was a "test by God of your worthiness" and that "I had to accept what God had given us" (Heller et al., 1994, p. 297). Euro-American families were more likely than Latino families to report that raising their son or daughter was more of a burden. Interestingly, however, the two groups did not differ on the basis of social supports.

The role of religion has also been investigated within African-American families who are raising a son or daughter with DD. Rogers-Dulan and Blacher (1995) provided a family framework based on an ecological perspective that can be applied to any family who is raising a child with a disability (Figure 11.1). The authors applied this model to African-American families (Figure 11.2) to highlight how religious, social, and family-level variables interact in the adaptation process of the family system. They argued that policy and practice to African-American families must be more culturally congruent. Specific recommendations included having the church play a more vital role in the provision of services to families. An example of a successful project that could be used as a model is Father George Clement's "One Church–One Child" project, which has involved child adoption services (Billingsley, 1992). Father Clement, an African-American priest, has demonstrated how the church

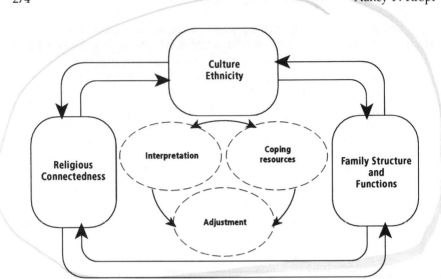

Figure 11.1. Religion, ethnicity, and disability: Families framework. Source: Rogers-Dulan and Blacher (1995). Adapted with permission.

can begin to help solve social problems. In Andrew Billingsley's recent book, *Climbing Jacob's Ladder: The Enduring Legacy of African American Families* (1992), he provided numerous examples of African-American congregations that are becoming leaders in community reform including sponsoring adopt-a-child family projects to battle poverty and offering nutrition, housing, and other social services to senior adults.

Cohort issues are also relevant to understanding function within the population with DD. Many people with DD have spent their formative years in institutional settings. Institutions were often extremely deprived environments, as chronicled by Blatt and Kaplan (1966) in their photo essay entitled *Christmas in Purgatory.* Many residents were separated from members of their families and had no connections to the world outside the institution. In a videotape entitled, *I Should Know a Lot, I Been Around So Long* (Howell, 1989), an older woman with mental retardation discussed her "admission" to an institution. As a young girl, her mother dressed the child in her best outfit and told her that she was going to a birthday party. Instead, the child was dropped off at an institution where she lived most of her adult life. Within the institutions, some residents formed close relationships that functioned as surrogate families. As people were deinstitutionalized, these relationships were often severed as residents returned to different communities and locations (Edgerton & Gaston, 1991).

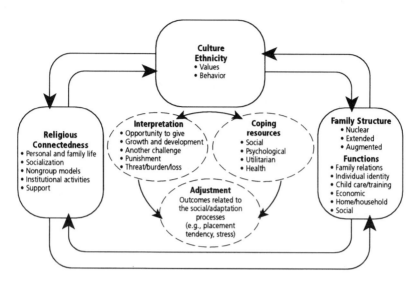

Figure 11.2. Religion, ethnicity, and disability: African-American families framework. Source: Rogers-Dulan and Blacher (1995). Adapted with permission.

Policies and Resources. The macrolevel also includes the policy issues about how resources are distributed and programs are structured for people with DD. One of the primary issues is the cost of caring for a person with DD—many individuals will require support services for their entire lives. The costs of care can be a hardship for families who must financially support a son or daughter by providing living expenses (e.g., clothes, shelter, or food) in addition to any extra expenses associated with the person's disability, such as structuring a barrier-free environment

> The supported living model allows people with DD to receive services in their own homes.

in the household. Jacobson et al. (1995) have described the economic plight of one mother who provided for an aging daughter with DD: "One thing that hurts is diapers. Sara uses diapers, and they are expensive. I had been using just a cloth diaper. I sew two together and buy Huggies and put it in. Of course, that's expensive too" (p. 26). In a study of out-of-pocket expenses paid by families who were supporting an adult with DD, findings revealed that the average cost of care per year was $6,348, with families reporting a range of $1,408 to $28,627 (SD = 3,339) (Fujiura, Roccoforte, & Braddock, 1994). These costs, though, last for a longer period than the costs of raising a child without a disability. Some families bear responsibility for their son's or daughter's basic expenses across the child's entire lifetime.

In an effort to support families in their caregiving responsibilities, some states have passed family support subsidies. Michigan, for example, enacted a cash subsidy program for families of children with DD. This program has been in operation since 1984, and families generally have reported that they were satisfied with the amount that they received per month (Herman, 1994). The local community mental health board is the point of contact for application, and eligibility is determined by the family's income (less than $60,000), age of child (must be younger than 18 years), residential status (must live with family), and disability (child must have severe mental retardation, severe multiple impairment, or autism). As reported by Herman, the average check is $256 per month.

Even when families receive support for the provision of care, resources available to people with DD may be unavailable or are inconsistent with the individual and family's goals and desires. For example, residential placements have been unappealing to many families who feel that their son or daughter would not do well in a communal living situation. In addition, a residential placement may be a distance from the new resident's family, friends, and services. Unfortunately, residential relocations of people with DD are often done with little preparation for the person or the new environment, which can lead to relocation trauma (Jacobson & Kropf, 1993).

An emerging service model is supported living for people with DD. Until recently, professionals typically have assumed that people with disabilities who do not reside with families should live in a facility such as an institution, nursing home, or group home. Today, more people with DD with the support of their families, are planning to live in their own homes within their own communities (O'Brien, 1994). In this service model, the client with DD receives services in his or her home, therefore making it unnecessary to relocate into a congregate living arrangement. The person with DD thus remains in familiar surroundings, establishes linkages in the communities, and has some control over his or her life.

IMPLICATIONS FOR SOCIAL WORK

Currently, the social work education curriculum offers little on DD despite the professional positions and opportunities available, even though this is an important group of people in need of social work intervention. The social work profession can assist this forgotten minority by improving the education of social work students.

—K. DeWeaver and N. P. Kropf, "Persons with Mental Retardation: A Forgotten Minority in Education"

Social work practitioners can provide a range of services and supports to people with DD and their families. On an individual level, practitioners can assist families to adjust to care provision for a son or daughter with DD. As the family ages, social workers can also be involved in decision-making around future care planning. Social workers, especially those in administrative positions, can work toward greater coordination between service systems. Practitioners in all roles need to be committed to promoting policies and programs that promote the dignity, worth, and autonomy of all client groups, including people with DD.

Individuals and Families. Across the life span, social workers have a role in supporting the well-being of families with a person with DD. However, their function also should be to provide initiatives to prevent developmental disabilities from occurring in the first place. Prevention efforts include educational programs to decrease the incidence of fetal alcohol syndrome in children; well-baby clinics that provide information and resources to keep babies healthy during critical developmental periods; and broker and advocacy services to help families acquire resources that will keep children safe, such as child car seats and bicycle helmets. Promoting healthy practices in families can prevent the acquisition of a developmental disability through a childhood accident or illness.

Families who do have a child with DD will also benefit from social work services. Social workers can inform parents about the services and educational system for people with DD including client involvement in individual education plans (IEPs) in the school programs as well as vocational options available when the child graduates from school. Regardless of the age of the son or daughter with DD, families need to begin future care planning. Social workers can be involved in this process by providing information; helping to clarify family values regarding different options; and acting as resources brokers, for example, by connecting a family to an attorney for estate planning.

In addition to these supports, practitioners may help families and the person with DD with psychosocial issues. When parents learn that their child has a disability, they may feel sad or experience a loss that can inhibit their ability to accept their child's strengths and talents. Social workers can provide education about the development of children with DD and foster a sense of hope that the child may achieve a degree of mastery and independence in his or her lifetime. Practitioners can also work with siblings to help them work through issues related to having a brother or sister with a disability. Siblings may benefit from group interventions that provide a normalizing environment in which group members share stories and experiences with other children in similar family situations (Levy, 1995).

In addition to interventions with families, social workers are also involved in direct practice roles with individuals who have DD. For instance, in the school situation, the social worker is part of the interdisciplinary planning process for educational and habilitation goals. As children with DD age, social workers may be involved in the children's transition to a work environment, serving as participants in a vocational program or working as job coaches in a supported employment setting. Social workers in other service settings besides the developmental disability services network may also work with people who have DD. Because people with disabilities are members of neighborhoods and communities, practitioners in other service settings such as hospital social work, mental health, aging, and public welfare can expect to work with clients who have some type of developmental disability.

Services. In addition to direct practice roles, social workers also must promote a comprehensive service system that is responsive to families and people with DD across the life span. Programs that are structured to meet the families' needs in one developmental phase may not be useful for families in other life phases. For example, one service that can provide support to families is respite, which offers caregivers a temporary break from their caregiving responsibilities. Research on respite care usage suggests that younger parents tend to use respite as a brief time-out; for example, they may go out with friends or doing something as a couple. Older families, however, tend to require respite as a replacement caregiving arrangement, such as the hospitalization of a caregiver (Lutzer & Brubaker, 1988). These findings suggest that respite care programs need to be flexible enough to be a useful resource for parents at different points in the life course.

Because people with DD can benefit from resources that are part of different service systems, social workers also need to promote collaboration among service settings. Sutherland et al. (1997) provided an example of a coalition forum to join aging and DD service providers. Such types of initiatives need to be replicated in other service systems, because people with DD are often considered under "the domain" of developmental disability services. Social workers in administrative positions are in prime roles to advocate for and create structures that do not segregate clients based on diagnostic labels such as a developmental disability.

Political Advocacy. Political advocacy is also a role that social workers can assume in eradicating barriers to full social participation for people with DD. In recent years, a rising social movement of people with disabilities has resulted in the demand for greater political resources and attention. For example, the community of people with disabilities was instrumental in achieving the passage of the Americans with Disabilities Act [P.L. No. 101-336, 104 Stat. 327 (1990)], which extends civil rights protection similar to the protection provided to individuals that is based upon race, gender, national origin, and religion.

Unfortunately, people with cognitive impairments (e.g., mental retardation) have low levels of self-determination as compared with people without disabilities (Wehmeyer & Metzler, 1995). *Self-determination* is the ability of a person to make choices regarding the direction of his or her life, and to be an active agent in determining the quality of life. Miller and Keys (1996) propose a model for assisting people with DD to reach higher levels of self-advocacy. As a way to promote macrolevel changes, practitioners can empower people with DD to assume a stronger self-advocacy role. As Miller and Keys stated, "Self advocacy offers opportunities for persons with developmental disabilities to work collectively to become advocates not just for themselves but for all individuals with developmental disabilities" (p. 317). The authors gave the example of Russell Daniels and Mark Samis, who lived in institutions for more than 10 years of their lives. Following discharge, they became involved in a self-advocacy movement called Operation Close Doors, which has the goal of closing all institutions and promoting community living for people with DD.

In summary, many of the problems experienced by people with DD are a result of the barriers experienced in social, economic, and political roles. Social work practice with people with DD and their families involves initiatives on many levels, including providing direct practice, working to promote effective service delivery, and promoting political changes to increase full participation of this population. With a greater awareness of the needs and strengths of this client group, practitioners can conduct assessments and structure service plans that eradicate impediments to full social participation of people with DD and their families .

REFERENCES

Ansello, E. F., & Rose, T. (Ed.) (1989). *Aging and lifelong disabilities: Partnership for the twenty-first century. The Wingspread Conference Report.* Baltimore: University of Maryland Center on Aging.

Baribeault, J. J. (1996). Clinical advocacy for persons with epilepsy and mental retardation living in community based programs. *Journal of Neuroscience Nursing, 28,* 359–372.

Beck, R. B. (1994). Diversity and populations-at-risk: People with disability. In F. G. Reamer (Ed.), *The foundations of social work knowledge* (pp. 391–416). New York: Columbia University Press.

Billingsley, A. (1992). *Climbing Jacob's ladder: The enduring legacy of African American families.* New York: Simon & Schuster.

Blacher, J. Shapiro, J., Lopez, A., Diaz, L., & Fusco, J. (1997). Depression in Latina mothers of children with mental retardation: A neglected concern. *American Journal on Mental Retardation, 101,* 483–496.

Blatt, B., & Kaplan, F. (1966). *Christmas in purgatory: A photographic essay on mental retardation.* Syracuse: Human Policy Press.

Carlson, B. E. (1997). Mental retardation and domestic violence: An ecological approach to intervention. *Social Work, 42,* 79–89.

Clements, C. (1994). *The arts/fitness quality of life project: Creative ideas for working with older adults in group settings.* Baltimore: Health Professions Press.

Demetral, G. D. (1994). Diagrammatic assessment of ecological integration of sex offenders with mental retardation in community residential facilities. *Mental Retardation, 32,* 141–145.

DePoy, E., & Miller, M. (1996). Preparation of social workers for serving individuals with developmental disabilities: A brief report. *Mental Retardation, 34,* 54–57.

DeWeaver, K. L. (1995). Developmental disabilities: Definitions and policies. In R. L. Edwards (Editor-in-Chief), *Encyclopedia of social work* (Vol. 1, 19th ed.) (pp. 712–720). Washington DC: Author.

DeWeaver, K., & Kropf, N. P. (1992). Persons with mental retardation: A forgotten minority in education. *Journal of Social Work Education, 28,* 36–46.

Edgerton, R. B., & Gaston, M. A. (Eds.) (1991). *"I've seen it all": Lives of older persons with mental retardation in the community.* Baltimore: Paul H. Brookes.

Feldman, M. A., Case, L., Towns, F., & Betel, J. (1985). Parent education project I: Developmental and nurturance of children of MR parents. *American Journal of Mental Deficiency, 90,* 253–258.

Freedman, R. I., Krauss, M. W., & Seltzer, M. M. (1997). Aging parents' residential plans for adult children with mental retardation. *Mental Retardation, 35,* 114–123.

Fujiura, G. T., Roccoforte, J. A., & Braddock, D. (1994). Costs of family care for adults with mental retardation and related developmental disabilities. *American Journal on Mental Retardation, 99,* 250–261.

Furey, E. M. (1994). Sexual abuse of adults with mental retardation: Who and where. *Mental Retardation, 32,* 173–180.

Gallimore, R., Weisner, T. S., Bernheimer, L. P., Guthrie, D., & Nihira, K. (1993). Family responses to young children with developmental delays: Accommodation activity in ecological and cultural context. *American Journal on Mental Retardation, 98*(2), 185–206.

Hand, J. (1993). Summary of national survey of older people with mental retardation in New Zealand. *Mental Retardation, 31,* 424–428.

Heller, T., Markwardt, R., Rowitz, L., & Farber, B. (1994). Adaptation of Hispanic families to a member with mental retardation. *American Journal on Mental Retardation, 99,* 289–300.

Herman, S. E. (1994). Cash subsidy program: Family satisfaction and need. *Mental Retardation, 32,* 416–421.

Hodermarska, M., Sherman, D., & Spiegel, M. (1997, May). In the desert at dawn: Issues of diagnosis and treatment of individuals with developmental disabilities who are alcohol and/or other drug-dependent. Paper presented at the 121st annual meeting of the American Association on Mental Retardation, New York City.

Howell, M. D. (Writer) (1989). *I should know, I've been around so long.* Videotape available from Joseph Kennedy Center, Center on Aging, University of Maryland, Baltimore.

Ito, K., & Nihira, K. (1997, May). Ecocultural study of Japanese-American and Euro-American families with developmentally disabled children. Paper presented at the 121st annual meeting of the American Association on Mental Retardation, New York City.

Jacobson, S., & Kropf, N. P. (1993). Facilitating residential transitions of older people with developmental disabilities. *Clinical Gerontologist, 14*(1), 79–94.

Jacobson, S. A., Stoneman, Z., & Kropf, N. P. (1995). *Aging caregivers of individuals with developmental disabilities in the state of Georgia.* Athens: Governor's Council on Developmental Disabilities and University of Georgia University Affiliated Program for Persons with Developmental Disabilities.

Janicki, M. P. (1994). Policies and supports for older persons with mental retardation. In M. M. Seltzer, J. W. Krauss, and M. P. Janicki (Eds.), *Life course perspectives on adulthood and old age* (pp. 143–165). Washington, DC: American Association on Mental Retardation.

Kaufman, A. V., Adams, J. P., & Campbell, V. A. (1991). Permanency planning by older parents who care for adult children with mental retardation. *Mental Retardation, 29,* 293–300.

Kelly, T. B. & Kropf, N. P. (1995). Stigmatized and perpetual parents: Older parents caring for adult children with life-long disabilities. *Journal of Gerontological Social Work, 24*(1/2), 3–16.

Keltner, B. (1994). Home environments of mothers with mental retardation. *Mental Retardation, 32,* 123–137.

Kopels, S. (1995). The Americans with Disabilities Act: A tool to combat poverty. *Journal of Social Work Education, 31,* 337–346.

Kropf, N. P. (1991). *Stress and social support of parents with an adult mentally retarded child.* Doctoral dissertation, Virginia Commonwealth University, Richmond. *Dissertation Abstracts International, 51,* (7-A), 2520.

Kropf, N. P. (1996). Infusing content on older people with developmental disabilities into the curriculum. *Journal of Social Work Education, 32,* 215–226.

Kropf, N. P. (1997). Older parents of adults with developmental disabilities: Practice issues and service needs. *Journal of Family Psychotherapy, 8*(2), 35–52.

Kropf, N. P., & DeWeaver, K. L. (1996). Social work practice with persons with developmental disabilities. In D. F. Harrison, B. A. Thyer, and J. S. Wodarski (Eds), *Cultural diversity and social work practice* (2nd ed.) (pp. 176–200). Springfield, IL: Charles C. Thomas.

Kropf, N. P., & Greene, R. R. (1993). Life review with families who care for developmentally disabled members: A model. *Journal of Gerontological Social Work, 21*(1/2/), 25–40.

Levy, J. M. (1995). Social work. In B. A. Thyer & N. P. Kropf (Eds.), *Developmental disabilities: Handbook for interdisciplinary practice* (pp. 188–201). Cambridge, MA: Brookline.

Lutzer, V. D., & Brubaker, T. J. (1988). Differential respite needs of aging parents of individuals with mental retardation. *Mental Retardation, 26,* 13–15.

Mackelprang, R., & Salsgiver, R. O. (1996). People with disabilities and social work: Historical and contemporary issues. *Social Work, 41,* 7–14.

McLaughlin, P., & Wehmann, P. (Eds.) (1996). *Mental retardation and developmental disabilities* (2nd ed.). Austin, TX: Pro-Ed.

Miller, A. B., & Keys, C. B. (1996). Awareness, action, and collaboration: How the self-advocacy movement is empowering for persons with developmental disabilities. *Mental Retardation, 34,* 312–319.

O'Brien, J. (1994). Down stairs that are never your own: Supporting people with developmental disabilities in their own homes. *Mental Retardation, 32,* 1–6.

Rasmussen, D. E., & Sobsey, D. (1994). Age, adaptive behavior, and Alzheimer's Disease in Down Syndrome: Cross-sectional and longitudinal analyses. *American Journal on Mental Retardation, 99,* 151–165.

Rogers-Dulan, J., & Blacher, J. (1995). African American families, religion, and disability: A conceptual framework. *Mental Retardation, 33,* 226–238.

Rusch, F. R., Heal, L. W., & Cimera, R. E. (1997). Predicting the earnings of supported employees with mental retardation: A longitudinal study. *American Journal on Mental Retardation, 101,* 630–644.

Seltzer, M. M., & Krauss, M. W. (1987). *Aging and mental retardation: Extending the continuum* (Monograph No. 9). Washington, DC: American Association on Mental Retardation.

Smith, G. C., & Tobin, S. S. (1993). Practice with older parents of developmentally disabled adults. *Clinical Gerontologist, 14*(1), 59–77.

Stoneman, Z., Brody, G. H., Davis, C. H., & Crapps, J. M. (1989). Role relations between children who are mentally retarded and their older siblings: Observations in three in-home contexts. *Research in Developmental Disabilities, 10,* 61–76.

Sundrum, C. J., & Stavis, P. F. (1994). Sexuality and mental retardation: Unmet challenges. *Mental Retardation, 32,* 255–264.

Sutherland, G. S., Thyer, B. A., Clements, C., & Kropf, N. P. (1997). The evaluation of coalition building training for aging and developmental disability service providers. *Educational Gerontology, 23,* 105–114.

Turk, M. A., & Machemer, R. H. (1993). Cerebral palsy in adults who are older. In R. H. Machemer and J. C. Overeynder (Eds.), *Understanding aging and developmental disabilities: An in-service curriculum* (pp. 111–129). Rochester, NY: University of Rochester.

Unger, O., & Howes, C. (1988). Mother-child interactions and symbolic play between toddlers and their adolescent or mentally retarded mothers. *Occupational Therapy Journal of Research, 8,* 237–240.

Wehmeyer, M. L., & Metzler, C. A. (1995). How self-determined are people with mental retardation? The national consumer survey. *Mental Retardation, 33,* 111–119.

Westermeyer, J., Phaobtong C., & Neidor, J. (1988). Substance use and abuse among mentally retarded persons: Comparison of patients and a survey population. *Journal of Drug and Alcohol Abuse, 14*(1), 109–123.

Wilhite, B., Keller, M. J., & Nicholson, L. (1990). Integrating older persons with developmental disabilities into community recreation: Theory to practice. *Activities, Adaptation, and Aging, 15,* 111–130.

Wilson, J., Blacher, J., & Baker, B. L. (1989). Siblings of children with severe handicaps. *Mental Retardation, 27,* 167–173.

Zuniga, M. E. (1992). Families with Latino roots. In E. W. Lunch and M. J. Hanson (Eds.), *Developing cross-cultural competence: A guide for working with young children and their families* (pp. 151–179). Baltimore: Paul H. Brookes.

12

Culturally Competent Research Protocols

WILLIAM H. BARTON

As researchers, we will always represent our own voices, and it would be naive to assume that we can ever simply present the voices of others. Nevertheless, it is possible to adopt a worldview that not only values diversity, but also requires researchers, scholars, interventionists, and policy makers to continuously ask, "Whose interests are being served?"

—J. Rappaport, "Empowerment as a Guide to Doing Research: Diversity as a Positive Value"

The ecological perspective brings cultural factors to the foreground, such that research from this perspective must be culturally competent. Culturally competent research involves more than just making sure that the language in questionnaires is appropriate for various groups. It means embracing and working within multiple perspectives at all phases of the research process. This chapter examines the many phases of the research process, from identifying the research question, organizing the logistics of a research effort, and choosing appropriate designs and methods, to reporting strategies, all through the lenses of cultural diversity and empowerment practice. The chapter first examines some paradigmatic assumptions of research from an ecological perspective. The aim of the chapter is to contribute to the reader's awareness of the implications of the many decisions made during the planning and conducting of research. More technical details regarding specific methodological procedures may be found in various social work and social sciences research texts.

RESEARCH ASSUMPTIONS

Traditional research texts in social work as well as the social sciences generally tend to be written primarily from a positivist perspective. Positivism assumes the existence of an external reality and the possibility of objective, context-free research yielding knowledge that at least approximates that reality. Accordingly, positivist researchers attempt to test propositions derived from theories postulating general, universal laws. Although nothing in positivist research protocols prevents consideration of diversity characteristics (e.g., race, gender, sexual orientation, social class, or culture), these characteristics simply become parameters to include in multivariate model specification.

In contrast, the ecological perspective directs our attention to the embeddedness of the individual-in-context, wherein the very essence of an individual's experience depends on the particular combination of social, cultural, and historical factors that condition the meaning as well as the operation of behavioral influences. According to Germain and Gitterman (1995), "The ecological perspective makes clear the need to view people and environments as a unitary system within a particular cultural and historic context" (p. 816). Social work research texts written explicitly from this perspective do not appear to exist, although some recent ones contain informative sections on diversity (e.g., Mark, 1996) or cultural factors (e.g., Grinnell, 1997), and many refer to nonpositivist paradigms (especially constructivism and its companion, qualitative methods), at least in passing.

In discussing social work research from an ecological perspective, one could take the position that ecologically appropriate research must focus literally on the transactions between people and environments—that the proper unit of analysis derives from neither the person nor the environment but from their intersection. This position asserts that it is not enough to look separately for potential causal influences from personal and environmental factors, but rather that research must focus on the unified, reciprocally causal unit as defined by Germain and Gitterman (1995). Such an extreme position appears to go even beyond examining *interactions* among elements (which can be accommodated by complex multidimensional research models). Yet it is unclear how research should characterize such person-environment units other than through potentially reciprocal, interactional models (see Phillips, 1987, for a trenchant critique of holism in social research).

A second approach would be to simply explicate the constructivist paradigm (e.g., Gergen, 1994; Guba, 1990; Guba & Lincoln, 1989) while outlining qualitative methods (e.g., Denzin & Lincoln, 1994) and perhaps advocating grounded theory (Glaser & Strauss, 1967). In contrast to positivism, constructivism begins with the assumption that reality is socially constructed, and hence varies across cultural place and historical time. Accordingly, most constructivist research uses qualitative methods that attempt to provide what Geertz (1973) has called "thick descriptions" of individuals' subjective perceptions and experiences. Constructivist research would at least document and give voice to the perspectives of diverse groups and avoid the stereotypical problems associated with the positivist inquiry imposition of its presumed reality across diverse groups.

A third approach, and the one adopted for this chapter, takes the explicitly political stance that culturally sound social work research from an ecological perspective should empower diverse groups in our society who have been oppressed by the existing power structure (e.g., Rappaport, 1994). From this view, research is a political act designed to "collaborate with people to create, encourage, or assist them to become aware of, obtain, or create the resources they may need to make use of their competencies" (Rappaport, 1994, p. 366). The emphasis is on the purposes of research, with epistemological and methodological considerations secondary and flexibly applied to the research context. Empowerment research is compatible with existing social work values (National Association of Social Workers, 1997) and the profession's current attention to the strengths perspective (e.g., Saleebey, 1992).

ECOLOGICAL PERSPECTIVE
AND CULTURAL COMPETENCE

The emphasis of the ecological perspective on the person-in-situation mirrors the multiculturalism assumption that behavior can only be understood within specific cultural contexts. What are relevant cultural contexts? When we think of the concept of culture, we tend to think of groups of people, usually identifiable by some broad characteristic such as race, ethnicity, religion, or nationality. However, each is a different concept, and to equate the concepts can lead to confusion. Soriano (1995) usefully defined *culture* as "distinct, preferred (idealized) or performed patterns of behavior . . . communication and cognitions held in common and accepted by members of a distinct group of people" (p. 98). Grinnell (1997) distinguished culture from race ("based on physical attributes"), nationality ("country of origin"), and ethnicity ("based on common ancestry and cultural heritage") (p. 606). Thus, people of a given race may be drawn from several nationalities, ethnic groups, and religions, each exhibiting distinct cultural patterns. Moreover, the list of culturally relevant characteristics goes well beyond those previously listed, and may include gender, sexual orientation, physical ability, age, education, income level, and perhaps others in the future that have yet to emerge as socially or politically salient.

We are all shaped by our cultural context, and have evolved particular sets of assumptions, values, and even meanings to apply to situations we encounter. To conduct culturally competent research, we must first recognize and acknowledge our own assumptions, understand that they may not be shared by others, and accept the possibility that what seems valid to us may not seem so to others. Failure to do so can lead to *cultural encapsulation* (Pedersen, 1988), in which we assume that all people use the same concepts in the same way, share definitions of what is normal, and characterize their existence similarly (e.g., as individual, autonomous beings, or alternatively as interdependent group members). Culturally encapsulated research produces gross distortions in which, among other things, cultural differences are likely to be interpreted as abnormalities or deficits.

> Culturally sensitive research embraces differences, involves participants, seeks to understand people within the context of their environments, and strives to empower participants.

STEPS IN THE RESEARCH PROCESS

Identifying the Research Question

Empirical studies of group dynamics in the United States began in the 1930s with the industrial management research of Mayo (1933), his colleagues Roethlisberger and Dickson (1939), the work of Sherif (1936) on group influence on social norms, and the studies of Lewin and colleagues on leadership and group climate (Lewin, Lippitt, & White, 1939; Lippitt, 1940). Why did research questions about group dynamics emerge at that time? The purpose of much of this research was to discover ways to enhance industrial productivity in the midst of the Great Depression and on the eve of World War II. An examination of the cultural and historical context of the emergence of many substantive themes in social research reveals a similar pattern.

The identification of research questions requires a confluence of researcher interest and available resources. Most of the funding for research comes from governmental or philanthropic sources. Although some research is investigator initiated, much arises in response to requests for proposals issued by funders. Thus, those groups in society who are less central to the governmental or philanthropic worlds have less voice in determining the direction of social research. Furthermore, to the extent that trained researchers are not drawn equally from all social groups, even the direction of investigator-initiated research is culturally limited. The result is that much, if not most social research serves to maintain the status quo in the interests of people with more power.

In addition, research questions often emerge from culturally encapsulated observations of "differences." Why do some people engage in behaviors that most of "us" think strange, unusual, amusing, or perhaps dangerous? Thus, social sciences journals are replete with studies of "deviants," however defined at the time. Even the names of journals or social sciences subdisciplines (e.g., *Abnormal Psychology, Criminology, Deviance, Mental Retardation, and Psychopathology*) reveal our fascination with the "others," whoever they may be at a particular place and time.

The ecological perspective offers several antidotes to such distorted research question identification. First, it directs our attention not to the implied deficits of difference but to a positive embracing of difference and to an appreciation of the interdependence of people and their environments. Second, if the purpose of research from an ecological perspective is empowerment, then research questions should seek knowledge that can be used by the participants to enhance their competencies. Third, the key stakeholders in research include the participants (usually called "subjects" in more traditional research), and they have a primary role in identifying the research question.

Research questions likely to emerge from this perspective include, among others:

- How do various groups perceive the effects of specific social policies, for example, welfare reform, and how are their lives affected?
- What strategies can neighborhoods use to enhance the lives of their residents?
- How can services be made accessible to diverse groups in the community?

Organizing the Research Effort

The first requirement of social work research from an ecological perspective, then, is that it be collaborative from the very beginning, that is, that the individuals who are being studied should have a stake and role in the identification of the research question. This can be accomplished in several ways. Some have stated that the researcher must be of the same cultural or racial group as those being studied. Thus, for example, Becerra

(1997b) presented the argument that "ethnic minority researchers must be the ones to study their own ethnic groups, because they bring an understanding and sensitivity to the research that only an 'insider' can provide" (p. 111). She viewed such understanding and sensitivity as essential for gaining access to communities as well as for developing culturally appropriate study instruments, data collection procedures, analyses, and interpretations of findings. The same writer (Becerra, 1997a) also presented the other side, countering that the real issues are trust and cultural appropriateness of methods, and that all good researchers are potentially capable of dealing competently with them.

Gross (1995), reflecting on research about American Indians, added that the "politically correct" position that only ethnic minority researchers can study their own groups can lead to a monolithic view of such groups that obscures diversity within ethnic minority populations. Consistent with the opinions of Rappaport, Gross advocated that researchers adopt a self-conscious and critical stance:

> There are guidelines that one can apply to one's own research or learning about practice with people of color. For example, Who is doing the analyzing and observing? What are their and my interests in pursuing the subject? Who will benefit from these writings and practices? How will the population at stake benefit. . . . What provisions are made for others to be heard? (p. 212)

de Anda (1997) has provided an appealing synthesis to this debate:

> I agree, then, with the position that a research partnership between ethnic and non-ethnic researchers in the study of ethnic populations is probably advantageous. I would only add one word of caution. This needs to be an equal partnership, in which the partners work from the inception of the research and throughout the research process to bring their particular perspective and expertise to the enterprise. . . . Finally, a third party needs to be included in the partnership, representatives from the population under study, whose input regarding the design and implementation of the research is important throughout the process. (p. 118)

How can such research partnerships be created? The social work researcher must begin with knowledge about the community or organizational context within which the research will occur. From this knowledge, it is possible to identify areas in which information may be useful for stakeholders as they attempt to enhance their community, organizational, or individual functioning. The social work researcher is just one more resource with particular expertise that he or she can bring to the table. In addition to technical knowledge of research methods, the social work researcher must possess good group facilitation skills. The first task is to identify the key stakeholders and develop egalitarian mechanisms for planning and conducting the research.

For example, consider research to evaluate the effectiveness of a neighborhood youth recreation center. The purpose of such research might be to assist stakeholders in strengthening the program as well as in enhancing its accountability to funders and the community. Key stakeholders might include agency administrators, staff, and neighborhood youth and their families, as well as the funders of the program, perhaps the local United Way or community foundations. Although all of these stakeholders may share a desire for an effective program, they may differ considerably in their definitions of effectiveness and in the priorities they place on various program goals. The evaluation researcher must help create a context for all relevant views to be heard and considered. This may mean creating one or more advisory or task groups, comprising representatives of the diverse stakeholders, to oversee the research process.

However, setting up representative task or advisory groups may not be sufficient in some instances. In large human services organizations, for example, the demographic composition of the various types of stakeholders may differ. The degree of power within the organizational context often mirrors that of diverse groups in society at large, so that the proportions of women, people of color, and people with fewer material resources may be higher among line staff than among supervisors or administrators, and higher among clients than among staff. In an advisory group, a lone line staff representative may not feel free to offer candid opinions in the presence of administrators. Similarly, the contributions of the client representative may be affected by the real or perceived possibility of changes in that person's access to or quality of services received. When such organizational power dynamics are further confounded by cultural dynamics, the ability of the research to empower diverse groups is compromised. Thus, simply creating an advisory group with a representative staff person and representative client may inadequately represent staff or clients' interests or perspectives. In such cases, the researcher must develop creative ways to circumvent these barriers. Perhaps there is an organization of line staff, and the researcher can ask to be placed on the agenda of a meeting to introduce the research and seek input and participation from line staff on their "turf." Perhaps there is a client advocacy organization that can be similarly invited to collaborate.

Selecting a Paradigm

For some researchers, the notion of selecting a paradigm after identifying the research question might seem odd. Epistemological paradigms, after all, reflect sets of assumptions about what reality is, what knowledge is, and how knowledge can be obtained. Although there are many varieties of such paradigms (see Morgan, 1983, for an extensive sampling), three major ones appear most frequently in the literature: (1) contemporary versions of positivism (often called postpositivism), (2) social constructivism, and (3) critical theory (Guba, 1990). The assumptions of each are contradictory. For example, the opposing views of reality of positivism and constructivism are such that strong adherents of these paradigms would argue that no approach to inquiry is possible other than their chosen one (e.g., for postpositivism, see Phillips, 1987; for constructivism, see Guba & Lincoln, 1989; for a feminist version of critical theory, see Harding, 1991). Paradigm debates have periodically appeared in the social work literature as well, most recently exemplified by the article written by more than 40 social work researchers (Grinnell, Austin, Blythe, Briar, Bronson, Coleman, et al., 1994) in response to Tyson's (1992) presentation of a constructivist "heuristic paradigm."

Constructivism has particular relevance for many research questions that might arise from an ecological perspective. The heightened focus on the social and cultural situatedness of diverse groups is congruent with constructivist assumptions regarding multiple, socially defined realities (Gergen, 1994), in which subjective "meanings" rather than objective factors govern behavior. Because such meanings are culturally and historically dependent, only research that seeks to give voice to the subjective experiences of diverse populations can adequately describe human behavior.

Some have argued that all knowledge must be population specific (e.g., Davis, 1994, and Reinharz, 1992, regarding gender; and Asante, 1990, Jones, 1986, and Ramirez, 1983, regarding race and ethnicity). Others (e.g., Watts, 1994) have countered that population-specific approaches run the risk of indefinite multiplication (that is, separate methodologies and theories for every combination of potential diversity markers such as race, ethnicity, gender, social class, sexual orientation, and physical ability). The ecological perspective provides a middle ground that acknowledges the richness of specific cultural contexts while allowing for the possibility of common patterns among them. Berry (1994), for example, has offered a nested methodological framework consisting of four levels:

1. the ecological context . . . relatively stable and permanent characteristics of the environment and the population that provide the context for human action . . .

2. the learning context . . . the pattern of recurrent experiences that provides a basis for individual learning . . .

3. the situational context . . . the limited set of environmental circumstances . . . that may account for particular behaviors at a given time and place. They include such features of a setting as roles or social interactions . . .

4. the assessment context . . . any environmental characteristics, such as test items or stimulus conditions, designed by the [researcher]. (pp. 128–129)

Research questions may evolve at any of these levels, and multiple paradigms and methodologies may be appropriate. For example, to understand the ecological context of a group, a researcher may wish to work within a constructivist framework. To understand the effects of contemporary situational context on behavior, the researcher may adopt a more positivist approach.

Some researchers (e.g., Creswell, 1994; Patton, 1997) have explicitly adopted this more pragmatic view, suggesting that different sets of assumptions and methods may be most useful for exploring particular research questions. Creswell (1994) has offered three models for combining paradigms:

1. the two-phase design, for example, an exploratory qualitative phase followed by a quantitative phase;
2. the dominant-less dominant design, for example, a qualitative interview component embedded within a larger survey design;
3. the mixed-methodology design, which combines inductive and deductive inquiry throughout.

Such pragmatic options are consistent with the ecological perspective. If the research is guided by empowerment principles with collaborative planning and implementation, it can use any paradigm with cultural competence, assuming that diversity issues continue to be addressed in the design, information collection, and reporting stages as discussed in the sections that follow.

Designing the Research

Research design involves determining what information needs to be collected from what source(s) to answer the research question. Research texts typically provide details for sampling, group designs, single-subject designs, and so on, that may or may not be relevant for specific research efforts. No research design is perfect, yielding unassailable "truth." The design challenges researchers face are nicely captured by McGrath (1982) in his discussion of "dilemmatics." He observed that it is impossible for any single research study to optimize all three of the "desiderata" of research: (1) internal validity (the accuracy of causal model specificity); (2) external validity (generalizability of results to persons and groups other than those participating in the research); and (3) naturalism (fidelity to the phenomenological world of the research participants).

> When attention is given to stakeholders and their diversity issues, all research designs have the potential to be culturally competent.

Graphically depicting these desiderata as three equidistant points around a circle, McGrath illustrated the strengths and weaknesses of various research designs. For example, experimental laboratory research optimizes internal validity, but at the expense of limited generalizability and little naturalism. Ethnographic and many other qualitative designs, which maximize natural fidelity, sacrifice both internal and external validity. Large sample surveys, which emphasize external validity, are limited in their ability to test causal hypotheses (internal validity) and in their ability to reflect the perceived world of respondents (naturalism). In contrast to positivist calls for replication of studies, in which each succeeding study contains the same strengths and weaknesses, McGrath has urged that programs of research use multiple methodologies, such that each succeeding study compensates for the weaknesses of the preceding ones.

The previously described design dilemmas apply to all research, regardless of the population being studied or the paradigm selected. Some of the debates about the cultural competence of research seem to equate inadequate implementation of design and method with fundamental inadequacy of the design or methods themselves. For example, in arguing that research methodology should be adapted and modified to accommodate multicultural populations, Leslie and Gorey (1997) relied on critiques of biased measurement tools and grossly aggregated data analysis to make their case. On the other side of the debate, Franke (1997) concluded,

> However, it is not the methods themselves, either qualitative or quantitative, that determine the relevance to multicultural populations or inclusion of a multicultural perspective. That is determined by how the methods are instantiated in the particular evaluation by the evaluator/researcher. Thus it may be necessary to educate evaluators/researchers about the importance of considering multicultural issues in applying methods of evaluation. However, it does not require changing the methods themselves. (p. 130)

Overall, all designs have flaws, yet each may be suitable for addressing certain research questions. If the process of identifying the research question has been inclusive and guided by the empowerment principles described previously, any design has the potential for being culturally competent if carried out with attention to cultural issues and under the continued direction of the stakeholder partnership.

There are specific concerns, however, regarding studies that involve conducting surveys with samples representing a particular population. Consider a neighborhood assessment survey designed to document residents' perceptions of local resources, opportunities, and problems. A simple random sample will provide representative information about the neighborhood as a single aggregation of people. But such an aggregation may be meaningless if the neighborhood comprises several distinct groups, each having unique perspectives. If some groups are relatively small, a sample large enough for aggregate estimates may contain too few members of the smaller groups to provide any useful information about their perspective. Researchers must identify all relevant subgroups in a population and design sampling strategies that yield large enough numbers of each to provide meaningful information about them. Stratified samples and oversampling of small subgroups are ways to address these design concerns.

Collecting Information

The phase of information collection is when the researchers most obviously interact with individuals who are providing the information. Thus, researchers must exert great care to interact in a mutually respectful and comprehensible manner. Furthermore, they must tailor data collection procedures and instruments to the cultural context of the research. It is assumed in what follows that a culturally relevant partnership has initiated the research, whatever the method, and that the purposes of the research are nonexploitative of the individuals from whom information is being collected. It is also assumed that researchers follow standard ethical guidelines in their research protocols. Following a brief review of basic ethical issues pertaining to all research protocols, the chapter examines specific issues that arise in research evolving from the ecological perspective.

Universities and most other major research organizations have institutional review boards (IRBs) that serve as ethical gatekeepers for research conducted under their auspices. Basic "human subject protections," as they are usually called by IRBs, include avoidance of harm to participants, informed consent, participants' rights to discontinue participation, and confidentiality guarantees. Extending a framework developed by Kitchener (1984), Newman and Brown (1996) have outlined five ethical principles applicable to evaluation research: "autonomy, nonmaleficence (doing no harm), beneficence (doing good), justice, and fidelity" (p. 38). A consideration of these principles extends the usual protections to include the requirement that the research provide some real benefits for the participants. Moreover, these principles are congruent with the collaborative and empowerment emphases recommended in this chapter.

Major methods of information collection that require interaction include observation (covert observation is not considered in this chapter), interviews, and survey questionnaires. Observation can be intrusive and reactive, but in some circumstances, may be the only method for obtaining firsthand knowledge of behavior. Whether researchers intend to participate as well as observe, they should acknowledge their presence and purpose, and they should share with participants their emerging understandings of their observations.

Interviews and questionnaires are alternative ways to ask people for information about their perceptions, attitudes, and experiences. Traditional research texts present the choice of these alternatives in terms of resources (interviews are more labor intensive, hence expensive) and the depth (interviews) versus breadth (questionnaires) of information collected. However, participants who come from collectivist cultures are more likely to respond to personal contact than to impersonal surveys (Marin & Marin, 1991). Furthermore, interviewers need to know the language and culture of the research participants, and this is more likely to be the case when they are members of the same cultural group (ibid.). However, simply speaking the same language is not enough, because there is considerable variation within the same language. For example, both Grinnell (1997) and Soriano (1995) have illustrated language misunderstandings that occurred between Spanish-speaking people from different parts of Latin America.

Regardless of the data collection method, the wording of questionnaires or interview schedules must consider the participants' culture. The ideal process for translating a data collection instrument, as presented in detail by Grinnell (1997), includes these six steps:

1. translation by two or more translators familiar with the target population;
2. assessment of clarity and equivalence, provided by representatives of the target population;
3. back-translation, in which the translated version is retranslated back into the original language;
4. field-testing with monolingual individuals from each language and from bilingual people;
5. assessment of reliability;
6. interpretation, that is, discriminating between extraneous factors and translation problems. (pp. 621–622)

In addition to language issues, data collection instruments reflect concepts and assumptions that may be specific to the researcher's culture and may reflect biases that harm and offend others. For example, information about an individual's relationship status may be important to collect to help understand the social or familial context of the individual. Many questionnaires include an item, often termed "marital status," that contains response options such as "married," "divorced," "separated," "widowed," "never married." What does the presence of this item communicate to a gay or lesbian person who may now be or have been in a committed relationship? Similarly, in research regarding people with HIV or AIDS, instruments that include the phrase "AIDS victim" are offensive. People who have contracted HIV do not consider themselves "victims," but rather people who are living and actively coping with a virus.

The best protection against culturally inappropriate methods and measures is provided by collaborative research partnerships that draw members from the cultural groups relevant for the particular research context. The team can collectively review and arrive at a consensus about information collection, measures, language, and other issues.

Analyzing Information

If the research planning, design, and information collection phases have evolved from the collaborative partnership process previously described, the analysis phase should present few major difficulties beyond those associated with any analysis endeavor. A key concern is that the researchers must examine the data for the possibility of subgroup differences. Moreover, there may be several dimensions to consider simultaneously, such as gender, race, ethnicity, and other factors, as relevant to particular studies. Although there may be patterns of results that apply across diversity dimensions, researchers must not assume such universality. Subsequently, if subgroup analyses reveal clear differences between groups on a dimension, such as ethnicity, researchers must explore the possibility that ethnicity may be confounded with some other dimension, urban versus rural settings perhaps, and that ethnicity may or may not be the characteristic most closely linked with the observed difference. Compromises inevitably made during the design phase may limit the extent to which researchers can examine all possible combinations of characteristics.

> In analyzing information, the researcher must be alert for subgroup differences, but must be cautious that group differences are not overemphasized or confounded.

At the other extreme, researchers should not overemphasize group differences and neglect the possibility for shared perceptions or experiences across diversity dimensions. Grinnell (1997) argued that common themes may underlie diverse cultural patterns; therefore, ignoring them may contribute to biases and confusion. Grinnell also urged researchers to consider the potential for variation within cultural groups. Gross (1995), in her review of research with American Indians, made a compelling argument for attending to within-group differences.

As the analysis phase unfolds, the academically trained researchers, as resources to the partnership, may need to educate other team members about the technical details of various analysis strategies. In turn, as every analysis step raises as many questions as it answers, the other members need to educate the academics regarding the cultural implications of various analyses and provide guidance for the next steps.

Reporting Results

Data seldom, if ever, speak for themselves. The chapter author once conducted an evaluation of juvenile intensive probation programs in a major midwestern city (Barton & Butts, 1990, 1991). Although the main research question concerned the viability of the in-home programs as alternatives to incarceration, a secondary question concerned identifying which youthful offenders could best be served by the programs to assist the juvenile court in making future referrals to the programs. One way I addressed this question was through a comparative analysis of youths who successfully completed the intensive programs with those who did not. The main factors associated with program success turned out to be age (older youths were more likely to succeed) and the number of prior adjudications (those youths with fewer "priors" were more likely to succeed). I also found that, controlling for those and many other factors, race was associated with program success (Caucasian youths were more likely than African-American youths to successfully complete the programs). When I present this example to social work students, they are quick to suggest external interpretations: the programs might have been culturally biased or the police may have been racist in their arrest practices. In the context of the juvenile court in that city at that time, many would have been quick to suggest an internal interpretation, attributing the failure to the African-American youths or their families. In presenting these findings, I had to carefully point out the ambiguity and caution stakeholders against using these results to screen out African-American youths from the programs.

Without more information, it is impossible to settle on the one, correct interpretation of a finding such as the preceding one. More information may strengthen or weaken the case for some competing interpretations (e.g., some of the programs were designed and operated by African-Americans and employed relatively young staff who had grown up in the same neighborhoods as the youths), but some uncertainty always remains. Researchers must acknowledge such uncertainty and seek input from stakeholders in generating and critically analyzing potential interpretations.

You may have seen or heard of weighty final reports of research studies that stand unopened, gathering dust on someone's bookshelves. The "final report," although necessary as a complete documentation of a research effort, is neither the sole nor best reporting mechanism. Reporting is a process rather than a product, and involves dialogue and several iterations. Ideally, researchers present analysis results (these may take the form of narrative stories, data tables, or charts, as relevant) and solicit ideas from stakeholders as to what they might mean. Researchers may need to make a series of presentations to various groups. As stakeholders offer interpretations and raise questions, the researchers may need to conduct additional analyses. A consensus interpretation may or may not arise. If not, the researchers' report can acknowledge alternative interpretations, their sources, and evidence.

SUMMARY

The ecological perspective requires that social work researchers consider the cultural embeddedness of individuals' perceptions and experiences. Relevant research questions arise from practice in specific settings at specific times in history, thus affecting and being affected by particular cultural groups. Culturally competent researchers are aware of the cultural (or multicultural) context of their research and seek to conduct inquiry that is collaborative and empowering at all stages in the research process.

They begin by establishing collaborative partnerships in which members, drawn from all relevant stakeholder groups, share in the planning, implementation, and use of the research. These partnerships clarify the research questions, select appropriate paradigms of inquiry, design the information collection procedures and measures, direct the analyses, and provide interpretations of findings in which all relevant perspectives are considered. It is this process, rather than the dogmatic use of particular methods, that characterizes culturally competent research.

EXAMPLE OF CULTURALLY COMPETENT RESEARCH

The research on families of people with HIV or AIDS (see Chapter 14) is an example of the kind of research discussed in the present chapter. The study (Marshall, Barton, Roberts, Stephany, Pickett, & Carter, 1995) evolved from the practice context of the principal investigator (Marshall) as he became aware of the efforts made by significant others to provide care to people with HIV in the absence of supportive services. Along with other stakeholders, including the state department of health, he wanted to learn more about the perceptions and experiences of these significant others so that the information could be used to direct the development of services that would enhance their ability to provide care. He assembled a research team and constituted an advisory group consisting of social services and medical professionals who worked with individuals with HIV and AIDS, religious leaders who were especially active in helping people with HIV and AIDS in their communities, and nonprofessionals who themselves were significant others of people with HIV. The research team and advisory panel included members of the gay community, people of color (African-Americans and Latinos being the relevant groups in this context), and individuals from different regions of the state (see chapter 14).

The study used a mixed-method design with the following three phases:

1. in-depth, qualitative interviews with a small number of respondents;
2. focus groups, each having members who had a specific type of relationship to a person with HIV (e.g., parents, gay partners, heterosexual partners), members from a particular geographical region of the state, and members of a particular race or ethnicity (e.g., African-American, Caucasian, or Latino);
3. structured interviews, with a larger sample drawn to be representative of the family caregivers in the state in terms of their relationship type, race or ethnicity, and geographical region.

The collaborative team provided input at all stages of the research. They helped ensure that study participants were invited to participate using culturally appropriate recruitment channels, that the interview schedules were worded appropriately and translated accurately as needed, and that the information was analyzed with attention to the many dimensions of diversity present.

The research questions themselves reflected the ecological perspective, focusing on the types and quality of formal and informal support used by caregivers, the effect of the experience on the caregivers and their families, and differences in perceptions and experiences across geographic region, relationship type, and race or ethnicity. The final phase of this research has not yet been completed, but the study has great potential to support significant others of people with HIV by increasing awareness and programmatic support for them as they provide care to their loved ones.

REFERENCES

Asante, M. K. (1990). *Kemet, Afrocentricity, and knowledge.* Trenton, NJ: Africa World Press.

Barton, W. H., & Butts, J. A. (1990). Viable options: Intensive supervision programs for juvenile delinquents. *Crime and Delinquency, 36,* 238–256.

Barton, W. H., & Butts, J. A. (1991). Intensive supervision alternatives for adjudicated juveniles. In T. Armstrong (Ed.), *Intensive interventions with high-risk youths: Promising approaches in juvenile probation and parole* (pp. 317–340). New York: Criminal Justice Press.

Becerra, R. (1997a). Can valid research on ethnic minority populations only be conducted by researchers from the same ethnic group? No. In D. de Anda (Ed.), *Controversial issues in multiculturalism* (pp. 114–117). Boston: Allyn & Bacon.

Becerra, R. (1997b). Can valid research on ethnic minority populations only be conducted by researchers from the same ethnic group? Yes. In D. de Anda (Ed.), *Controversial issues in multiculturalism* (pp. 110–113). Boston: Allyn & Bacon.

Berry, J. (1994). An ecological perspective on cultural and ethnic psychology. In E. Trickett, R. Watts, and D. Birman (Eds.), *Human diversity: Perspectives on people in context* (pp. 115–141). San Francisco: Jossey-Bass.

Creswell, J. W. (1994). *Research design: Qualitative and quantitative approaches.* Thousand Oaks, CA: Sage.

Davis, L. (1994). Is feminist research inherently qualitative, and is it a fundamentally different approach to research? Yes. In W. Hudson and P. Nurius (Eds.), *Controversial issues in social work research* (pp. 63–69). Boston: Allyn & Bacon.

de Anda, D. (1997). Rejoinder to Dr. Becerra. In D. de Anda (Ed.), *Controversial issues in multiculturalism* (p. 118). Boston: Allyn & Bacon.

Denzin, N. K., & Lincoln, Y. S. (Eds.) (1994). *Handbook of qualitative research.* Newbury Park, CA: Sage.

Franke, T. (1997). Do methods of evaluating practice need to be adapted for multicultural populations? No. In D. de Anda (Ed.), *Controversial issues in multiculturalism* (pp. 125–130). Boston: Allyn & Bacon.

Geertz, C. (1973). *The interpretation of cultures.* New York: Basic Books.

Gergen, K. (1994). *Realities and relationships: Soundings in social construction.* Cambridge, MA: Harvard University Press.

Germain, C. B., & Gitterman, A. (1995). Ecological perspective. In R. L. Edwards (Editor-in-Chief), *Encyclopedia of social work* (19th ed.) (Vol. 1, pp. 816–824). Washington, DC: NASW Press.

Glaser, B. G., & Strauss, A. L. (1967). *The discovery of grounded theory: Strategies for qualitative research.* Chicago: Aldine.

Grinnell, R. (1997). *Social work research and evaluation: Quantitative and qualitative approaches* (5th ed). Itasca, IL: F. E. Peacock.

Grinnell, R., Austin, C., Blythe, B., Briar, S., Bronson, D., Coleman, H., et al. (1994). Social work researchers' quest for respectability. *Social Work, 39,* 469–470.

Gross, E. (1995). Deconstructing politically correct practice literature: The American Indian case. *Social Work, 40,* 206–213.

Guba, E. G. (Ed.) (1990). *The paradigm dialog.* Newbury Park, CA: Sage.

Guba, E. G., & Lincoln, Y. S. (1989). *Fourth generation evaluation.* Newbury Park, CA: Sage.

Harding, S. (1991). *Whose science? Whose knowledge? Thinking from women's lives.* Ithaca, NY: Cornell University Press.

Jones, J. (1986). Racism: A cultural analysis of the problem. In J. Dovidio and S. Gaertner (Eds.), *Prejudice, discrimination and racism* (pp. 279–314). San Diego, CA: Academic Press.

Kitchener, K. (1984). Intuition, critical evaluation and ethical principles: The foundation for ethical decisions in counseling psychology. *Counseling Psychologist, 12*(3), 43–56.

Leslie, D., & Gorey, K. (1997). Do methods of evaluating practice need to be adapted for multicultural populations? Yes. In D. de Anda (Ed.), *Controversial issues in multiculturalism* (pp. 120–124). Boston: Allyn & Bacon.

Lewin, K., Lippitt, R., & White, R. (1939). Patterns of aggressive behavior in experimentally created "social climates." *Journal of Social Psychology, 10,* 271–299.

Lippitt, R. (1940). An experimental study of authoritarian and democratic group atmosphere. *University of Iowa Studies in Child Welfare, 16*(3), 43–195.

Marin, G., & Marin, B. (1991). *Research with Hispanic populations.* Newbury Park, CA: Sage.

Mark, R. (1996). *Research made simple: A handbook for social workers.* Thousand Oaks, CA: Sage.

Marshall, E., Barton, W. H., Roberts, T., Stephany, C., Pickett, W. E., & Carter, S. (1995). *Families and HIV/AIDS: A statewide needs assessment. Research project preliminary report.* Indianapolis: Indiana State Department of Health.

Mayo, E. (1933). *The human problems of an industrial civilization.* New York: Macmillan.

McGrath, J. (1982). Dilemmatics: The study of research choices and dilemmas. In J. McGrath, J. Martin, and R. Kulka (Eds.), *Judgment calls in research* (pp. 69–102). Beverly Hills, CA: Sage.

Morgan, G. (Ed.) (1983). *Beyond method: Strategies for social research.* Beverly Hills, CA: Sage.

National Association of Social Workers (1997). *Code of ethics of the National Association of Social Workers.* Washington, DC: Author.

Newman, D., & Brown, R. (1996). *Applied ethics for program evaluation.* Thousand Oaks, CA: Sage.

Patton, M. Q. (1997). *Utilization-focused evaluation: The new century text* (3rd ed.). Thousand Oaks, CA: Sage.

Pedersen, P. (1988). *A handbook for developing multicultural awareness.* Alexandria, VA: American Association for Counseling and Development.

Phillips, D. C. (1987). *Philosophy, science, and social inquiry.* Oxford, England: Pergamon.

Ramirez, M. (1983). *Psychology of the Americas: Mestizo perspectives on personality and mental health.* Elmsford, NY: Pergamon.

Rappaport, J. (1994). Empowerment as a guide to doing research: Diversity as a positive value. In E. Trickett, R. Watts, and D. Birman (Eds.), *Human diversity: Perspectives on people in context* (pp. 359–382). San Francisco: Jossey-Bass.

Reinharz, S. (1992). *Feminist methods in social research.* New York: Oxford University Press.

Roethlisberger, F., & Dickson, W. (1939). *Management and the worker.* Cambridge, MA: Harvard University Press.

Saleebey, D. (Ed.) (1992). *The strengths perspective in social work practice: Power in the people.* White Plains, NY: Longman.

Sherif, M. (1936). *The psychology of social norms.* New York: Harper.

Soriano, F. (1995). *Conducting needs assessments: A multidisciplinary approach.* Thousand Oaks, CA: Sage.

Tyson, K. (1992). A new approach to relevant scientific research for practitioners: The heuristic paradigm. *Social Work, 37,* 541–556.

Watts, R. (1994). Paradigms of diversity. In E. Trickett, R. Watts, and D. Birman (Eds.), *Human diversity: Perspectives on people in context* (pp. 49–80). San Francisco: Jossey-Bass.

13

Culturally Sensitive Policy

CAROL T. TULLY

Social policy . . . goes beyond the enactments at the various levels of government to include procedures and policies established in the private sector by businesses, educational institutions, and other private associations that have crucial social implications and may or may not be monitored and shaped by governmental force.
—A. Hartman, "Social Policy as a Context for Lesbian and Gay Families: The Political Is Personal"

Social welfare policy provides the legal and moral basis for the social services that are provided, the social problems that are identified and addressed, and under what auspices programs will be provided. As one of the primary areas of both the baccalaureate- and master's-level social work curriculum and a pathway for advocacy and the creation of social change, the arena of public policy, although perhaps not as appealing to some social workers as clinical intervention, provides a dynamic and powerful activity center for interested participants. Because public policy, by definition, must accommodate all people within a heterogeneous social setting, a natural question arises: Is it realistically possible to create culturally sensitive public policy? Moreover, if a policy is sensitive to one minority culture, does it discriminate against others?

This chapter explores the feasibility of creating public social policy that is culturally sensitive. It also defines key terms related to social policy and society, analyzes the concept of social policy, and discusses how social policy is actually created. Furthermore, the chapter explores whether it is realistic to expect that culturally sensitive policy can be created and addresses issues related to the development and implementation of such policy.

SOCIAL POLICY AND SOCIETY

Many . . . have noted the failures of the American Dream ideology, and have
suggested that value readjustments are going to be necessary even if the
processes used to achieve such changes are far from traditional or nonviolent.
—R. C. Frederico, *The Social Welfare Institution: An Introduction*

There is general acceptance of the idea that because humans have inhabited this planet they have lived in some type of communal clusters with rules to regulate their conduct. The oral tribal customs and behaviors of early humankind gave way to the written codes of Hammurabi in 1750 B.C. These customs and behaviors, in turn, yielded to the Greek, Chinese, and Roman political and social traditions that predated the birth of Jesus. The legitimization of Christianity in 313 A.D. by Constantine further codified social policies and provided laws that determined the conduct of individuals (Barker, 1995; Trattner, 1994). The next several centuries saw an increase in the development of social welfare programs that included the creation of hospitals, orphanages, taxes, almshouses, and a growing philosophy that people who are able to must care for individuals who are unable to care for themselves (Barker, 1995). By 1531, England had enacted its first statute dealing with the poor population, providing begging licenses to some disabled and aged people. The English Henrican Poor Law of 1536 and Parish Poor Rate of 1572 provided the framework for the Elizabethan Poor Law of 1601. The 1601 legislation became the major policy related to poor people and lasted for more than 200 years (Barker, 1995; Trattner, 1994). Administered at the local level, the 1601 law taxed individuals in each parish; the monies collected were used to provide local paupers with funds, create workhouses and programs for children, and punish the ablebodied poor population (Barker, 1995; Trattner, 1994). Many of the social welfare policies found in the United States today have their roots in the Elizabethan Poor Law of 1601.

Social policy evolves from the philosophical concept of social welfare. Were there no concern for social welfare, there would be no concern for public policy. *Social welfare* is a philosophical construct in which the focus is on the institutional aspects of social life with an emphasis on society's concern for the well-being of its members as individuals, families, and groups of communities. Within society, there is a system of interlocking preventative and protective laws and organizations unified by a societal commitment to common goals, values, and operating principles designed to provide, at a minimum, universal access to the mainstream of society (Axinn & Levin, 1993; Dye, 1987).

Because society is a series of interdependent, multifaceted and multi-level social systems, conflicts or social problems exist. A *social problem* is an individual or collective unmet need, the solution to which is perceived to be the responsibility of a social institution (Gilbert & Specht, 1974). It is generally thought that a social problem is one that cannot be solved with available social resources and poses a threat to the function of society (Barker, 1995). A social problem may be conceptualized as manifesting human need that is universal or singular and has causes and consequences. It is a condition of institutional dysfunction, presents both challenges and opportunities, and requires some sort of social welfare solution in the area of services or intervention (Axinn & Levin, 1993; Dye, 1987).

What Is Social Policy?

Social problems are usually addressed through the development and implementation of social welfare policies that create solutions and direct how those solutions will be reached. *Social policy* has been variously defined as a product created by lawmakers (Lindblom, 1968), but such a singular definition seems to severely limit the construct. Therefore, for the purposes of this chapter, social policy is defined as a philosophical statement, a political process, a product, a practice, and a pathway for action (see Table 13.1).

Table 13.1. The Five Ps of Social Policy[1]

Social Policy is a

Philosophical statement. It defines what needs to be done.

Political process. It reality tests how realistic is it to actually do what needs to be done.

Product. It legally defines how what needs to be done gets implemented.

Practice. It is the operationalization or actual way the product gets implemented by organizations.

Pathway for action. It is the ongoing evaluation of the implementation of the policy that creates actual societal changes.

[1] The author is uncertain of the source of this table, which she has been using in her teaching for more than 20 years. Undoubtedly, it has its roots in the author's own social policy experience at Virginia Commonwealth University, Richmond, where she completed her MSW and Ph.D. degrees.

Philosophical Statement

Social policy derives from the collective wisdom of members of societal institutions and political groups who jointly seek to provide solutions for social problems. An example is the 1997 debate about the provision of federal funds to the flood-ravaged Midwest. The social problem identified is the lack of adequate housing and other community structures resulting from the floods that hit the area in early 1997. One solution has been an effort to get federal dollars appropriated to those people in need as quickly as is possible. Thus, the philosophical statement of social policy asks, What needs to be done?

Political Process

Social policy also is the means by which decisions related to a specific course of action are determined, promoted, and formulated. Using the midwestern floods as an example, although the House of Representatives and the Senate have passed legislation ensuring the distribution of funds to the flood-ravaged areas, the president vetoed the bill because of unwanted amendments. What ensued was a battle between the Democrats (the Democrats stayed up the night of June 10, 1997, to protest Republican amendments) and the Republicans (who have said they will not remove the amendments). By June 17, 1997, the Republicans had removed the objectionable amendments, the president had signed the bill, and the people in need received the first check of several million dollars. So, the political process of creating social policy asks, How realistic is it to actually do what needs to be done?

Product

Social policy comprises the laws, rules, regulations, and procedures that are promulgated as a direct result of the political process. Once passed, legislation is enacted and sent to a federal agency that writes the rules and regulations about how to implement the law and forwards them to the appropriate state agencies for further policy development and implementation. State agencies then develop specific policies related to their unique needs and transmit those policies to the regional or local level for implementation. Hence, the product defines how what needs to be done should be implemented.

Practice

Once the law has been passed and the policies about how to implement the law promulgated and disseminated, the policies and procedures are put into action. The practice of public policy describes how the solution to the social problem is pragmatically handled. Eventually, the moneys designated for disaster relief are distributed to those people in need, but it is a long journey from Capitol Hill in Washington, D.C., to a washed-out home owner in Iowa. The practice of public policy also evaluates the equity of the policy: Are some in need not covered? Do some groups get more than others? Who is eligible? Who is not? In sum, the practice of social policy asks, How is what needs to be done actually implemented? It is at this phase that social programs and social services designed to alleviate social problems are developed, implemented, and constantly evaluated to ensure compliance with the policies and procedures.

Pathway for Action

Just as the Elizabethan Poor Law of 1601 created a base for the future development and implementation of social welfare policies, social welfare legislation that is passed today will affect the future development of social welfare legislation. The development of social policy is not static; rather it tends to mirror the changing social structures, albeit more slowly. But with ever-evolving social welfare legislation come changes to the existing social structures that are affected by law. A recent example is the legislation designed to end employment discrimination against lesbians and gay men. The U.S. Senate in 1996 narrowly failed to pass this measure, known as the Employment Non-Discrimination Act (ENDA). The defeat was not surprising; what was surprising was how close the legislation came to being passed. The vote was so close that an ENDA-type bill may very well be passed by the Senate during the 1998 legislative session. This is notable simply because, only 3 decades ago, a bill banning employment discrimination against gays would never have been introduced at the federal level, much less moved out of committee and onto the floor for a vote.

Having defined social policy as a philosophical statement, a political process, a legal product, a practice, and a pathway for action, it is important to fully understand the creation of social policy. The following brief review should facilitate a more comprehensive understanding of the culturally sensitive model of policy development.

Creating Social Policy

The two most common approaches to policy creation are the "rational" and the "political"; the rational approach is much preferred over the political approach. Policy developers who use the rational approach tend to have a thorough understanding of the social problem that necessitates the development of social policy. Once there is an understanding of the dilemma, policy creators identify several alternative methods for solving the problem and finally choose the

> In creating social policy, it is vital that policy developers comprehend society's dominant culture and its various subcultures.

most logical and rational approach. In contrast, those people in power who use the political approach simply define and implement policies they believe are important, with little or no regard for people without political clout. Table 13.2 explores the rational approach for the creation of social policy. Closely linked with the definition of policy as a philosophical concept, political process, product, practice, and pathway for action, the following seven steps for creating social policy are relatively straightforward.

First, policy creators identify a social problem, the magnitude of which is sufficient to warrant the development and implementation of social policy. For example, in New Orleans and other parts of Louisiana, there have recently been a series of hate crimes directed at African-Americans, Vietnamese immigrants, lesbians, gay men, prostitutes, tourists, and members of the transgender community. This social problem was at such a significant level that many citizens called for legislation to increase the penalties for convicted hate criminals. Begun as a grass roots campaign in the gay community, the idea for hate crimes legislation became important to members of oppressed minorities, who have been routinely targeted and victimized by such crimes.

The second step in policy formulation centers on the development of various strategies to deal with the issue. In the hate crimes example, a major obstacle was that many hate crimes likely were not reported because members of the minority community perceived that such crimes would be treated as if they were of little importance, that the penalties would be minimal, and that reporting the crimes would not be worth the hassle. The thinking of advocates was that, if the penalties were increased and if there were appropriate legislative support for such legislation, the number of hate crimes reported and prosecuted would increase. However, in conservative Louisiana, the hope for passage of such a law seemed remote, even with an obvious social need.

The third and fourth steps are often taken concurrently, that is, as policy developers are forming coalitions to support the policy incentive and drafting position papers, they also may be seeking legislative support. In the hate crimes example, the gay community gathered support from other minority communities who were also affected by hate crimes and formed coalitions with those communities. Together, these coalitions

Table 13.2. Seven Steps for Creating Social Policy Using the Rational Approach

1. Identify a social issue or problem that is of a significantly social nature that it is considered important enough to warrant the development of public policy.

2. Identify a variety of creative strategies to deal with the problem.

3. Develop position papers related to the issue and form coalitions to support the solutions.

4. Move her or his thoughts and actions into a political arena by finding a sponsor to develop legislation related to the issue.

5. Act as an advocate for the issue by lobbying legislators, testifying before legislative committees, drafting more position papers to answer questions related to the issue, and facilitating the movement of the bill through the House and Senate.

6. Become a spokesperson—once the bill is signed into law—for the development of rules, regulations, policies, and procedures related to how her or his solution will be implemented at the grass roots level by responding to inquiries related to policies associated with the legislation. Continually monitor the implementation of the law—after the law has been implemented and a social services agency is, in actuality, providing a solution to the social problem—to be certain that the policies and procedures are being addressed as required by law.

7. Help keep the policies current by updating the law to be as current with social mores as is possible. Start the process over as time passes and social customs evolve and change.

drafted position papers and legislative briefs and began the hunt for appropriate sponsorship in both the state house and senate. Eventually, they found sponsors who would support and help draft legislation to increase the penalties for hate criminals. As a result state senators introduced S. 914 (1997) into the Louisiana Senate.

Step five of creating social policy—advocacy and lobbying—can be the most fun, most exasperating, most challenging, and certainly most exciting part of the process. It involves becoming active at the legislative level, which can mean organizing a telephone tree for the purposes of lobbying legislators, visiting state capitals to meet with legislators, or testifying at legislative hearings. Letter writing, the preparation of legislative testimony, and the organization of supporters are also important aspects of the advocacy or lobbying effort. In the hate crimes example, the policy developers engaged in activities to ensure the passage of the hate crimes legislation as soon as the bill was sent to its first senate committee. They telephoned members of the senate committee and received letters of support. Moreover, advocates (pro and con) attended public hearings to present testimony on the benefits of the proposed legislation. Narrowly passing the senate committee, the bill went to the senate floor. Lobbyists (pro and con) met with senate members to discuss the good and bad points of the proposed legislation. From outside the capital, supporters of the legislation made more telephone calls, wrote more letters, and provided more testimonials to each state senator. A major sticking point for some people in relation to S. 914 (1997) was its inclusion of homosexual sexual orientation as a protected minority. For example, members of the Christian Coalition, who have stated that a homosexual sexual orientation is an aberrant behavior, sought to strike the words sexual orientation from the bill on the basis of biblical scripture (Broderick, 1996; Louisiana Electorate of Gays and Lesbians, 1997). The bill managed to pass the senate and went to a house committee where, because of continued telephone calls, letters, and meetings with committee members, it passed and was sent to the floor of the house for a full vote. With continued pressure from lobbyists and individuals, S. 914 (1997) was passed in the house with a 61–37 vote and returned for final approval to a senate committee, which forwarded it to the governor for his signature (Anderson, 1997; Louisiana Electorate of Gays and Lesbians, 1997).

The entire lobbying effort associated with this single bill took several months of actual planning and implementation and was the culmination of at least 6 years' work (Louisiana Electorate of Gays and Lesbians, 1997). Similar legislation had been introduced in the Louisiana legislature annually since 1991. Clearly, because of previous efforts, continued advocacy efforts by a number of people and groups, and the support of a number of key legislators, the bill was passed in the 1997 legislative session, and signed into law by Governor Foster.

The sixth step of policy creation is to develop appropriate rules, regulations, procedures, and policies that are designed to implement the legislation. For instance, the hate crimes legislation in the previous example calls for an additional 6 months in prison and a fine of $500 for misdemeanors and up to 5 years in jail and fines up to $5,000 for felony crimes motivated by race, age, gender, sexual orientation, gender, or religion. Although relatively simple in scope, it is necessary that the policy creators monitor the implementation of the new law to ensure that it is being followed.

This monitoring is the seventh step, which involves updating current policies as necessary. In the example, the hate crimes legislation updates current Louisiana legislation related to misdemeanors and felonies by specifying particular oppressed minorities who have been and continue to be targets of crime and by increasing the penalties for the commission of those crimes. This clearly represents a shift in the social consciousness of the Louisiana legislature, which since 1991 had failed to act on this issue.

Using the preceding steps on how to define and rationally create social policy as a reference point, it is important that policymakers have an understanding of society in terms of its dominant culture as well as its variety of subcultures. Although many social policies seem to reflect the white, male, heterosexual viewpoint, this perspective is changing through the development and implementation of more culturally sensitive or minority friendly social policies.

Distinguishing between the Dominant Culture and Subordinate Subcultures

The fabric of U.S. culture comes from the early English settlers who provided the first written codification of social policy. There is little remembrance, however, of the social structures and culture of the Native Americans who inhabited North America before 1607, and what has evolved from the colonial period still reflects patterns of the dominant culture. To use an old, but serviceable definition, *social structures* refer to those regularities, patterns, and configurations found in social life (Blau, 1975) and are usually defined in terms of familial, economic, religious, educational, political, and social welfare (Vander Zanden, 1979). Social institutions that have evolved to support these six structures have created the arena in which life tasks are "organized, directed, and executed" (Vander Zanden, 1979, p. 621) and are identifiable systems of interconnected relationships in which all people in the society function (Blau, 1975). In the United States, the dominant culture has been defined almost exclusively, until recently, by white, male, heterosexual people who developed and implemented public social policy based on their values, with little thought of the values and needs of others. These "others," by definition, became minority groups assigned to subculture membership. A *subculture* is simply a group within the main culture that is differentiated from the larger culture by certain distinguishing features (e.g., ethnicity, race, age, or sexual orientation) that functionally unites the group and acts as a cohesive factor in joining its members together (Berube, 1985).

No accurate numbers are available of the total membership of minority citizens currently residing in the United States, nor is there an accurate count of the variety of minority groups existing in this country today. Although it is outside the scope of this chapter to define each oppressed minority, the chapter does explore concepts related to minorities of color, ethnic minorities, sexual minorities (e.g., lesbians, gay men, bisexuals, and transgender people), women, and older people. Each of these groups has a long tradition of being oppressed and members of these groups certainly need to be considered when examining culturally sensitive policies.

The term *minorities of color* seems troublesome and lacks even face validity because it defines people on the basis of skin tone or color. As a social construct, it tends to divide people into categories ranging from black to white and including such other definers as yellow, high yellow, red, bronze, copper, or brown. *The Social Work Dictionary* (Barker, 1995) confirms this definition and explains that, "in the United States, the term usually refers to African Americans, Asian Americans, American Indians, and certain other groups" (p. 236). No mention is made of mixed race "colors" nor is there an estimate of how many minorities of color reside in the United States. Furthermore, the definition lacks any pragmatic way to operationalize it. Thus, on the surface, it seems not only artificial but a crude way on which to base political decisions and social policy. Nevertheless, political decisions and social policies have been defined in terms of skin color.

As troubling as the construct of minorities of color is the construct *ethnic minorities.* An ethnic minority is categorized as a minority group or subculture that has distinct characteristics such as language, customs, religion, race, origin, or culture (Barker, 1995). Ethnic minorities, then, might include Italians, Irish Catholics, black Muslims, Jewish people, Chinese-Americans, African-Americans, Mexican-Americans, Vietnamese immigrants, and countless others. What becomes immediately obvious is that the concepts of minorities of color and ethnic minorities are not mutually exclusive. This definition, like the one for minorities of color, lacks an appropriate way to measure it and is open to various interpretations of its exact meaning. Again, to base political and social policy decisions on the basis of ethnicity alone seems a peculiar way to conduct business; however, it seems to be the norm.

Sexual orientation minorities such as lesbians, gay men, bisexuals, and transgender people may be a bit easier to define, but are virtually invisible within the dominant culture—no data are available on their total number in society. Furthermore, those people whose sexual orientation differs from the nongay population are also members of other groups that would provide them either status as a member of the dominant culture or as a member of an additional minority subculture. Besides membership in a subculture that is defined by sexual orientation, this group is anything but homogeneous (Tully, 1994). Women, too, face the same dilemma. Although it has been generally estimated that about 52% of the American population is female, women as a group are as heterogeneous as the rest of society. The classification, "older people" though, seems easily defined. However, the social concept of age is variously defined by chronology, physical ability, mental acuity, or a combination of these (Busse & Pfeiffer, 1977).

What is apparent is that the definitions generally in use today that create the framework for the creation and implementation of social policy related to traditionally disenfranchised minorities are basically flawed. But, even with the limitations of the definitions, each group shares some common characteristics. It is well accepted that each group previously mentioned does represent a minority that has been systematically marginalized and historically kept from power (see chapter 4). Furthermore, membership in one or more of these groups does constitute membership in at least one subculture, if not several (e.g., the 80-year-old African-American lesbian), and requires consideration in the creation of public policy. The remainder of this chapter explores the creation of culturally sensitive policy by positing a model and then analyzing it to determine if it is pragmatically possible or even desirable to create culturally sensitive social policy.

CREATING CULTURALLY SENSITIVE POLICY: REALITY OR MYTH?

> *There is . . . a large and persistent gap between the law as authoritatively uttered and the law as it finds its way to the public.*
> —N. Dorsen, *The Rights of Americans: What They Are—*
> *What They Should Be*

Theoretical Framework: Ecological and Empowerment Perspectives

Two major conceptual frameworks support the proposed model: (1) ecological and (2) empowerment. The ecological framework emphasizes the interrelationships between people and their environments, in which importance is placed on the transactions that occur between the individual and the situation in which the person finds herself or himself. This perspective evolved from the older general systems theory, which emphasizes the complex interactions that occur between social systems (Germain & Gitterman, 1995). The ecological perspective accepts that individuals are involved in multifaceted social environments, that each individual has a variety of human relationships that last throughout a lifetime, and that individuals continually adapt to ever-changing environments (Compton & Galaway, 1994; Germain & Gitterman, 1995).

Equally important to the conceptual framework that supports the creation of culturally sensitive policy is the empowerment perspective (Lee, 1994; Simon, 1994, Solomon, 1976, 1985; Tully & Walker, in press), or what Saleebey (1992) has called the strengths perspective. Like the ecological perspective, the empowerment perspective is concerned with the person-in-environment and accepts the continuous ability of the individual to adapt to ever-changing environmental situations as well as the reality that people are involved in many complex relationships at various levels across the life span (Lee, 1994; Saleebey, 1992; Simon, 1994; Solomon, 1976; Tully & Walker, in press). The empowerment perspective is distinct from the ecological perspective and general systems theory in its commitment to working with stigmatized, oppressed, disenfranchised populations and its concern with the promotion of social and economic justice through individual and collective means. It uses the general theoretical approach of the ecological perspective but builds on those constructs by also using constructs from other theoretical frameworks including human behavior, personality development, ego functioning, learning theories, feminism, and postmodernism (Tully & Walker, in press). In addition, the empowerment perspective is dedicated to working collaboratively with others in an effort to change oppressive environments and social structures. Synthesizing the ecological and empowerment perspectives provides an excellent framework for the development of a policy creation model that is culturally sensitive.

Policy Creation and Analysis Model

Members of minority groups function in the larger, dominant society as well as within various subcultures. Within both the dominant culture and subcultures are three generally accepted levels of interactions, those at the micro-, mezzo-, and macrolevels. For the purposes of this chapter, the term *microlevel* means those interactions that occur with individuals, families, or small groups and the related professional social work activities. *Mezzolevel* relationships are relationships and professional intervention at the community level, and *macrolevel* refers to activities related to the large social institutions created and supported by customs (Tully & Walker, in press). Given these broad operational definitions, it is assumed

> Social policy in the United States must reflect the diverse cultures in this society.

that individuals function in micro-, mezzo-, and macrolevel settings in both their minority subculture as well as within the larger, dominant society (Figure 13.1). It is also assumed that social policy is created for the purpose of regulating interrelationships among individuals, groups, communities, and social institutions and, as such, represents values and customs of the society. Social policy is also designed to define the number of resources available to ensure the greatest good for the greatest number. Because the United States is a multicultural entity, social policy that reflects this heterogeneity is vital.

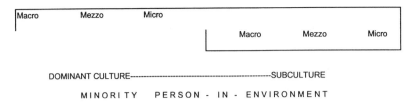

DOMINANT CULTURE--SUBCULTURE

MINORITY PERSON - IN - ENVIRONMENT

Figure 13.1.   Minority person-in-environment.

The steps for creating culturally sensitive policy are similar to those for developing any type of public policy but are more sensitive to the multicultural dimensions of our society. Because not all minority groups are equally represented in the policy formulation forum, it is increasingly important for those people involved with policy development and implementation to adhere to the principles presented in the earlier section entitled Creating Social Policy. Table 13.3 examines questions that policy developers must answer when creating culturally sensitive public policy.

The first step in creating culturally sensitive public policy is to examine the social issue in terms of its antecedent roots to provide documentation as to the origins of the social issue. For example, Hawaii is close to passing public policy that would allow same-sex marriages. While no state currently permits same-sex unions, 11 states currently have policies that ensure nondiscrimination based on sexual orientation ("New Hampshire Chief Signs Gay Rights Bill," 1997), and countless municipalities, companies, and universities have similar domestic partnership policies that provide spousal benefits to same-sex couples (Achtenberg & Newcombe, 1991; Stratton, 1996). Three same-sex couples (two female and one male) in Hawaii decided to challenge state policies regarding marriage (Ramsey, 1996), which led to Hawaii's examination of its marriage laws. To support the issue, historical analysis of same-sex marriage revealed that same-sex unions were not unheard of in ancient times (Boswell, 1994; Brooten, 1996) and that the early church conducted and celebrated such marriages (Boswell, 1994).

Once policymakers thoroughly understand an issue in terms of its antecedent roots and are aware of previous attempts to address the problem the policy is designed to ease, they must define what services the policy will provide and who will be served by the policy. In the case of same-sex marriages, the only minority group to be served by the intended policy would be same-sex couples who want to legally solemnize their relationship and then be legally entitled to spousal benefits as are nongay married couples. Policymakers then must ask, "Does this policy discriminate?" It could be argued that every public policy is discriminatory at some level; for example, children cannot purchase liquor, public welfare

Table 13.3.   Questions to Consider When Formulating Culturally Sensitive Public
   Policy

Where did the need for new policy come from? What are the historical antecedent roots of the originating issue? What social problem necessitated the policy?

Specifically what services will be provided by the policy? Who is it intended to cover? Does it discriminate?

What is the cost of the proposed policy? How will it be funded?

What are the long- and short-term effects of the policy? What are its unintended consequences?

How will the policy be implemented? What agencies will be used? How accessible are the agencies?

Who is responsible for the evaluation of the policy? How will the policy be evaluated?

---

is unavailable to all people, Medicare is based on age, and teens in New Orleans have a curfew. Given that discrimination seems to be a reality in public policy, how much discrimination is acceptable to ensure that the policy is culturally sensitive? Answers will vary depending on the level of public acceptance and values associated with a given issue. Currently, antigay sentiment from the Religious Right is at a level not seen since the early days of the civil rights movement of the 1960s. Many people have expressed their belief that same-sex marriages pose a threat to family values and that policies to allow same-sex marriages go against the will of God (Broderick, 1996). The consequence of these beliefs is an intolerance of same-sex marriages and an insistence that policies banning such marriages must be enacted (Purdum, 1996). Following this path to its logical conclusion would mean that legislation proscribing single-sex marriages should be enacted, thereby continuing discrimination against same-sex couples wishing to marry. Many people agree with this position and many states are moving to ban same-sex marriages (Broderick, 1996; Louisiana Electorate of Gays and Lesbians, 1997; National Gay and Lesbian Task Force, 1996; Purdum, 1996). So, to create policy that is sensitive to a particular minority culture, in this case the gay culture, there must be a political base in place that is strong enough to thwart attempts to derail the policy initiative before it can be implemented.

Assuming the policy passes legislative and public scrutiny and becomes law, the next step is to understand the cost of implementing the policy and how such implementation will be funded. Because few costs are associated with the issue of same-sex marriage, consider another example. In its 1997 legislative session, the Louisiana legislature passed a bill requiring that all people who receive "anything of economic value" (Anderson, 1997) from the state be required to undergo random drug testing. This bill would include welfare recipients, state college students, state employees, state retirees, people with state contracts, and people with state loans. The total number of persons eligible for drug testing would be an estimated 1 million, or about 25% of the entire state population (ibid.). The cost for each drug test would be an estimated $30, but it has not been determined who will pay that fee. At one point during legislative debate on this bill, a legislator suggested that the people being tested pay for the tests. That suggestion seemed unjust; the discussion then shifted to having the state assume the cost for testing. Given the fiscal problems in Louisiana that proposal seemed impossible, and the policy measure was passed without money for implementation. With no money to implement the policy, it will not be put into effect (ibid.).

An immediate question arises as to the cultural sensitivity of the proposed drug testing policy. The policy is not culturally sensitive to members of minority groups such as the poor and elderly populations or women. However, were such a broad-based drug testing policy implemented, what would its long- and short-term consequences be? Would there be unanticipated consequences to the implementation of the policy? Policymakers need to examine these questions as the next phase of policy creation. The authors of the bill want to ensure that those people who are abusing drugs are not receiving state benefits. For a drug abuser to continue to receive state benefits, the offender would have to be enrolled in a substance abuse program. On the surface, this looks like a simple matter, but on closer scrutiny, some difficult questions must be addressed before such random drug tests are implemented. For example, Who will assume responsibility for the children of single public welfare recipient mothers or fathers who are placed in a drug abuse program? If, following treatment, individuals are not rehabilitated and lose benefits, by what means would they be able to care for themselves or their family? Who will be responsible for the work of state employees during their stay in rehabilitation? Who will look after the disabled spouses of state retirees who are found to be addicted to prescription medications? Who will pay for substance abuse rehabilitation? How will substance abuse programs be able to deal with increased numbers of clients?

Once the short- and long-term effects of a policy are analyzed and the policymaker defines the unanticipated consequences of policy implementation, it becomes necessary to pragmatically define which agency or agencies will actually implement the policy. In the example of the random drug testing policy, the plan is to implement the policy in phases. The first people to be tested include public welfare recipients who either have been arrested on drug charges or whose social workers suspect they may have a substance abuse problem. This means at least two systems are involved: the legal system and the public welfare system. Although it could be argued that each of these socially sanctioned systems is readily accessible to people who use the services provided by each, jails and public welfare offices often are at inconvenient locations. These frequently difficult-to-find locations no doubt serve the "public good": Who wants a jail in their backyard? However, that jails and welfare offices are inaccessible also sends a message about the type of people who are perceived to use both the city lockups or public assistance offices. This message has not been, and continues not to be, culturally sensitive.

The final step in the public policy creation process is to determine who will be responsible for evaluating the policy. Because the random drug testing policy has not been implemented and there has been no mention of formal evaluation of its success, consider another example. The Council on Social Work Education (CSWE) is a nationally recognized accrediting board that is federally sanctioned to develop, implement, and evaluate criteria related to the educational training of social work professionals (CSWE, 1994). As such CSWE accredits baccalaureate and master's programs in the United States and Canada through a system of program self-study and peer evaluation. Its policies tend to be culturally sensitive (e.g., mandating curricular content in the areas of ethnic minorities, women, lesbians and gay men and with an emphasis on social and economic justice and disenfranchised minorities) and it has the responsibility of measuring compliance of social work programs to specifically mandated standards (or the periodic evaluation of adherence to criteria). This evaluative process, CSWE's primary reason for existence, is accepted by programs in social work as a necessary activity to ensure a general uniformity in social work education across the country.

An example of this type of policy evaluation follows. The 1994 CSWE handbook related to accreditation standards has mandated that content on women be included in the baccalaureate- and master's-level curricula. How this policy is pragmatically operationalized within a curricular structure has been left to the discretion of the individual program, but the program must demonstrate compliance with the policy or risk the possibility of unfavorable action by the CSWE Commission on Accreditation. The actual evaluation of the policy is tripartite in nature: the program, through a self-study process, evaluates its compliance with the policy; a site visitor committee evaluates the implementation of the policy and, through a written report, documents what it finds during the site visit; and finally, the CSWE Commission on Accreditation deter-

Table 13.4. Ensuring the Cultural Sensitivity of Policy[1]

It is not always an easy task to ensure that a policy is culturally sensitive. However, answers to the following questions considered when evaluating any public policy will help determine if the policy is as culturally sensitive as possible:

Specifically what minority groups are impacted by the policy? Does it favor the majority view? How inclusive is the policy?

Who actually benefits from the policy (minorities or the majority)? What specific benefits exist?

What barriers are there to the implementation of the policy? What cost, distance, and time factors associated with the receipt of intended services?

What role do those people who are affected by the policy have in its evaluation?

[1] The author has been using this material in her teaching for more than 20 years and acknowledges that some of the ideas herein come from materials in Dahlke, Carlton, Itzkovitz, and Madison (1980).

mines whether the program is in compliance with the policy. As with all good evaluative procedures, the process is clearly defined and well documented.

The evaluative process, although perhaps not culturally sensitive itself, can—and should—evaluate the policy in terms of its cultural sensitivity in relation to its development and implementation. To ensure that a policy is culturally sensitive, several questions should be considered (Table 13.4). Because social policies are designed, among other reasons, to present solutions for societal inequities, specifically what minority groups are affected by the policy and how does the policy create a solution? How inclusive is the policy? Does the policy actually make a difference in the lives of those people for which it is designed, or is it merely an attempt by those in power to subjugate minorities? How do those people for whom the policy is intended actually benefit? What barriers may hamper the full implementation of the policy? Are the implementing agencies easily accessible the target population? How long does it take to get the services intended by the policy? How much does it cost for the intended recipients to acquire the benefits? What role do those people for whom the policy is created have in the implementation and evaluation of the policy? Were they consulted before the development and implementation of the policy? Do they have a means by which their issues and concerns can be included in the evaluative process of the policy?

In sum, the assurance of culturally sensitive public policy is a challenging process that requires diligent and constant monitoring at all phases, but especially during the evaluation phase of the policy. The answer to the question of whether it is realistic or mythical to create culturally sensitive policy is left to the conscience of those people who will identify, develop, implement, and evaluate public social policy.

REFERENCES

Achtenberg, R., & Newcombe, M. (Eds.) (1991). *Sexual orientation and the law.* New York: Clark, Boardman, Callaghan.

Anderson, E. (1997, June 22). Broad drug testing ok'd. *Times Picayune,* p. 1.

Axinn, J., & Levin, H. (1993). *Social welfare* (3rd ed.). New York: Longman.

Barker, R. L. (1995). *The social work dictionary* (3rd ed.). Washington, DC: NASW Press.

Berube, M. S. (Ed.) (1985). *American heritage dictionary* (2nd ed.). New York: Houghton Mifflin.

Blau, P. (Ed.) (1975). *The approaches to social structure.* New York: Free Press.

Boswell, J. (1994). *Same-sex unions in premodern Europe.* New York: Villard.

Broderick, G. R. (1996). The religious right. In *Queer resources directory religious right pages* (on-line). Available at http://qrd.tcp.com/qrd/www/RRR/rrr-page. html.

Brooten, B. J. (1996). *Love between women: Early Christian responses to female homo-eroticism.* Chicago: University of Chicago Press.

Busse, E. W., & Pfeiffer, E. (Eds.) (1977). *Behavior and adaptation in late life.* Boston: Little, Brown.

Compton, B. H., & Galaway, B. (1994). *Social work processes* (5th ed.). Pacific Grove, CA: Brooks/Cole.

Council on Social Work Education (1994). *Handbook of accreditation standards and procedures.* Alexandria, VA: Author.

Dahlke, O., Carlton, T., Itzkovitz, C., & Madison, T. (1980). *A foundation for social policy analysis* (rev. ed.). Lexington, MA: Ginn.

Dorsen, N. (Ed.) (1971). The rights of Americans: What they are—What they should be. New York: Vintage.

Dye, T. R. (1987). *Understanding public policy.* Englewood Cliffs, NJ: Prentice Hall.

Frederico, R. C. (1973). *The social welfare institution: An introduction.* Lexington, MA: D.C. Heath.

Germain, C. B., & Gitterman, A. (1995). Ecological perspective. In R. L. Edwards (Editor-in-Chief), *Encyclopedia of Social Work* (19th ed., Vol. 1) (pp. 816–824). Washington, DC: NASW Press.

Gilbert, N., & Specht, H. (1974). *Dimensions of social welfare policy.* Englewood Cliffs, NJ: Prentice Hall.

Hartman, A. (1996). Social policy as a context for lesbian and gay families: The political is personal. In J. Laird and R. J. Green (Eds.), *Lesbians and gays in couples and families* (pp. 69–85). San Francisco: Jossey-Bass.

Lee, J. A. B. (1994). *The empowerment approach to social work practice.* New York: Columbia University Press.

Lindblom, C. (1968). *The policy making process.* Englewood Cliffs, NJ: Prentice Hall.

Louisiana Electorate of Gays and Lesbians (1997). *Hate crime bill finally passes* (on-line). Available at http://members.aol.com/legalinc.

National Gay and Lesbian Task Force (1996). *Same-sex marriage* (on-line). Available at http://www.ngtf.org.

New Hampshire chief signs gay rights bill (1997, June 8). *New York Times,* p. 23.

Purdum, T. S. (1996, September 22). Gay rights groups condemn Clinton on same-sex unions. *New York Times,* p. 1.

Ramsey, T. (1996). *Court TV to broadcast Baehr v. Miike* (on-line). Available at http://qrd.tcp.com/qrd...rriage.update/08.05.96.

Saleebey, D. (Ed.) (1992). *The strengths perspective in social work practice.* New York: Longman.

Simon, B. L. (1994). *The empowerment tradition in American social work: A history.* New York: Columbia University Press.

Solomon, B. B. (1976). *Black empowerment: Social work in oppressed communities.* New York: Columbia University Press.

Solomon, B. B. (1985). Community social work practice in oppressed communities. In S. H. Taylor & R. W. Roberts (Eds.), *Theory and practice of community social work* (pp. 217–257). New York: Columbia University Press.

Stratton, L. D. (1996). EEO/orientation list (on-line). Available by e-mail from larry@bradley.bradley.edu.

Trattner, W. I. (1994). *From poor law to welfare state* (5th ed.). New York: Free Press.

Tully, C. T. (1994). Should only gay and lesbian community organizers operate in gay and lesbian communities? In M. J. Austin and J. I. Lowe (Eds.), *Controversial issues in communities and organizations* (pp. 86–96). Boston: Allyn & Bacon.

Tully, C. T. & Walker, E. J. (in press). *Empowering gays and lesbians: A social work perspective.* New York: Columbia University Press.

Vander Zanden, J. W. (1979). *Sociology* (4th ed.). New York: Wiley.

14

Ecological Approach to Families Living with HIV Disease

ELDON MARSHALL, THERESA L. ROBERTS, WILLIAM BARTON,
CAROLYN STEPHANY, and BRAD LIGHTY

> *At points during the life cycle of the disease, persons with [HIV/]AIDS are*
> *overwhelmed with stressful life events and fears for which they and their loved*
> *ones require specific information and help with developing strategies to cope and*
> *to reduce the stress they are experiencing. Thus, the challenge for social workers,*
> *like that for other helping professionals, is to provide services in an accepting,*
> *responsive, and nonthreatening manner.*
> —C. G. Leukefeld and M. Fimbres, *Responding to AIDS:*
> *Psychosocial Initiatives*

A MOTHER'S STORY

What follows is the story of one wife's encounter with AIDS. It reflects
both her psychosocial struggles along with the family and community
dimensions of her experience. The story was told by Mary, mother of
three young children and wife to Michael, who was HIV-infected. Mary
shared her story in a group of other heterosexual spouses of HIV-infected
males. Tears spilled from Mary's eyes as her narrative unfolded. Her
ordeal began in a small rural community of the state and exemplified the
worst kinds of stigma and discrimination:

> It's been very emotional for us. My husband and I have been married 15
> years and have known each other since we were little kids. Michael worked
> as a funeral director and did the blood work and embalming. Because of his

325

profession, in the past 8 years, he has had an annual physical and HIV test, which has always been negative. More recently he began experiencing severe headaches and a temperature of 103 degrees. After many tests and hospitalizations, the doctors decided that he had encephalitis and sent him home with medication. He was somewhat better until September, when he had to be hospitalized again. This time, they decided he had meningitis, even though there was no evidence of bacteria. Finally, we went to Mayo Clinic and, after obtaining repeated negative blood results, they did a comprehensive test including a 6-week blood culture, and on my 35th birthday, they called to say that Michael's test was HIV positive. We just held each other and cried when we found out.

When Michael, who had worked at the funeral home for 10 years, told his boss that there was no doubt he had contracted HIV through work there, the boss fired him, and our health and life insurance policies through the funeral home were terminated. The doctors have said that Michael was probably infected earlier in the year, but his boss has been telling people that he has had the virus for years and it is a life-style thing, even going so far as to name two men with whom Michael has supposedly been intimate. I guess he is just so scared that he created lies, because he doesn't know how else to handle it.

There doesn't appear to be anything we can do. Our lawyer said that when a business has fewer than six employees, the boss can fire you for any reason. The boss is an entrepreneur and is protected by the law. We were helped, though, by the unemployment office, which said that firing Michael was unfair, so they have given us unemployment compensation until we can get disability. It's like the ultimate betrayal: the boss who has almost been like your dad in the past turns his back on you. He won't talk to us or even look at us, and in December told us that we had to get out of the house we rented from him for 8 years. Right now, our stuff is stored in 12 different places, but we have finally found a one-bedroom basement apartment in which Michael and I and our three kids, aged 12, 9, and 7 years, all live.

After Michael was fired, I knew that I would immediately have to start making some money, so I took a factory job. It's an industry where I work on an assembly board and I have to keep moving from 3:30 P.M. until 1:00 A.M. I come home and cry at night because my feet hurt so bad. When Michael is gone, it is going to be so hard to work and raise three kids by myself. I'm really scared about it because he is progressing so fast. His doctor said that if his T cell count keeps varying like it is, he may not be here in 18 months. This would make him go from being infected to death in only 2 years.

Some of the people in our church have been supportive, but we have had our car windows smashed by people in the community, and last week someone spray painted these words in our yard with white paint: "HIV kills. Keep your kids safe. Stay aware." It was a direct hit on us. I wish the general public could be more educated and not so ignorant about this virus. We are trying to sell our minivan because we can't keep up the payments.

Somebody put $500 down on it, but when they found out what illness Michael has, they screamed, got out of the van, and said, "Oh, my God, don't touch anything." Then, the dealer who was helping said, "Hey, all I can tell you is to get in touch with your doctor." Needless to say, we haven't been able to sell the van. The other night, Michael started crying and said, "It's just so bad when people act like this and don't believe me. It's very painful to always be defending myself as to how I got this thing."

The emotional distress experienced by Mary is in part a function of the multiple stressors within her social environment. Among these are the anxiety surrounding her husband's deteriorating health, fears and worries for her children's, employment discrimination resulting in loss of job and income, neighborhood rejection and persecution, problems with the health care system, and community ignorance and misinformation about AIDS. These ecosystems-induced stressors have combined in ways to compromise Mary's functioning both socially and emotionally.

As the AIDS epidemic moves into its second decade, it leaves in its wake more than 360,000 dead in the United States [Centers for Disease Control (CDC), 1997] and an estimated 11.7 million dead throughout the world [World Health Organization (WHO), 1997, p. 359]. Moreover, more than 562,000 people in the United States are currently estimated to carry HIV (CDC, 1997) and an estimated 30.6 million people presumed to be living with HIV infection or AIDS worldwide (WHO, 1997, p. 359). AIDS is a public health problem of national and international scope and import. Beyond the toll already exacted in human lives, the psychosocial costs for those infected people living with the illness are enormous, and the human costs are expanded substantially given the thousands of family members affected by the disease. The extent to which the family is affected and number of family members touched by the illness can be partially grasped if one multiplies the number of all people who are or have been infected by HIV by their many biological and functional family member ties. In this context, for the many family members who have confronted AIDS and those people who are presently living with the illness, AIDS is a family crisis of major proportions.

Understandably, in the early phase of the epidemic, efforts of the medical and social services establishments centered primarily on individuals with the disease. More recently, however, as the epidemic has unfolded, there has been an increased awareness of its effects on the family. Some of these effects have been well-documented in the clinical literature (Barth, Pietrzak, & Ramler, 1993; Boyd-Franklin, Steiner, & Boland, 1995; Brown & Powell-Cope, 1992; Geballe, Gruendel & Andiman, 1995b; Macklin, 1989; Walker, 1991). In addition, a small but growing body of research has illuminated many family dimensions of the disease (Bor, Miller, & Goldman, 1993; Brown & Powell-Cope, 1991, 1993; Marshall, Barton, Roberts,

Stephany, Pickett, & Carter, 1995; Powell-Cope, 1995; Powell-Cope & Brown, 1992; Wardlaw, 1994).

As the number of individuals and families affected by HIV multiplies, the mental health and social services professions will increasingly be called on to respond to the challenges confronting families affected by the illness. The helping professionals will need to be highly knowledgeable about the disease and the many ways it affects families, as well as competent in intervening effectively on behalf of those people living with the illness. If the needs of families are to be well served, the demands on the organizations and professionals delivering services will be great. This chapter addresses some of the requirements. Viewing the overall practice challenge within an ecological and cultural context, the chapter sets forth an empirically based ecological framework for practice, presents overarching practice guidelines, outlines a structure for comprehensive services, highlights needed macrolevel policy and program initiatives along with issues in this area, and projects training and research directions that will be needed.

DEFINITION OF FAMILY

Definition of *family* in the context of HIV is complicated by the traditional narrow definitions of the term, which focus on blood relationships or the idea of a common household, or emphasize the social network that may include any provider of social support (Bor et al., 1993). A broad conceptualization of the family is needed, given the anticipation that practitioners will be working with a variety of people including partners, members of the family of origin, extended families, close friendship networks (family-of-choice), and families of caregivers.

The following are among the differing family configurations with which a practitioner may work: the traditional intact, two-parent family with children with an infected child or parent; the single-parent family, with an infected mother; gay/bisexual couples, with an infected partner; the family-of-choice context, in which one member is infected; and infected individuals who are disconnected from family ties of any sort. In the context of the discussion in this chapter, *family* is viewed as encompassing both biological (blood) and social (chosen) relationships. Furthermore, this chapter adopts the definition suggested by Levine (1990), that is, family members are viewed as "individuals who by birth, adoption, marriage, or declared commitment share deep, personal connections and are mutually entitled to receive and obligated to provide support of various kinds to the extent possible, especially in times of need" (p. 36).

ECOLOGICAL FOUNDATION FOR FAMILY PRACTICE

The ecological perspective constitutes a major vantage point for understanding the nature of human behavior and experience. It has evolved into a major approach to social work practice with its basic tenets well-explicated in the life model (Germain, 1979; Germain & Gitterman, 1980, 1986). Central to the model is the importance placed on the environment and social context in which people find themselves. An ecological orientation "recognizes the enduring and transient relationships between and

> The concomitant psychosocial and health issues connected with HIV disease has a multisystemic affect and the illness is particularly stressful for caregivers.

among individuals, families, other groups, institutions, and society at large; and that transactions between or among these systems have a profound effect on human behavior and functioning" (Caple, Salcido, & di Cecco, 1996, p. 373). Few perspectives on human behavior fully encompass the living reality and totality of a family member's experience as does the ecological model. The relevance of this framework to understanding the effects of HIV on families and organizing practice efforts in their behalf is strongly supported in the practice and research literature.

During the early stages of the epidemic, most of social workers' understanding of the family dimensions of HIV came from clinical practice (Ackerman Institute for Family Therapy, 1989; Kaplan, 1988; Mohr, 1988; Patten, 1988; Walker, 1988). The clinical literature pertaining to work with HIV-affected families made clear that the social and psychological status of people with HIV and their families were integrally and reciprocally connected, and that family members' well-being was profoundly influenced by the quality of their relationship with multiple systems in their social context. Research into the effects of HIV on families tended to follow social practice initiatives. In the earlier stages of the epidemic, few studies could be found, and existing studies varied greatly in focus, sample surveyed, and methodological adequacy. More recently, somewhat paralleling the increased awareness of the effects of HIV on the family and appreciation of the family's role in care and support of people with AIDS (PWAs), there has been an emerging body of family-oriented research. In a comprehensive review of research during the first decade of the HIV epidemic, Bor et al. (1993) highlighted the multiple focal points and themes that emerged during this period. The studies they surveyed provided some beginning empirical documentation of the multisystems influence of HIV on the family. The authors' analysis pointed out significant areas of individual stress and burden experienced by family members, alterations in family structure and functioning that sometimes occur, and changes in social network relationships that often evolve. Bor et al.

also underscored the strains that may arise between families and the human services organizations that serve these families, as well as the sociocultural factors that can profoundly influence a family's experience (e.g., social stigma and discrimination).

Recent studies have contributed substantially to further understanding of the effects of HIV on the family and have underscored its multisystem repercussions. In a study of 125 informal family caregivers who provided support to people with AIDS, McCann and Wadsworth (1992) found that partners and friends assumed responsibilities ranging from the provision of emotional support to assistance with household tasks (e.g., shopping, cooking, cleaning, or making repairs) and personal tasks (e.g., getting in or out of bed, bathing, and dressing). Speaking to their own concerns, family members identified their needs for emotional support from friends and families, practical assistance in a variety of areas such as transportation and legal concerns, and special services such as individual and couples counseling to address their individual needs. Reporting on one of the most comprehensive family-oriented investigations conducted to date, Wardlaw (1994) summarized the experiences of 642 informal family caregivers of people with HIV. Findings documented the widely ranging physical, emotional, and economic effects of HIV on traditional and non-traditional family caregivers. Many of the family members surveyed assumed heavy caregiving responsibilities, providing assistance with emotional support, instrumental activities of daily living, legal and financial matters, management of personal affairs, and in-home medical care, among other tasks. The research provided substantial documentation of the multiple burdens family caregivers often experienced. The observed stressors centered on emotional vacillations throughout the caregiving process (e.g., regret, anger, or guilt), a pervasive sense of loss and uncertainty about the future, disruptions in personal life and pressures resulting from being on call (e.g., altered vacation plans and deferred activities), conflicts between and among family members, altered social relationships and contacts with friends and family, work-related strains (e.g., balancing caregiving demands with employment, as well as fears of job loss), financial costs (e.g., using their own personal income to meet medical costs), and changes in living arrangements (e.g., physical relocations to be more accessible to a loved one).

To investigate the effects of HIV on individual family caregivers and relationships with their loved ones with AIDS, Brown and Powell-Cope (1991) conducted extensive interviews with 53 individuals who were providing in-home care for a person with HIV (i.e., lovers, spouses, parents of either adults or children with AIDS, siblings, and friends). Living with uncertainty was found to be the core social-psychological struggle of family members as they navigated six core psychosocial processes centered on (1) managing initial reactions, (2) managing and being managed by the illness, (3) living with loss and dying, (4) renegotiating relationships, (5) disclosing the illness to others, and (6) containing the spread of HIV. Family members were challenged by specific tasks as they confronted each of these processes.

In extending and building on the preceding study, Powell-Cope (1995) explored the experiences of nine gay couples in which at least one partner was diagnosed with symptomatic HIV or AIDS. The overall experience of the couples was marked by transition and multiple losses including those related to life, relationships with friends and family, pre-AIDS life-style, health, and financial status. Among the relationship-related losses were those of independence, roles and role expectations, intimacy, freedom of sexual expression, altered boundaries, and uncertainty about their future as a couple. Life as a couple was marked by three major transitional processes: (1) hitting home (responses evolving out of awareness of loss), (2) providing mutual protection (responses oriented to forestalling loss), and (3) moving on (the strategies partners used to continue on with life in the face of significant losses). Specific tasks challenged partners as they confronted each of these three core psychosocial processes.

In 1995, the authors Marshall et al. launched a major statewide-oriented research initiative assessing the effects of HIV on the family. This comprehensive and socioecologically oriented investigation sought to accomplish the following: obtain a statewide (Indiana) perspective of the psychosocial needs of family members who are affected by HIV and the effects of the disease on family system multiple levels ranging from partners, parents, grandparents, adult siblings, and friends; determine the social systems composing the ecological world of a family member's experience; appraise the nature and quality of the social support network surrounding family members as well as the resources available to them; and determine the kind and quality of programs and services used by family members and ascertain the gaps in resources. Data from the study testified to the ecosystemic effects of HIV on those family members most affected by the illness. The data added to the knowledge about families acquired from earlier studies. Among the prominent themes, major stressors were found to center on the following: pervasive emotional strain and a sense of uncertainty, heightened family tensions and instability, heavy caregiving pressures and demands, life adjustments and transitions, fears or anxieties related to disclosure, deficits relative to social supports or services, and discrimination and oppression. The research provided further insights into the ecological dimensions of a family member's experience with living with HIV and the major supports and sources of strain in the individual's larger systems environment. Furthermore, the research serves as the foundation for the discussion that fol-

lows. This chapter speaks specifically to data acquired from the focus
group phase of the research, which not only provide empirical grounding
for an ecologically and culturally sensitive approach to family work but
also inform recommendations related to policy and program development on behalf of family members who are living with AIDS.

FAMILY STUDY AND CONTEXT

The Families and HIV/AIDS Study (Marshall et al., 1995) combined
qualitative and quantitative methods in a three-phase process. In phase 1,
the researchers conducted in-depth interviews with 26 family members
(caregiving partners, parents, grandparents, adult children, and siblings)
balanced to include both rural and urban families. Phase 2 encompassed a
series of 13 focus groups held with family members throughout the state.
In phase 3, a comprehensive, structured questionnaire was individually
administered to 214 family members representing various regions of the
state.

In relation to previous research on families, the study was unique in its
comprehensive, statewide focus. Beyond the aforementioned research objectives, it was anticipated that the ecological approach would yield a
number of benefits and that the study would serve the following broader
purposes: lead to the development of a model needs assessment process
potentially adaptable to other states interested in obtaining data on the
effects of HIV/AIDS on families; provide systematic documentation of
the family members' social and mental health needs, which is basic to
effective program initiatives aimed at prevention; establish an information database, which is essential to the development of well-targeted
services oriented to families' clearly identified needs, which is essential
and necessary for policymaking and program planning on their behalf;
provide a comprehensive picture of current patterns in the use of social
and mental health services by family members; and heighten community
consciousness of the needs of family members affected by the illness.

FAMILY'S ECOLOGY

Early in the research, it seemed essential to establish the social parameters composing the totality of the family's social environment because one
cannot begin to fully understand the experience of a family member
living with HIV without viewing that experience through an ecological

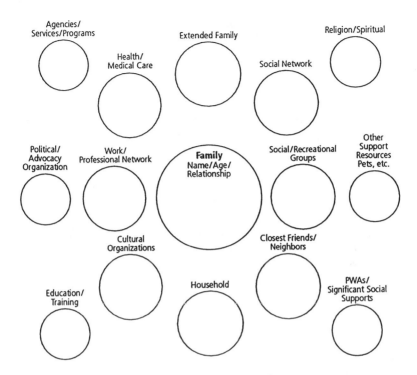

Figure 14.1. Family ecogram. Note: From Marshall et al. (1995). Reprinted with permission.

lens. As shown in the familygram in Figure 14.1., the ecosystems environment in which family members live is a potentially complex one. The transactions that occur between family members and the many subsystems composing the ecological world in which they are embedded can profoundly affect their overall sense of well-being and ability to cope, as is well illustrated in the stories that follow.

One Gay Couple's Experience

Rick, a Caucasian gay male, aged 43 years, was a partner of Roger, aged 40 years, a gay, PWA. They had lived together for 7 years in a home (left to Rick by his grandmother) with their two cats, who were "very near and dear to them." Also living in the area were Roger's parents, two sisters, and a brother-in-law, as well as Rick's parents. Rick also had a brother and sister, both of whom lived out of state.

Roger tested positive for HIV in 1991 after an infection on his finger became rather severe. At the emergency room, the medical staff, as a "routine procedure," asked to include an HIV test in Roger's blood work. "He agreed to have a test because he'd never been tested before," Rick stated. "He was reluctant at first, but then finally consented. So he went ahead and signed the papers, and that's when he found out he was positive." When the results were in and after learning Roger was HIV positive, Rick said he became highly anxious, knowing in the back of his head that it would be the beginning of a long journey. He commented, "Having had friends sick with [AIDS] at that time, I'd only had one close friend die, so it was still somewhat foreign to both of us."

Even though distressed, Rick tried to be the "Rock of Gibraltar" for his partner. He shared that, early on in the hospital, "Roger was being pretty forthright with his parents and everybody else, even if this was not always appreciated by family members. He did not feel as though he had anything to hide. Eventually he even told his boss, and everybody at his place of employment knew he was sick." Unlike many of his friends, Roger never faced any "problems as to discrimination on the job. Most people were very sympathetic with his dilemma. Neither of us got any abuse, and it has been pretty smooth sailing. No one who knew us has ever given us any problems."

Roger's HIV status led him to a reexamination of values within his family of origin, which was Southern Baptist. One of Roger's stepsisters had made the comment once that if there was "no homosexuality, then there would be no AIDS." Her homophobia prompted such comments as, "Roger had this disease because of his horrible homosexual lifestyle." Rick noted that, despite this stepsister's negative reactions, Roger's family had become much closer and an important source of support. He stated, "Since the disease has devastated him, he's gotten to be closer with his parents and sisters, and they've spent a lot more time together and talked. The same has happened in my family."

The increased cohesion in each of these families has been a tremendous source of support as they both struggled to cope with AIDS. Rick has been Roger's primary caregiver:

> I have assisted him with changing his bandages, and even with getting him up and walking. I've helped him into the bed, or moved him out of the bed into the wheelchair. Basically, I've been his nurse, if you will. I prepare his meals, and encourage him to eat properly. In a way I feel badly, because maybe that's all he wants, and if that's all he wants, then that's all he wants. I can't force him, but I know it's not enough. So what do you do? I don't want to nag him, so I just drop it. It hurts me, though.

Roger's family has been helpful in running errands and taking him for medical appointments. However, Rick said that it is hard to let others help, and he sometimes feels guilty when they do.

Beyond the demands of daily caregiving, AIDS has forced a significant reversal and alteration in roles. Rick reported that divisions of labor in the household, wage earning, the paying of bills, intimacy, and so forth have been altered. As the disease has progressed, sexual intimacy has become less important, and the couple expresses intimacy in other ways. In that respect, Rick noted, "We've grown closer in a more spiritual or intellectual plane. I guess, in a way, by his being unable to have sex, you grow closer though just hugging and cuddling. I think that's what I've cherished. Roger sort of brought me down to earth and, if anything, mellowed me out and got me to a plateau in my life where I've never been happier. He's brought me the home I've always wanted."

This is not to say that everything has been easy. Shortly after learning of Roger's HIV status, both partners—at Roger's urging—joined a support group at a local AIDS service agency in their community. Rick said that the services provided helped both of them tremendously. The group has given Rick feedback that he is not the only one in this situation with these feelings. "Everybody's story [in the group] is kind of interrelated, and we can help each other. I look forward to the group, and it has proven very helpful." It gave him support and relieved some of his stress from caregiving.

Watching his partner slowly succumb to AIDS-related cancer has evoked highly intense emotions in Rick ranging from anxiety, concern, and anger, to relief. He noted, "As weird as it might seem, when the end comes, I feel that I will be very relieved, because I've done my hell, I've suffered my pain, and I've cried my tears. When he dies, I would like to rejoice in the thought that he is at peace. And I will be at peace, too. It's unbearable for me, living with him, to see him that way, suffering so much." Roger has given advanced directives, leaving Rick in charge through power of attorney. Rick feared that things might not go smoothly—he talked about the "horror stories" told by members of his family and support group and the court challenges that often occurred in relation to advanced directives. As he said, "You never can tell what will happen." Rick commented that it will be extremely hard after Roger dies. He shared, "I'll just be devastated, because we did not have everything together. You focus your whole life on this family you have built, and then it doesn't exist anymore. What do you do? It is just a matter of time, and I'll have to deal with it then."

In Rick's story, one can observe the social inequities that prevail in families of gay men and lesbian women compared with heterosexual couples. For example, the court's challenge to advanced directives and the resulting stress and fears experienced would be less of a concern for married heterosexual couples than they were for him. In addition to this kind of discrimination, the partners must contend with the aversive homophobic reactions of Roger's stepsister. Demands surrounding caregiving are most visible in the many tasks and responsibilities taken on by Rick in supporting his partner. Changes in the couple's relationship and the role reversal that occurs contribute further to partner stress in addition to tensions surrounding sexuality and interpersonal intimacy. Alongside the aforementioned stressors, however, are the significant resources residing within the family and the couple's social network that support them in their coping efforts. Still, the overwhelming harshness of AIDS takes its toll on all involved, and Rick acknowledged that assistance will be needed long after his partner has died.

One Father's Experience

Jeremy is 36 years old, African-American, and HIV positive. He grew up in a biracial family, later marrying an African-American woman. Jeremy had been an intravenous drug user and a heterosexual spouse of a family member who had died of AIDS. He lived with his two little girls, Tonya, a very bright 5-year-old, and Tammy, a 16-month-old. In 1995, Jeremy's wife, Sharon, who was pregnant with Tammy, became very ill with intestinal problems and went to the doctor for a checkup. After extensive tests, her physician discovered that she was HIV positive. The illness progressed rapidly from that time until 6 months later, when Sharon died on New Year's Day at age 27 years. In addition, when Tammy was tested at the age of 6 months, it was discovered that she was also HIV positive. Jeremy firmly believes that the disease progressed so quickly because of Sharon's fear about her pregnancy, her typically high stress level, and her tendency to overreact, which led to her refusal to take any medications prescribed by the family doctor. He felt that his hardest task during her illness had been that of trying to keep her strong by boosting her spirits so that she would not give up hope.

In speaking about the relationship with his wife, Jeremy noted, "We loved each other, and since I have probably been HIV positive for at least 8 years, Sharon knew about the risks, but said it didn't matter and made the decision to marry me anyway. She never blamed me when she found out she was sick; we were as close as ever." Unfortunately, this same acceptance was not present in the attitude of Sharon's African-American mother, who blamed Jeremy for every bad thing that had ever happened in her family, and pursued a personal vendetta to try and take Sharon, their children, and all his personal possessions and assets from him. His mother-in-law took out a restraining order against him, put out a warrant for his arrest, and refused to let Sharon see him after she found out about the illness. Jeremy was forced to leave their home and take up residence with his mother in another city to protect himself. With the help of his own mother, who provided transportation and child care, Jeremy and

Sharon visited one another as often as possible without the knowledge of Sharon's mother. He described the situation as really difficult: "I was both angry and sad to be kept from my wife and children, especially when Sharon was deteriorating so quickly and I wanted to be there to help and support her and spend every minute with her in those last months. I tried to keep her moving and active, so that she wouldn't just lie around waiting to die; I would take her to the zoo, children's museum, and park to try and make life positive for her."

Of further concern to Jeremy was that he felt Sharon had not received the services and professional care that she needed, because her mother felt a need to keep the disease a secret. Sharon's mother, who was prominent in the community and quite financially stable, lived in continual fear that someone might find out that her daughter had AIDS. For this reason, she would not secure outside services, and she tried to take care of Sharon's many physical problems with only the help of the housekeeper who had been in her employ for many years. It was only at the end, when Sharon was too ill to remain at home, that her mother secured a private room in the hospital, for which she personally paid, and in which Sharon died without the support and presence of her husband at her side.

In contrast to Sharon's African-American mother, who feared discrimination in her community if she were to talk about her daughter's illness, Jeremy's Caucasian mother had no hesitation about discussing the illnesses of her son and his wife and the predicament of the family. According to Jeremy, "She told everybody everything, including all our relatives who told everybody else, and then she joined a support group and of course shared her story there. We didn't appreciate this and Sharon was really upset about it because of her family's cultural beliefs. In fact, my mother tried to become too involved, and sometimes it was upsetting because she would worry about everything and wanted to make all our decisions for us."

After Sharon's death, her mother found a lawyer who would represent her in court in an attempt to gain custody of Tonya and Tammy. According to Jeremy, she told the court that he was never in the home while Sharon was living and did not want the children. Tearfully, he related how his mother-in-law had told Tonya, the oldest child, that Daddy didn't love Mommy and had killed her and didn't love his girls either and was going to kill Tammy as well. Jeremy knew that ultimately he would lose his life to AIDS, but he was concerned about the stress that he was experiencing from the court fight between the two grandmothers and the strain of continuing to live in his mother's home under these conditions. He felt that the stress could shorten the life that he had left to live and spend with his daughters.

Because his health was still good and he wanted to try and keep it that way for as long as possible, Jeremy decided that he should move into an apartment of his own. This was not an easy task to accomplish though, because he had been forced to leave his job as a time and motion analyst when he moved to his mother's home and he had no money left. Eventually, he was able to obtain Supplemental Security Income and Medicaid, but finding a place to live was another hurdle to overcome. He commented that,

> being Black, poor, and HIV positive is the cause of a lot of discrimination; when you don't have money, they try to put you in real bad places that are falling apart and full of drugs, rats, and such. Finally, after many months, a Shelter Plus Care program found this place for me and they pay everything except $104 per month, which I take care of. I'm really grateful for their help, because it gives me a chance to try and put my life back together. Now, the only thing left is to try and find work because I feel fine and I don't want to be in a position of just sitting around waiting to die. But, there is a problem here, too, because I can't make any more than $500 a month or I will lose all of my benefits, and it's really hard to find anyone who will hire me with my technical expertise for so few hours.

Jeremy expressed his concerns for the children growing up without their mother and the stress they were currently under. He worried greatly about his daughter, Tonya, and the stress she experienced because her grandmother told Tonya that her father, whom she adored, had killed her mother. In her confusion and sadness, she often awoke, crying and calling out for her mother to come back. Beyond the struggles confronting Jeremy, one could only wonder about the long-term affects of the illness on the children's well-being.

Jeremy's story clearly suggests that no one can begin to understand the totality of his experience without knowledge of the multiple systems affecting his life. Conflicts between him and his mother-in-law were intense, reverberating in ways that influenced his children's emotional well-being and left unresolved grief and loss in their wake. Strains surrounded his relationships with other systems including service organizations, employment, and the legal system. Discrimination and oppression emanating from the cultural context in which he lived further heightened his stress. Clearly, Jeremy's overall adjustment was profoundly affected by the ebb and flow of his interactions with the key systems composing his socioecological world.

FAMILY'S ECOLOGICAL NETWORK

The clinical literature pertaining to families and HIV contains a plethora of personal accounts about the multitude of ways in which families are affected by the many social systems that impinge on them. The stories of Mary and Jeremy reflect, in part, something of the ecological spectrum that may characterize a family member's experience. The Families and HIV/AIDS Study sought to learn more about the ecological terrain of family members, and from this context, examined major stressors and resources relative to the different social systems with which a family member interacted. The familygram (see Figure 14.1.) was designed to guide the researchers' exploration of the relationship between family members and social systems. A familygram provides practitioners a useful tool for conducting practice-relevant assessments of the client-environment situation and focuses interventions on those social systems of greatest clinical significance. The framework evolved from in-depth individual interviews with family members in which the researchers sought to stake out the key ecological parameters of family members' experiences and captured a wider range of data than that typically obtained from using ecomaps (Hartman, 1978). Based on focus group findings, the following discussion captures the major stressors and resources manifest at different system levels, namely, individual, family, social network, community, service agencies or organizations, and social or cultural institutions.

Individual Level

The individual experience of family members was often marked by a range of stressors centered on emotional distress, most commonly manifested in a pervasive sense of uncertainty about the future and a sense of helplessness and vacillating feelings; grief and sadness related to current and anticipated losses; disclosure-related struggles about when to tell, who to tell, and what to share; life adjustments and transitional crises; and caregiving demands ranging from providing emotional support, assisting with activities of daily living, and managing personal affairs, to assisting with in-home medical care.

Comments from family members poignantly reflected the dimensions of their stress. As one mother noted, "When your son lives with you, the most stressful thing is seeing him suffer so much. I mean it is just more than you can almost stand sometimes. I just had to go in the other room and cry." Another mother observed, "The most stressful thing for me in caring for him was the emotional part of listening to a young person talk about his death. He needed someone to be honest with him, and to stay open with someone when your heart is breaking is the hardest thing to do. Then, when he'd say, 'Mom, I know this is my last Christmas,' and it was, that's really hard to talk." One Latino parent shared, "We kept asking our son if there was anything we could do and he said, 'No, I just want to sleep.' You feel so helpless. There's nothing you can do." Speaking about the life adjustments brought about by the illness, one parent put it this way, "The illness really disrupts the prime time of your life just as you are trying to get settled." Or, as another family member observed, "We had no life for 2 years other than our son. He was our total focus. It just consumes you."

Although the stress of living with a person with HIV may be great, findings have richly detailed the strength possessed by family members, most especially their adaptability and resilience, openness to make major accommodations in life patterns and routines, and commitment to stand by their loved ones, oftentimes in the face of large personal, social, and economic costs. Many family members drew on a rich reservoir of personal and inner resources in the process of coping, finding strength through spiritual beliefs, and specific self-care strategies that worked for them, and altered beliefs and outlooks regarding their situation.

Family Level

Findings have clearly documented that the effects of HIV may extend to all levels of the family system, thus heightening family members' stress and threatening family stability. Although breakdowns in communication between family members tended to be among the more commonly cited problems, numerous other problems in family functioning were acknowledged, especially those related to parenting, making needed role adjustments, resolving conflicts, coping with negative emotional reactions, making decisions about care, and making plans. As one parent commented, "I have another son who is straight who never really understood his brother's life-style, and it really tore our relationship apart for a while. He didn't want his brother to come to his college graduation because he was embarrassed that he looked so bad at that time. He didn't want him there. That broke my heart." In talking about her family relationship, one sister shared, "My brother and mom had a very stressful relationship. When he was hospitalized and she was told he was dying, she wouldn't call him. She would not acknowledge his illness. My mom didn't want us to tell extended family and I got to the breaking point. My two other brothers were concerned about me and my stress level."

Despite the varied strains emerging in family relationships, many family members could point to positive developments in their relationships over time. Most notable among the improvements cited was increased emotional support and bonding that often developed between different members within the family system. The crisis around coping with HIV tended to pull many families closer as they faced the illness. As one sister observed, "Before my brother passed away, we made Wednesday our family day. It never failed, rain or shine: we'd pick him up, go to lunch, then shopping. It seems like the sicker he got, the more time we spent with him." One Latino aunt remarked that her nephew "took his two nieces and nephew on a vacation. This will be something the kids will remember all their lives and they will remember their uncle." As another family member observed, "Sometimes the illness does bring the family closer together, probably because the family knows that time is limited."

Social Network

Although social support has long been recognized as a key buffer against stress, the kind and quality of support received may vary widely. For some family members, social support was either totally lacking, difficult to access, or limited in kind and amount. As one sibling of a PWA noted, "I didn't really have support. I was a supporter for my mom and dad." Or, as a friend said, "The people I have been the closest to and those who have been the most supportive are gone [deceased]." Attesting to the value of one's social network, a mother noted, "It makes me stronger just knowing how close we all are." Or, as another observed, "Just being able to air my frustrations with my friends helps so much." When family members were asked directly, typically they acknowledged family and friends as among their most valued sources of support in their lives, significantly enhancing their coping. At the same time, for some family members, relationship disconnections and a general lack of support from others represented their most stressful experiences with living with HIV.

Community Level

The familygram reflects the potential range of community organizations and institutions with which a family member may be connected beyond those specifically concerned with delivery of social, mental health, and health care services. The diversity of connections that family members had with the larger community ranged from religious organizations to recreational agencies and sports-related groups such as organized athletic teams (e.g., bowling leagues and ball teams). Relationships with these organizations were generally for better or worse, that is, either a source of support or strain. House of worship, for instance, was a source of spiritual renewal and faith-building for some people, while for others it was a place where family members felt judged, discriminated against, and socially ostracized. Stories documenting each type of experiences were numerous. Overall, resources in the larger community represented a potential source for broadened social and emotional support and coping skills.

Service Agency/Organization Level

In the process of living with HIV disease, PWAs and their families must draw on a range of services from AIDS service organizations, community mental health centers, and health care organizations. Many testimonials from family members underscored the importance of these agencies and the services they provided. Speaking about his support group, one person noted, "The support groups are just invaluable in the help they provide to me." Relative to her experience with a hospital, one family member shared, "The doctor was just wonderful. He became very close to the family, and the nurses just went overboard to be helpful." Reflecting on his experience in counseling, one father said, "The counseling is what got us through. Before that, we didn't know how to talk about our feelings or resolve conflicts." Findings clearly indicate that the quality of interactions between family members and the service organizations with which they related had—for better or worse—consequences for their social and emotional well-being. Family members tended to be specific in their evaluations of care providers' behavior and service delivery practices in terms of helpfulness, effectiveness, or aversiveness. Typically, knowledge, attitudes, and interpersonal competence figured prominently in family member evaluations of their experience with care providers. In general, they were most appreciative of providers who manifested an accepting and caring attitude, respected and listened well to their concerns, and treated their loved ones in a respectful manner. They were most critical of those providers who communicated in a disrespectful manner, treated them impersonally, and performed their work incompetently.

Factors most commonly viewed as compromising the quality of services were professional ignorance and fears about HIV, which sometimes led to refusal of service, and discrimination; the limited quantity and quality of services typically found in rural areas; homophobic attitudes and behaviors of care providers as well as discriminatory practices against sexual minorities; ineffective dissemination of information about HIV-related sources; constraints in terms of access to services; and poverty, which limited the options and quality of services available.

Societal Level

A person cannot begin to fully understand the experience of a family member living with AIDS outside the cultural milieu in which he or she lives. The stigma and discrimination surrounding AIDS continues to oppress many of those people most affected by it. There were numerous reports of discrimination encountered in interactions with specific service providers as well as in the community at large. As one mother observed, "He'd go to the hospital and there were a couple of nurses who rarely came into his room, and when they did, they looked like they were going to Mars. They'd have the booties, the gown, the gloves, and the masks. They'd be scary." One family member who used to attend churches with primarily African-American congregations, said, "If I did go to a black church, you would never ever under any circumstances stand up and say, "My brother has AIDS, my lover has AIDS, or anyone else in my family for that matter." It just wouldn't be tolerated. There are a lot of black ministers who preach from their pulpit that AIDS is God's punishment for gays. These people are getting what they deserve." Manifestations of discrimination ranged from blatant to subtle and could be recognized in a multitude of ways, from barriers encountered in efforts to access services or outright refusals to provide services, to negative interpersonal interactions.

CULTURAL CONTEXT OF FAMILY WORK

Mary's, Rick's, and Jeremy's narratives poignantly articulated how HIV/AIDS have affected the very existence of their family systems. Mary's life story highlighted the complexities of the regional and economic context—the "hypervisability" of a rural family affected by HIV disease and living in poverty. Her narrative illustrated themes associated with powerlessness, overwhelming stresses, and the resilience of women in HIV-related caregiving roles. Along with the multiple stressors commonly encountered by family members living with AIDS, the social inequities faced by sexual minorities and aver-

> The multiple stressors commonly encountered by people and their families living with HIV or AIDS are exacerbated by social and economic inequities and discrimination.

sive effects of homophobia were evident in Rick's experience with the disease. Jeremy's circumstances illustrated challenges in negotiating the boundaries between family subsystems with radically different cultural beliefs about help-seeking, help-giving, and use of external supports. This racial and ethnic diversity was exacerbated by class and economic differences. As Jeremy observed, the lens through which he viewed his experiences were shaped by "being Black, poor, and HIV positive," underscoring the significance of the cultural context of his families' reality. His experiences as an intravenous drug user were played out in an urban context.

In less progressive ecological frameworks, the cultural context of family work may be limited to superficial acknowledgment that diversity is merely one element of the family's environment. Clearly, such recognition would not be sufficient to understand the concerns, needs, and efficacies of families such as Jeremy's and Mary's. However, this perspective is common in applications that are at the culturally blind or cultural pre-competence level. These "generic" approaches to practice, although touting an objective, unbiased stance, in reality promote orthodox, Eurocentric models of practice with a cursory admonition to be culturally aware and sensitive (Reid-Merritt & Mathis, 1997). Typically, traditional paradigms have emphasized separateness and a lack of connection among families, groups, communities, macrosystems, and the larger society. They have failed to affirm the richness, history, culture, values, strengths, and experiences of persons of color, women, gay men and lesbian women, younger and older persons, individuals with diverse physical and mental abilities, economically oppressed persons, and similar groups (Schriver, 1995). Ironically, these often marginalized groups are among the very populations significantly affected by the HIV/AIDS pandemic (Bethel, 1995; Boyd-Franklin et al., 1995).

More recently there has been a shift toward more progressive, alternative ecological paradigms that give primacy to the individual's perspective of his or her cultural realities and the implications for social work practice. These frameworks value revision as well as interpretation, feminism, diversity, and integrative, personal conceptualizations of the cultural context of family work (Schriver, 1995). There is clear support from a number of professionals who have asserted that competent practice, research, and evaluation must be contextualized in the social, cultural, political, and economic context of the people with whom practitioners work. For example, Akbar (1984), Schiele (1996, 1997), and Reid-Merritt and Mathis (1997) have formulated social sciences and social work models that affirm African-centered worldviews of collective identity, the primacy of spirituality, and the vitality of affective knowledge. Other scholars have specifically applied culturally grounded, ecological approaches. Particularly informative, in this regard, are the works of Logan and Joyce (1996) on African-Americans; Mancoske and Lindhorst (1995) on gay men, lesbians, and their significant others; Gillman and Newman (1996) on women; Linsk (1994) on older persons; and Anderson and Shaw (1994) on regional diversity.

The Families and HIV/AIDS Study maximized opportunities to address the cultural context of practice while giving primacy to specific ecological considerations. In this regard, attention was given to assessing the extent to which multiple cultural factors influenced the experiences of family members who cared for or supported persons with HIV. There was a fundamental commitment to ensuring that diversity characterized the research team, staff, and advisory group members, as well as the theoretical frameworks grounding the research to ensure the communication of respect and understanding for the communities the team sought to engage. This effort offered rich opportunities to operationalize an inclusive conceptualization of the cultural context and to embrace the diversity of families throughout the state who were affected by HIV disease. The research in and of itself was empowering in that it provided opportunities for caregivers to share their expertise and concerns with state-level policymakers.

Marshall et al. (1995) integrated a variety of strategies enabling caregivers to voice their perspectives on the significance of diversity in their experiences. The researchers put diversity on "the table" by specifically exploring the strengths and challenges associated with diversity throughout each phase of the study, including the interviewer training sessions. The primary focus was on the dimensions of race, ethnicity, language, sexual orientation, gender, age, socioeconomic class, religious or spiritual beliefs, disability or health status, political affiliation, intravenous drug use, and urban and rural living areas. King's (1990) interactive model of multiple jeopardy was useful in conceptualizing the complexity and interactive effects of multiple oppressions as experienced by families in the study. For example, one individual may be an African-American, bisexual grandmother living in a poor, rural community, who is HIV positive, and is serving as the primary caregiver for a significant other with HIV/AIDS. The study moved beyond a mere additive approach to understanding multiple strengths and challenges associated with cultural dimensions of families' lives to embrace a culturally competent ecological perspective. The following discussion briefly highlights the cultural dimensions that bore on the family members experiences.

Ethnicity/Race

In the study, there was diversity as to how families restructured their lives to incorporate HIV as a crisis, challenge, or opportunity. An African-American mother, reflecting on her crisis, noted that professionals need to be more understanding of the accessibility for diverse populations:

> I think they need to realize Black males, especially, are uncomfortable or embarrassed that they'll be labeled as being homosexual. . . . Being a straight Black male has kept him from the group, I think. This has bothered

him and I think it's a male thing. He wants to come to the meetings, but I think he felt he didn't want people to think he was gay.

Sexual Orientation

Varied stories surfaced about parents' coming to terms with their son's homosexuality while simultaneously learning about the son's HIV status. In addition, the fallout from homophobia within the family system sometimes eventuated in major conflicts and cutoffs between members of the family. In the case of some members, coming to terms with their son's sexual orientation was a growth-enhancing process. As the mother of a gay son shared, "I think the illness forced us to become more accepting of our son and his life-style. We just came from such conservative backgrounds, whereby we kept wanting to deny who he was. Finally, we said this is the way he is, and became closer to him at that time."

Gender

The cultural context for women affected by HIV paralleled the same gender-related issues that exacerbated their lives before HIV (Gillman & Newman, 1996; Taylor-Brown, 1992; Land, 1994). The stress on women in caregiving and supporting roles was great. Their distress was often compounded by struggles related to parenting, poverty, housing, substance abuse, isolation and invisibility, racist and sexist stereotypes, and power inequities, which further disenfranchised those women. Despite the enormity of their burdens, they often evidenced phenomenal inner resources of the kind reported by Gillman and Newman (1996): "strength, courage, kindness, devotion to family and children and an uncanny will to live and reestablish priorities for survival in spite of the paucity of services for them" (p. 130).

Age

In her study of informal caregivers of people with HIV, Wardlaw (1994) found that one of the most profound age-related issues was the predominance of "out of sequence" life transitions, such as parents who served as caregivers and grieved about the death of an adult child with AIDS. These transitional and bereavement crises were common in family members' stories. One adult child of a PWA reflected on the role reversal and lack of peer support: "I think there are some people who are unsupportive, even though they don't intend to be. It's a hard thing to be supportive, especially when I'm talking about people in my age group, talking about parents dying. It's a hard thing to be supportive about that." In another instance, a grandparent found anticipatory grief for her son a challenge, but confronting the future of her granddaughter made it extremely difficult for her to bond with the infant. "It's awful about the baby. She was really ill when she was born. She only weighed 10 pounds when she was 6 months old. Now she's so big and fat. We don't want to get attached to her. But I think my oldest granddaughter is going to be devastated. I think she can part with her mother and dad but with her sister it's going to be greater."

Other examples of age-related considerations concern the benefits and challenges of intergenerational caregiving, such as children who care for their parents with HIV, older grandparents who care for grandchildren who are living with AIDS, and other role reversals. Linsk (1994) examined the often neglected experiences of the elderly population with HIV/AIDS, and called for greater attention to their unique concerns as persons living with HIV as well as to the concerns of intergenerational caregivers.

Region

Regional considerations were especially salient to the cultural context of some family members. In discussing their practice with family members in rural areas, Anderson and Shaw (1994) detailed the common concerns of family members living in rural settings, including circumscribed social networks, isolation and fear of ostracism, compelling issues regarding confidentiality, location security and visibility, service access and transportation, safety, homophobic attitudes, political conservatism, and limited public information. As one mother put it, "It's really tragic that there are people who need help and they might have to go as far as 50 miles away to get it because there's only one persons whom they can see here in my small hometown." Another sibling lamented that there was only one "generic" support group in the community: "I just didn't feel like I fit in. I was the only one there who was a sibling and my issues were so different. I didn't feel like I belonged in that group, but there wasn't another group for me to go to." In contrast with rural areas, urban communities tend to have greater numbers of AIDS-service organizations and resources; although it certainly cannot be assumed that there is universal access nor that parallel issues will not emerge given the greater demands for service in larger communities (Wilson, 1995).

PRACTICE IMPLICATIONS

The statewide Families and HIV/AIDS Study afforded much learning about the many ecological and cultural dimensions composing the experience of family members who have lived with AIDS. A number of practice implications emerged out of this learning.

Ecological Assessment and Treatment

Earlier discussion highlighted the multisystem complexity of the family members' experience. Enhancing the goodness-of-fit between them and the significant social systems in which they live requires focusing assessment and treatment through an ecological lens. Familygrams and ecomaps (Hartman, 1978) are useful guides for mapping out significant social systems surrounding and converging on the family, identifying main resources among these larger systems, and pinpointing major sources of strain. This kind of ecosystem assessment makes it possible to target interventions on those systems of greatest clinical significance. Practice interventions will need to be oriented to bringing about more optimal ecological conditions on behalf of family members, moderating constraints and sources of stress, and building on resources. Hence, practitioners must be highly skilled in working with larger systems and competent at moving flexibly into the multiple roles of counselor, teacher, coordinator, broker, mediator, and advocate.

> Social work practice in the area of HIV or AIDS is most effective when it is strengths-based and culturally-sensitive. Assessment and intervention is a seamless process involving multiple services as appropriate.

Culture-Sensitive Intervention

A broad conceptualization of culture must be applied in the assessment of family members and intervention on their behalf. This conceptualization must be multidimensional to include ethnicity, race, sexual orientation, gender, age, physical and mental ability, health status, socioeconomic class, religion, and language. Core to cultural competence are knowledge of the significant ways in which diversity influences the experiences of families affected by HIV and acquisition of skills basic to engaging them in culturally sensitive and responsive ways. Practitioners must develop what Caple et al. (1996) referred to as a *culture-sensitive perspective*, which is distinguished by appreciation of the following: (1) there is no single American culture; (2) members of each cultural group are diverse; (3) acculturation is a dynamic process; and (4) diversity is to be acknowledged and valued (p. 373). At the interactional level, practitioners must be able to understand the multidimensional cultural context of family members, effectively apply cross-cultural communication skills, perceive problems from the individual's cultural perspective or reality, and make effective use of interpreters when necessary (Ivey, 1988; Pedersen, 1988). Culture-responsive interventions are likely to involve work with extended families, respected leaders in an individual's community, and sometimes natural helpers (Caple et al., 1996). Useful culture-oriented guidelines for family work have been set forth by Breunlin, Schwartz, and MacKune-Karrer (1992), in which they proposed that, among their tasks, practitioners must assess the salient cultural dimensions bearing on an individual's problems, evaluate constraints along with opportunities residing in these areas, and plan interventions oriented to lessening the hold of constraints and building on culture-based strengths and opportunities.

Strengths-Based Approach

The personal strengths and resilience of family members were remarkably evident as they shared their stories about living with HIV. Many strengths were found to exist within their family relationships and social networks beyond the kind and scope observed within individuals. Practice with family members should identify, draw, and build on these many personal and social resources in support of growth and improved coping. By adapting a strengths-based practice orientation as defined by Saleebey (1996), practitioners would emphasize a family member's unique traits, talents, and resources; they would develop interventions that are possibility and solution focused; they would reinforce aspirations of individuals and their families; individuals and families would be their own experts in the helping process; opportunities for choice and control would be created; and individual families' adaptive skills and capacities and social networks would become resources in support of coping.

Policy and Program Development

Effectively addressing the needs of HIV-affected families will require a well-defined policy and comprehensive service infrastructure. The policies of service delivery organizations along with policies at the state and national governmental levels must provide the context that both encourages and mandates advancement of services to this long-neglected population. Policies must be of the kind and scope that provide solid underpinning for the development of a comprehensive continuum of services responsive to the families' psychosocial needs (Boyd-Franklin & Boland, 1995; Geballe, Gruendel, & Andiman, 1995; Harvey, 1995; and National Coalition on AIDS and Families, 1989). Services must be multisystem oriented in scope and delivered in a coordinated fashion (Gruendel & Anderson, 1995). The collective voice of family members represented in the Marshall et al. (1995) study speaks to the necessity for improved services addressed to family members' needs and urges that resources be more accessible to those people who need them. Family members' needs have been translated into policy and program recommendations at the state and local levels that call for the kinds of program and macrolevel initiatives as follows.

SERVICES

Because AIDS influences family members in multisystemic ways, a broad spectrum of programs and services is needed to adequately address family members' psychosocial and mental health needs in their formal and informal caregiving or supportive roles with persons with HIV disease. The following are among those recommended to the state.

Outreach Services

Although in some communities, needed services are simply unavailable, with the general exception of HIV service organizations, there oftentimes has been a conspicuous lack of family member use of the wider network of existing social and mental health services. In the Marshall et al. (1995) study, family members documented a variety of constraints that limited their use of existing services: actual or anticipated discrimination; fears of social stigma and rejection; inadequate knowledge about available resources; lack of understanding about the nature and value of different services; and culturally insensitive or exclusive practices that characterized some agencies and programs. Because of these factors and others, access to services clearly will require significant outreach efforts on the part of those agencies and programs purporting to serve the families of people with HIV.

Case Management

Since the beginning of the AIDS epidemic, case management has been integral to the effective care of persons with HIV and a context for assessing needs, linking PWAs to services, empowering them, and advocating on their behalf. Although case management has been a key ingredient in the network of services for PWAs, for the most part these services have been unavailable to family members. Family members' initial reactions and adjustment struggles following disclosure of their loved one's HIV status make the social worker keenly aware of the need for early access to services. Common challenges confronting family members in the post-disclosure period include physical and emotional distress, specific disclosure-related conflicts and anxieties, and stress related to caregiving and life-adjustment crises created by the illness. Given these multiple stressors, family-centered case management centered on needs assessment, information dissemination, and appropriate referral would serve families well.

Clinical guidelines set forth by the U.S. Department of Health and Human Services (1994) strongly affirmed the role of families in the care of PWAs and recommended the inclusion of families in the case management process. Adapting the recommendations to families would result in a case management process consisting of the following: an assessment of the family context (both immediate and extended family), current resources being used, areas of greatest stress, current family resources and supports, and specific needs; a written plan for addressing needs and taking action; referral to the appropriate resources and advocacy, when necessary, on behalf of family members; a reassessment of needs within an established time frame; and disposition and termination based on agreed-upon criteria for concluding services.

Psychoeducation Groups

When family members first learn about a loved one's HIV status, they experience social and emotional stress of considerable proportions. Moreover, their needs for information about the illness and how to best cope with it are extensive. Short-term psychoeducational groups (i.e., 6 to 8 sessions) can be a cost-effective and useful intervention that provides family members with basic information about the illness and equips them with essential survival skills for coping with the effects of the illness. The effectiveness of family psychoeducation with diverse mental health problems has been well documented (Nichols & Schwartz, 1995). In a program that served family members affected by AIDS, Pomeroy, Rubin, and Walker (1995) found an 8-week psychoeducation and task-centered group intervention format to be effective in alleviating stress, perceived stigma, depression, and anxiety among 33 family members of persons with HIV disease. Psychoeducation groups can be delivered in daylong workshops or in an ongoing series format. They are typically organized around specific educational themes. One such program developed by the senior author of this chapter covered the following themes: the nature of the disease including cause, symptom picture and prevailing treatments, the psychosocial dimensions of the illness; the effects on the family; how to confront grief and loss; sexual orientation and related issues; alcohol and other substance abuse; techniques for coping with a chronic illness; and resources for the family. Content presented in psychoeducation groups should be specific to the needs of all family member types and responsive to issues of diversity, especially ethnicity, gender, sexual orientation, age, and literacy level.

Individual Counseling

The stress experienced by some family members can reach a level and intensity that requires more specialized or intensive therapeutic help to cope with the multiple stressors and threats to family stability encountered in the course of living with the illness. Findings of Marshall et al. (1995) revealed that, for some family members, the problems reach clinical proportions encompassing depression, suicidal behavior, and alcoholism. For instance, one mother shared, "I started going to counseling this week because I just can't deal with it. I'm not dealing with my kids. I almost feel abusive to my children. I don't hit them, but I yell at them all the time." In another situation, a spouse shared, "The thing is that I have tried to commit suicide twice because of family reactions. They don't want to eat off the same table that I've touched. They don't want to hug me." In such situations, the social worker needs to connect individuals to therapeutic resources that will provide them the psychological or psychiatric help that is indicated. Furthermore, mental health agencies need to be more proactive in reaching out and making their services known to family members.

Family Counseling

As detailed earlier, the effects of HIV reverberate across all levels of the family system, from partners, parents, adult children, siblings, children and adolescents, to extended family and friends. Given its multisystemic influence, family therapy represents a resource of central importance in helping PWAs and their families cope with the challenges presented by the disease. In discussing its contributions, Walker (1992) underscored that a systemic model of family intervention can serve the following therapeutic purposes: empower the family to trust in its own capacities; normalize the effects of the illness; reframe family narratives from problem-generating to growth-enhancing ones; facilitate identification and use of family resources; mobilize extrafamilial supports; impart essential information in such areas as symptoms, expected course, requisites for optimal living, and environmental sources of exacerbation; support restoration of family functioning to preillness levels of adaptation; and enable planning for the future (pp. 39–64). The practice and research literature has strongly suggested that social workers may help families to navigate transitional crises, address psychosocial tasks associated with the process of living with a chronic illness, and make adaptations necessary for effective coping (Bor & Elford, 1994; Brown & Powell-Cope, 1992; Walker, 1992).

Support Groups

For many family members in the Families and HIV/AIDS Study (Marshall et al., 1995), support groups represented the social life blood that sustained them and bolstered their efforts to cope throughout the course of the their loved one's illness. Family members ranked these groups among their more valued social resources. The social and therapeutic value of support groups has been well-documented in the practice literature (Anderson & Shaw, 1994; Gomez, Haiken, & Lewis, 1995; Kelly & Sykes, 1989; Land & Harangody, 1990; Monahan, Greene, & Coleman, 1992; Toseland, Rossiter, Peak, & Smith, 1990). Among their many uses, support groups provide a context in which family members may obtain basic information about the illness and available resources, learn to live with the illness and the uncertainty that surrounds it, experience valued socioemotional support, learn effective ways of coping with problems encountered, and develop a sense of empowerment and hopefulness. Family members in the study urged that multiple kinds of support groups be available to address needs specific to different family member types (i.e., partners, parents, siblings, adolescents, and so on).

Supportive Resources

In the process of living and coping with HIV disease, family members typically need to draw on a variety of services. Specific service needs, of course, will depend largely on the unique situation of each family unit and the particular stage of the disease process. Individual professionals, agencies, organizations, and communities must be sensitive and responsive to each family's unique needs. A standard "cookbook" approach to care that offers services based on population norms will not do. Within a case management context, ongoing assessment and monitoring of family members can occur so that supportive resources are appropriately matched to currently identified needs. Family members in the Marshall et al. (1995) study identified the following resources as among those they most needed and were likely to access during their provision of care and support to their loved one: in-home health care, homemaker or house-keeping assistance, home-delivered meals, transportation, emergency financial assistance, financial and legal counseling, out-of-home adult day care, respite care, and child-care.

MACROPOLICY AND INTERVENTION

One of the strengths of an ecological approach is that it provides an opportunity to embrace alternative practice paradigms centered around empowerment and social change. Nowhere is this more needed than in relation to families living with HIV disease. Schriver (1995) defined *empowerment practice* as "the essence of the purpose of social work: to preserve and restore human dignity, to benefit from and celebrate the diversities of humans, and to transform ourselves and our society into one that welcomes and supports the voices, the potential, the ways of knowing, the energies of us *all* (p. 16, emphasis in the original). The voices of the families resounded with accounts of distress associated with resource constraints, barriers, and discrimination (Marshall et al., 1995). Those voices seem to suggest that achievement of the broader purposes of social work requires attention to macrolevel policy and intervention. The following discussion integrates macrolevel policy and intervention themes emerging from the Families and HIV/AIDS Study, highlighting specific principles derived from the literature that promote greater accountability to families confronted by HIV and AIDS.

Policy and Program Development

Family member comments regarding agency experiences confirmed that, when at their best, AIDS service organizations are a source of refuge, support, and resources. As one participant observed, "It's like a second family, you know you're in a safe place and everything is going to be all right." Another communicated relief at finding respect and compassion from a competent provider: "It was just unbelievable to find a loving, caring atmosphere." At their worst, the very service delivery system designed to serve families exacerbated their stress and pain. As one caregiver lamented, "I keep thinking that he has options. And, he should have, no matter what he's dying of—he should have options and choices." Their worst experiences were associated with a lack of respect and acceptance, dehumanizing bill-collecting procedures, lack of follow through, discrimination by staff, and profound program and service deficits.

The National Coalition on AIDS and Families (1989) offered a comprehensive set of general principles for practice that recognize the strengths, diversity, and complexity of families affected by HIV disease. These guidelines have great potential to revitalize policy and program development in AIDS service organizations. They include the following:

- AIDS affects families and not just the individuals who contract the disease.
- The family plays a key role in education, prevention, and attitude change regarding AIDS.
- Social services and health providers must view family as the unit of care in the treatment of AIDS. Families need to be educated regarding this role and be provided the support required to be effective.
- The effect on the family continues beyond the illness and death of the infected member.
- Special attention must be given to the needs of low-income families and minority families because these families, with multiple burdens, suffer severely from the AIDS epidemic.
- The effects of the AIDS epidemic on families, and the reaction of families, will vary according to ethnicity, religion, race, and social class.
- Efforts must be made to reduce the stigma, discrimination, and isolation of families with an HIV-infected member.
- Preventative and educational efforts must be rational, pragmatic, and supportive of healthy sexuality.
- Decisions regarding the psychosocial aspects of prevention and treatment must be based on solid theory and research.
- Social policy regarding AIDS must recognize and respond to the strengths and needs of families (pp. 269–270).

These guidelines provide useful broad and overarching directions for policy and program development. Their implementation will require adaptations responsive to specific state and local circumstances and needs.

Education and Training

Family members in the HIV/AIDS study were adamant regarding the need for education of professionals, volunteers, community members, and families affected by HIV (Marshall et al., 1995). Specifically, they underscored the importance of continuing education and training for social service and health providers to enhance their knowledge base, technical skills, and interaction skills. One individual spoke to the issue of cultural competency: "If you only spoke Spanish, it would be hard to get help. People aren't bilingual. If they can't even help people who speak English, how can they speak to Spanish-speaking people?"

Given the predominance of participant concerns about social worker competency, Marshall et al. (1995) recommended that the state departments of health and mental health develop instructional resources to use in the training of professionals and volunteer workers regarding effective methods of work with families. The researchers suggested these departments also provide support staff training and development workshops with an emphasis on dissemination of relevant practices to effectively serve this population. Policymakers were urged to ensure that training and services be grounded in empowerment and cultural competence practice standards and principles (National Association of Social Workers, 1993; Child Welfare League of America, 1993). These standards are congruent with the ecological perspective of individuals, families, and communities as dynamic interacting systems and potential collaborators, not merely recipients of AIDS-related services. Furthermore, Marshall et al. (1995) recommended the use of assessment tools such as *The Questions of Diversity* (Simons & Abramms, 1994), *Cultural Competence Self-Assessment Instrument* (Child Welfare League of America, 1993), and *Sexual Orientation in the Workplace* (Zuckerman & Simons, 1994). These instruments facilitate organizational cultural audits to assess the extent of diversity principles in agency policies, procedures, governance, administration, program and policy development, service delivery, staffing, and relations with clients and the community. This affirmative approach is salient to all human services organizations, and especially those serving families affected by HIV and AIDS.

Advocacy

Data from the research gave support to empowerment practice with caregivers (Marshall et al., 1995). Family members found that negotiating services was made more difficult by deficiencies in the service delivery system, such as limited information about services and a lack of personal validation from those people working in the system. They sought confirmation of their perspectives, experiences, and needs and valued opportunities to provide input regarding services and policies.

Moses Newsome (1996), president of the Council on Social Work Education, asserted that, "because of the epidemic nature of AIDS and social work's tradition of helping the underserved, we must not be remiss in preparing students for practice with families who are either directly or indirectly affected by this devastating disease. . . . [T]he mandate is clear from all directions [that the profession must respond to this] 'matter of life and death'" (p. 1). He called for a balanced response to fulfill the urgent need for advocacy and service.

Saleebey (1996) reiterated that, realistically, social workers must recognize that true advocacy requires risk-taking, a willingness to share power, and an ability to assume the learner's stance. The foundations of his strengths perspective parallel the advocacy-related recommendations of the statewide Families and HIV/AIDS Study (Marshall et al., 1995). In that study, there was strong family receptivity for interventions that enhanced families' abilities to build on their strengths, collaborate with necessary resources and supports, and become better advocates for themselves as well as others affected by AIDS. One primary context for accomplishing this goal is through use of groups that educate family members about strategies for organizing for community change and use of political advocacy to influence and enhance the HIV and AIDS service delivery system.

CONCLUSIONS

Findings from the Families and HIV/AIDS Study (Marshall et al., 1995) made clear that HIV affects the family in psychologically and socially significant ways. The effects are felt throughout the family system by partners, parents, siblings, children and adolescents, extended family, and friends. Results strongly suggested these effects can be for better or worse, and can act to either compromise or enhance the well-being and quality of care provided to the infected family member. Considerably more needs to be learned about the important family dimensions of HIV and role of families in the health and care of persons with the disease. In this regard, sufficient funding is needed to support qualitative and quantitative research aimed at furthering understanding of several areas. They are the following: the number and roles of family members affected by HIV; relation between an infected person's family support networks and the quality of care provided to him or her; differential effects of HIV on the mental health and psychosocial functioning of family members in caregiving and noncaregiving roles; long-term effects of HIV on family members who serve as primary caregivers; interrelationship between family structure and functioning and the well-being of persons with HIV; social and mental health impact of HIV on children and adolescents of infected parents or siblings; effects of loss, grief, and bereavement on families, including multiple family losses; appropriateness of fit between available services and needs of women, African-Americans, Latinos or Hispanics, and other ethnic communities; and behavior and attitudes within the community and families that affect help-seeking behavior and service delivery.

According to the World Health Organization (WHO), as of 1997, 1.7 million cumulative cases of AIDS in adults and children have been officially reported by countries throughout the world (WHO, 1997). An incidence of this magnitude strongly suggests the extent to which family members of HIV-infected persons have been touched by the illness. Estimates of these numbers within the United States are high. Relative to this population, an important issue is whether and how well the helping professions will be prepared to respond to the needs of HIV-affected families. The growing numbers of those people affected by the virus will call for approaches that effectively respond to the ecological, cultural, and political dimensions of the problem. Furthermore, it will be incumbent on the social work profession to advocate for the policy and program initiatives so necessary if practice with these family members is to be advanced and their needs effectively addressed.

REFERENCES

Ackerman Institute for Family Therapy (1989). *AIDS and families: Facilitator's workbook.* New York: Author.

Akbar, N. (1984). Africentric social sciences for human liberation. *Journal of Black Studies, 14,* 395–414.

Anderson, D. B., & Shaw, S. L. (1994). Starting a support group for families and partners of people with HIV/AIDS in a rural setting. *Social Work, 39,* 135–138.

Barth, R., Pietrzak, J., & Ramler, M. (1993). *Families living with drugs and HIV: Intervention and treatment strategies.* New York: Guilford.

Bethel, E. R. (Ed.) (1995). *AIDS: Readings on a global crisis.* Needham Heights, MA: Allyn & Bacon.

Bor, R., & Elford, J. (Eds.) (1994). *The family and HIV.* London: Cassell and Collier Macmillan.

Bor, R., Miller, R., & Goldman, E. (1993). HIV/AIDS and the family: A family review of research in the first decade. *Journal of Family Therapy, 15,* 187–204.

Boyd-Franklin, N., & Boland, M. G. (1995). A multisystems approach to service delivery for HIV/AIDS families. In N. Boyd-Franklin, G. L. Steiner, and M. G.

Boland (Eds.), *Children, families, and HIV/AIDS: Psychosocial and therapeutic issues* (pp. 199–215). New York: Guilford.

Boyd-Franklin, N., Steiner, G. L., & Boland, M. G. (Eds.) (1995). *Children, families, and HIV/AIDS: Psychosocial and therapeutic issues.* New York: Guilford.

Breunlin, D. C., Schwartz, R. C., & MacKune-Karrer, B. (1992). *Metaframeworks: Transcending the models of family therapy.* San Francisco: Jossey-Bass.

Brown, M. A., & Powell-Cope, G. A. (1991). AIDS family caregiving: Transitions through uncertainty. *Nursing Research, 40,* 338–345.

Brown, M. A., & Powell-Cope, G. A. (1992). *Caring for a loved one with AIDS: The experiences of families, lovers, and friends.* Seattle: University of Washington Press.

Brown, M. A., & Powell-Cope, G. (1993). Themes of loss and dying in caring for a family member with AIDS. *Research in Nursing and Health, 16,* 179–191.

Caple, F. S., Salcido, R. M., & di Cecco, J. (1996). Engaging effectively with culturally diverse families and children. In P. L. Ewalt, E. M. Freeman, S. A. Kirk, and D. L. Poole (Eds.), *Multicultural issues in social work* (pp. 366–381). Washington, DC: NASW Press.

Centers for Disease Control (1997). *HIV/AIDS Surveillance Report, 8*(2), 1–39.

Child Welfare League of America (1993). *Cultural Competence Self-Assessment Instrument.* Washington, DC: Author

Geballe, S., Gruendel, J., & Andiman, W. (1995). Agenda for action. In S. Geballe, J. Gruendel, & W. Andiman (Eds.), *Forgotten children of the AIDS epidemic* (pp. 50–63). New Haven, CT: Yale University Press.

Germain, C. B. (Ed.) (1979). *Social work practice: People and environments, an ecological perspective.* New York: Columbia University Press.

Germain, C. B., & Gitterman, A. (1980). *The life model of social work practice.* New York: Columbia University Press.

Germain, C. B., & Gitterman, A. (1986). The life model approach to social work practice revisited. In F. J. Turner (Ed.), *Social work treatment: Interlocking theoretical approaches* (3rd ed.) (pp. 618–644). New York: Free Press.

Gillman, R. R., & Newman, B. S. (1996). Psychosocial concerns and strengths of women with HIV infection: An empirical study. *Families in Society, 77,* 131–141.

Gomez, K. A., Haiken, H. J., & Lewis, S. Y. (1995). Support group for children with HIV/AIDS. In N. Boyd-Franklin, G. L. Steiner, and M. G. Boland (Eds.), *Children, families, and HIV/AIDS: Psychosocial and therapeutic issues* (pp. 156–166). New York: Guilford.

Gruendel, J. M., & Anderson, G. R. (1995). Building child- and family-responsive support systems. In S. Geballe, J. Gruendel, and W. Andiman (Eds.), *Forgotten children of the AIDS epidemic* (pp. 165–189). New Haven, CT: Yale University Press.

Hartman, A. (1978). Diagrammatic assessment of family relationships. *Social Casework, 59,* 465–476.

Harvey, D. C. (1995). HIV/AIDS and public policy: Recent developments. In N. Boyd-Franklin, G. L. Steiner, and M. G. Boland (Eds.), *Children, families, and HIV/AIDS: Psychosocial and therapeutic issues* (pp. 311–324). New York: Guilford.

Ivey, A. E. (1988). *Intentional interviewing and counseling: Facilitating client develop-
    ment.* (2nd ed.). Pacific Grove, CA: Brooks/Cole.
Kaplan, L. S. (1988). AIDS and guilt. *Family Therapy Networker, 12*(1), 40–41.
Kelly, J., & Sykes, P. (1989). Helping the helpers: A support group for family
    members of persons with AIDS. *Social Work, 34,* 239–242.
King, D. K. (1990). Multiple jeopardy, multiple consciousness: The context of a
    Black feminist ideology. In M. R. Molson, E. Mudimbe-Boyi, J. F. O'Barr, and
    M. Wyer (Eds.), *Black women in America: Social science perspectives* (pp. 265–
    295). Chicago: University of Chicago Press.
Land, H. (1994). AIDS and women of color. *Families in Society: 75,* 355–361.
Land, H., & Harangody, G. (1990). A support group for partners of persons with
    AIDS. *Families in Society, 60,* 471–482.
Leukefeld, C. G., & Fimbres, M. (Eds.) (1987). *Responding to AIDS: Psychosocial
    initiatives.* Silver Spring, MD: NASW Press.
Levine, C. (1990). AIDS and changing concepts of the family. *Milbank Quarterly,
    68*(Suppl. 1), 33–58.
Linsk, N. L. (1994). HIV and the elderly. *Families in Society, 75,* 362–372.
Logan, S. L., & Joyce, J. (1996). Helping Black families who are providing care to
    persons with AIDS. In S. L. Logan (Ed.), *The Black family: Strengths, self-help,
    and positive change* (pp. 53–66). Boulder, CO: Westview.
Macklin, E. (Ed.) (1989). *AIDS and families.* New York: Haworth.
Mancoske, R. J., & Lindhorst, T. (1995). The ecological context of HIV/AIDS
    counseling: Issues for lesbians and gays and their significant others. In G. A.
    Lloyd and M. A. Kuszelewicz (Eds.), *HIV disease: Lesbians, gays and the social
    services* (pp. 25–40). New York: Haworth.
Marshall, E., Barton, W., Roberts, T. L., Stephany, L., Pickett, E., & Carter, S. (1995).
    Families and HIV/AIDS: A statewide needs assessment (Research Project Prelimi-
    nary Report). Indianapolis: Indiana State Department of Health.
McCann, K., & Wadsworth, E. (1992). The role of informal carers in supporting
    gay men who have HIV related illness: What do they do and what are their
    needs? *AIDS Care, 4*(1), 25–34
Mohr, R. (1988). AIDS: Deciding what's do-able. *Family Therapy Networker, 12*(1),
    34–36.
Monahan, D. J., Greene, V. L., & Coleman, P. D. (1992). Caregiver support groups:
    Factors affecting use of services. *Social Work, 37,* 254–260.
National Association of Social Workers (1993). *Code of ethics and practice standards.*
    Washington, DC: Author.
National Coalition on AIDS and Families (1989). National Coalition on AIDS and
    Families: Goal statements and general principles. In E. Macklin (Ed.), *AIDS
    and families* (pp. 269–270). Binghamton, NY: Haworth.
Newsome, M. (1996). From the president: A matter of life and death. *Social Work
    Education Reporter, 44*(1), 1–14.
Nichols, M. P., & Schwartz, R. C. (1995). *Family therapy: Concepts and methods* (3rd
    ed.). Needham Heights, MA: Allyn & Bacon.
Patten, J. (1988). AIDS and the gay couple. *Family Therapy Networker, 12*(1), 37–
    39.

Pedersen, P. (1988). *A handbook for developing multicultural awareness.* Alexandria, VA: American Association for Counseling and Development.

Pomeroy, E. C., Rubin, A., & Walker, R. J. (1995). Effectiveness of a psychoeducational and task-centered group intervention for family members of people with AIDS. *Social Work Research, 19*(3), 142–152.

Powell-Cope, G. M. (1995). The experiences of gay couples affected by HIV infection. *Qualitative Health Research, 5*(1), 36–62.

Powell-Cope, G. M., & Brown, M. A. (1992). Going public as an AIDS family caregiver. *Social Science Medicine, 34*(5), 571–580.

Reid-Merritt, P., & Mathis, T. P. (1997, April). *National Institute for African-Centered Social Work.* Paper presented at the annual meeting of the National Association of Black Social Workers, Detroit.

Saleebey, D. (1996). The strengths perspective in social work practice: Extensions and cautions. *Social Work, 41*, 296–305.

Schiele, J. H. (1996). Afrocentricity: An emerging paradigm in social work practice. *Social Work, 41*, 284–294.

Schiele, J. H. (1997). The contour and meaning of Afrocentric social work. *Journal of Black Studies, 27*, 800–819.

Schriver, J. M. (1995). *Human behavior and the social environment: Shifting paradigms in essential knowledge for social work practice.* Needham Heights, MA: Allyn & Bacon.

Simons, G. F., & Abramms, B. (1994). *The questions of diversity.* Amherst, MA: ODT.

Taylor-Brown, S. (1992). Women don't get AIDS: They just die from it. *AFFILIA, 7*(4), 96–98.

Toseland, R., Rossiter, C., Peak, T., & Smith, G. C. (1990). Comparative effectiveness of individual and group interventions to support family caregivers. *Social Work, 35*, 209–217.

U.S. Department of Health and Human Services (1994). *Clinical practice guidelines: Evaluation and management of early HIV infection* (AHCPR No. 94-0572). Rockville, MD: Author.

Walker, G. (1988). An AIDS journal. *Family Therapy Networker, 12*(1), 20–33.

Walker, G. (1991). Pediatric AIDS: Towards an ecosystemic treatment model. *Family Systems Medicine, 9*, 211–227.

Walker, G. (1992). *In the midst of winter.* New York: W.W. Norton.

Wardlaw, L. A. (1994). Sustaining informal caregivers for persons with AIDS. *Families in Society 75*, 373–384.

Wilson, P. A. (1995). AIDS service organizations: Current issues and future challenges. In G. A. Lloyd and M. A. Kuszelewicz (Eds.), *HIV disease: Lesbians, gays and the social services* (pp. 121–144). New York: Haworth.

Zuckerman, A. J., & Simons, G. (1994). *Sexual orientation in the workplace: Gays, lesbians, bisexuals & heterosexuals working together.* Santa Cruz, CA: International Partners.

Biographical Sketches of the Contributors

Glenna Barnes received her MSW in 1978 from the University of Maryland. She is a doctoral student at the Indiana University School of Social Work. She has worked in academia, as a nurse and as a social worker. Currently she coordinated the FIMR project at the Marion County Health Department.

William H. Barton is an Associate Professor of Social Work at Indiana University, Indianapolis, where he teaches courses in program evaluation methods, the philosophy of science, and juvenile justice policy. Publications include a co-edited book on juvenile detention, a chapter on juvenile corrections in the 1995 edition of the *Encyclopedia of Social Work*, and several journal articles based on research, consultation and training projects he has conducted with juvenile justice agencies throughout the United States. His current focus is on program evaluation, need assessment, and policy research in human services, especially in the areas of juvenile justice and youth development.

Lorraine C. Blackman is an Assistant Professor of Social Work at Indiana University. Prior to joining the university faculty, she practiced social work as a therapist specializing in individual, marriage, and family therapy in settings ranging from a psychiatric institution, mental health center, domestic violence shelter, and veterans medical center. Currently she is developing social work practice models in family life education.

Gayle J. Cox, Ph.D., is an Associate Professor of Social Work at Indiana University. She is a former school social worker and has also done extensive work in gerontology. She has presented at numerous professional conferences on these subjects as well as those related to issues of diversity and cross-cultural relationships.

Gail Folaron is an Associate Professor at the School of Social Work, Indiana University. Her area of focus is on family reunification. She is the co-author with Peg Hess of several articles on unsuccessful reunification. Her dissertation is a qualitative review of successful reunifications. She teaches child welfare practice and policy. Prior to receiving her doctorate, Dr. Folaron worked for seven years in a child welfare agency and two years in a mental health agency serving abused and neglected children and their families.

Elsa Iverson is Director of Field Instruction at Indiana University School of Social Work. She teaches in the area of practice, especially practice with families.

She has a long-standing interest in social work academic-community-agency/
organization collaborations to enrich teaching and practice.

Nancy P. Kropf is Associate Dean and Associate Professor in the School of
Social Work at the University of Georgia. She has authored several articles and
chapters on gerontology, developmental disabilities, and social work education. In
addition, she has a co-edited text on aging and a second on interdisciplinary
practice in developmental disabilities. Dr. Kropf is a member of both the Gerontology and the University Affiliated Program (UAP) for Disabilities faculty at the
University of Georgia.

Brad Lighty is a graduate of the Indiana University School of Social Work. He
has worked the last four years at The Damien Center in Indianapolis, Indiana. The
Damien Center is the state's largest AIDS Service Organization.

Luisa Lopez is special Assistant for Affirmative Action National Association of
Social Workers.

Eldon Marshall is an Associate Professor, Indiana University School of Social
Work. He has held prior positions with the schools of social work at Saint Louis
University and the University of Tennessee and has served on the faculty of the
University of Oklahoma, Department of Psychiatry and Behavioral Sciences. For
the past ten years, emphasis in his teaching, practice, and research has centered in
the area of families and HIV/AIDS. During this time he has been actively involved in the development of social service programs oriented to family members
impacted by the disease. Since 1995 he has been Principal Investigator of a major
study of the effects of HIV/AIDS on families. Conducted under the auspices of
the Indiana State Department of Health and Indiana University School of Social
Work, this research seeks statewide documentation of the psychosocial effects of
HIV disease on families and establishment of a database to guide policy and
program development in behalf of this population.

Lisa McGuire is a Teacher-Practitioner with the Indiana University School of
Social Work, coordinating an intensive field unit in the Indianapolis Housing
Agency. Her research interests include practice/policy in poverty and social field
education. She is currently a doctoral candidate at Mandel School of Applied
Social Sciences, Case Western Reserve University where she has been awarded a
HUD Doctoral Dissertation Grant to complete her research on the welfare-to-work
transition with public housing residents.

John G. McNutt is Assistant Professor of Social Work in the Graduate School of
Social Work at Boston College. A specialist in macrosocial work, social policy,
technology and nonprofit organizations, Dr. McNutt taught at Indiana University
before coming to Boston College in 1996. Dr. McNutt holds an MSW from the
University of Alabama and a Ph.D. in Social Work from the University of
Tennessee.

Gerald T. Powers is a professor and Director of the Ph.D. Program at the
Indiana University School of Social Work. His perspective on school social work

has been shaped by his direct practice experience and several consulting positions in a variety of different urban school settings. His research includes a number of investigations into issues involving the compatibility of student/teacher learning styles as a variable in the teaching/learning process. His publications reflect his dual interest in school social work and practice sensitive research and appear in a variety of scholarly journals, monographs, and a coauthored text entitled *Practice-Focused Research.*

Irene Queiro-Tajalli is associate dean for systems and baccalaureate program director at Indiana University School of Social Work. Her topics of research, professional presentations, and writing include aging, social work practice and education in Latin America, social welfare policies, health care utilization among Hispanic women, and Latino issues. Her international perspective is based on her social work practice experience in working with American Indian, Iranian, and Latino communities. She has extensive experience in accreditation of social work programs.

Theresa L. Roberts is an Assistant Professor at the Indiana University School of Social Work. She teaches in the MACRO Practice concentration with an emphasis on contemporary paradigms of organizational and community practice, administration in a diverse society, program planning and development, and human behavior in macro systems. Her current research foci address cultural competency advocacy and training, Afrocentric practice and teaching paradigms, African American communities, and social support and HIV/AIDS. She has provided extensive community service and advocacy through organizations such as the National Association of Black Social Workers, Indianapolis Chapter.

Linda Anderson Smith is an Assistant Professor at the Indiana University School of Social Work. A graduate of Hunter College/CUNY doctoral program, she has extensive experience in urban social work practice. She teaches interpersonal practice and social policy. Her current research addresses practice with overwhelmed populations, particularly those with severe and persistent mental illness and those affected by racism.

Carolyn Stephany is a Research Assistant with the Families and HIV Study, Indiana University School of Social Work. She also works as a clinical social worker in family and youth programs serving agencies in the Indianapolis area. Previous work includes: individual/group sexual abuse counseling and conference presentations; facilitation of psychoeducational groups for battered women, and co-facilitation of support groups and psychoeducational groups for families living with HIV/AIDS.

W. Patrick Sullivan is an Associate Professor at the School of Social Work at Indiana University and the Director of the Indiana Division of Mental Health. He has published extensively in the area of mental health, substance abuse treatment, case management and rural practice. He has also worked to develop and describe the strengths perspective of social work practice both in theory and practice.

Carol T. Tully is an Associate Professor of Social Work at Tulane University in New Orleans. Dr. Tully's primary areas of research are in the areas of gerontology, gay and lesbian issues, and higher education curriculum development and implementation. Past work has been related to social support systems of older women, elder abuse, aging and homelessness, social work faculty qualifications, issues associated with the social supports of hearing impaired lesbians and gay men, lesbian functioning in a heterosexist culture, curriculum development, accreditation issues, and social work practice. She is currently involved in the development of a lesbian and gay public policy institute at Tulane. She teaches at both the master's and doctoral levels in the area of policy.

Rebecca Van Voorhis is an Assistant Professor at Indiana University School of Social Work. She is also an adjunct member of the Women's Studies' faculty and has served as director of the Women's Studies Program at Indiana University-Purdue University at Indianapolis.

Marion Wagner is an Assistant Professor at Indiana University School of Social Work, teaching in the areas of Macro Practice, Social Policy, Community Organization, and Human Behavior in the Social Environment. Prior to her academic experience she worked for 15 years in public and private child welfare services in California, Oregon, and Indiana.

Marie Watkins is a Research Associate at Indiana University School of Social Work. In addition to this role, Dr. Watkins teaches graduate and undergraduate courses related to social work practice with individuals, families and groups. Dr. Watkins also teaches courses on oppression and understanding diversity in a pluralistic society. Dr. Watkins' academic education includes a doctorate in Child and Family Studies, College of Human Development, Syracuse University and a Master of Social Work, School of Social Work, Syracuse University. Dr. Watkins has 25 years of practice experience in the application of youth development principles across diverse populations of youth; agency administration; and child, adolescent and family counseling.

Index